I0815392

KKAA

KENGO KUMA & ASSOCIATES

Other Schiffer Books on Related Subjects:
Innovations in Mass Timber: Sequestering Carbon with Style in Commercial Buildings, Boyce Thompson, 978-0-7643-6743-4

Mies van der Rohe's Farnsworth House, Paul Clemence, 978-0-7643-2443-7

Library of Congress Control Number: 2024932776

Edited by Jesse J. Marth
Designed by Molly Shields

Type set in Runda/Cambria

ISBN: 978-0-7643-6680-2

Printed in China

10 9 8 7 6 5 4 3 2 1

Published by Schiffer Publishing, Ltd.
4880 Lower Valley Road
Atglen, PA 19310
Phone: (610) 593-1777; Fax: (610) 593-2002
Email: info@schifferbooks.com
Web: www.schifferbooks.com

KKAA

KENGO KUMA & ASSOCIATES

THE DETAILS OF DESIGNING SOFT AND SMALL

4880 Lower Valley Road • Atglen, PA 19310

CONTENTS

FOREWORD

THE ARCHITECTURES OF KENGO KUMA

BY MICHAEL J. CROSBIE

THE ARCHITECTURE OF THE HANDMADE

A handmade architecture composed of natural materials is a signature of the architect Kengo Kuma. What is so important about handmade architecture? "An architecture shaped by human hands gives us comfort and rich experiences," Kuma observes. "I believe that such architecture is more like a living creature than an artificial object. Human hands give life to the building and people are nourished by it." For Kuma, a wooden railing shaped by human hands, or buffed again and again by the hands of others, takes on a luster akin to long, silken hair lovingly brushed over and over. A stone wall that bears the marks of the mason's chisel or an iron gate shaped with the blows of the metalworker's hammer reveals the personalities of those who wrought them. "I emphasize the emotions that humans can get from natural materials," explains Kuma, "which can create a sense of delight and comfort or even change one's perception of the world."

For Kuma, the places in which he builds speak. As he has worked on sites farther afield from his native Japan (he currently has projects in about two dozen counties), his approach to the design of place has evolved with a consistency. He concludes that a country as an architectural entity is an abstraction. What is meaningful and rewarding is to make architecture in each locale by using materials and talent unique to the location. His approach is to walk the site—slowly. "It is not easy for architects to be humble," Kuma reflects, but good design demands a certain humility. Kuma must touch the ground with his own feet, touch the trees with his own hands, to feel the reality of a locale. "That is the start of the conversation with a place," he explains.

To achieve a handmade architecture, Kuma collaborates not only with his colleagues at Kengo Kuma & Associates, but also with those who craft his designs. His method is to work closely with craftspeople who are indigenous to whatever place he is designing for. He describes such homegrown craftspeople as "the bridge or the medium between the architecture and its location. Craftspeople can give a soul to an artificial structure." How does he discover these gifted fabricators? Kuma employs a variety of methods: conversations with the client and local people often uncover these creators. (Kuma likens the process to that of a good Buddhist priest, who gently visits a place and spends time honestly speaking with the people of that place.) But sometimes even an internet search might uncover potential collaborators. "When I work with the craftspeople, I would never force or insist on my idea with them," says Kuma. "I try to know their work as much as possible and bring out their skills and ideas to the maximum." In a sense, Kuma uses the design to conjure the best work out of the native craftspeople that he works with.

Kuma collaborates with craftspeople in many ways, but never through words alone. A turning point in his evolution as an architect was to relocate his practice in the early 1990s from Tokyo to the countryside. For a decade he worked intimately on small-scale projects with craftspeople, which changed his work and how he collaborated with "native geniuses" (to use Sibyl Moholy-Nagy's term). "I often draw new sketches specifically for them to show what sort of details we aim for," Kuma explains. "At a certain point in the construction we build a full-scale mockup and check it carefully with them." He is wary of using three-dimensional computer renderings or models in this process—he views them as abstractions that do not reveal the soul of the design in its details. Full-scale fabrications in the materials to be used are Kuma's preferred way of collaborating with colleagues and craftspeople. Of the five senses, he relies most on visual and tactile sensibilities.

THE ARCHITECTURE OF SMALL, GENTLE, SOFT

Kuma came of age as an architect in Japan as the figures of modern architecture reached their apex—architects such as Kenzō Tange, Arata Isozaki, Fumihiko Maki, and Tadao Ando—whose works were often hard edged and unrelenting, made of anonymous materials such as steel, glass, and concrete. As Kuma matured, he came to perceive such architecture as disconnecting people with nature, cutting them off from life-giving qualities that can be found in such materials as stone, paper, textiles, and especially wood. "Wood is always small, gentle, and soft," Kuma observes. "Wood is humble."

Such natural materials were also the setting of Kuma's childhood, particularly his home in the suburbs of Tokyo. In the late 1950s and '60s he was brought up in satoyama—small, hilly woods that exist in suburban areas of Japan. He grew up next to a farm, feeling close to the animals the farm family kept there, and the surrounding woodlands. Kuma relates that as an architect he has benefited from these memories. His own family's home was a 1940s traditional house, a single-story wooden structure, to which over the years his father added a series of extensions. "My father asked me to design and even build the structure together with him," Kuma reflects, "so we shared the process of house making, which eventually contributed to the way I work as an architect."

It was a house of wood, paper, and tatami, and even today he recalls the scent of its materials, their textures—memories that can be triggered in the olfactory aftermath of a rainstorm. In Kuma's recollection, one cannot help but hear echoes of childhood recollections that shaped other designers, such as the Finnish architect Juhani Pallasmaa, who shared in his book The Eyes of the Skin: "I cannot remember the appearance of the door to my grandfather's farmhouse from my early childhood, but I do remember the resistance of its weight, the patina of its wood surface scarred by decades of use, and I recall especially vividly the scent of home that hit my face as an invisible wall behind the door."

THE ARCHITECTURE OF GENTLENESS AND SHADOW

Kuma's increasing attention to humble, natural materials has yielded a theoretical posture that embraces what he has called "Defeated Architecture," one in opposition to the "Victorious Architecture" that characterized twentieth-century modernism. Such architectural heroism, writes Kuma, resulted in buildings that used "the hard, strong, heavy material of concrete as a means of defeating the environment." While I accept Kuma's dichotomy of "defeated" versus "victorious," and its architectural implications, I believe that better descriptors are at hand: an architecture that is compliant, an architecture of gentleness, buildings of compromise, environments of surrender.

Kuma believes that when he wrote his book Architecture of Defeat more than twenty years ago, his theory and thought outpaced his actual work. Today he believes that projects completed in the past two decades reflect in one way or another an architecture that bends to touch the human spirit in tender ways, that has a spiritual dimension no matter what its function. We see abundant evidence of this in the projects in this book, such as Mêmu Meadows, an experimental residence of textiles and wood, designed to safely respond to local seismic threats; Coeda House, made of randomly stacked cedar boards that appear to grow into a single, spreading bough supporting a delicate, sheltering pyramidal roof; the Portland Japanese Garden Cultural Village, a congeries of deferential pavilions gently inserted into the existing, wooded natural environment to create a courtyard that opens on one side to gardens; and the Community Market Yusuhara, a farm market enclosure with a façade of thatch that recalls the roofs of traditional Cha Do tea houses that long ago provided hospitality to weary travelers.

As related to environments of compromise and the architecture of gentleness, Kuma detects a connection between such buildings and how they influence the people who encounter them, inhabit them, work and play in them. "It is often said that the people whom you've met make you who you are," Kuma notes, perceiving his buildings as persons. "You are shaped by the people surrounding you . . . if you have family and friends who are gentle and kind, you should naturally be influenced by them, and that is the same for architecture. That is one reason I tend to choose soft and weak materials for my projects."

Kuma's architecture of gentleness, compromise, and servitude is infused with the qualities of wabi-sabi—the Japanese aesthetic "of things modest and humble, imperfect, impermanent, and incomplete," as described by the writer Leonard Koren. "Things wabi-sabi are usually small and compact, quiet and inward oriented. They beckon: get close, touch, relate." Koren notes that such qualities reduce the psychic distance between people and objects, as well as between people and nature. In its soundless directness, Kuma's architecture is enveloped in mystery, things implied and not seen, merely hinted at. In this way, shadows play an important role in his work. Often Kuma creates a weave of solids and voids, light and shade, material nets that capture the magic of shadows like fish. Sunny Hills Japan is such a weir—its intricate wooden members employing a "jigoku-gumi" construction technique. The Exchange, a project in Australia, has a similarly woven quality, clad with spirals of wooden "threads" that alternate light and shadow as it filters through this basket of a building. The Kadokawa Culture Museum, although appearing like a solid crag of magma emerging from a plateau, contains within it towering stacks of shelves akin to shadow boxes, rising up to a dark heaven.

Other projects manipulate light and shade to create dappled patterns on floors, walls, and the people who move under their stippled cascades. The delicate, three-dimensional wooden screen canopy of the Huruki Murakami Library bathes the entrance in patterns of light, creating a sense of hamorebi—light filtered through the leaves of trees. The same can be experienced when you enter the courtyard of Kuma's Nagaoka City Hall Aore—you find yourself in a virtual forest clearing, with sunlight and shade sifting down through layers of wooden slats. Kuma cloaks these spaces in the mystery of shadow and shade, creating what the author Jun'ichirō Tanizaki described as the "beauty not in the thing itself but in the patterns of shadows, the light and the darkness, that one thing against another creates. Were it not for shadows, there would be no beauty." Kuma has observed of his own architecture: "No shadow means no spirit."

THE ARCHITECTURE OF BIOPHILIA

The pandemic of the past few years has sharpened Kuma's view of architecture's role in the future. He sees the global health crisis as a warning of what human activity is doing to the planet, but he also observes the pandemic as an opportunity to change our mode of thinking in a postindustrial world. "We could let this pandemic be a new start," he notes, "a turning point." In its aftermath, he expresses a desire to meld his architecture even closer to nature, making it more kind to it. Biophilic design results in environments where human beings are brought into intimate approximation to nature, its healing powers, and its spiritual nourishment. Research has already shown that biophilic design can reduce anxiety in people through inclusion of nature or design with natural features.

Kuma's oeuvre is already abundant with biophilic architecture. His newly completed Hans Christian Andersen Museum in Odense, Denmark, has many biophilic qualities, bringing people and nature into familiar immediacy. The boundaries of the museum buildings are porous, accentuating the interplay of interior and exterior. An undulating hedge wall meanders around and through the complex, creating caressing spaces. On the scale of the city, the complex serves to seam together disjointed parts of the old medieval city and its newer urban core.

"Andersen's work projects the duality of the opposites that surround us: real and imaginary, nature and man-made, human and animal, light and dark," says the architect. The H. C. Andersen Museum is a place of repose, of nature, of mystery. It is an environment that both contrasts and unites, as does much of Kengo Kuma's architecture.

Michael J. Crosbie, PhD, FAIA, NOMA, DPACSA, is professor of architecture at the University of Hartford. He is the sole author, editor, or contributor to more than seventy-five books on architecture. He has published hundreds of articles on architecture, design, and practice; is a frequent contributor to international print and online publications; and lectures on architecture throughout the US and abroad.

PREFACE

Architecture is currently at a large inflection point. Rather than a simple transition, the history of architecture created by humankind has reached a significant turning point. New details are needed to make softness and smallness possible. If these new details are not created, softness and smallness cannot be achieved, and the entire movement will end as an empty theory.

The history of Homo sapiens over tens of thousands of years can be summed up as the history of the transition from dispersion to concentration. From the age of hunter-gatherers, during which small groups of people continued to move around in the vast wilderness, people were concentrated into larger groups with the advent of agriculture, bringing about a transition in how people worked and lived. Subsequently, there were repeated transitions as people moved from villages to towns, and from towns to cities, resulting in a continuing progression of the trend from dispersion to concentration. The skyscrapers that were built at the beginning of the twentieth century represent the final form of these transitions. Everyone believed that concentrating large numbers of people in high towers was the most efficient way to work, and that this would make people the happiest.

The coronavirus pandemic taught us and confronted us with the fact that this level of concentration exerts stress on our bodies and our minds. Many people who had obtained various digital technologies knew that there was a more creative way to work in a dispersed manner from long before the coronavirus pandemic, moving freely about in nature in a way similar to how people moved about during the hunter-gatherer age, rather than being crammed into high-rise buildings to work.

However, most likely due to the slow rejuvenation speed of hardware, competition to build the highest skyscraper continues without anyone being able to stop the vector oriented toward concentration, and humankind continues to strangle itself, resulting in continued destruction of the global environment. The basic principle of the hardware that has continued to rush toward even further concentration became even larger and stronger. Buildings cannot be made larger if they are not made stronger, and the stronger buildings that resulted from this closed people inside and decisively moved them farther away and cut them off from nature.

In order to reverse this trend, buildings must be made softer and smaller. Architecture that is soft and small will reconnect people with nature and is a tool that is necessary to achieve a new dispersed lifestyle that will release people's bodies and minds from stress, and it is this architecture that will bring about a rebirth of human beings.

As a matter of fact, traditional Japanese architecture has many hints for soft and small architecture. For example, floors in Japanese houses are made by using tatami, which are woven from soft rush, making them soft, and I occasionally have nostalgic recollections of the soft, warm feeling of tatami floors because of the unique fragrance, which is reminiscent of lying down in a grassy field.

There were almost no walls between rooms, and movable partitions made from shoji screens or fusuma panels, which are made from paper and wood frames, were used to separate the rooms. In particular, shoji screens are made using soft white paper that is so thin that it will break if too much force is applied, requiring care when these partitions are opened and closed. Soft architecture requires people to be soft and gentle, and has the ability to change the behavior and character of people.

Softness also has a deep connection to variability and flexibility. Light shoji screens, which are made from thin paper and wood frames, can be moved with a single finger, and rather than composing a portion of the architecture, they feel as if they are a part of your body. Glass was not used to separate the inside from the outside until the end of the nineteenth century. Wooden shutters called Amado were pulled out from door pockets when the sun went down, as well as during typhoons. Light items like this were frequently used, creating a lifestyle that continued to change according to the change of the seasons and nature.

And surprisingly, even the floors continue to move. It is unclear whether or not this is the result of Japan being the country that has the most earthquakes in the world, but the floors in traditional Japanese houses are flexible. Tatami mats are compressed when stepped on, and slowly return to the original shape when the load is removed. Even for places where wood floors were used in Japan, people often requested thin floors that were soft, which would squeak when walked on. The reason for this is that by making a noise, the floor lets you know that someone is approaching, even that the person is a man or a woman. On the contrary, thick floors were disliked because people thought that they were tiring. The sense of values at the time was completely opposite from the modern sense of values, where people think that thicker materials are more high class. In that age, materials and details were very carefully determined.

In addition to softness, smallness was something that was important in Japan. In the same manner that softness is needed to reduce the distance between nature and people, smallness is important to bring people closer to nature. First, by making the overall structure intimate and small, the distance between people and nature is dramatically reduced. Whether it was in a rural or urban area, small architecture was dispersed in nature. Even in cities that appeared to have high density, the architectural unit was small, and there is space between each small architectural unit where greenery is planted, allowing a pleasant breeze to pass through.

When a building needs to be made large, various innovations were made to maximize the length of the lines that are in contact with nature, and in turn to minimize the distance between people and nature by creating a floor plan with many corners, called the goose-flying plan, which was adopted at Katsura Imperial Villa and Nijo Castle. I adopted the goose-flying plan for the Portland Japanese Garden and various other projects.

In addition to making the overall building small, architects were required to make each individual component that composed the structure small. Since wood, a natural material, is used to build wooden structures, there is a limit to the thickness of the columns and beams, inevitably resulting in smaller components. However, compared to China and Korea, which have a similar tradition of building wooden structures, the size of the parts used in wooden structures in Japan is strikingly smaller. This increases the transparency of the space and reduces the obstructions to the flow of wind and entrance of light, making the space feel closer to nature.

The effect of utilizing small components does not end here. By using wood that is small, structures can be built with timber that is cut when thinning forests, without cutting down thick trees that take hundreds of years to grow, and this practice continued to protect forest resources. The fact that forests cover 70 percent of the land in Japan, which is unprecedented in a developed country, is the result of the unique wooden-construction system, which is based on the use of small-sized materials. The use of small-sized wood enables wooden structures to be incorporated in a naturally sustainable cycle, which seamlessly connects forests and buildings.

Due to the fact that, in Japan, metallic material is not used for the joints between members in wooden structures, which instead is assembled with small wooden members, this created a system where the joints were used as a type of shock absorber. A system called Kumiki was used to join the ends of members together rather than using metal fittings, eliminating deterioration resulting from rusting of the metal and increasing aseismic performance by reducing earthquake load. This is seismic-resistant design that was way ahead of its time.

The thing that is even more surprising about this wooden-construction system based on small members is the fact that it used the rational standard dimensions proposed by twentieth-century modernist architects, known for their adoption of the modular system. Le Corbusier and various other twentieth-century architects dreamed of rationalizing the production of structures, reducing costs, and shortening building schedules by comprehensively standardizing all dimensions used for buildings.

However, the modular system that they proposed ended up becoming an armchair theory and was not actually used on construction sites. The reason for this was the fact that structural materials have various thicknesses, which results in gaps where members with different thicknesses are joined together, making it impossible to use units that are manufactured with standard dimensions.

The first people who realized this were carpenters in Japan. Building wooden structures in the Middle Ages required components called tatamis, which had a standard dimension of approximately 90 × 180 cm. This was the first time that dimensions for architecture were standardized. However, since all the materials in a delicate wooden structure in Japan have a certain thickness, structures cannot be built by drawing a grid with 90 cm modules. It was necessary for the carpenters to absorb the errors due to thickness in various portions of the structure.

This was the reason that the modular system proposed in the twentieth century failed. Nevertheless, the problem of errors in wooden structures was brilliantly solved on-site by carpenters by means of fine adjustments, such as shaving and cutting to the length and thickness of wooden members, while striving to facilitate rationalization, streamlining, and low cost. In addition to being small, wood is a soft material, which resulted in a flexible modular system that was unprecedented anywhere in the world way before the age of industrialization.

With its softness, standardized architecture in Japan created buildings that had a pleasant and beautiful rhythm and at the same time achieved a system that was efficient and rational and could stand the passage of time. With wooden buildings being soft and flexible, it is relatively easy to extend and renovate them. Concrete and steel buildings, in contrast, have a narrower future.

The system that was created and perfected in Japan provided me with many hints for post-coronavirus-pandemic architecture at a time when the world is headed toward the adoption of softness and smallness. Naturally, the traditions that were used in Japan cannot be adopted to the various conditions required by modern society and unpredictable climate change without modification. However, I would like to count on the fact that flexibility is the essence of Japanese architecture. I believe that it can adapt and persevere in order to create new solutions to problems, no matter how demanding and severe the situation.

INTRODUCTION

BY JOE BOSCHETTI

In the first few years of the 2000s, in my junior days as an editor in architecture and design publishing, I boldly invited Kengo Kuma to write the foreword to a book about architectural detailing and was both surprised and delighted when he generously agreed. At the time, I was fascinated by Kengo Kuma's own projects that featured in the book, in particular stone walls that looked soft, like they were constructed from wood.

Moving forward twenty-four years since then, the world has survived a pandemic, and like many of us, our thoughts have turned toward finding spaces that are comforting and enveloping. I found myself reflecting on architecture, and back to the days when I would edit books about details in architecture and thought immediately about Kengo Kuma-san. In this book, Professor Kuma writes in the introduction to the first chapter, "Fabric," that buildings are like clothes: "Buildings are created between the bodies of people and the external environment in order to mediate between them. This definition is in essence the definition of clothes. I think that architecture and clothes are essentially the same. It should be possible to transform architecture into a form that is gentler to people if lessons are learned from the flexibility and softness of clothes."

It has been a pleasure to watch this book emerge from an idea. I am grateful to Kengo Kuma for boldly accepting the challenge, again, to be involved with a book on which I am working. I am grateful to Pete Schiffer and the professional and creative team at Schiffer Publishing, and to the talented and professional team at Kengo Kuma Architects and Associates who were so obliging to coordinate all content.

CHAPTER 1 FABRIC

I've long wanted to create structures that function like clothes, mediating between the human body and the external environment—much like clothing itself does. This notion aligns with my belief that architecture and clothes share an essential similarity; they both act as intermediaries, providing protection and comfort. I am convinced that by adopting the flexibility and softness characteristic of textiles, architecture can be transformed into a form that is more accommodating and gentler to people.

This intersection of architecture and textile has intrigued other architects as well. A notable figure in this realm is Gottfried Semper, a pivotal architect in nineteenth-century architectural theory. Semper made significant contributions to the design sections of the Great Exhibitions at the Crystal Palace in London. His profound studies of Indigenous dwellings from around the globe led him to propose a groundbreaking definition of architecture in his work The Four Elements of Architecture. Semper's use of the term ""weaving," a concept borrowed from the textile and clothing industries, highlights his innovative approach to integrating textile principles into architectural practices. This idea underscores the potential for a symbiotic relationship between the disciplines of architecture and textile design, suggesting that both can benefit from the insights and techniques of the other.

While Gottfried Semper was deeply embedded within Western culture, he ambitiously sought to redefine architecture by stepping outside the conventional Western methods of stone and brick masonry. It's often said that modernist architectural theory began with Semper. However, despite his attempts to break away from traditional masonry structures, modernist architecture ultimately remained tethered to frame structures made of concrete and steel. This observation suggests that Semper's vision might have extended far beyond the confines of modernism and even traditional architectural practices.

Recently, it feels as if Rem Koolhaas has the strongest interest in the potential of fabric. He stated that Philip Johnson told him that when designing the main building of the Kröller-Müller Museum (1938), the architect made a full-scale mockup of the museum using fabric to verify its size and space. This brings to mind the use of cloth for the wrapping of architecture by Christo and Jeanne-Claud. In fact, the unique fabric designed by Petra Blaisse, Rem Koolhaas's partner in his personal and professional life, often appears in his architecture. It consists of a new type of cloth that needs a different name, which is not used for curtains or applied to the walls like wallpaper.

However, it feels that Rem has a low level of interest in creating entire buildings with cloth. I dream that the age of concrete and steel will be followed by an age of wood, which is softer, and that this will give way to an age of cloth architecture, which is even softer.

FABRIC 1: CASA UMBRELLA

Completion year: 2008
Location: Milan, Italy
Structure: steel
Building type: pavilion

This project was initiated with the aim of reimagining the concept of a "temporary house," focusing on ease of construction and the use of readily available materials. The selected product, an umbrella, is already engineered to be lightweight, easily foldable, portable, and effective at repelling rain. By employing umbrellas in a novel, three-dimensional manner, we envisioned creating a new type of architectural product.

In our design, called Casa Umbrella, each triangle of a regular icosahedron structure is replaced with an umbrella. The "bones" of the umbrellas serve as a truss structure, with every component adapted from common umbrella designs. For connecting these umbrellas, we utilize water-cutoff fasteners typically used in diving suits. This allows for the rapid assembly of a new space in an open area simply by opening the umbrellas and fastening them together with zippers.

The umbrellas' size is determined by the scale of the space intended to be created. For instance, a few umbrellas can form a small roof or a partition, while fifteen umbrellas can construct a more substantial shelter. The material covering the umbrella is Tyvek, a polyethylene nonwoven fabric produced by DuPont, known for its excellent waterproofing and moisture-proofing qualities, which also meshes well with zippers for easy sewing.

Casa Umbrella adapts to the weather conditions: on rainy days, it serves as a rain shelter, while on sunny days, it can transform into a small arbor by unzipping sections to allow natural light and air to flow through. This design not only challenges traditional architectural concepts but also offers a practical, adaptable temporary housing solution for varying conditions.

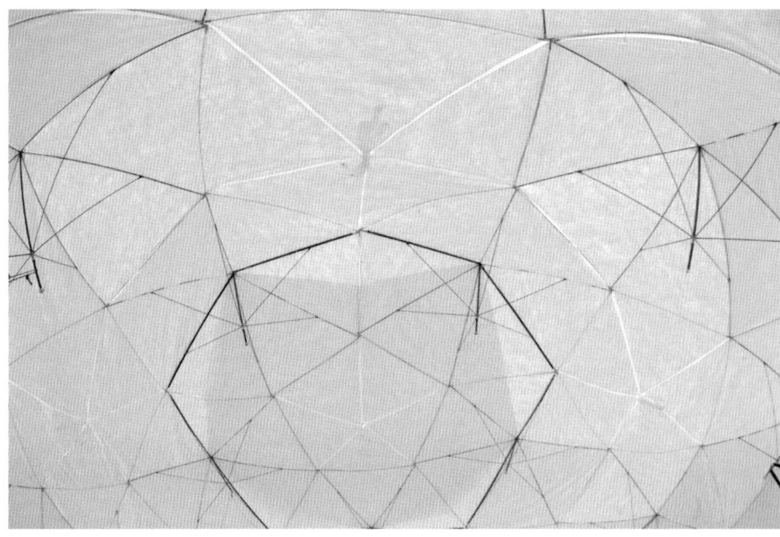

The structural integrity of Casa Umbrella, despite its resemblance in size to a standard umbrella, is enhanced by the adoption of a Tensegrity structure—a concept promoted by Buckminster Fuller that involves tensional integrity. This structure uses the tension of the membrane material, specifically a Dupont Tyvek waterproof sheet, in balance with the compression forces of a steel frame, enabling a delicate yet robust architectural system.

Buckminster Fuller was also instrumental in conceptualizing the use of geometric structures such as icosahedrons for creating domes, famously known as Fuller domes. However, he did not integrate the Tensegrity structure into these domes. As a result, Fuller domes lacked the lightweight, tentlike feel of portable structures and presented a more complex visual image. In contrast, Casa Umbrella aims to capture the portability and lightness of nomadic gers (yurts), facilitating easy transport and assembly.

Envisioned as a practical solution for emergency situations, these umbrellas could be stored at home entrances, ready to be used by residents needing to evacuate during disasters such as earthquakes or tsunamis. If fifteen people were to come together with these umbrellas, they could quickly assemble a temporary communal dwelling. This concept was practically demonstrated when fifteen students in Milan constructed the Casa Umbrella. They successfully used it for a gathering and stayed overnight, highlighting the design's functionality and communal potential.

01 Separate Center Shaft

02 Add Supporting Ribs

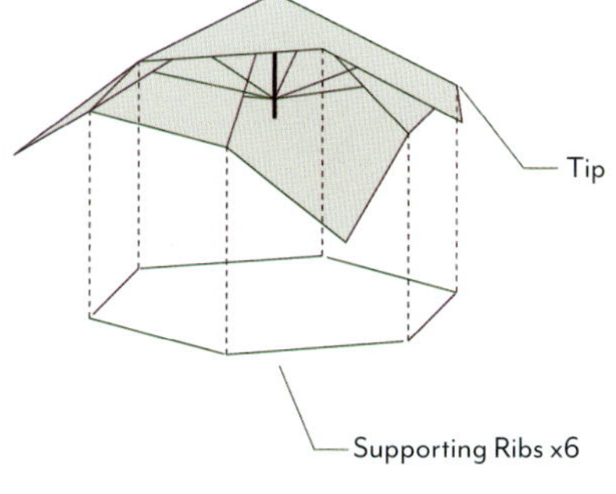

03 Zip Umbrellas

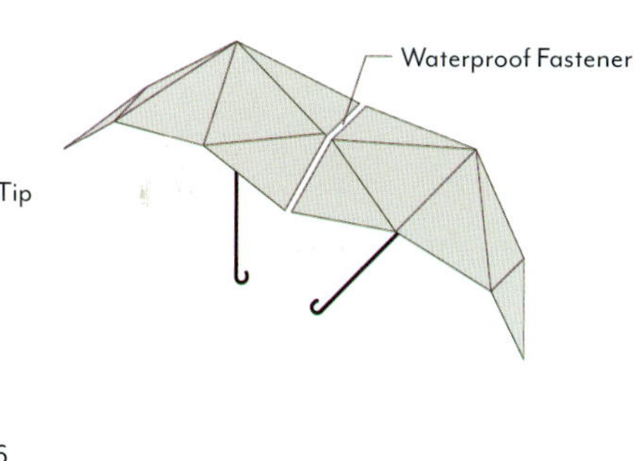

Separatable shaft

Supporting ribs hidden inside shaft

Tip invented to be connected with supporting ribs

Waterproof fastener

Assembly

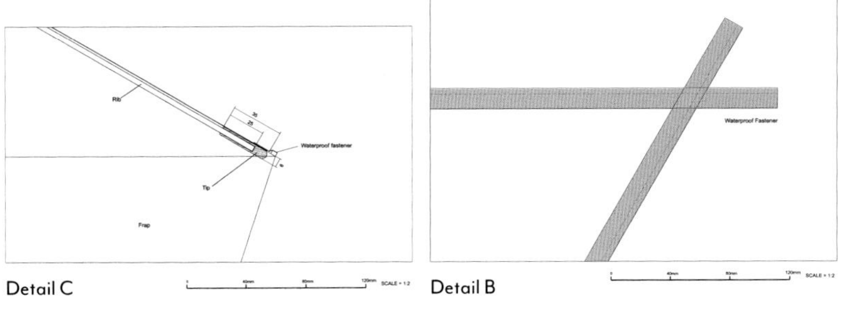

Detail C

Detail B

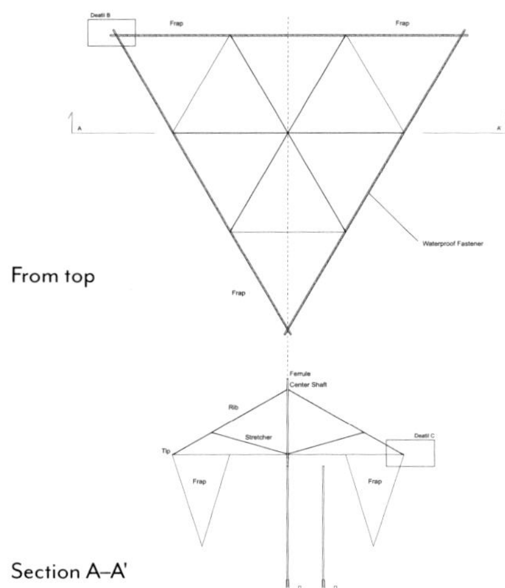

From top

Section A–A'

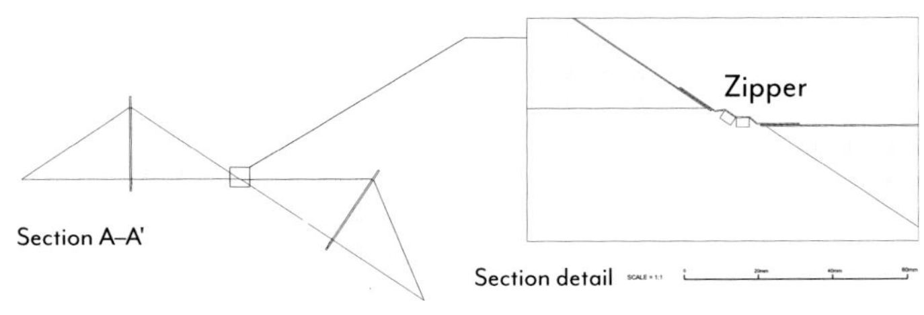

Section A–A'

Section detail

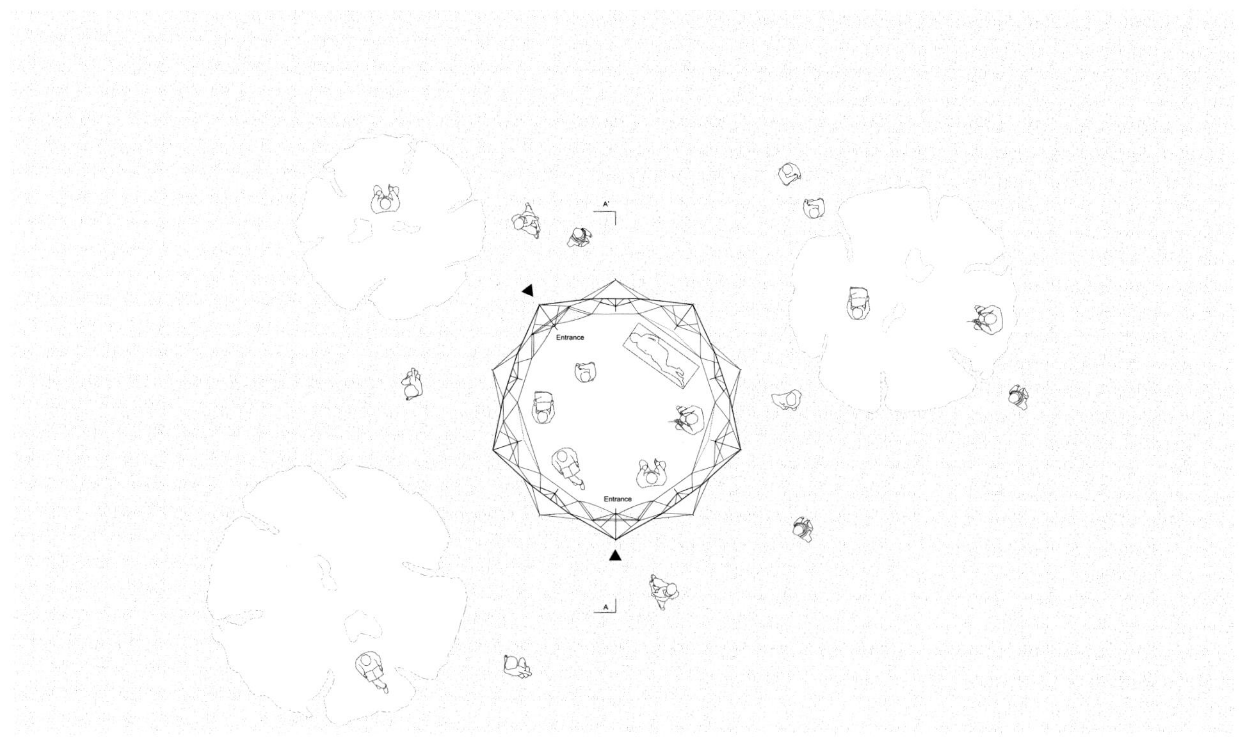

Plan

0 1M 3M 5M

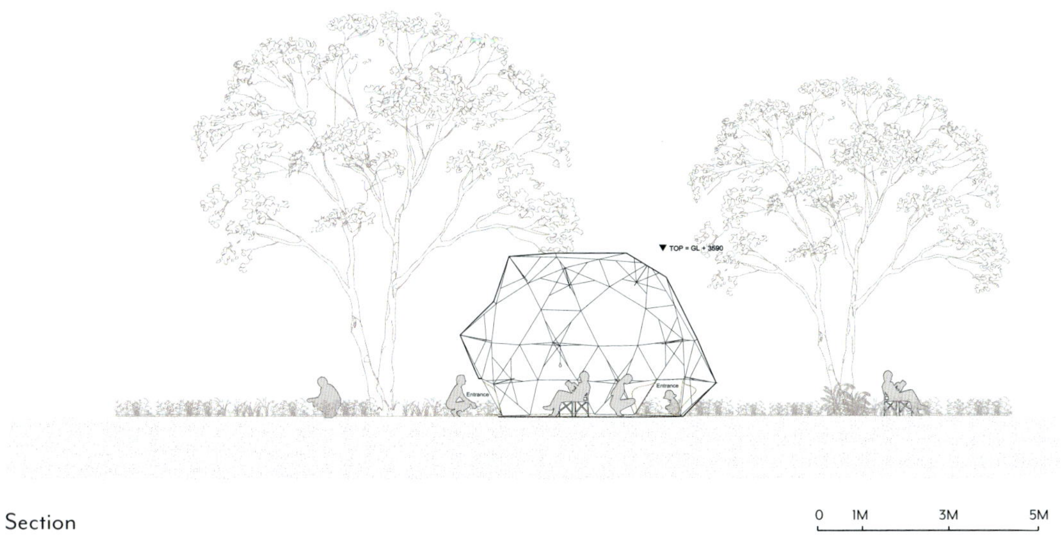

Section

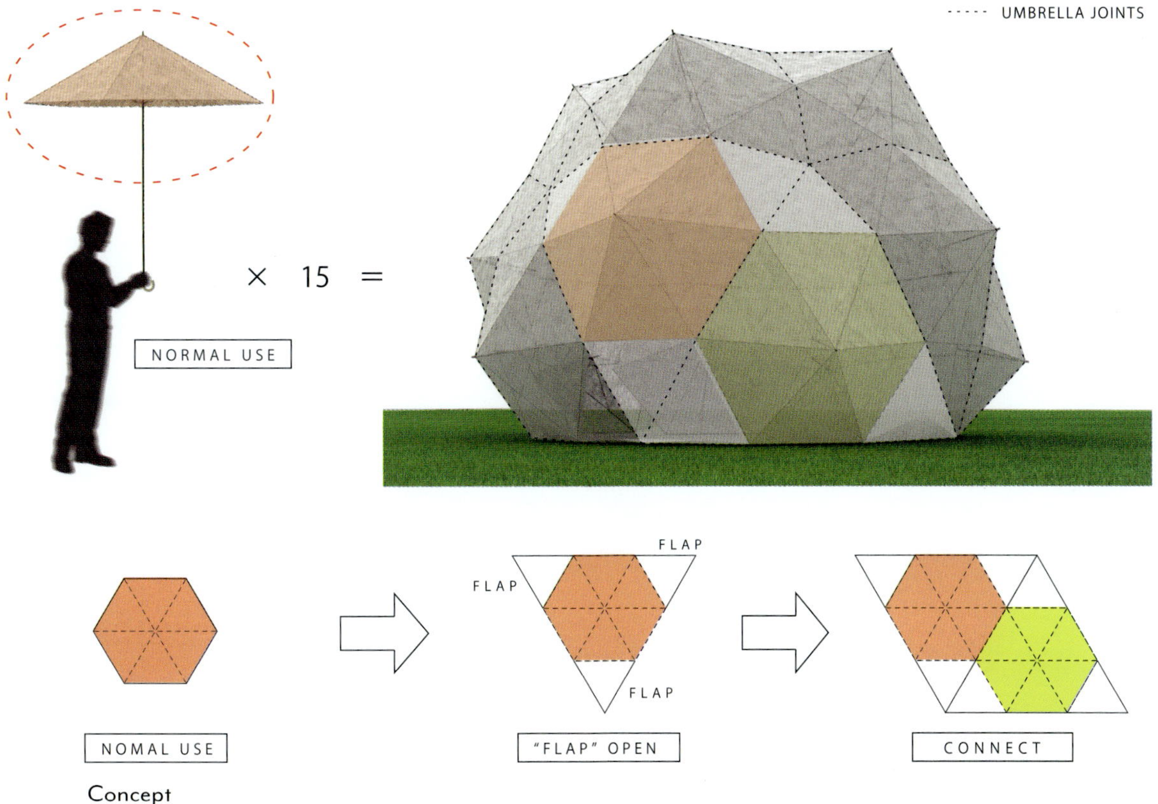

Concept

FABRIC 2: MÊMU MEADOWS

Completion year: 2011
Location: Hokkaido, Japan
Structure: wood
Building type: experimental house

Mêmu Meadows, formerly known as Taiki Farm, a farm for racehorses, has undergone a remarkable transformation into a hub for research, education, and training focused on sustainable architecture and urban solutions. This ambitious project comprises two key components: the construction of experimental houses within the grasslands, and the adaptive reuse of former horse stables and an indoor riding arena into university laboratories, accommodations, and training facilities.

The renovation of the former stables represents a symbolic shift from housing for horses to housing for humans. Portions of the expansive indoor arena, complete with its circular 30 m long track, have been repurposed into a vibrant restaurant and bar. These adaptive transformations are underpinned by state-of-the-art environmental technologies, ensuring sustainability and efficiency in design and operation.

The inception of the experimental house initiative dates back to 2011, with subsequent years seeing the realization of winning designs from a competitive process. Notable contributions include projects from esteemed institutions such as Waseda University (2011), Keio University (2012), Harvard University (2013), and the University of California, Berkeley (2014). Crucially, students have actively participated in the construction process, gaining invaluable hands-on experience.

Looking ahead, the vision for Mêmu Meadows is to evolve into a pioneering sustainable-housing village, offering a model unlike any other in the world. Nestled amid the picturesque prairies, this innovative community will serve as a beacon of sustainable living and design excellence.

The primary structural framework was constructed using wood, and a crane was utilized to sheath the framework with a PVC membrane. This membrane, resembling the action of donning a raincoat, was presewn in a factory.

Comprising two layers—a PVC film exterior and a nonflammable fiberglass film interior—the membrane incorporates a 100 mm thick air layer. Warmed air circulates within this layer, enabling winter endurance in Hokkaido without the need for bulky insulation. The inner fiberglass film is affixed with Velcro, facilitating easy attachment and removal.

The Indigenous Ainu people of Hokkaido historically employed Kuma bamboo grass leaves for roofing and walling their dwellings. They continue to reside in traditional Chise houses, characterized by an exceptionally soft texture. Inspiration for employing the aforementioned membrane was drawn from the texture of these Chise dwellings.

Central to a Chise is a hearth, leveraging the ground itself as a thermal reservoir by maintaining a continuous fire during summer, thereby enduring winter cold. Similarly, at Mêmu Meadows, a hearth occupies the center, with the concrete floor slab ingeniously designed to serve as a thermal reservoir.

Ceiling Section Detail

roof:
membrane
ceiling hanger
wooden ceiling joist
ceiling hanger
hook-and-loop fastener
15
15
glass fiber cloth

Ceiling: Wall Section Detail

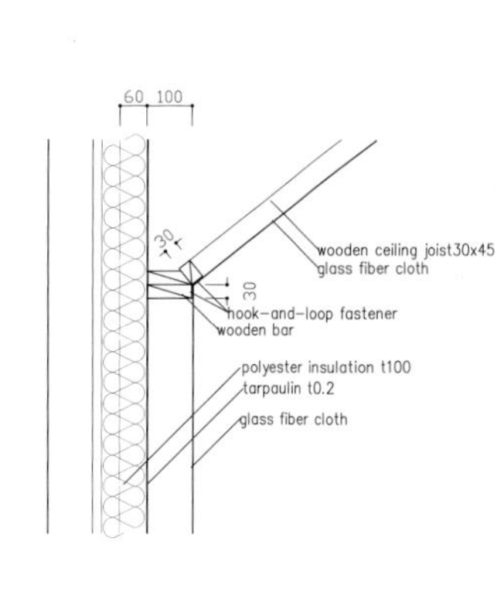

Wall Plan Detail

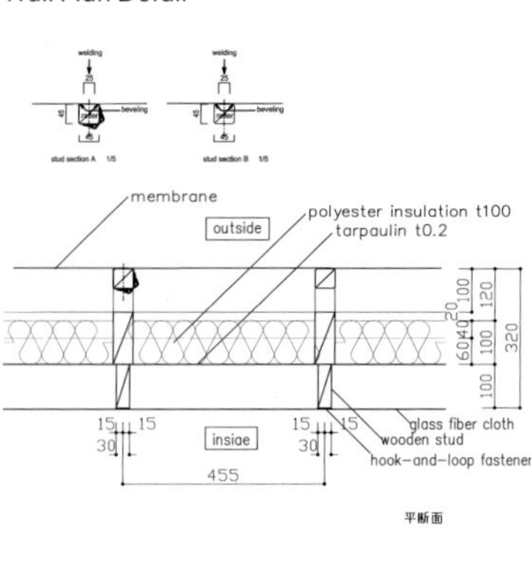

Corner Plan Detail

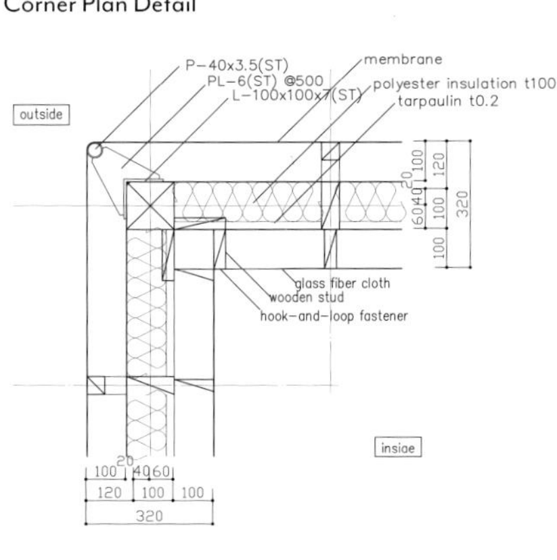

Roof: Wall Section Detail

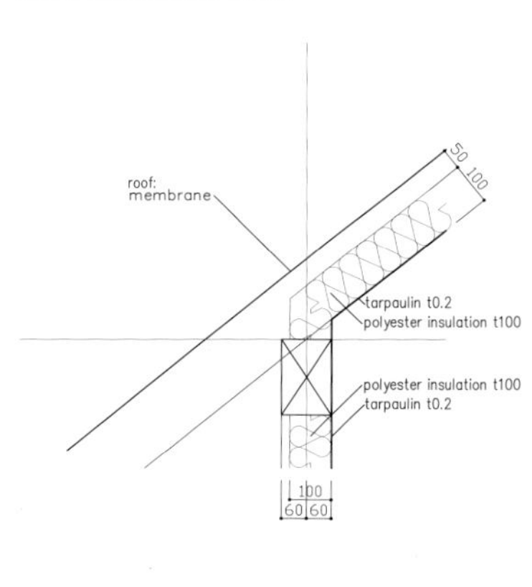

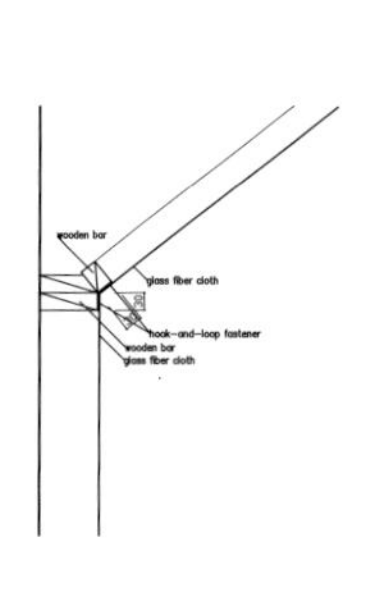

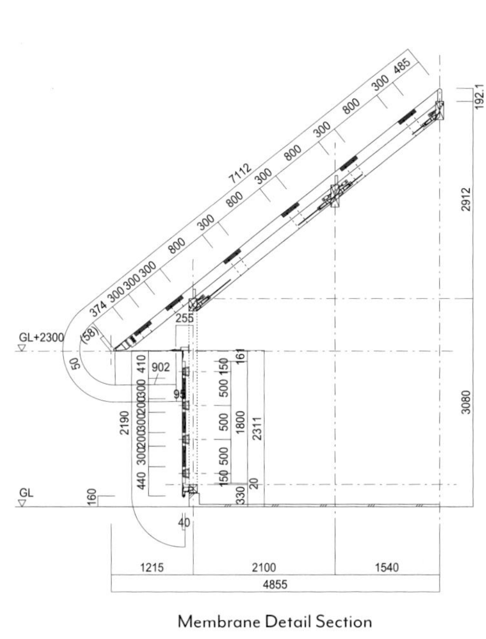

Membrane Detail Section

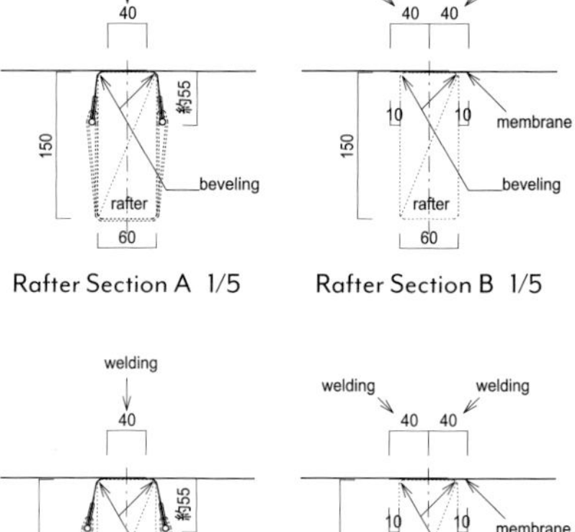

Rafter Section A 1/5

Rafter Section B 1/5

B A
membrane
grommet#3(SUS)
rope
75 150 75
300

Rafter Elevation 1/5

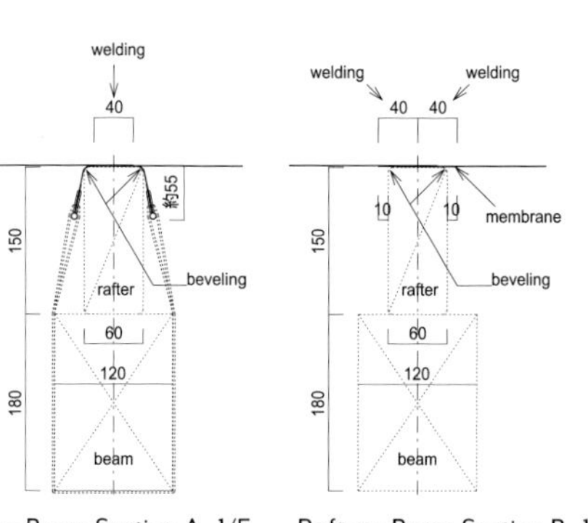

Rafter + Beam Section A 1/5

Rafter + Beam Section B 1/5

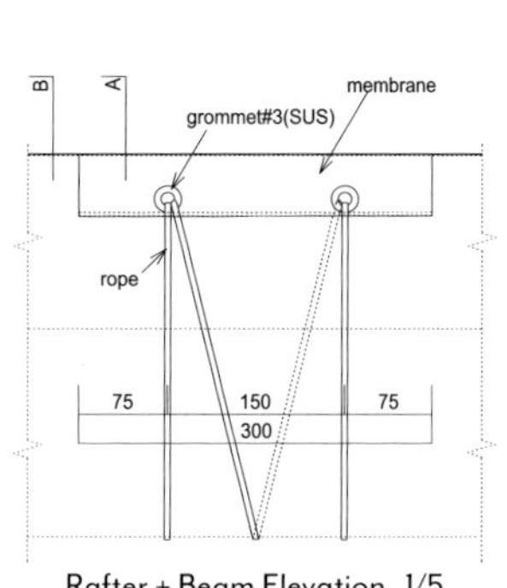

Rafter + Beam Elevation 1/5

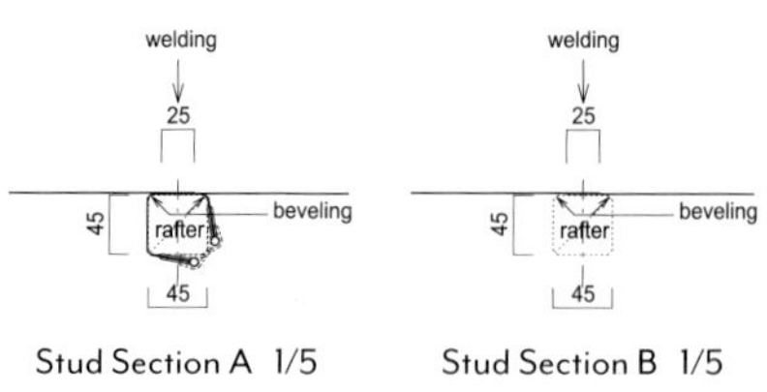

Stud Section A 1/5

Stud Section B 1/5

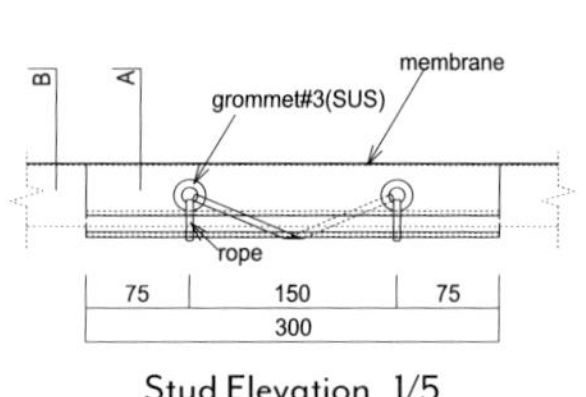

Stud Elevation 1/5

Section Details

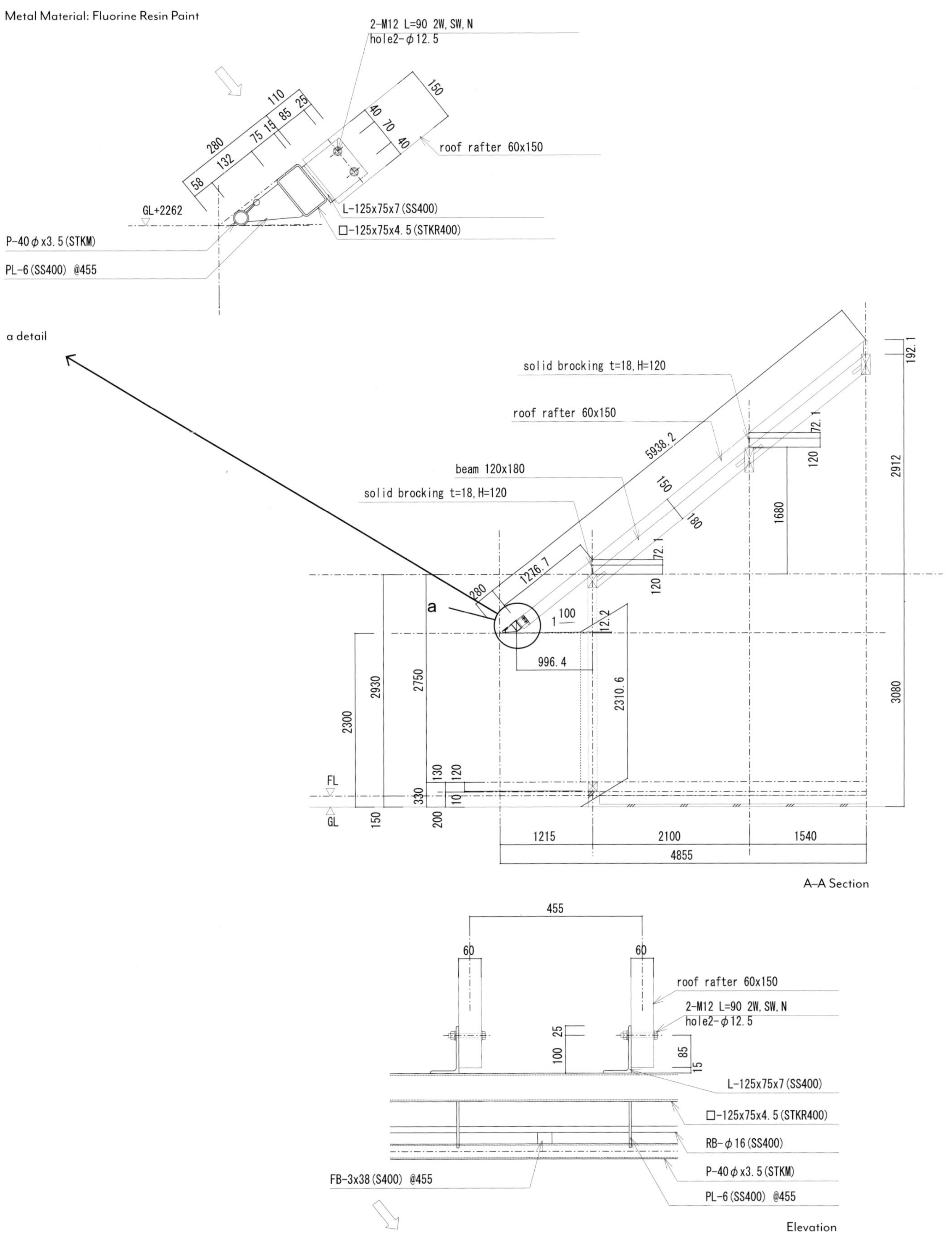

Metal Material: Fluorine Resin Paint
2-M12 L=90 2W, SW, N
hole2-φ12.5
roof rafter 60x150
L-125x75x7 (SS400)
□-125x75x4.5 (STKR400)
GL+2262
P-40φx3.5 (STKM)
PL-6 (SS400) @455
a detail
solid brocking t=18, H=120
roof rafter 60x150
beam 120x180
solid brocking t=18, H=120
FL
GL
A–A Section
roof rafter 60x150
2-M12 L=90 2W, SW, N
hole2-φ12.5
L-125x75x7 (SS400)
□-125x75x4.5 (STKR400)
RB-φ16 (SS400)
P-40φx3.5 (STKM)
PL-6 (SS400) @455
FB-3x38 (S400) @455
Elevation

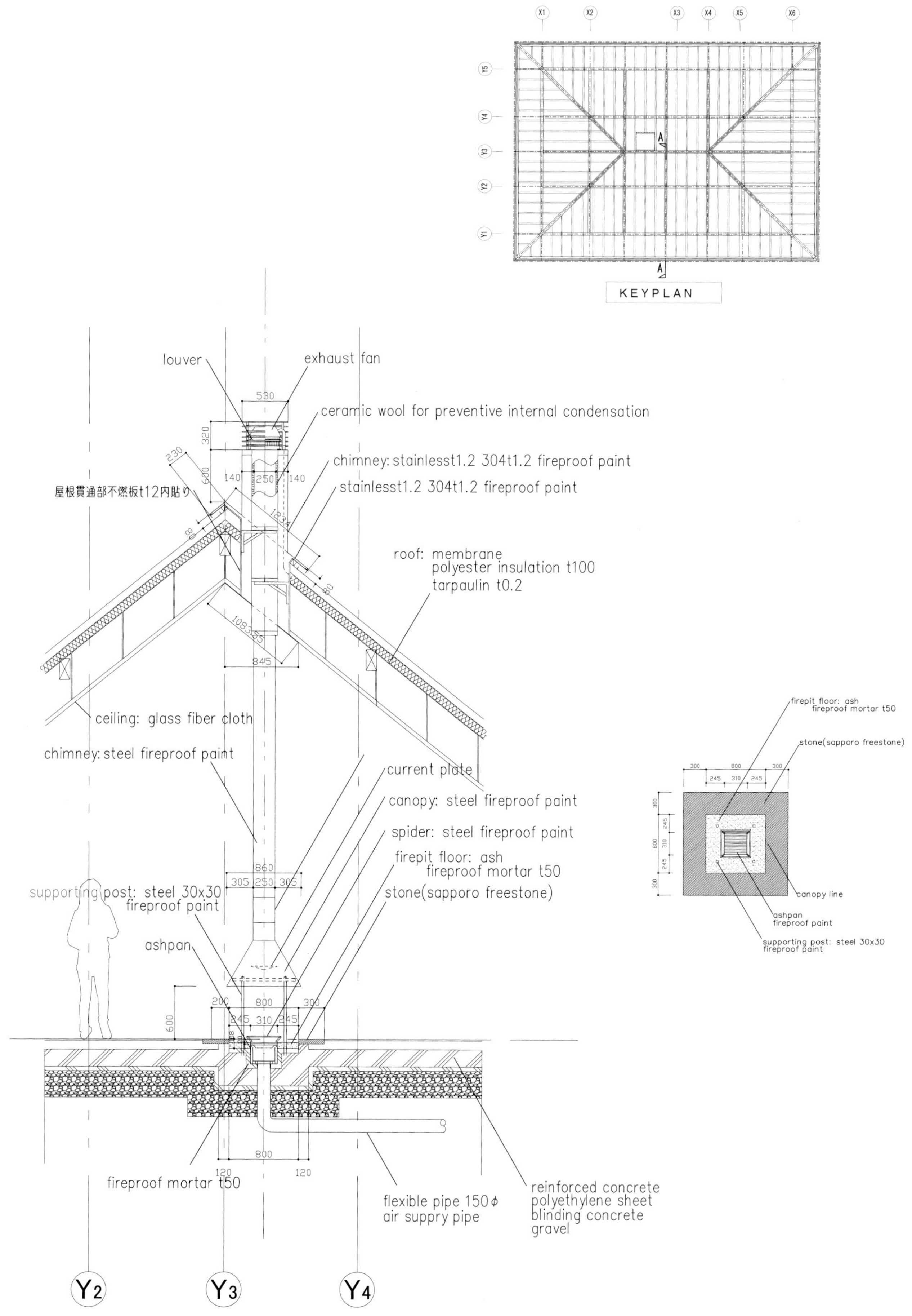
KEYPLAN
louver
exhaust fan
ceramic wool for preventive internal condensation
chimney: stainlesst1.2 304t1.2 fireproof paint
屋根貫通部不燃板t12内貼り
stainlesst1.2 304t1.2 fireproof paint
roof: membrane
polyester insulation t100
tarpaulin t0.2
ceiling: glass fiber cloth
chimney: steel fireproof paint
current plate
canopy: steel fireproof paint
spider: steel fireproof paint
firepit floor: ash
fireproof mortar t50
stone(sapporo freestone)
supporting post: steel 30x30
fireproof paint
ashpan
FL
fireproof mortar t50
flexible pipe 150ϕ
air suppry pipe
reinforced concrete
polyethylene sheet
blinding concrete
gravel
Y2
Y3
Y4
canopy line
ashpan
fireproof paint

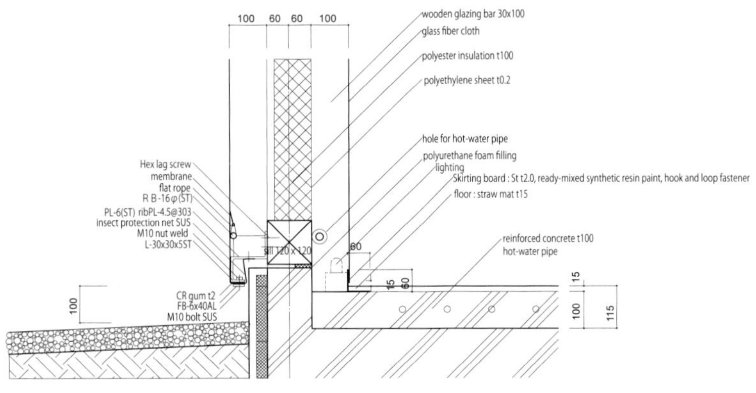

Detail Section

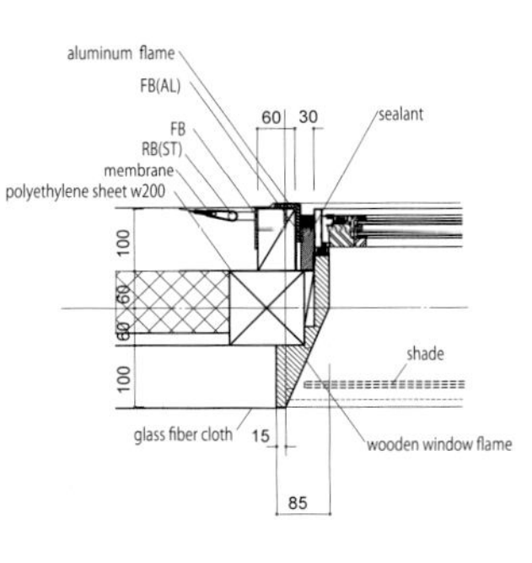

Window Horizontal Section Detail

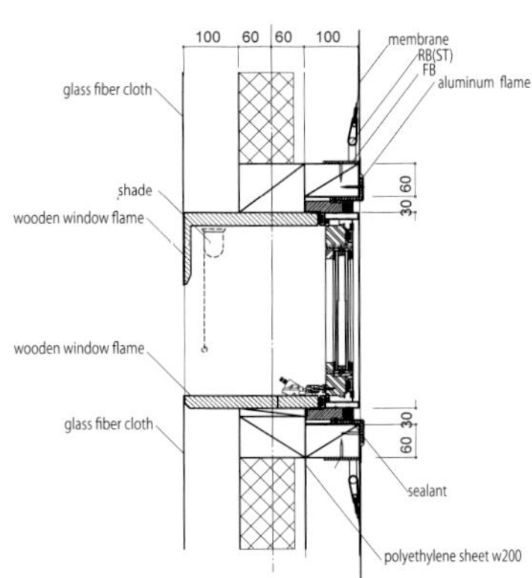

Window Vertical Section Detail

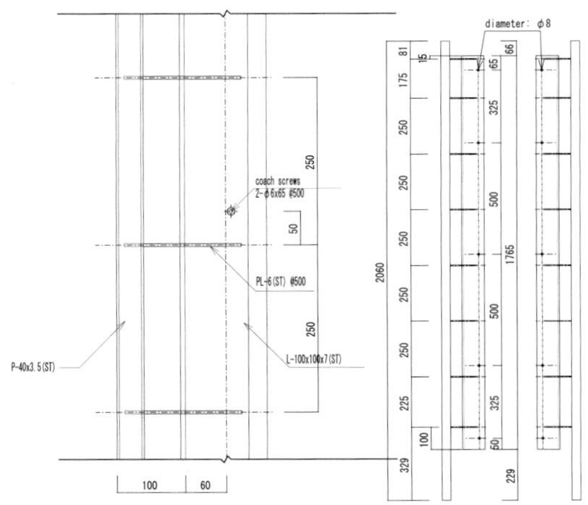

Elevation

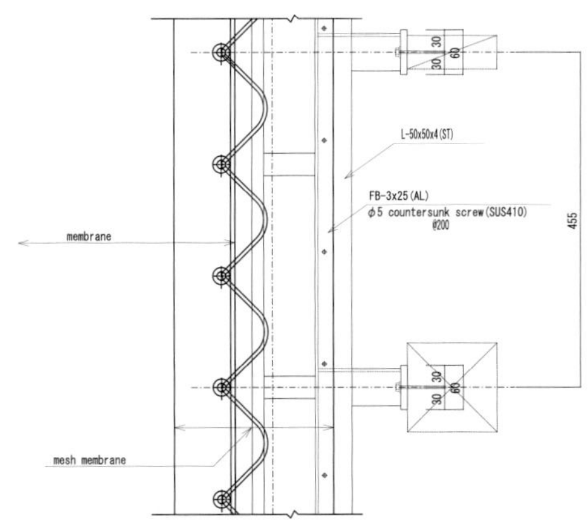

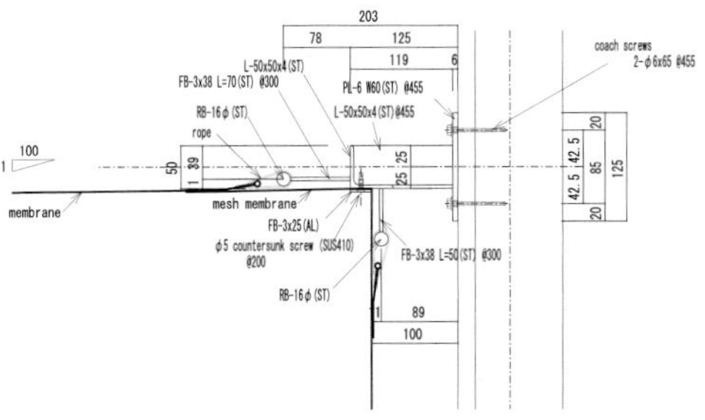

Wall Upper Part Detail

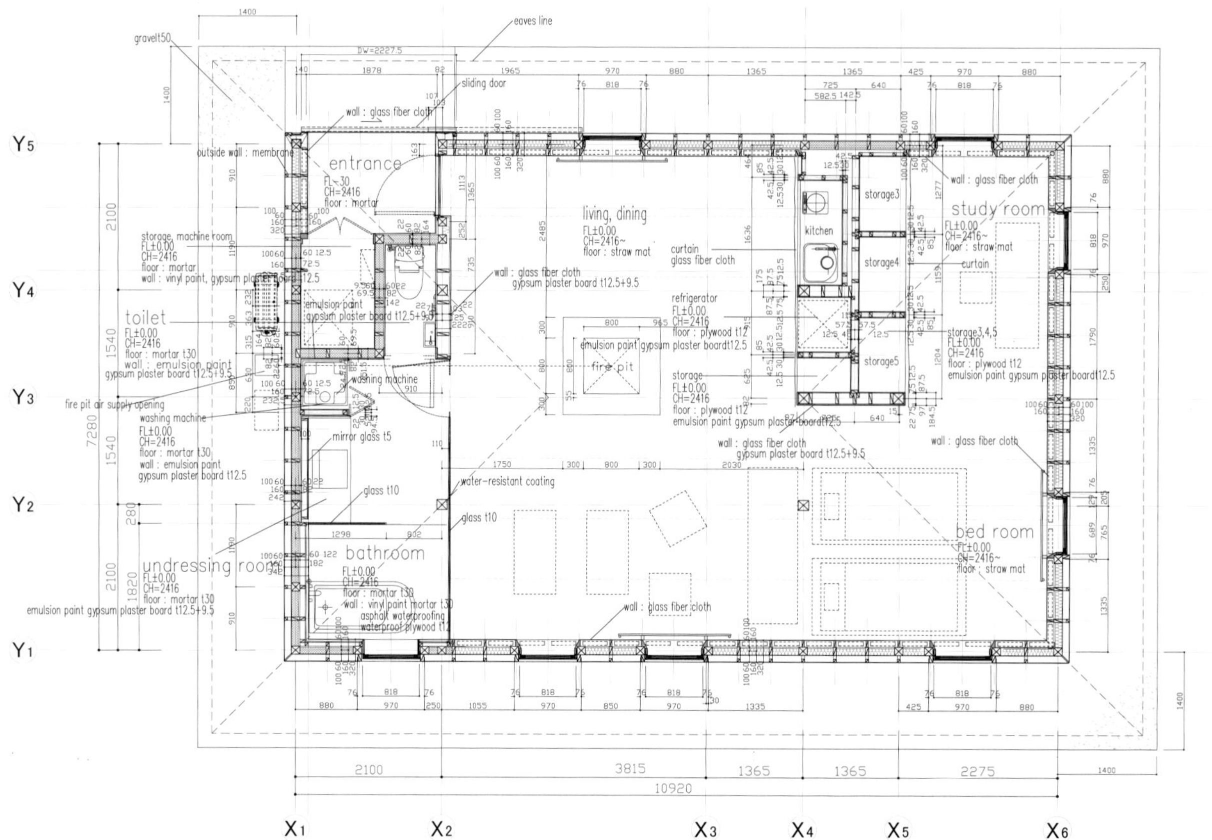

Plan

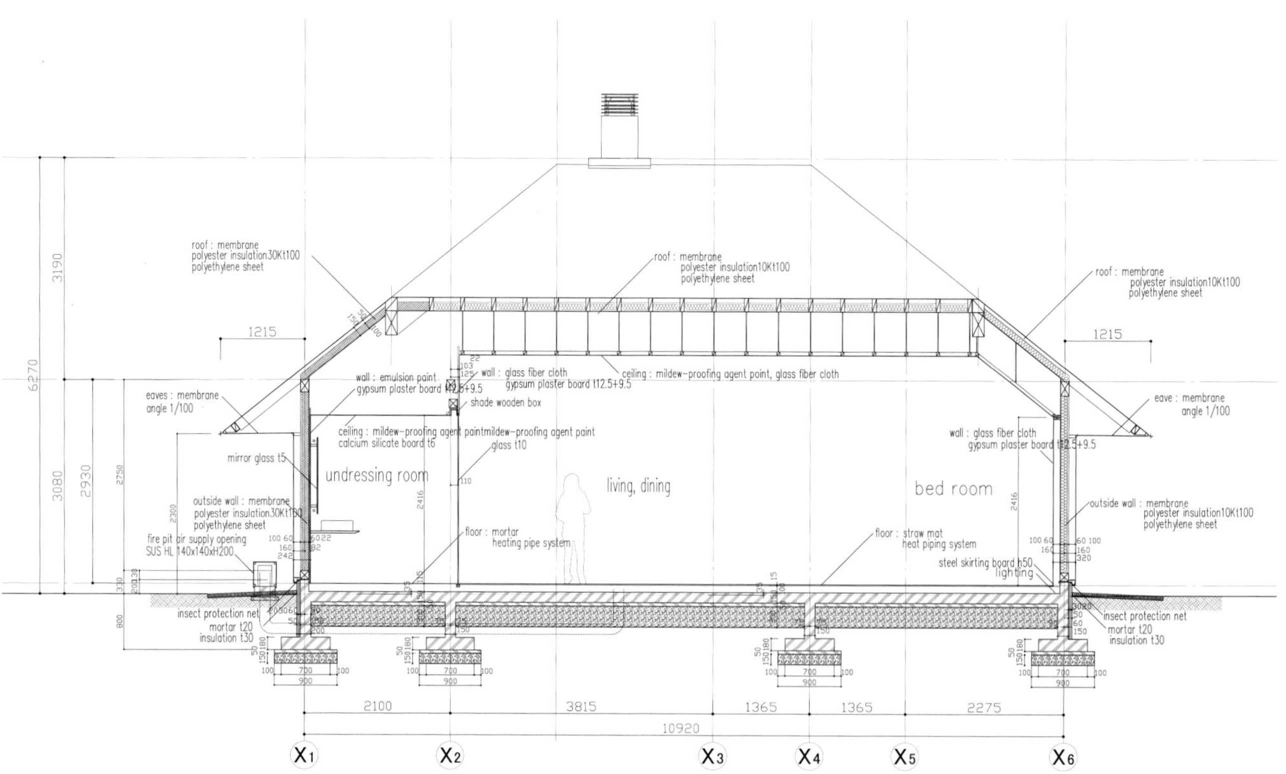

Section

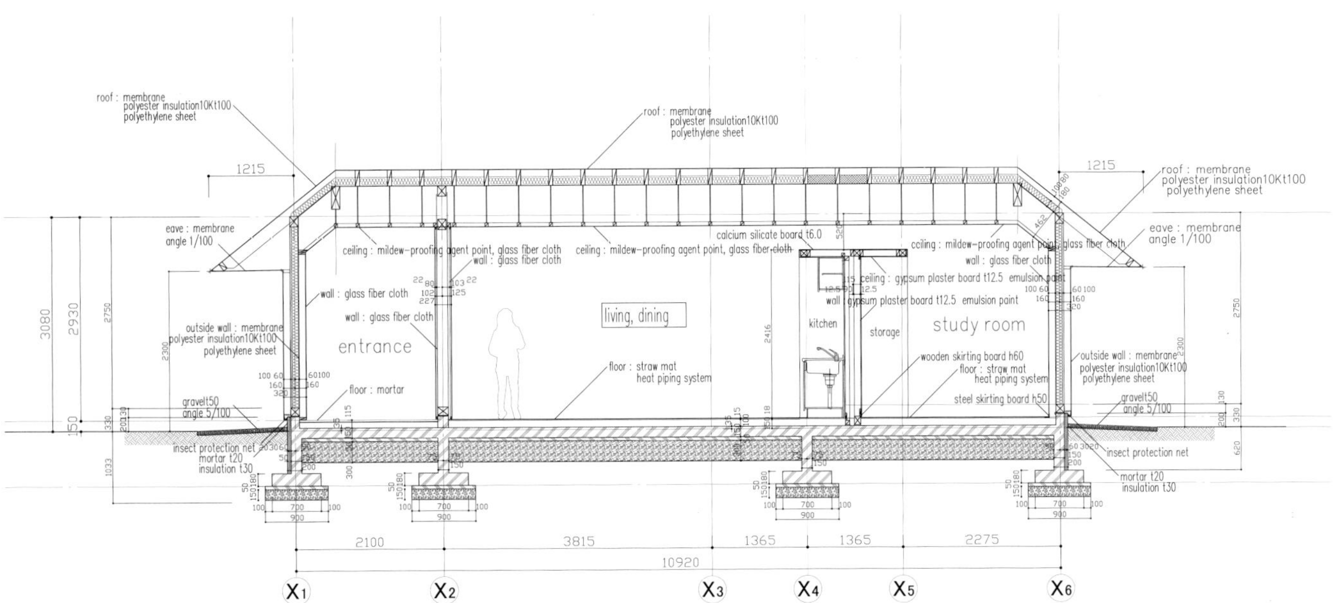

Section

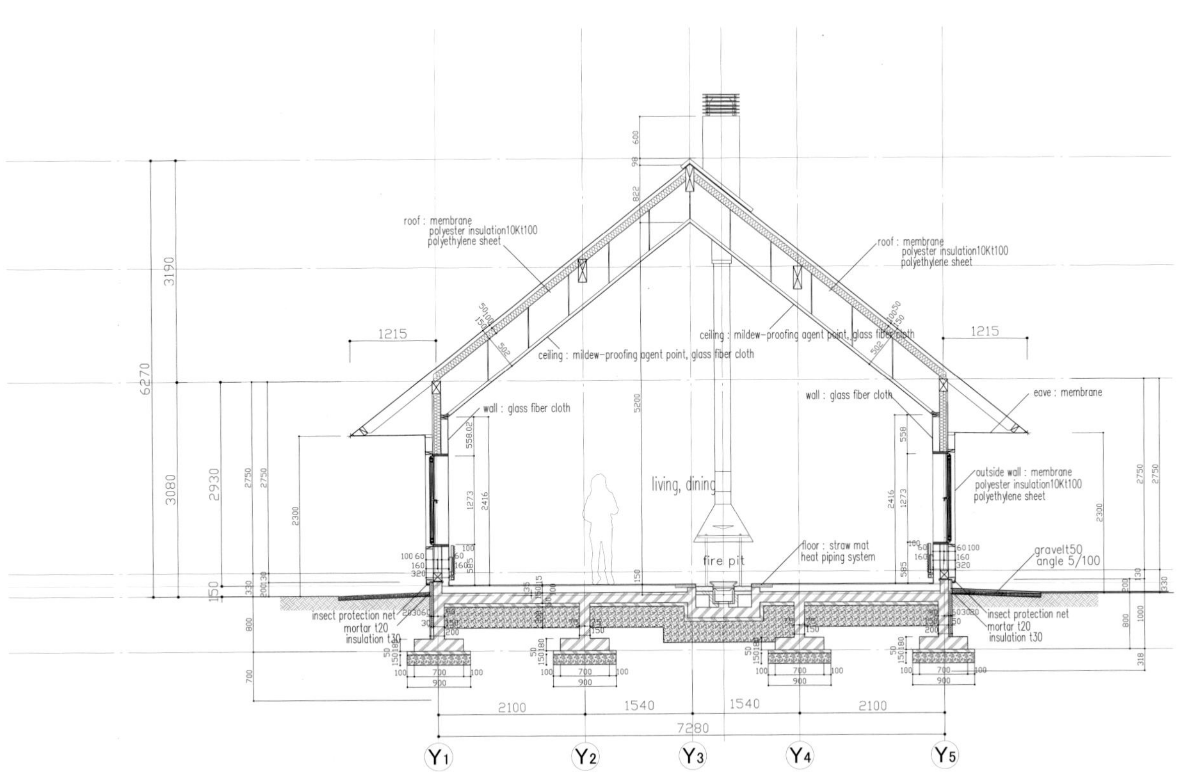

Section

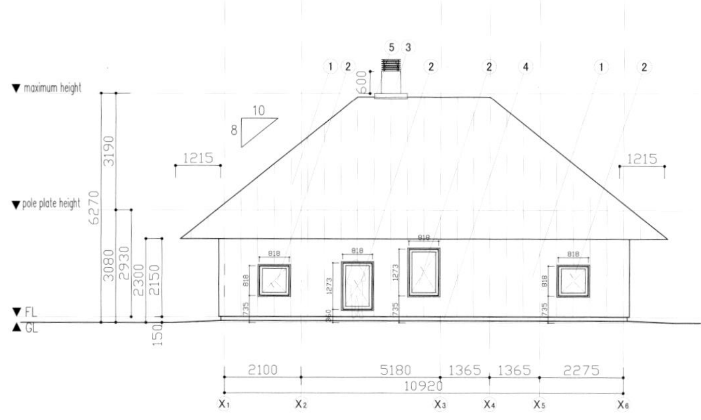

South Elevation

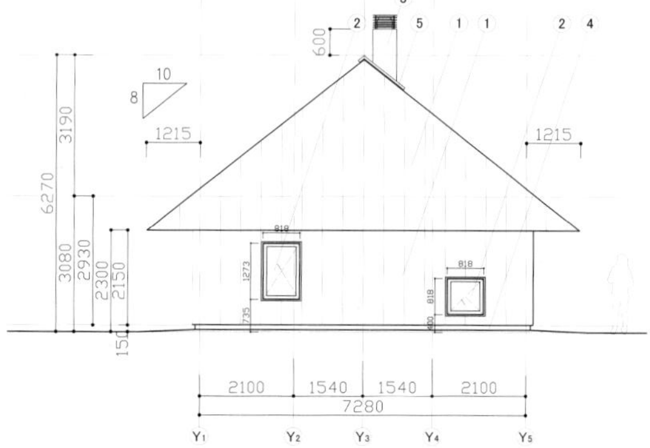

East Elevation

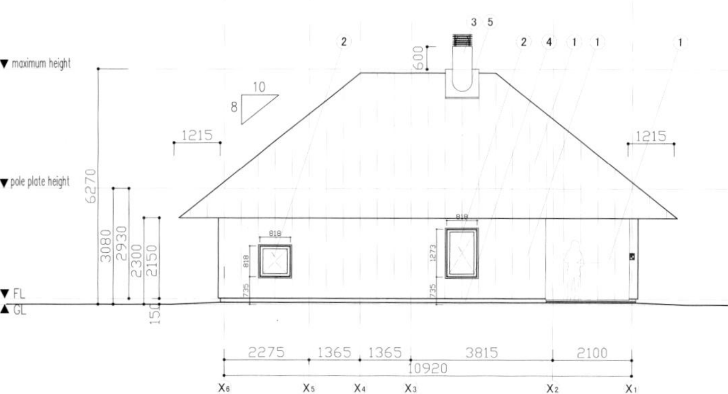

North Elevation

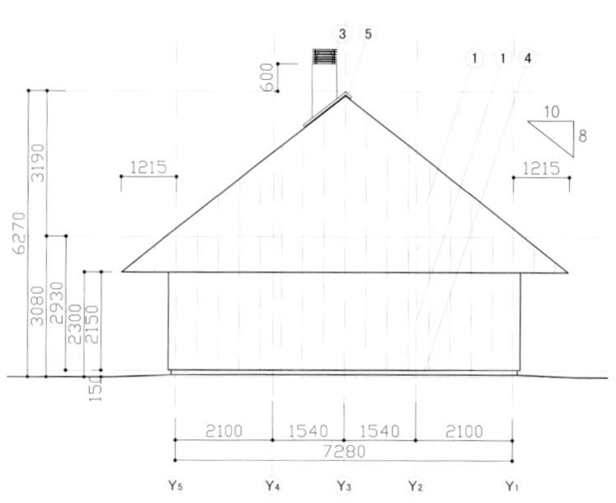

West Elevation

No.	Finish
1	Membrane
2	Double-glazed glass
3	Steel heat-resistant paint
4	Mortar
5	Galvanized sheet iron

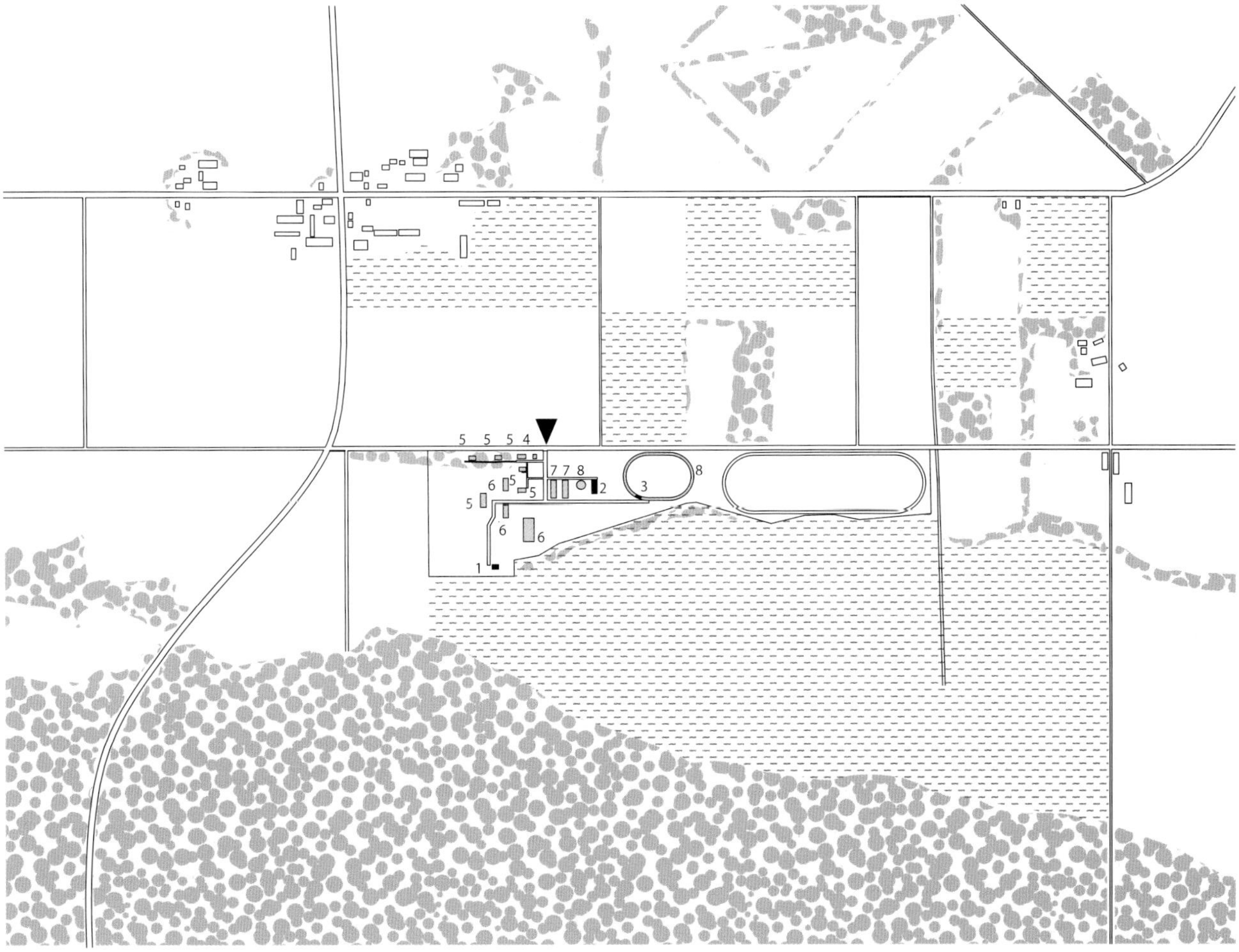

Site Plan 

1. MÊME (experimental residence)
2. Accomodation, laboratory (renovated stable block)
3. Restaurant (renovated indoor track)
4. Office (existing building)
5. Residence (existing building)
6. Store house (existing building)
7. Stable block (existing building)
8. Indoor track (existing building)

FABRIC 3: KOMATSU SEIREN FABRIC LABORATORY FA-BO

Completion year: 2015
Location: Ishikawa, Japan
Structure: RC/SRC (reinforced concrete / steel-reinforced concrete)
Building type: office

This project entails the renovation of an office building with a rigid-frame reinforced-concrete (RC) structure, aimed at enhancing its seismic resilience through the application of carbon fiber. Simultaneously, the interior is being converted into a museum named Fab Labo, dedicated to showcasing the technological advancements of Komatsu Seiren, the client company. The design leverages a local technique of rope braiding, with additional flexibility being ingeniously integrated into the carbon fiber.

Remarkably, the strength of the fiber rod reportedly surpasses that of iron by a factor of ten, marking the inaugural utilization of this material for earthquake reinforcement purposes. Exploring the potential of this lightweight and pliable fiber extends beyond structural enhancement to various applications within the building.

Internally, fiber is utilized for lighting ducts, while atop the building, experimental greening initiatives are underway that use porous ceramic panels known as Greenbiz. These panels are derived from the fiber production process, demonstrating a holistic approach to sustainability and innovation.

In the past, the transportation and installation of carbon fiber rods exceeding 10 m in length, such as those utilized in this project, posed significant challenges due to the inherent rigidity of carbon fiber. To address this limitation, the ancient technique of rope braiding, a tradition passed down through generations in the Hokuriku region, renowned for its textile industry since antiquity, was adapted for use with carbon fiber. This innovative approach endowed the rods with flexibility, thereby simplifying their transport and installation and facilitating the application of carbon fiber for seismic reinforcement.

H beams were strategically embedded around the perimeter of the building and linked to the foundation. The ends of the carbon fiber rods were affixed to these H beams, imparting a visual effect akin to the building being gently enveloped by the rods, reminiscent of a veil.

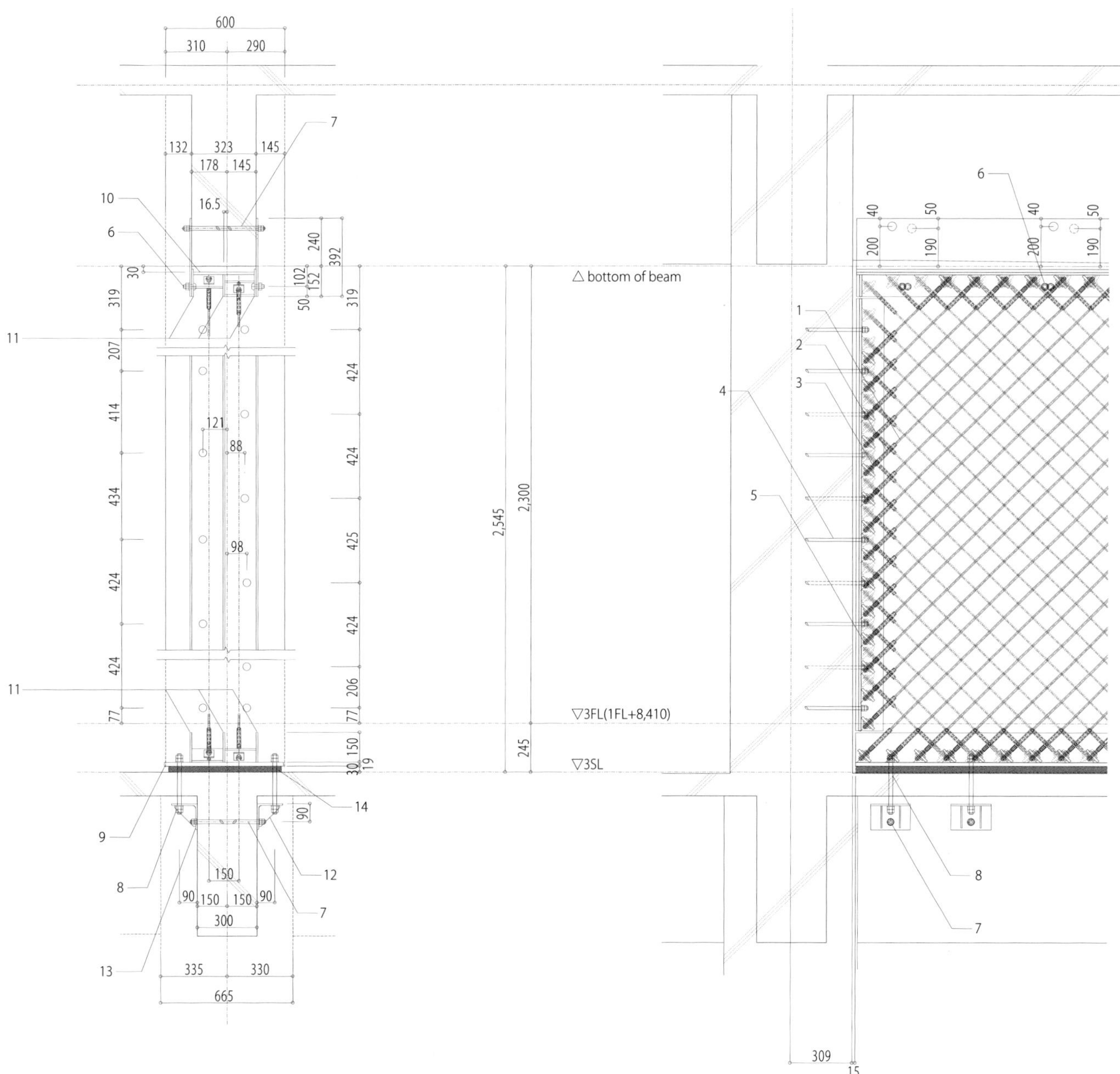

1. Carbon fiber rod φ 9 mm
2. Steel pipe, adhesive
3. Threaded bolt M16
4. Postconstruction anchor 2-M16
5. Bolt M20
6. High-strength bolt M20
7. Postconstruction anchor M20
8. Slab penetrating bolt M20
9. Steel plate t19 mm
10. Steel plate t12 mm
11. Steel plate t9 mm
12. Steel rib plate t6 mm
13. Steel L-shaped angle t9mm
14. Nonshrinkable mortar

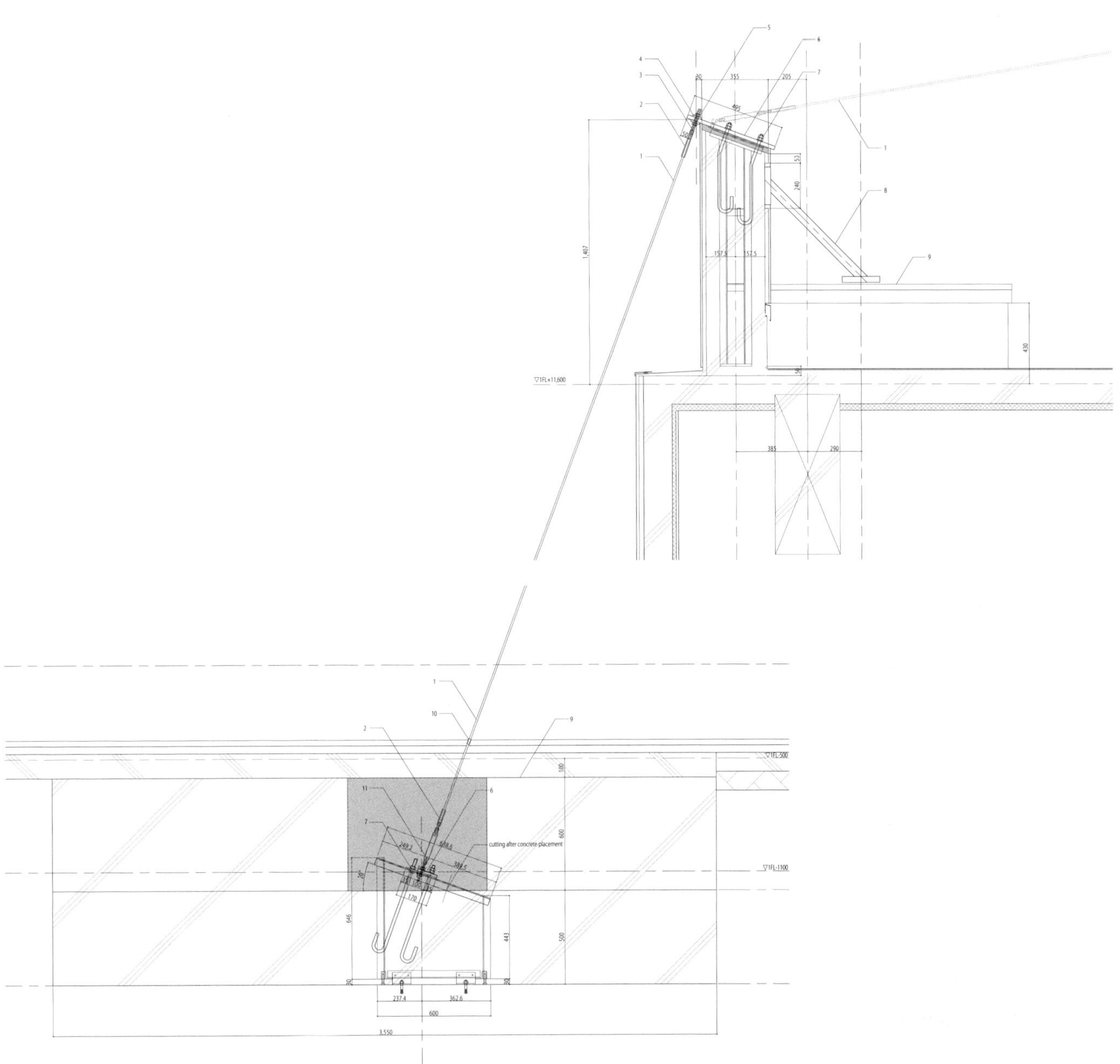

1. Carbon fiber rod φ 9 mm
2. Steel pipe, adhesive
3. Threaded bolt M16
4. Tapered washer
5. Bolt M20
6. Steel plate t19 mm
7. Anchor bolt 2-M16 @500
8. Steel round bar 40 mm
9. RC foundation
10. Sheath pipe
11. Pipe turnbuckle

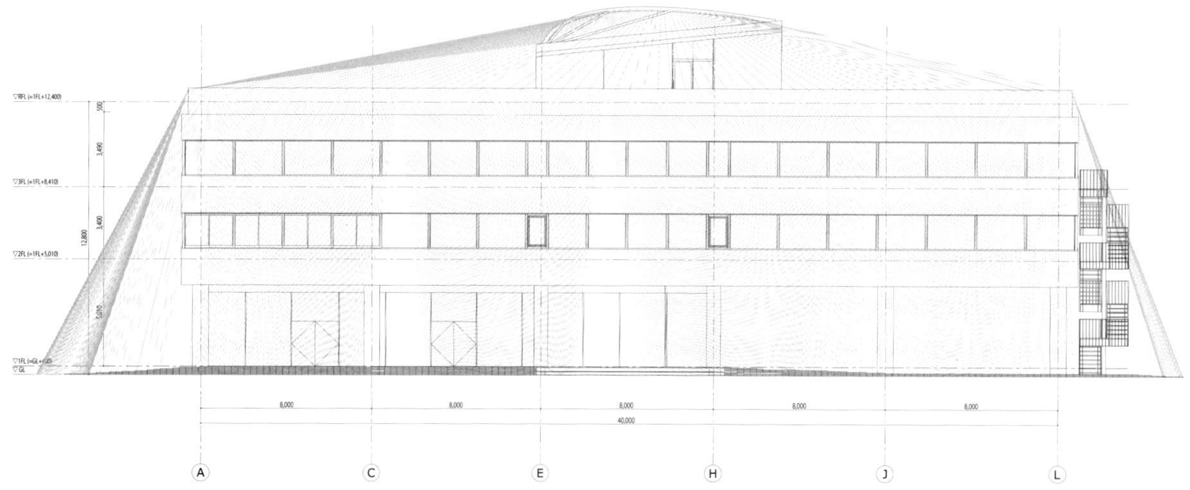

Elevation

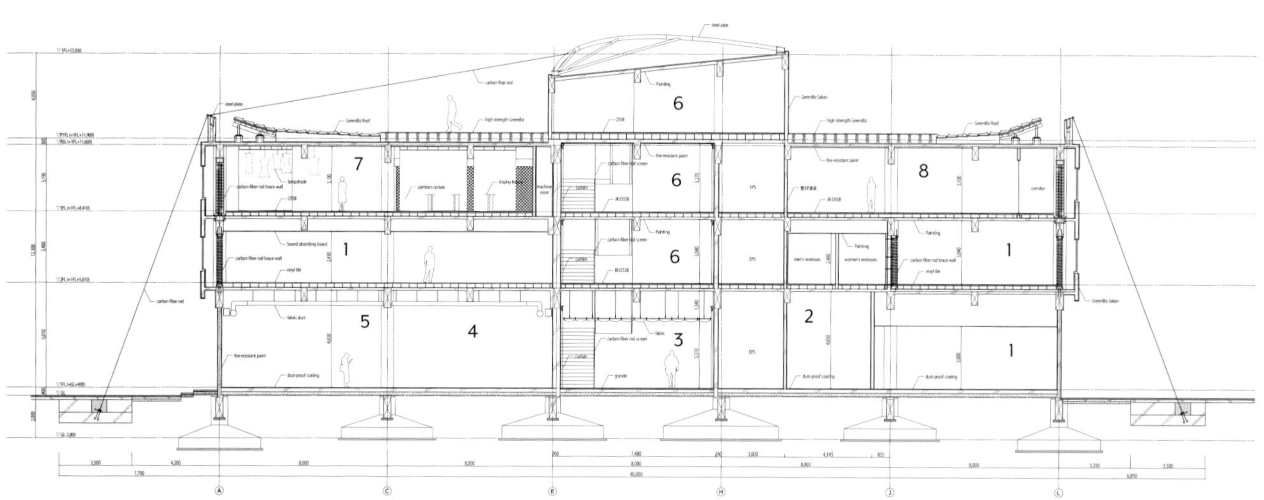

Section

1. Office
2. Warehouse
3. Entrance hall
4. Laboratory
5. Cafe
6. Hall
7. Exhibition room 1
8. Archive space

1. Office
2. Warehouse
3. Entrance hall
4. Laboratory
5. Cafe
6. Terrace
7. Conference room
8. Hall
9. Meeting room
10. Archive space
11. Exhibition room 1
12. Exhibition room 2
13. Rooftop garden
14. Rooftop terrace

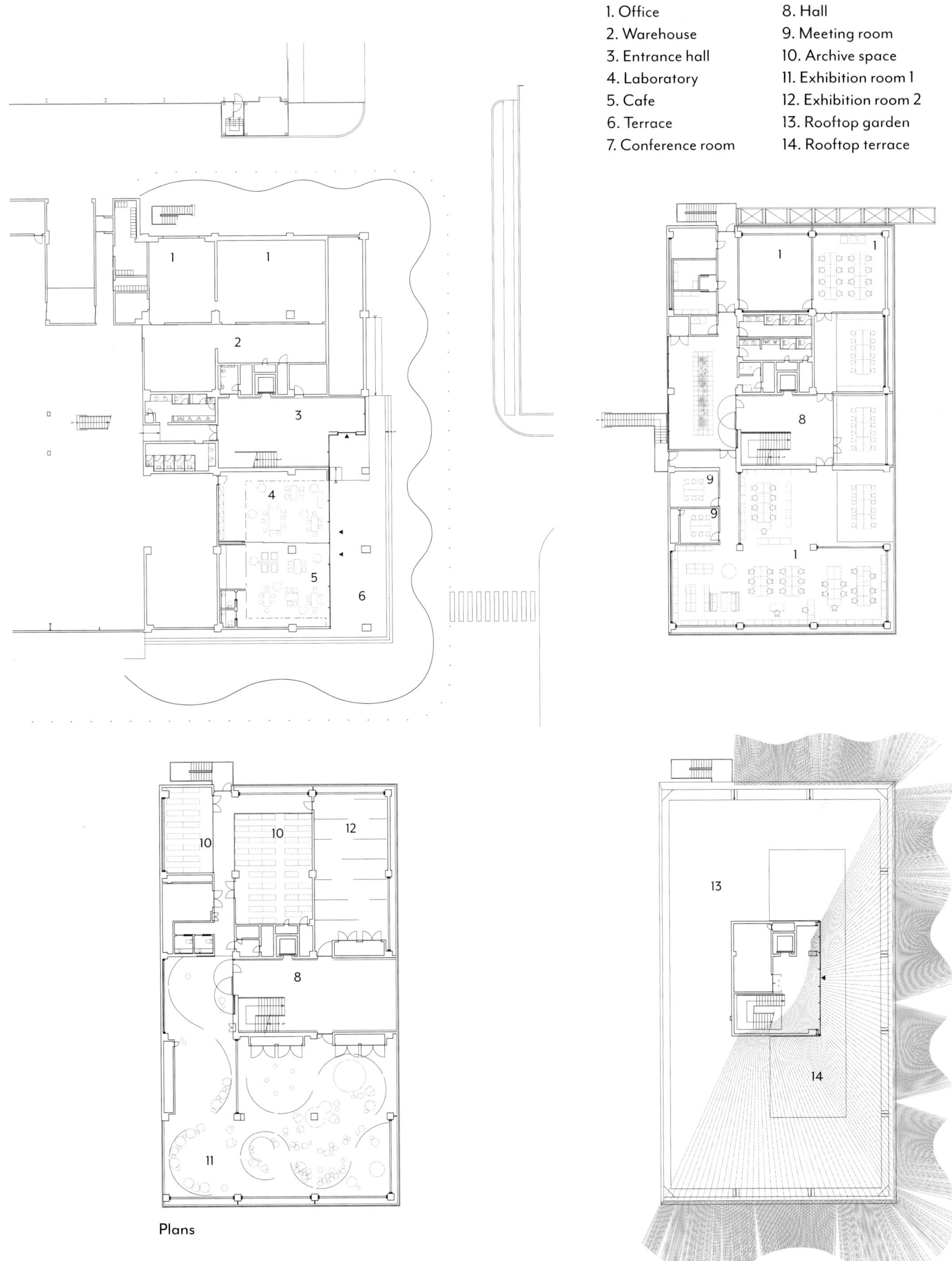

Plans

FABRIC 4: TAKANAWA GATEWAY STATION

Completion year: 2020
Location: Tokyo, Japan
Structure: steel
Building type: station building

A new addition to Tokyo's Yamanote Loop line, this station marks the line's thirtieth stop. Originally scheduled to coincide with the 2020 Tokyo Olympics, it commenced operations in March 2020. The station's name reflects its envisioned role as a pivotal sea and land gateway for Tokyo, seamlessly integrated with the adjacent "New Town" development, spanning a 13-hectare (32 acre) site.

A striking feature of the station and surrounding town is the expansive membrane structure roof, serving to unify the two spaces. Supported by an origami-inspired frame crafted from steel beams and laminated Japanese cedar members, the roof embodies a harmonious blend of modern engineering and traditional craftsmanship.

In contrast to conventional stations, the interior of this station boasts a spacious, well-lit environment with lofty ceilings. The combination of the wooden frame and white membrane invokes the aesthetic of "shoji screens," ubiquitous in Japanese architecture, characterized by the use of Japanese handmade paper.

Further enhancing the station's ambiance is the incorporation of the traditional "yamato-bari" technique for the walls. This method involves applying wooden boards to create an uneven surface, resulting in a welcoming, intimate atmosphere seldom found in standard station designs.

I wanted to design a station reminiscent of grand European terminal stations, characterized by soaring ceilings and expansive interiors. However, I also sought to infuse the space with the organic geometry of origami, creating a sense of natural fluidity by interspersing trees throughout the interior, allowing their branches to sprawl freely like those of a forest.

This geometric approach, comprising numerous small triangular shapes reminiscent of mountainous terrain, imbues the station with a sense of intimacy and human scale, despite its vast proportions.

For the roofing material, fiberglass membranes coated with fluoroplastic were predominantly utilized. This choice enables passengers on the platform to observe changes in the sky and the subtle movements of clouds. Additionally, transparent membranes made from ETFE were strategically incorporated at various points, enhancing natural light penetration and further connecting the interior space with the surrounding environment.

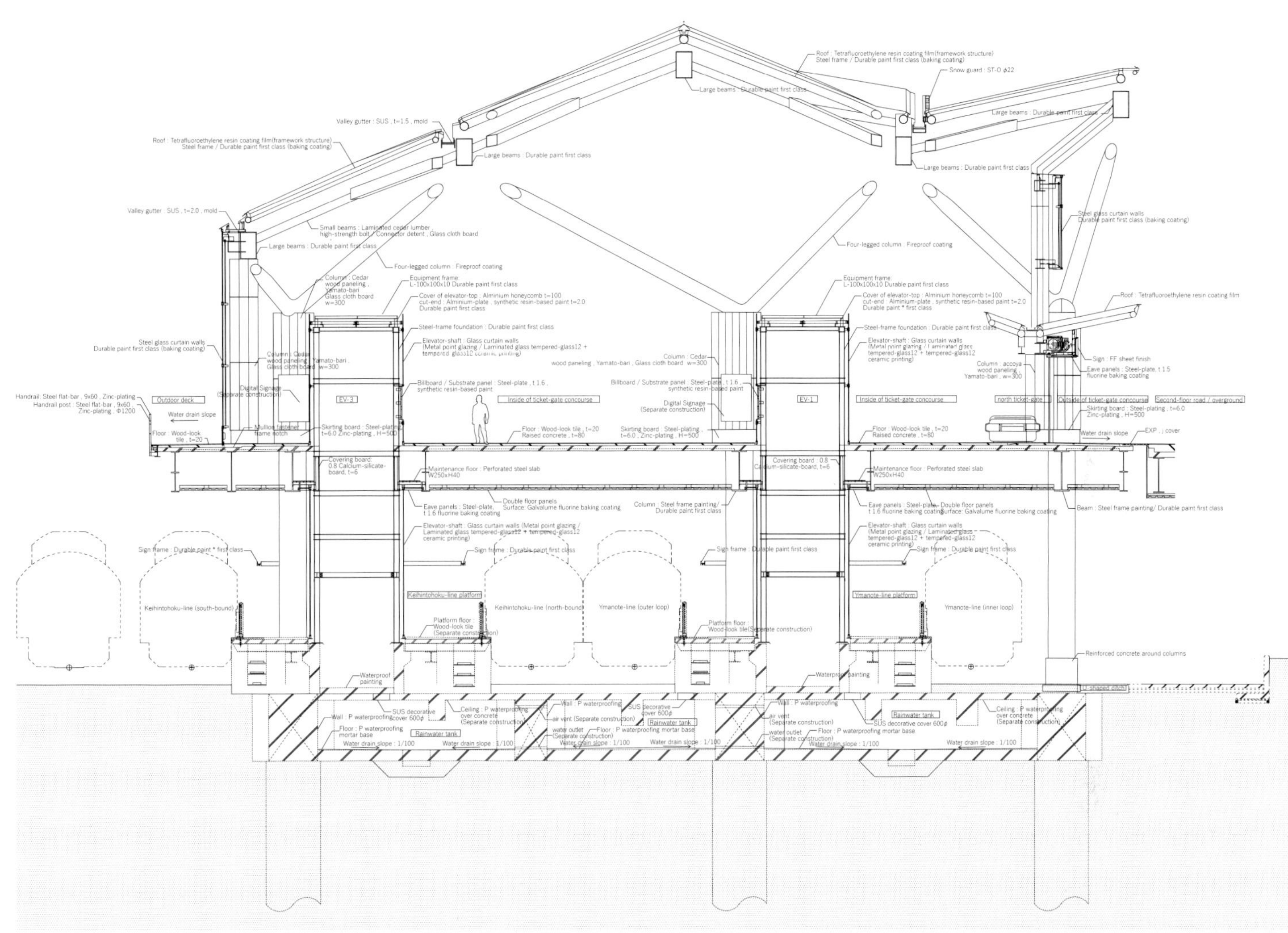

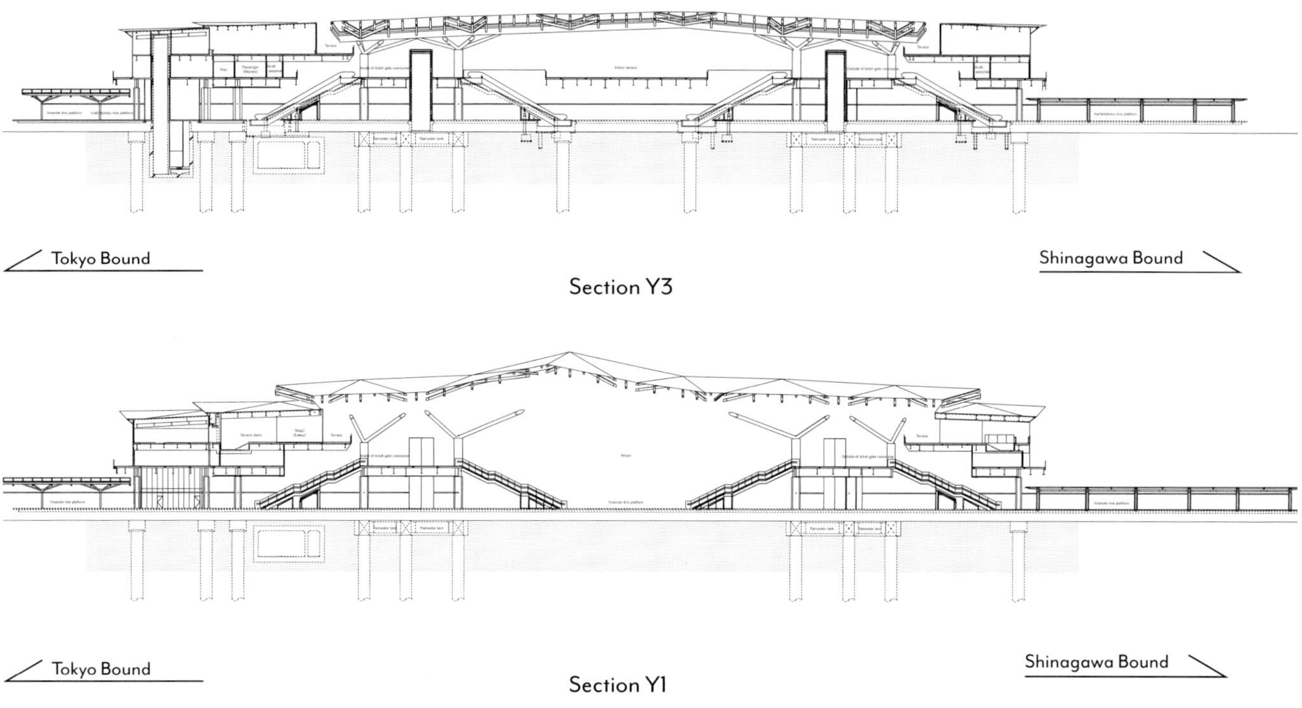

Section Y3

Section Y1

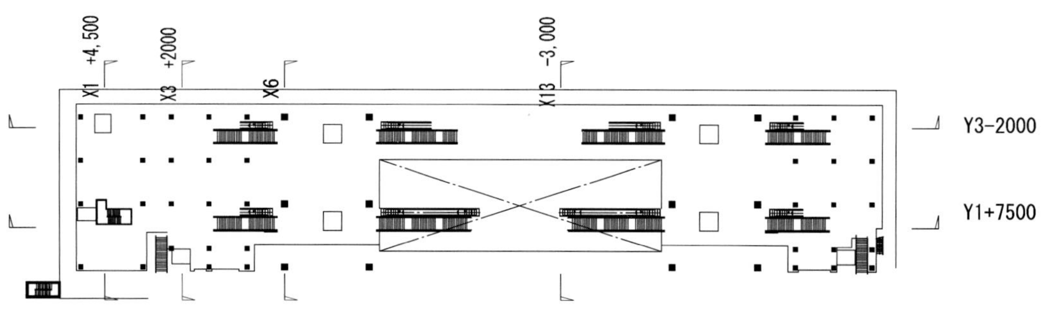

Keyplan

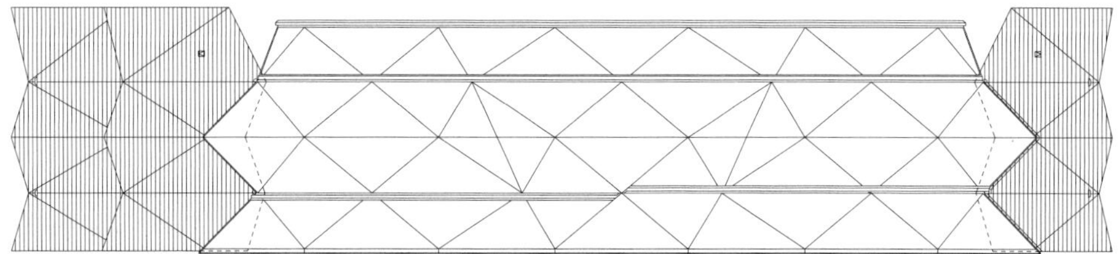

Roof Plan

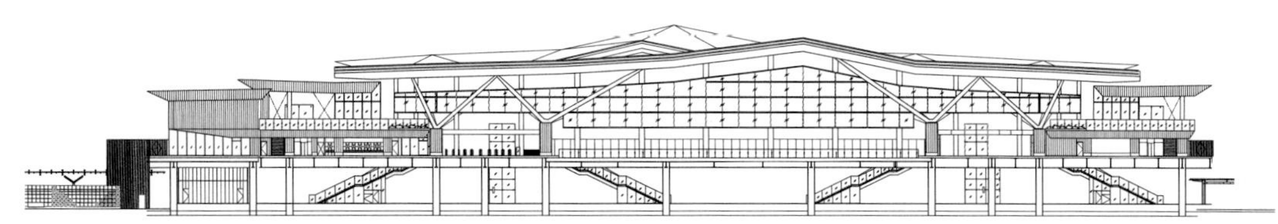

Tokyo Bound

West Elevation

Shinagawa Bound

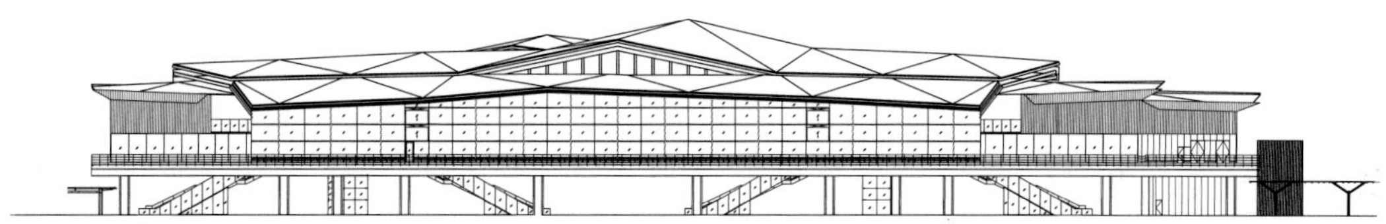

Shinagawa Bound

East Elevation

Tokyo Bound

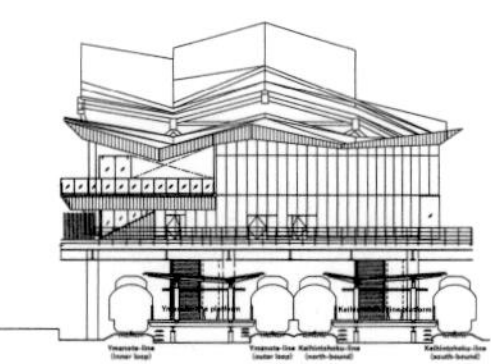

South Elevation

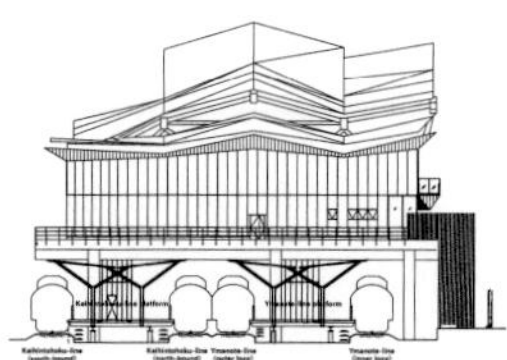

North Elevation

FABRIC 5: ONE HEALTH CARBON GATE

Completion year: 2022
Location: Fukuoka, Japan
Building type: monument

We conceived a spiral-shaped monument, crafted from eco-friendly carbon fibers, to grace the entrance of Chikugo Regional Park in Fukuoka Prefecture. Our design embodies the principle of "One Health," emphasizing the interconnectedness of human, animal, and environmental well-being.

In contrast to conventional imposing gates, our structure is light and ethereal, evoking a sense of weightlessness as if poised for flight. This design approach aims to seamlessly integrate the monument into its natural surroundings, nestled amid the tranquil river and lush greenery of the park.

Crafted from braided carbon fiber tubes measuring 15 mm in thickness, the structure forms a double helix that gracefully coils into a torus shape. By elevating two sides of the torus, it transforms into a double arch resembling a Möbius loop. This distinctive form is achieved through the repetition of individual elements, each spanning one-third of a circle's circumference. Precision in connecting these elements at twenty-nine optimized angles not only enhances structural integrity but also streamlines construction, minimizing both cost and timeline.

Functionally, this flexible gate allows the gentle breeze to permeate freely, fostering a sense of connection between the ground and visitors. Aesthetically, it harmonizes with the park's natural elements, blending seamlessly with the azure waters, verdant foliage, and expansive skies of the Chikugo region.

We wanted to create this monument in the great outdoors to be as transparent and light as possible, while ensuring that its shape and expression would be perceived differently from various angles. The result is an ephemeral form that blurs the boundary between the material and the immaterial.

This fleeting presence was made possible through the use of carbon fiber, valued for its light weight and high strength. Thanks to Norihiro Ejiri, a structural engineer with extensive experience in using carbon fiber to reinforce wooden structures considered national treasures, an unprecedented monument has been realized.

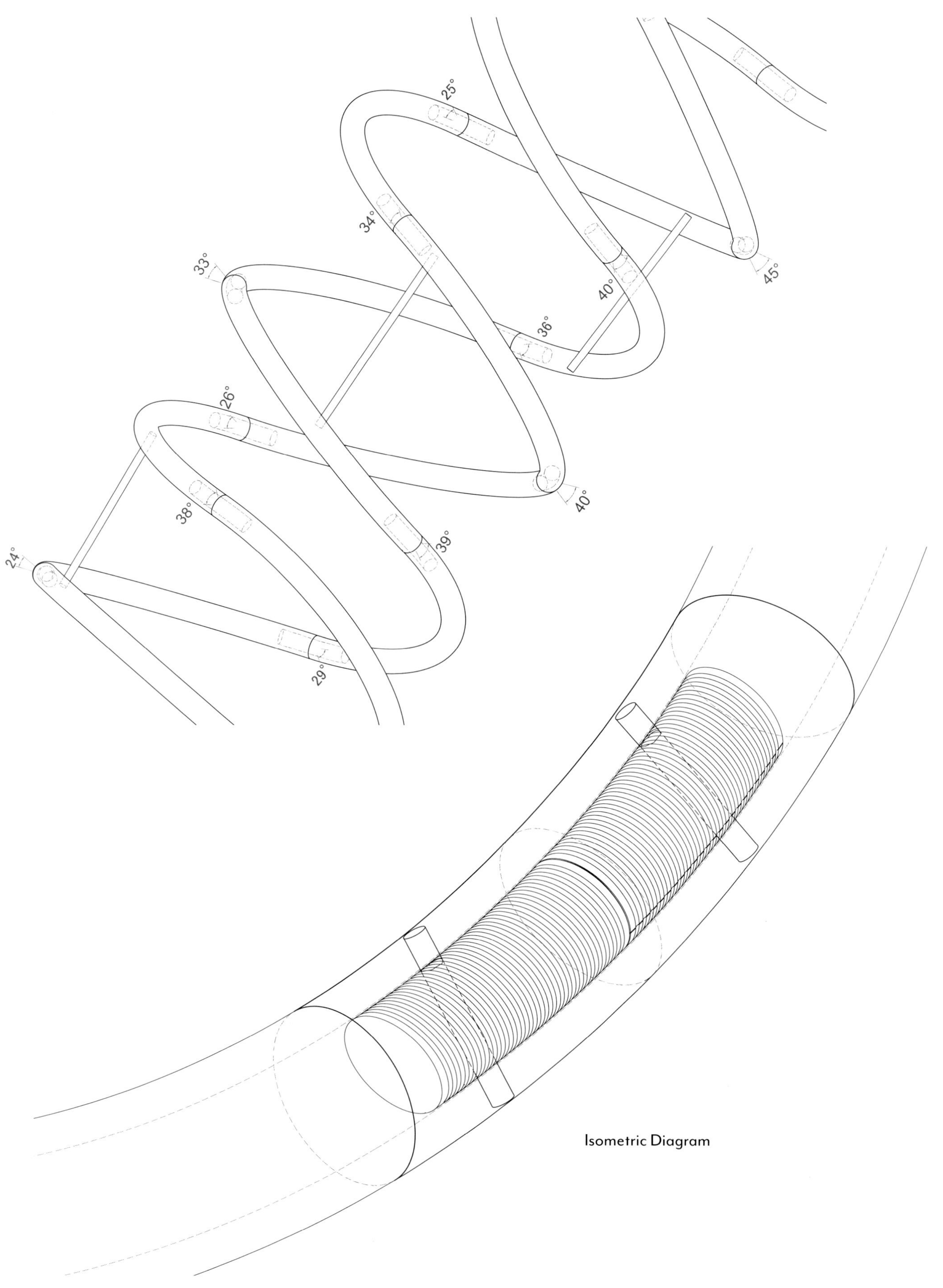

Isometric Diagram

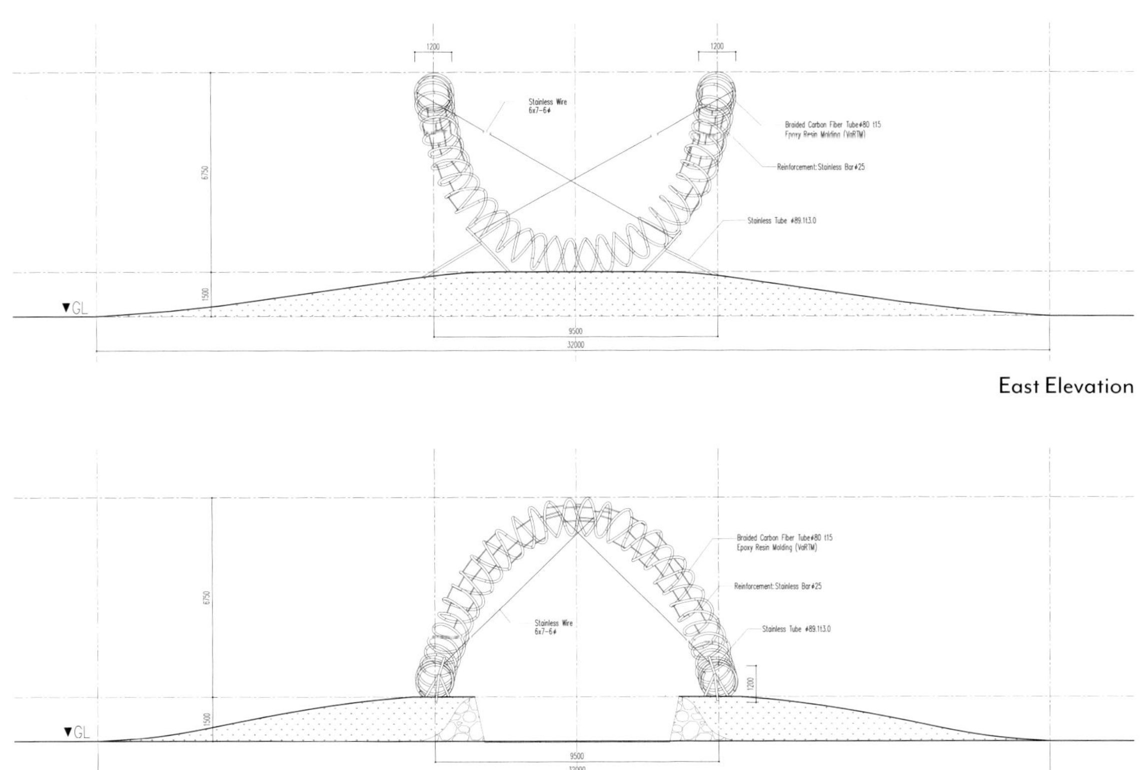

East Elevation

North Elevation

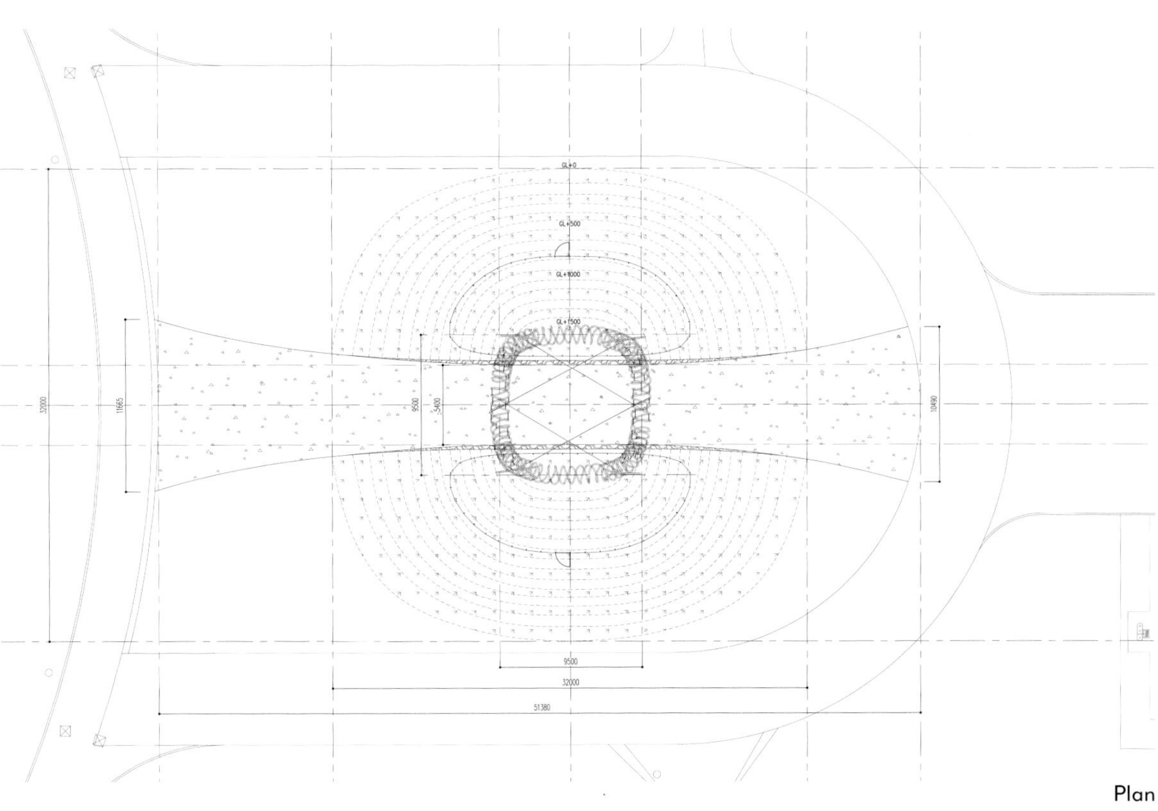

Plan

CHAPTER 2 MINERAL

When concrete became the main material used for architecture in the twentieth century, thinly slicing various minerals and attaching these sheets to the surface of concrete, in a manner similar to putting on makeup, became a general practice. This felt like a desecration of the mineral to me. Minerals originally had a deep spiritual connection with people. From ancient times, people have believed that stones have permanence, and have protected and prayed to stones. There is a deep relationship between holy places and stones, and many holy places have been established on top of special minerals. Shrines in Japan have a deep relationship with stones and mineral veins, and Western holy sites such as in Jerusalem also have a deep relationship with stones and mineral veins.

Japanese culture is said to be a culture of wood, but the Japanese people have actually had a special sensitivity to stones and objects from ancient times. Large, magnificent stones have been the subject of faith, people have believed that a god resides in these stones, and these stones have been called "iwakura" (stone repositories). Before wooden shrines were built, people prayed to stones on top of holy places. People believed in stones before the age of wood. Therefore, stones played an important role before architecture existed.

Ise Grand Shrine is the shrine for the emperor's family, making it the top shrine out of all shrines in Japan. The simple, beautiful wooden structure directly standing on the ground, which consists of thick cypress pillars, is renowned, but I think that the white and black cobblestones spread around the wooden structure are the source of the holiness of the shrine.

This shrine is rebuilt every twenty years, but the white and black cobblestones, which were spread out on the two sites prepared for this purpose, remain, so the cobblestones continue to exist at each site as the structure continues to move between them. The wooden structure of the Ise Grand Shrine is a symbol of transient nature that continues to change, but the cobblestones are a symbol of the permanence of nature, which stands on top. The Japanese people have this type of sensibility with respect to stones.

My desire to bring back this type of sensitivity to life in the present age through architecture is directing me toward minerals.

MINERAL 1: STONE MUSEUM

Completion year: 2000
Location: Tochigi, Japan
Structure: masonry, steel
Building type: museum

The Stone Museum repurposes eighty-year-old stone buildings, originally used for rice storage, as exhibition spaces for arts and crafts made from stone. Beyond featuring stone-themed items, the museum explores stone's new and emerging potential as an architectural material. We have utilized the interior areas for displays and designed the pathways between the three stone warehouses as semi-outdoor spaces, creating a seamless flow between the inside and outside.

Ashino stone, the same type used in the original warehouses, was employed for new architectural details that connect these areas. To achieve a unique lighting effect inside, we incorporated two types of design features: horizontal stone louvers and porous masonry, from which approximately one-third of the pieces have been removed.

I embraced the challenge of utilizing stone as a three-dimensional mass with texture in a building project, moving beyond the cosmetic use prevalent in contemporary architecture, where thin, 30 mm thick stone sheets are merely attached to concrete surfaces.

In the main area, we strategically opened holes in the stone, removing 25 to 30 percent of the mass, to allow light and wind to penetrate without compromising structural integrity. This was achieved by cutting the stone to a thickness of 50 mm and a depth of 30 mm and stacking them by using the traditional masonry method that has been in use since ancient times. At specific locations, thin (6 mm) marble sheets of Bianco Carrara were incorporated, enabling visitors to enjoy the soft light filtering through the stone.

For the entrance, we used bar-shaped stone with a cross section of 40 × 120 mm to create "stone louvers." These structures are light and transparent, challenging traditional perceptions and exploring new potential uses for stone.

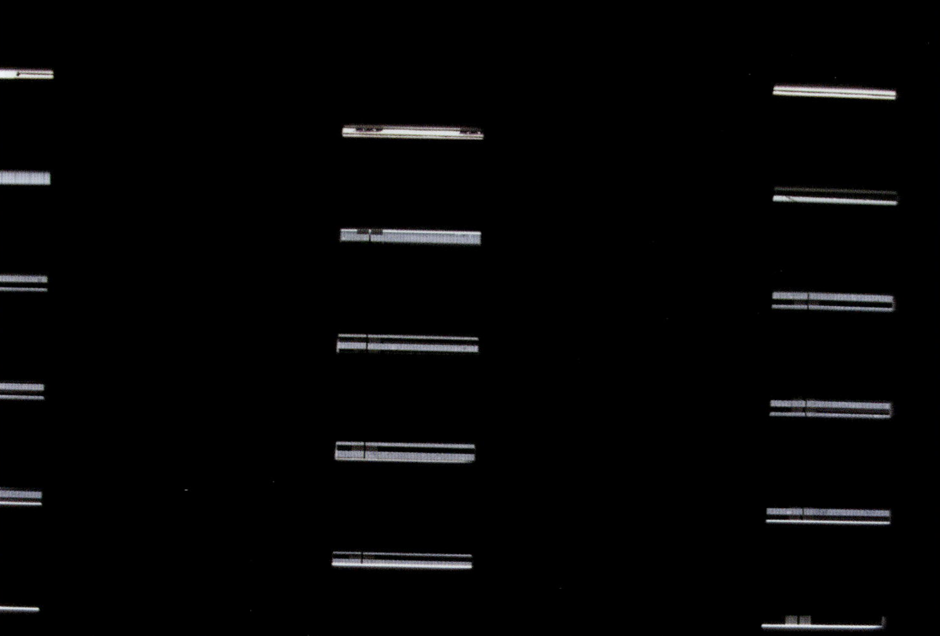

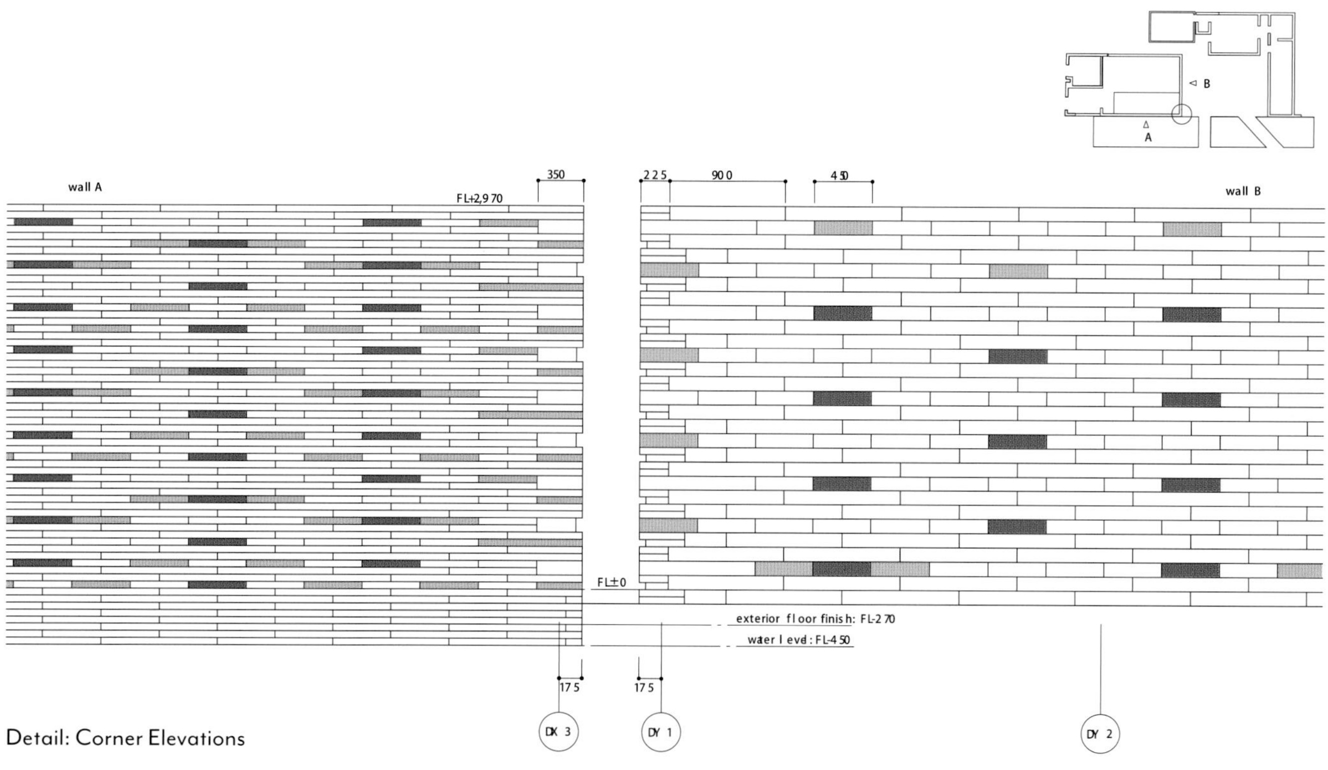

Detail: Corner Elevations

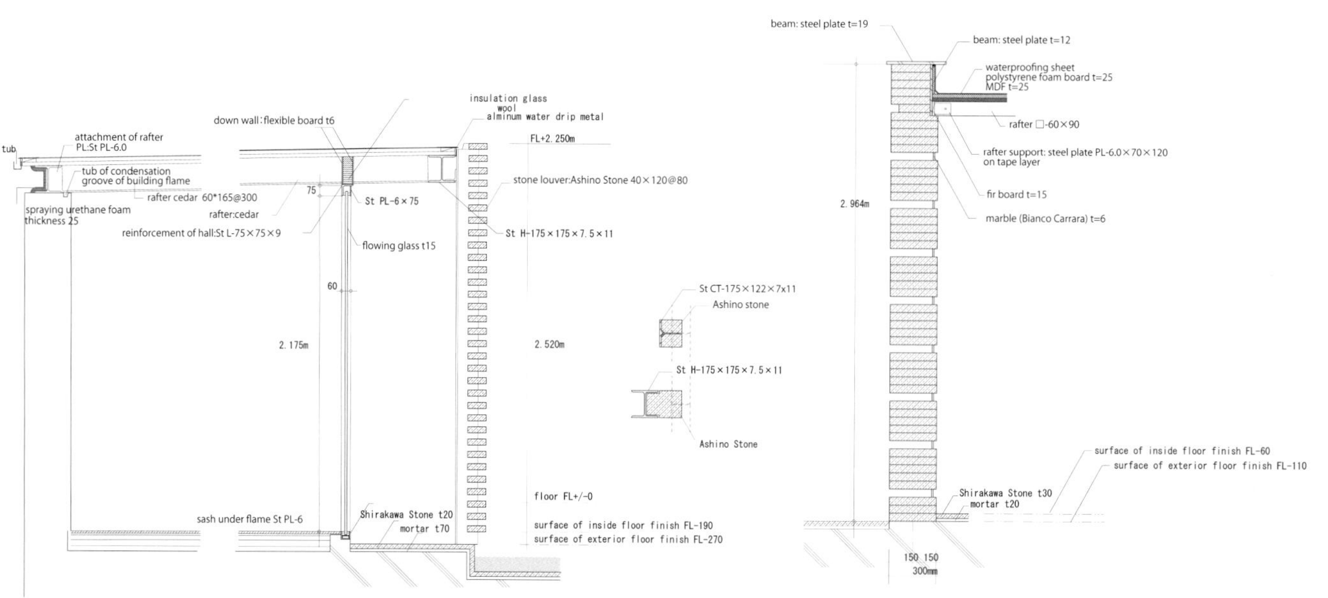

Detail Section: Stone Wall

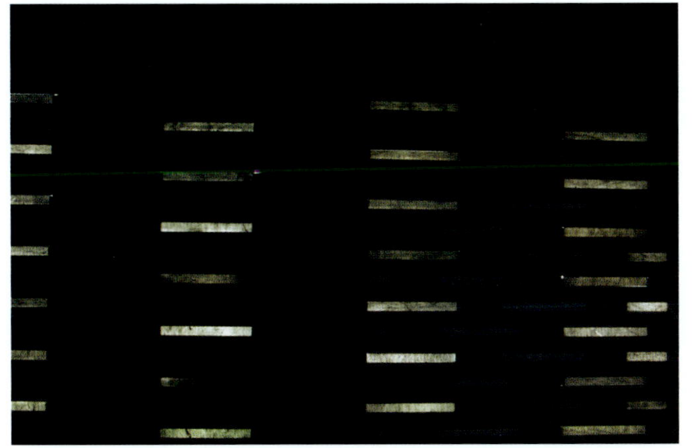

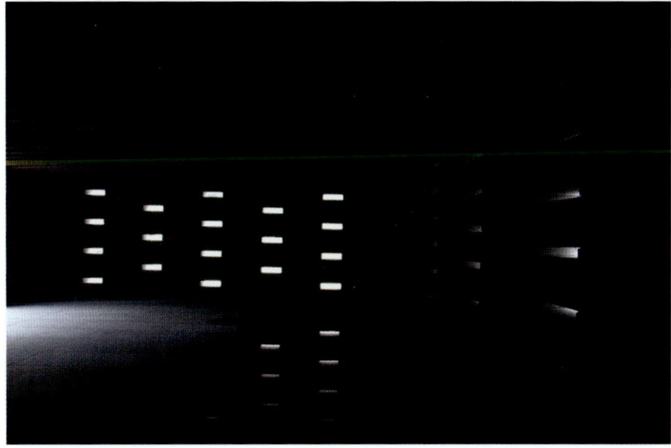

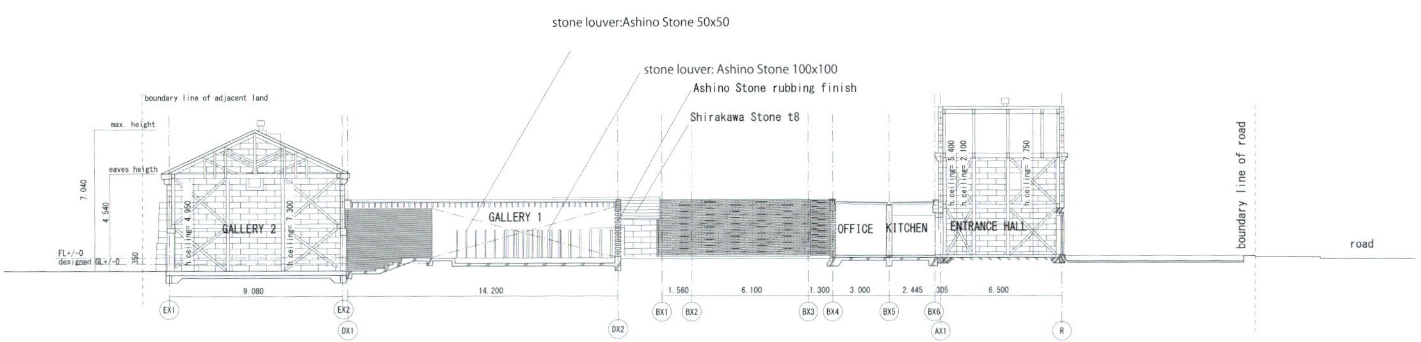

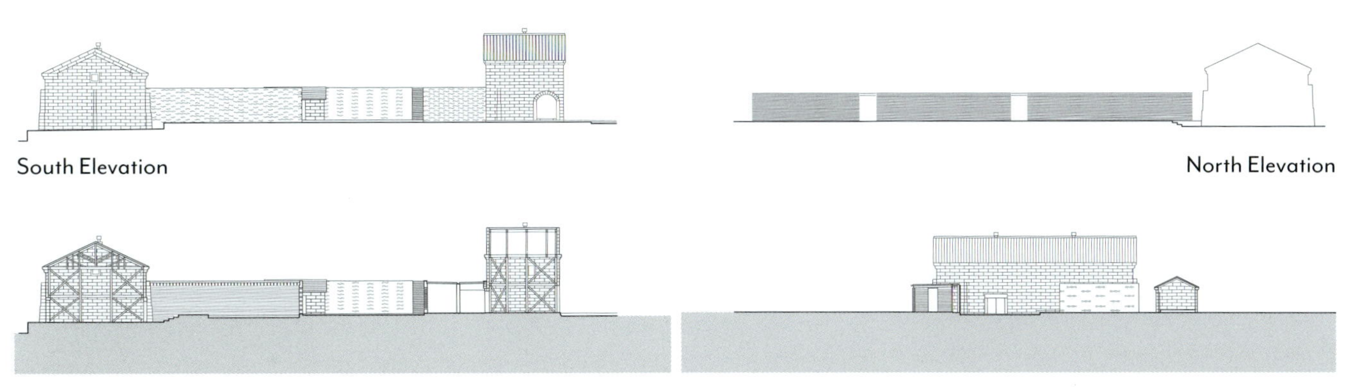

South Elevation

North Elevation

Sections

MINERAL 2: CHOKKURA PLAZA

Completion year: 2006
Location: Tochigi, Japan
Building type: plaza

This project aimed to create a new station plaza that would become a central hub for community activities, centered on a preserved Oya stone masonry storehouse.

Debris from the Oya stone of the storehouse was reused and combined with steel plates arranged diagonally. This design was intended to enhance transparency and make the most of the material's natural texture, creating a visually appealing and functional communal space.

Upon discovering that the mixed structure of stone and steel used in an Oya stone storehouse, structurally designed by Masato Araya, sustained almost no damage during the Miyagiken-oki earthquake in 2005, we decided to explore the unconventional use of a mixed stone-and-steel structure.

The construction process involved opening holes in the stones that were stacked, with 6 mm thick steel plates welded in between—a method known as "partner work." While this technique typically reduces working efficiency, we embraced this challenge to achieve what we termed a "transparent masonry structure."

Frank Lloyd Wright famously chose Oya stone for the Imperial Hotel in Tokyo in 1923, appreciating its soft texture and gentle hue, which he believed suited the Japanese environment. Historically used mainly for storehouses in the Utsunomiya region, this "weak" stone subsequently gained wider application across Japan. In our project, we used Oya stone to create a porous wall, both as an attempt to further highlight the stone's softness and as an homage to Frank Lloyd Wright.

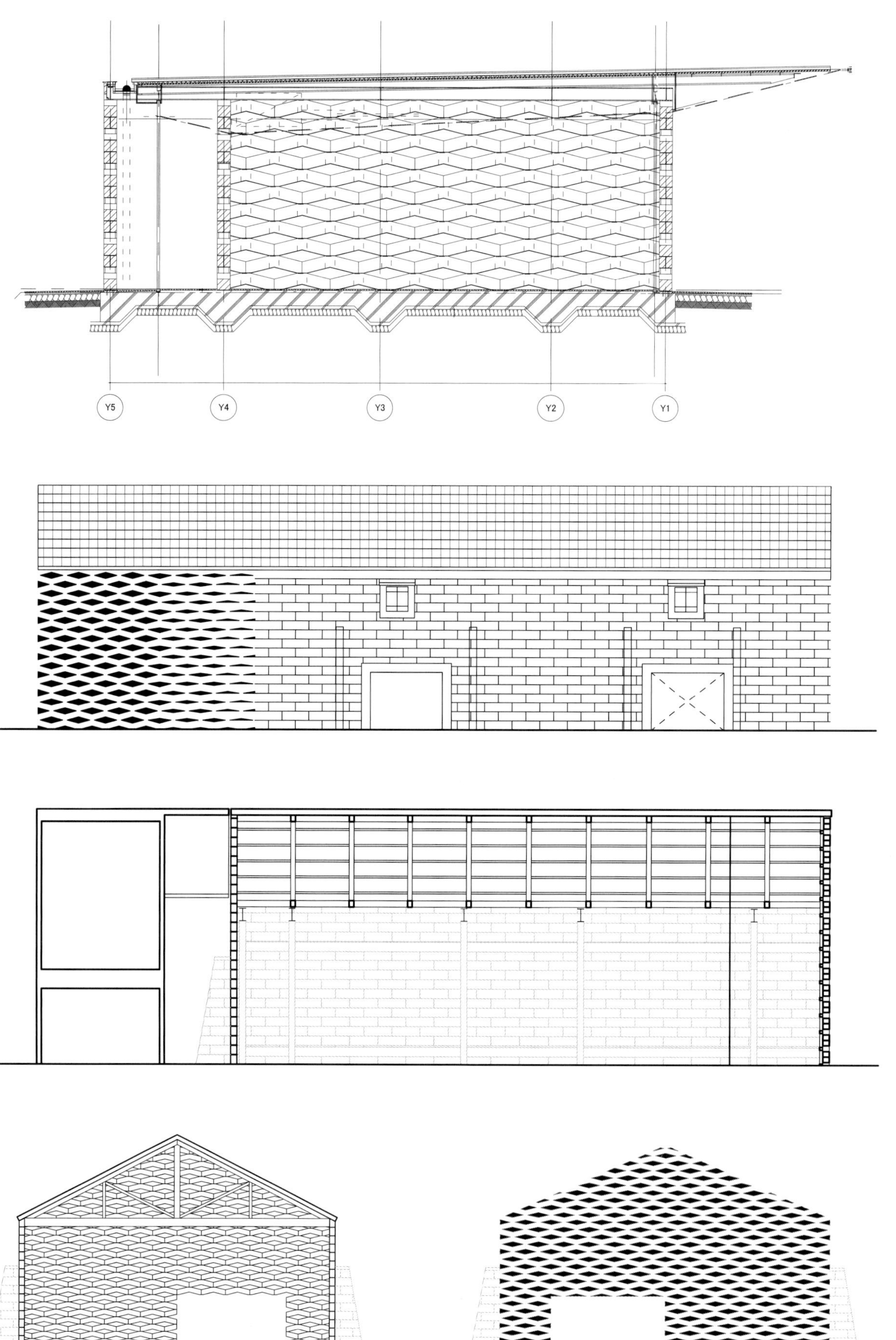

Sections / Elevations

1. Multipurpose Exhibition Hall
2. Anteroom
3. Bathroom
4. Chokkura Hall
   (Warehouse in existence)
5. Storage
6. Lavatory
7. Bamboo Grove

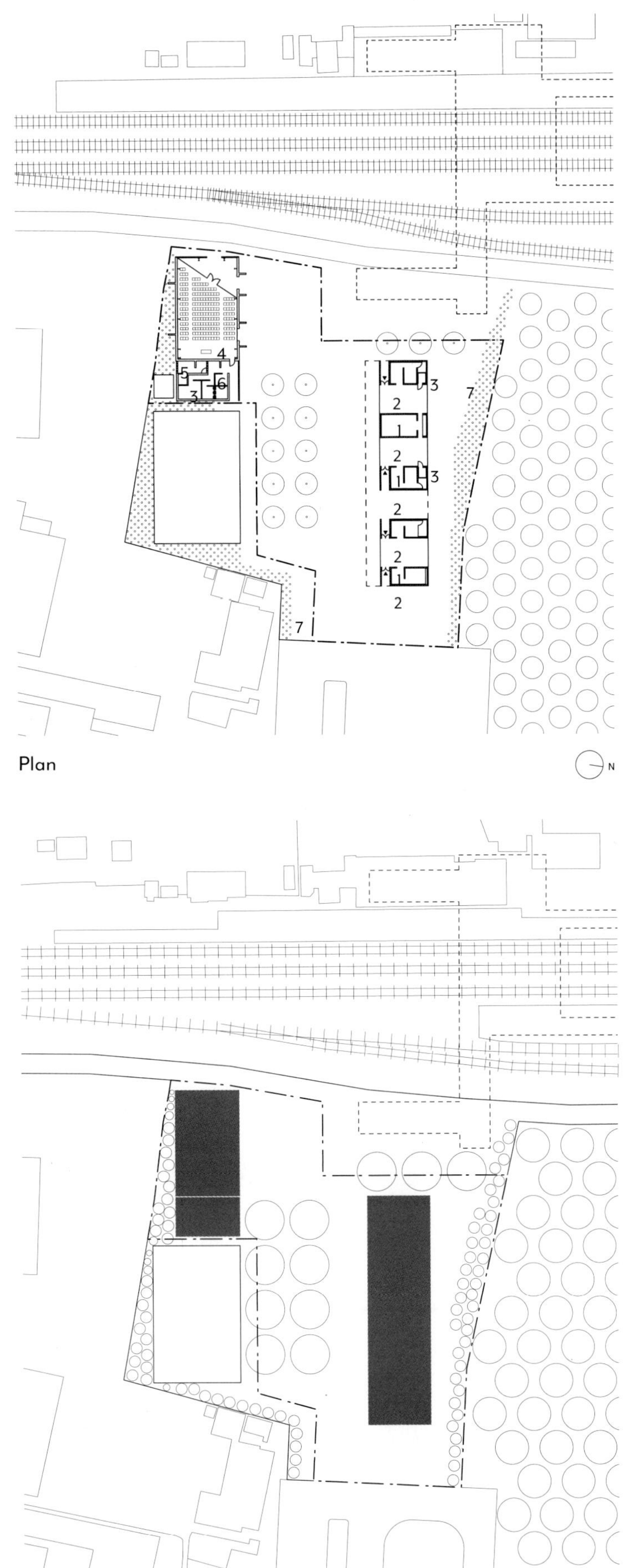

Plan

Site Plan

MINERAL 3: CERAMIC CLOUD

Completion year: 2010
Location: Reggio Emilia, Italy
Building type: monument

We were tasked with creating a monument in a road roundabout in Casalgrande, an area in Reggio Emilia celebrated for its rich tradition and advanced technology in ceramics. This roundabout, nestled within the stunning landscape typical of that Italian region, presented a unique opportunity.

Instead of using ceramic tiles merely as cladding, we embraced the challenge of making them a fundamental architectural element. After developing a specific method for paneling and connecting standard ceramic tiles, we realized the possibilities of assembling them to form various structures.

Our vision for the monument was to integrate it seamlessly with its surroundings, rather than it standing out as a central focal point. Thus, we designed a wall that simply divides the site into two, giving the space a dual character that diverges from typical, mundane roundabouts. Our antimonumental approach extended to aligning the ceramic wall with the approaching road, making it nearly invisible upon approach. Drivers would perceive only a vertical divide in the roundabout. However, as they navigate around it, the wall's full 45 m length gradually reveals itself, in sync with the movement of their vehicle.

In our buildings, we often explore concepts such as antidimension or antivolume, but this project, situated uniquely in a roundabout accessible only by car, allowed us to experiment with these ideas in relation to dynamic principles such as time, movement, and sequential perception.

Throughout the construction period, we observed the dynamic interaction of the wall's light structure, its transparency, and the subtle reflections of its fine-glazed white ceramic with the surrounding landscape and changing weather conditions. This dynamism manifested as a unique, soft, light, and ever-changing phenomenon, which we aptly named the Ceramic Cloud.

A fiberglass sheet was sandwiched between two large 14 mm thick tiles to create a 30 mm thick panel. These panels were then assembled into a composite structure using 20 mm diameter stainless-steel pipes. The tops of these pipes are threaded, allowing the units of pipes and panels to be stacked and secured by applying torque to the top of each joint. This method compresses the assembly, providing a rigid and durable connection between the units.

At the base of the monument, white cobblestones were spread out to enhance its aesthetic and symbolic significance. A wavy pattern, reminiscent of those found in the ponds of Japanese gardens, was employed to seamlessly integrate the water's surface with the cobblestones. This design element not only beautifies the space but also delineates the sacred area surrounding the monument, echoing the use of white cobblestones at the Ise Grand Shrine.

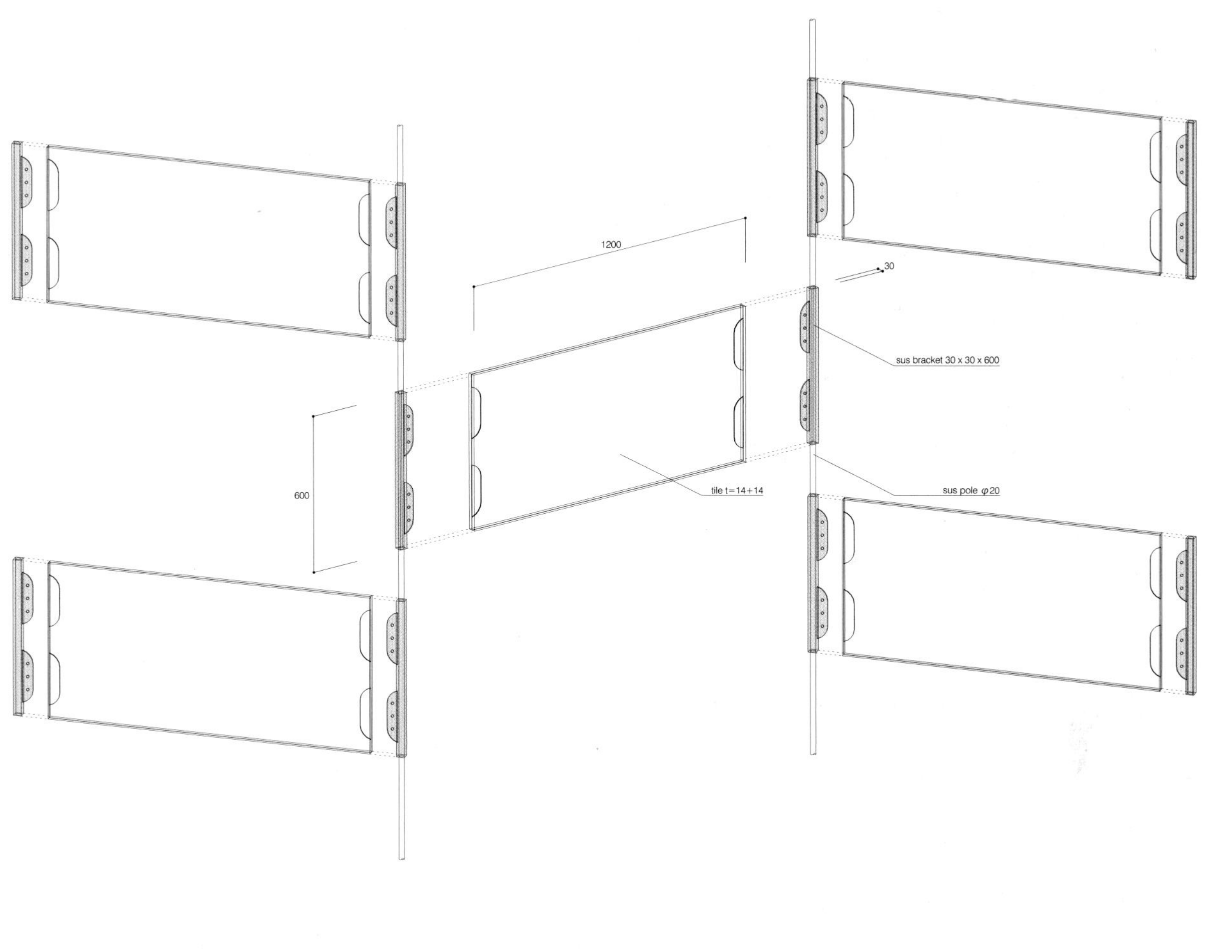

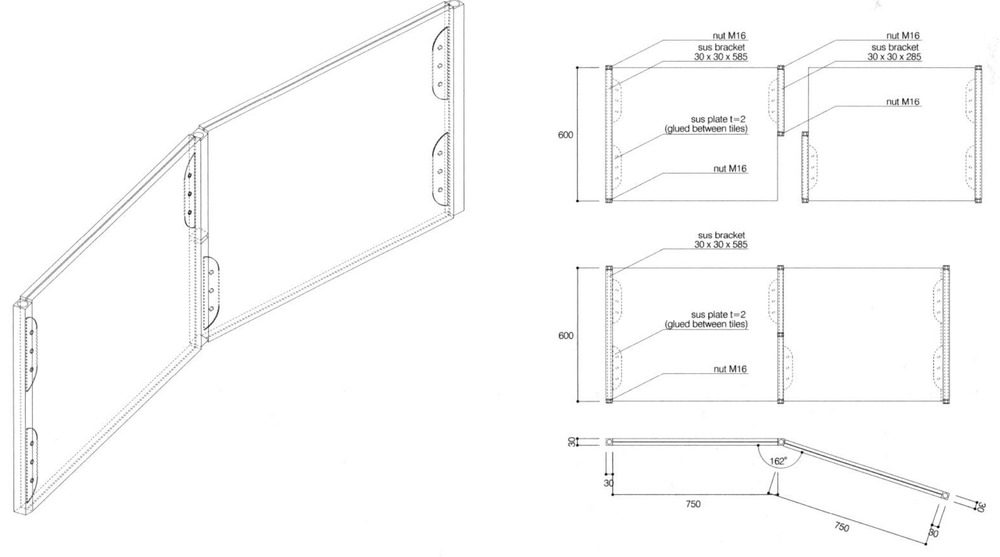

Isometric Diagram

45510
5400

row 9
8
7
6
5
4
3
2
1
row 9(GL+5,300)
row 5(GL+2,900)
row 8(GL+4,700)
row 4(GL+2,300)
row 7(GL+4,100)
row 3(GL+1,700)
row 6(GL+3,500)
row 2(GL+1,100)
row 1(GL+500)
1230
45510

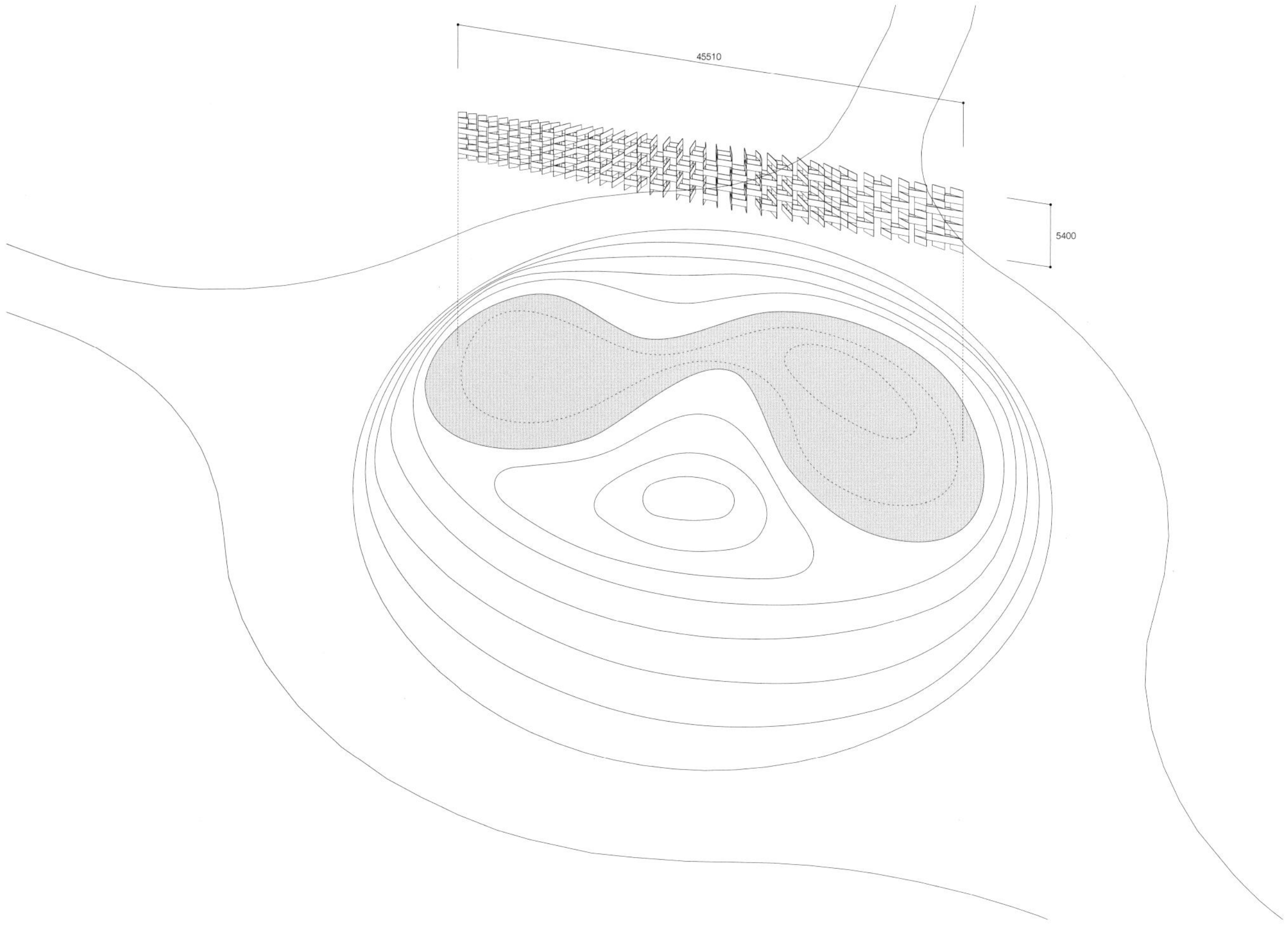

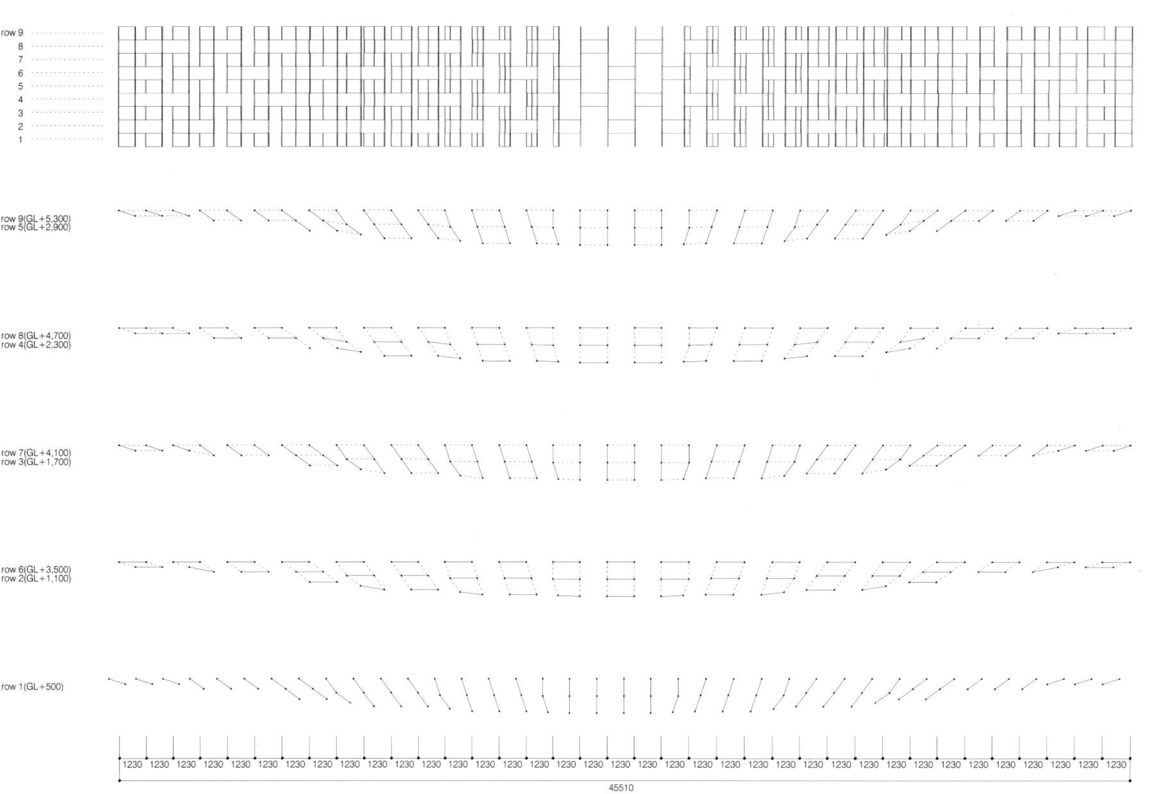

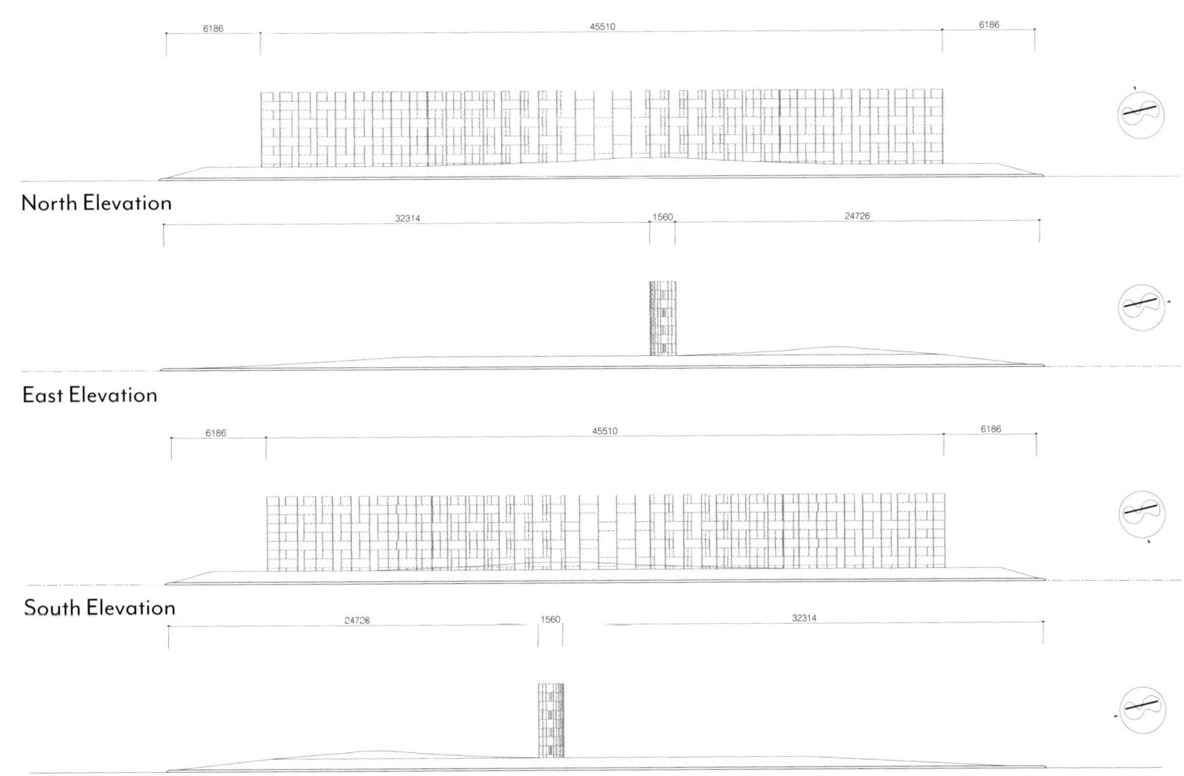

North Elevation

East Elevation

South Elevation

West Elevation

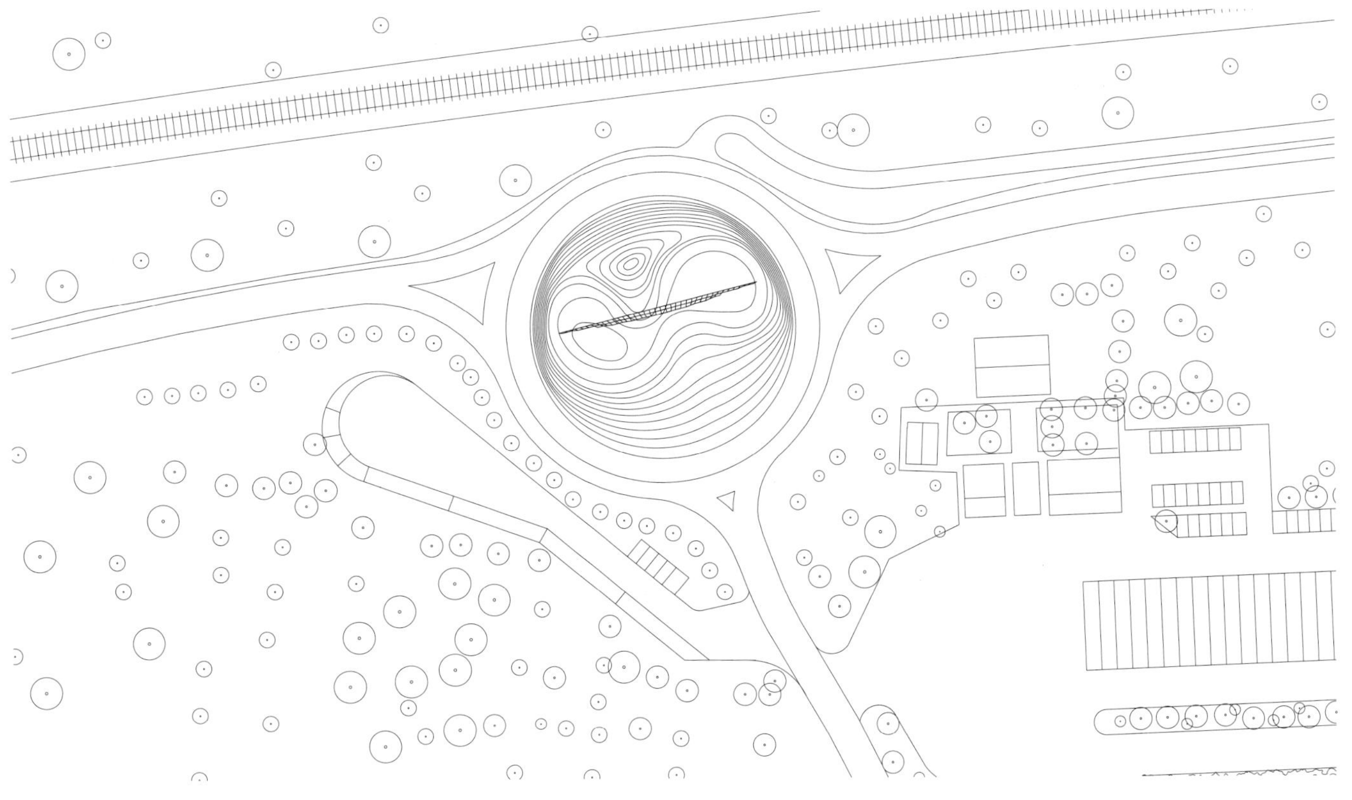

Site Plan

MINERAL 4: FRAC MARSEILLE

Completion year: 2013
Location: Marseille, France
Structure: RC/SRC (reinforced concrete/steel-reinforced concrete), steel
Building type: gallery

In line with France's cultural policy, FRAC (Fonds Régional d'Art Contemporain, or Regional Contemporary Art Collection), established in 1982, art facilities have been distributed throughout the Provence-Alpes-Côte d'Azur (PACA) region. FRAC, a community-based organization, was created to nurture young artists and foster new art. Embracing the FRAC philosophy, we aimed to design architecture that is open and accessible to the local community, moving away from the traditional, closed-off, box-shaped art museum model. This approach ensures that the spaces not only showcase art but also invite community interaction and engagement, reflecting the dynamic spirit of contemporary art within the region.

Located in the waterfront district of Marseille, the site is distinctively triangular, bounded by two roads. Rather than constructing a traditional, enclosed box-shaped display space, we developed a plan where the building interacts with the streets, transforming them into a three-dimensional display area. This initiative aimed to replicate the communal corridors or alleys reminiscent of Le Corbusier's Unité d'habitation (1952). A new concept of spiral corridors was adopted as a three-dimensional expression of alleys.

FRAC

An open-air terrace is provided at one corner and along the sides facing the streets, serving as a multipurpose space for outdoor art production, displays, and various gatherings and events.

The façade is clad in enamel glass designed to resemble a collection of particles, softening the building's appearance. These glass panels are mounted at slightly varying angles, diffusing the intense Mediterranean sunlight into fine particles. Whereas Le Corbusier addressed the challenge of light with brise-soleil, which deflects sunlight, we approached it through the use of particles (panels). Inspired by André Malraux's concept of an "art museum without walls," proposed in 1947, we further developed this idea by creating an "ambiguous façade," thereby redefining the boundaries between the museum and the public space.

Impressed by the milky-white glass that resembled oysters at a glass-recycling factory in Marseille, I was inspired to use enamel glass for the façade. Marseille, not Paris, was the city I first visited as a student, and the memorable taste of the oysters I enjoyed there has lingered with me. This façade can be seen as a culmination of that memory.

To enhance the strength of the panels, an EVA film was sandwiched between two sheets of enamel glass. The panels are mounted using the DPG technique with stainless-steel dot-shaped fixtures, which are designed to be invisible from the front, maintaining a clean and uninterrupted surface.

At night, the effect of the enamel glass is reminiscent of Japanese shoji screens, since the light diffuses softly through the panels, creating a tranquil and inviting glow that enhances the building's aesthetic appeal.

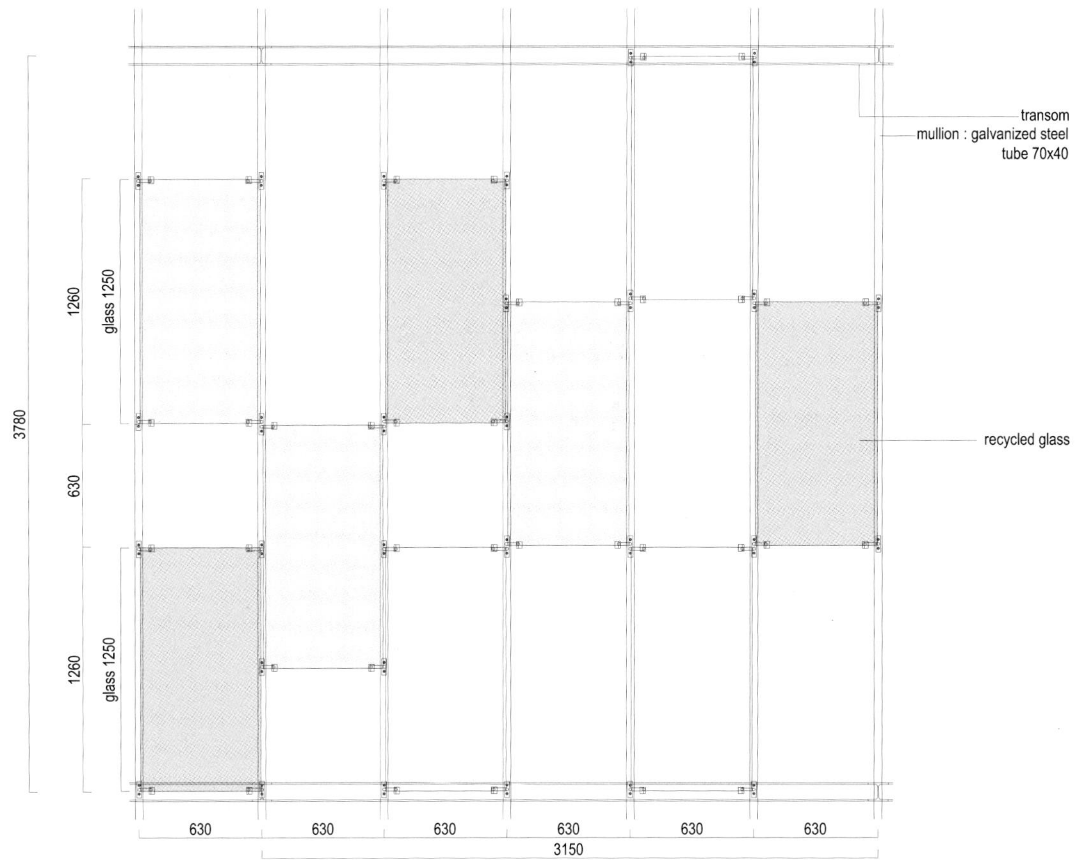

Elevation

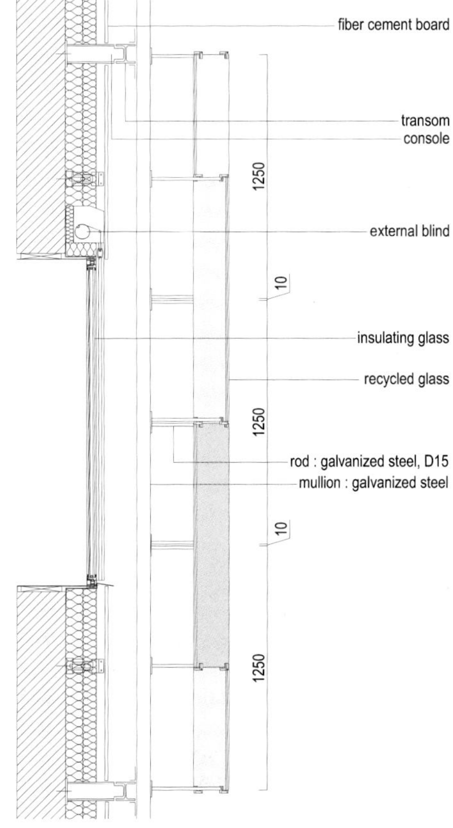

Section Detail

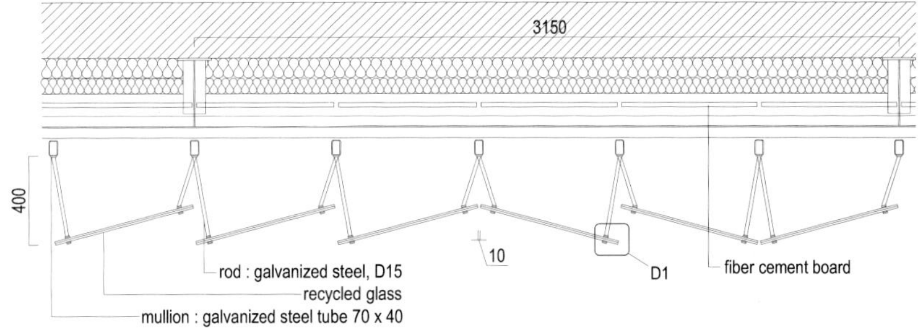

Plan Detail

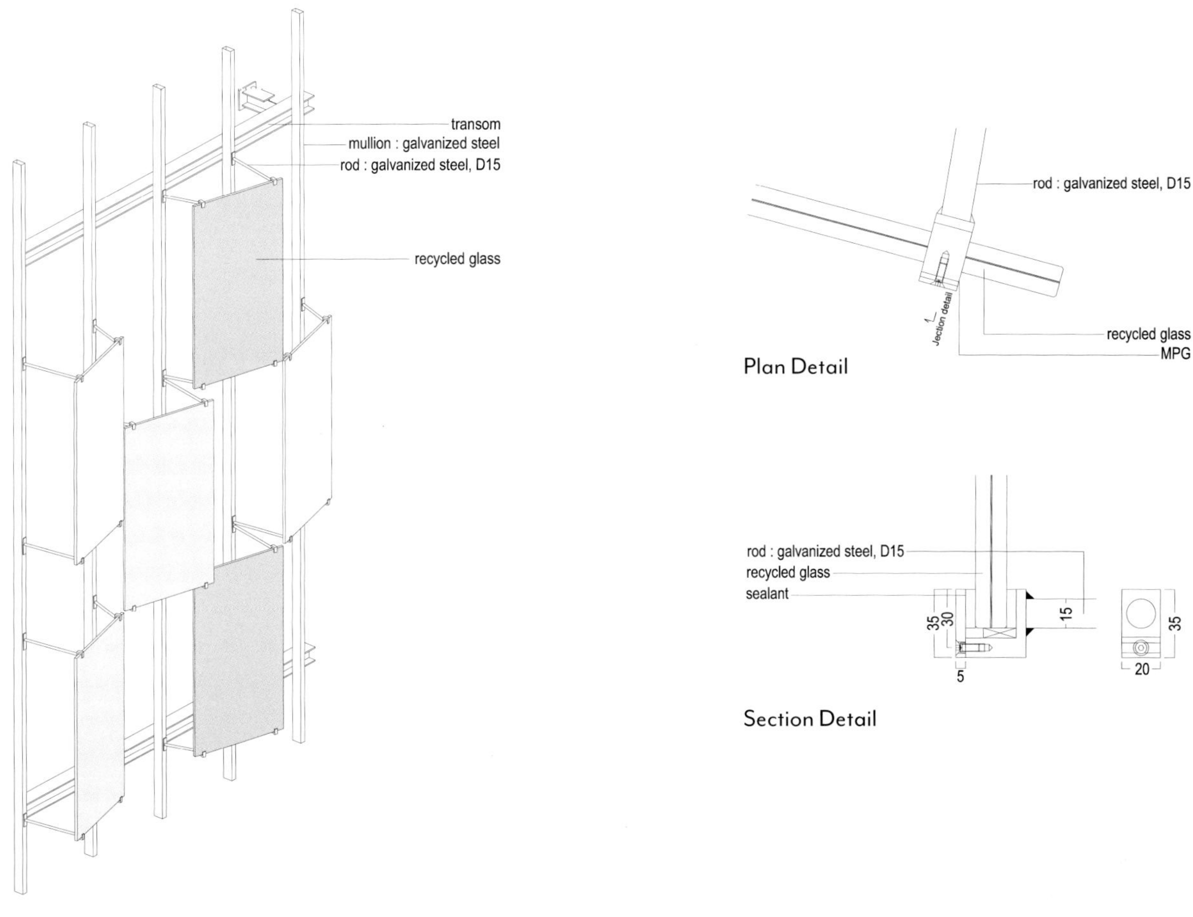

Plan Detail

Section Detail

Axonometry

1. Archive
2. Entrance
3. Café
4. Reception
5. Exhibition 1
6. Conference room
7. Foyer
8. Exhibition 2
9. Assembly
10. Control room
11. Apartment
12. Urban terrace
13. Resource center
14. Atelier for children
15. Roof terrace
16. Office
17. Exhibition 3
18. Technical room

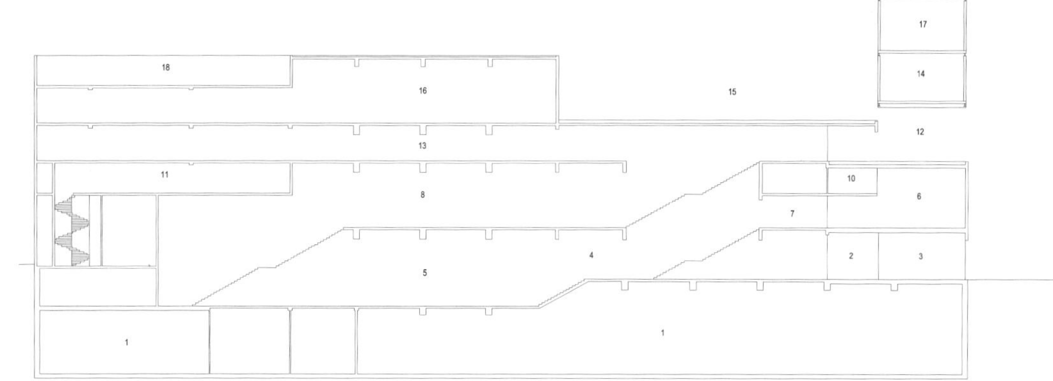

Section

Elevation

1. Entrance
2. Café
3. Reflecting pool
4. Reception
5. Shop
6. Exhibition 1
7. Atelier
8. Delivery
9. Conference room
10. Foyer
11. Sculpture garden
12. Exhibition 2
13. Assembly
14. Urban terrace
15. Resource center
16. Atelier for children
17. Terrace
18. Office
19. Exhibition 3
20. Roof photovoltaic

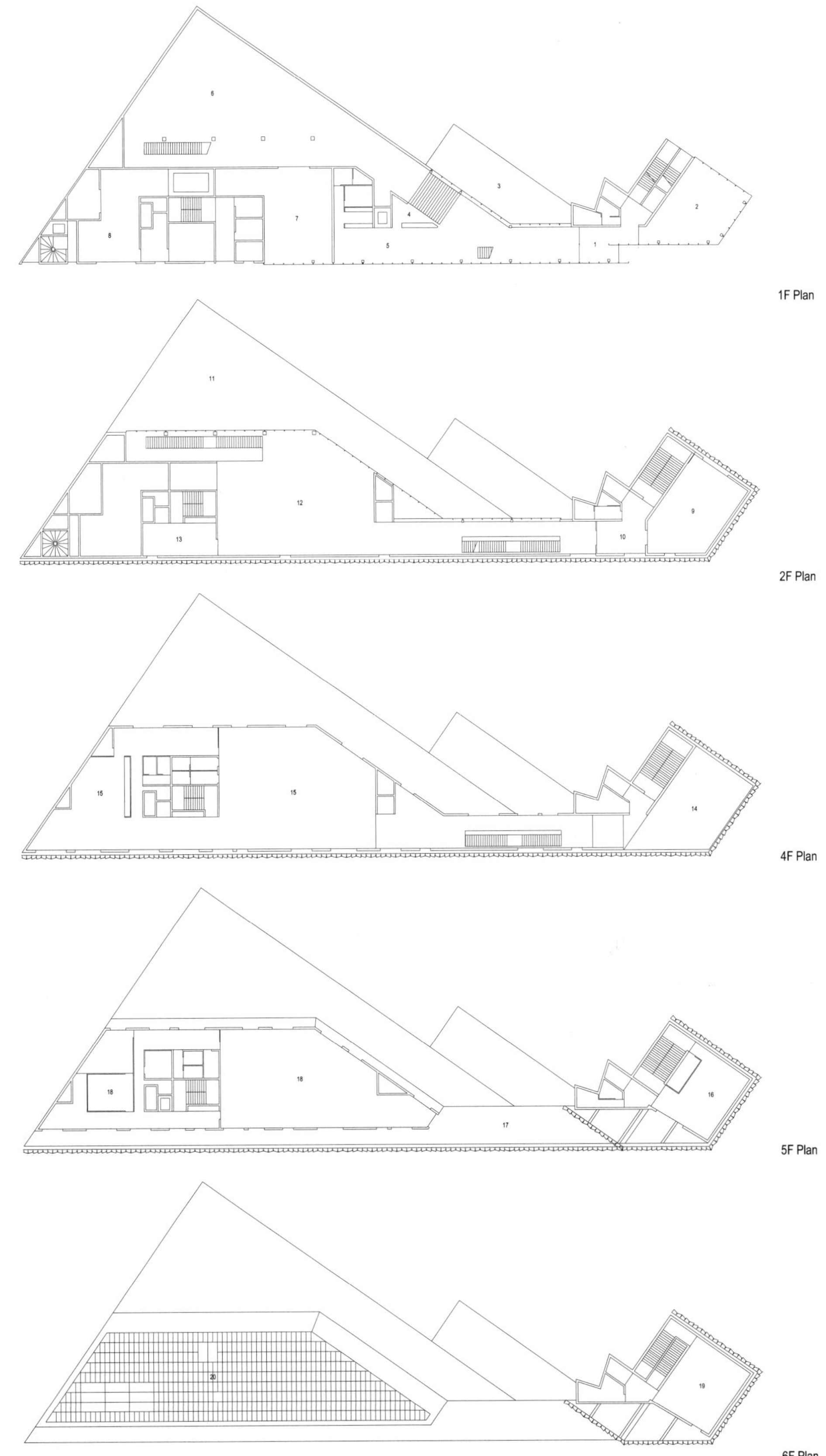

MINERAL 5: CHINA ACADEMY OF ART'S FOLK ART MUSEUM

Completion year: 2015
Location: Hangzhou, China
Structure: steel
Building type: museum

The Folk Art Museum is situated within the campus of the China Academy of Arts in Hangzhou, occupying a scenic hillside that was once a tea field. Our design philosophy centered on creating a museum that embodies the natural undulations of the landscape beneath it. The building's floors gently rise and fall in alignment with the slopes, establishing a profound connection with the terrain.

The museum's layout utilizes a geometric system based on parallelogram units, specifically chosen for their ability to adapt to the complex topography of the site. Each unit is topped with a small individual roof, giving the museum the appearance of a village with an expanse of tiled roofs.

The external walls are adorned with a screen made of tiles, hung on stainless-steel wires. This innovative feature not only adds a unique aesthetic but also plays a functional role in controlling the sunlight entering the rooms. The tiles used for both the screen and the roof were sourced from local houses, varying in size to enhance the building's natural integration with its surroundings. This thoughtful use of materials reinforces the museum's connection to local heritage and landscape.

Old tiles from local folk houses in China were repurposed for the roof, wall screens, and external structure of the museum. The varied shapes and colors of these old roof tiles lend the building an appearance reminiscent of an ancient grove, suggesting that it has stood as part of the landscape for a long time. This use of reclaimed materials not only preserves a piece of local heritage but also helps the structure blend seamlessly with its natural surroundings, enhancing its historical and aesthetic value.

The traditional roofs of folk houses in China are typically covered with curved cross-section tiles, layered in a manner similar to those found along the Mediterranean coast in Europe. These tiles, with their pronounced convex and concave sections, create a visually striking contrast. The more formal, convex tiles are often used in dignified structures, such as temples, in both China and Japan, underscoring their ceremonial importance.

In contrast, during the middle of the Edo period around 1674, an industrialized version known as the pantile was developed. This type of tile integrates both convex and concave shapes, which enhances installation efficiency and improves waterproofing capabilities. Pantiles became widely used across most houses due to these practical benefits. However, from an aesthetic standpoint, I find pantiles somewhat lackluster and industrially unappealing. This sentiment guided my decision to use the more traditional and visually appealing roof tiles from Chinese folk houses as the central architectural theme, aiming to capture their rich cultural significance and unique beauty in the overall design of the museum.

To construct the tile screen wall, a foundational diamond-shaped screen was first crafted from stainless-steel wire. This provided a robust and flexible base for attaching the roof tiles. We employed a traditional, albeit primitive, method for securing the tiles: using piano wire threaded through holes made on all four sides of each tile. This approach proved particularly effective for accommodating roof tiles of various sizes, ensuring a secure and aesthetically pleasing arrangement. The choice of such a method not only facilitated the physical construction but also preserved the authenticity and rustic charm of the tiles, integrating them seamlessly into the overall design.

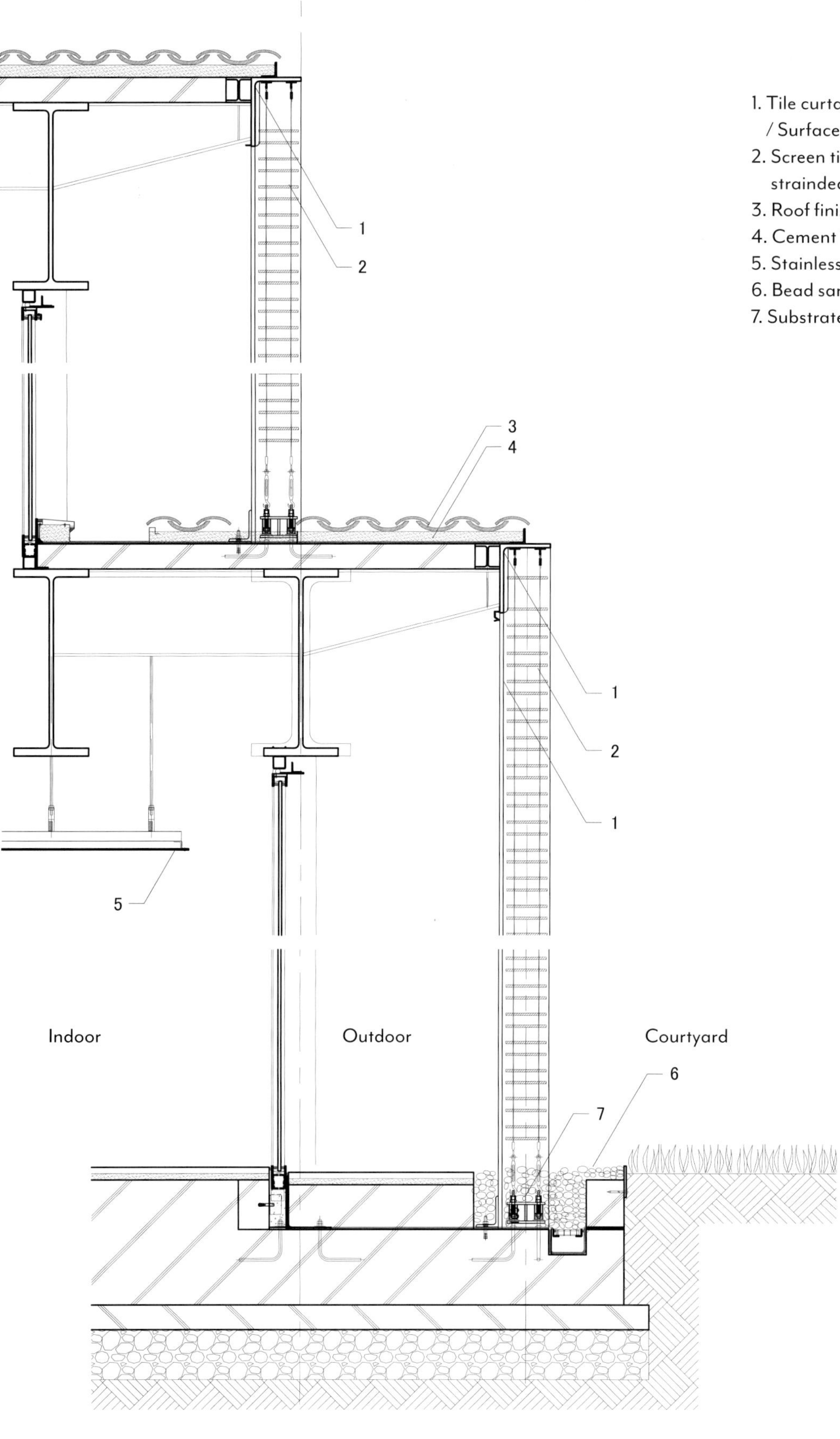

1. Tile curtain wall fixed steel frame / Surface fluorocarbon coating
2. Screen tiles Φ2.0 mm stainless steel strainded wire
3. Roof finish
4. Cement T30 - 50
5. Stainless steel mesh
6. Bead sand stone
7. Substrate

Section Detail

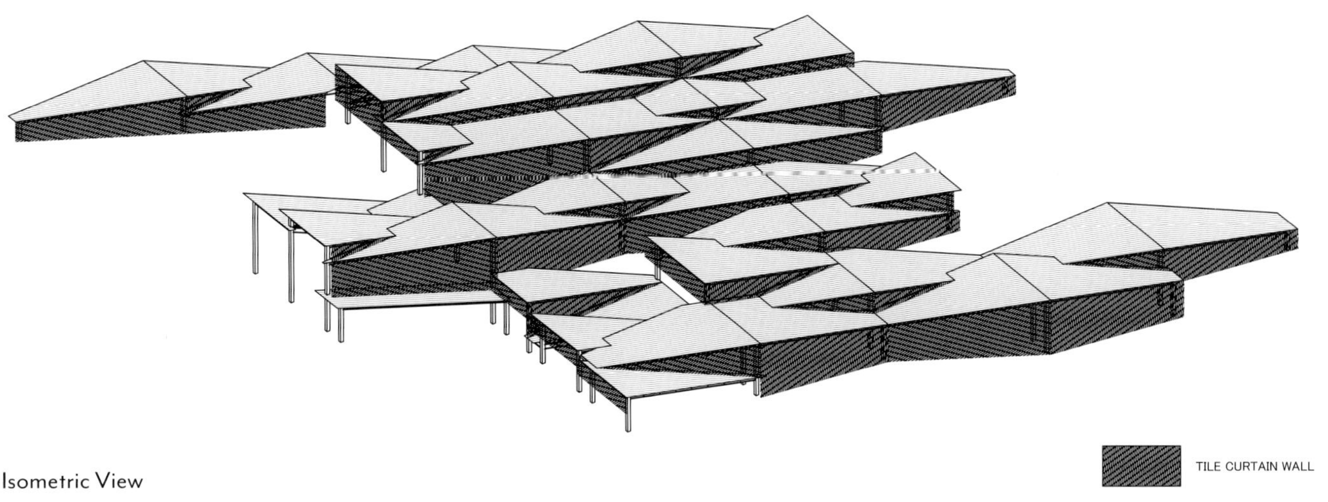

Isometric View

1. Conference room
2. Meeting room
3. Exhibition room
4. Water feature
5. Corridor
6. Machinery room
7. Courtyard

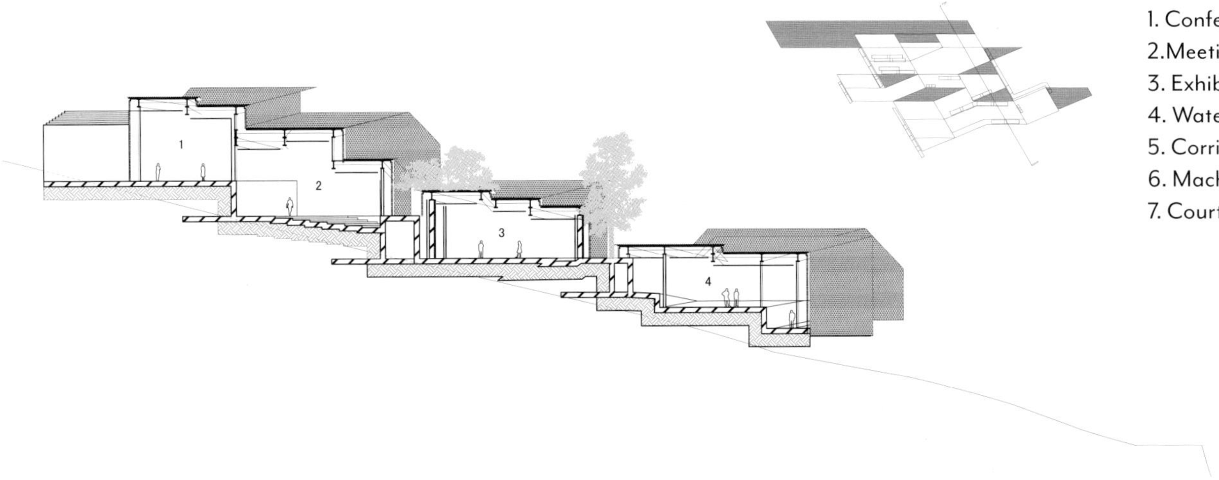

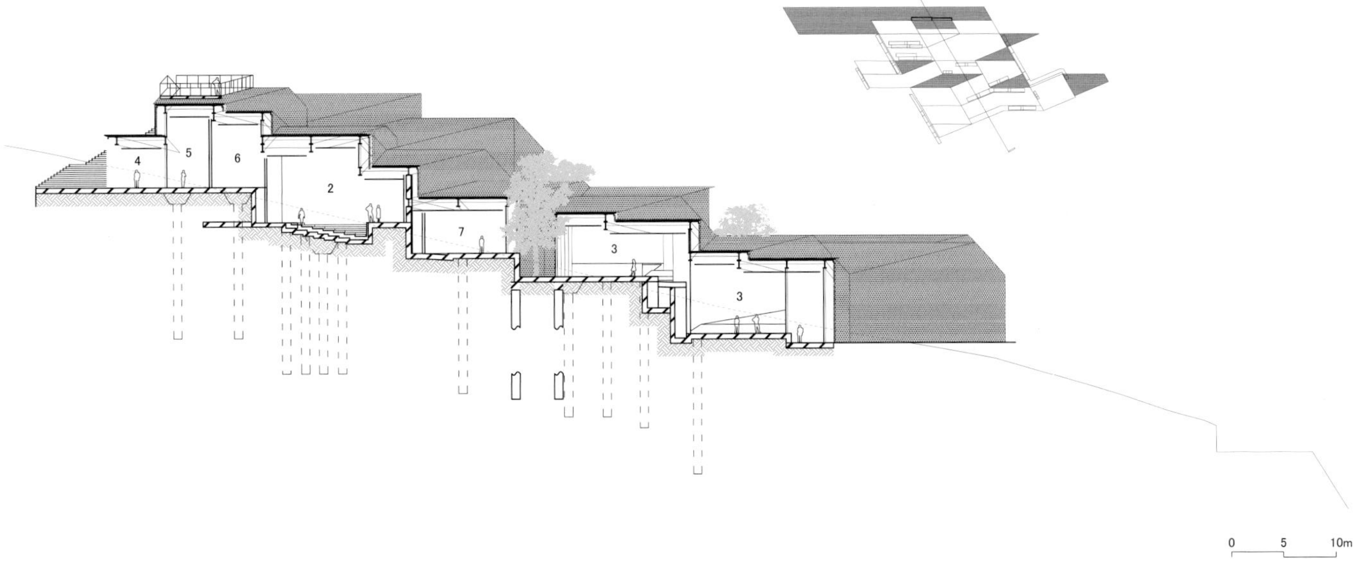

0 5 10m

Sections

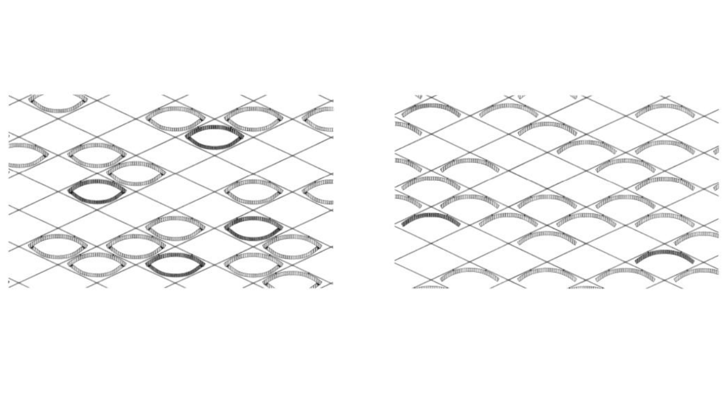

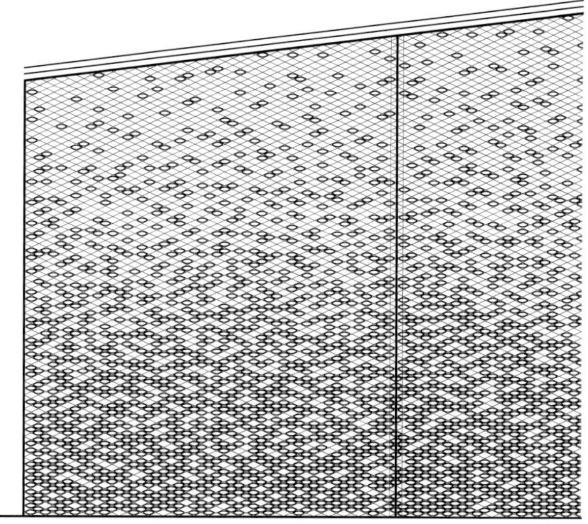

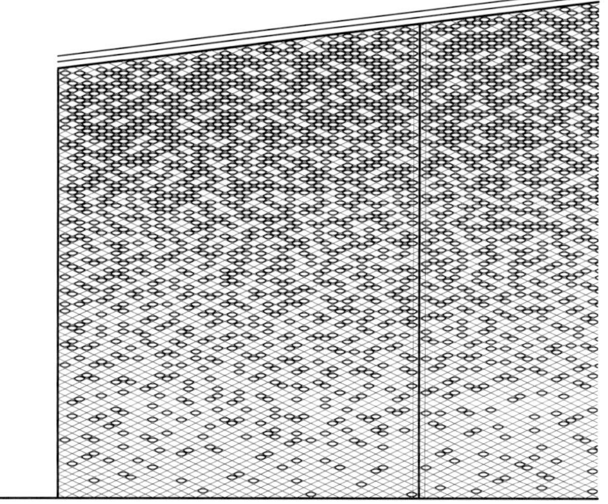

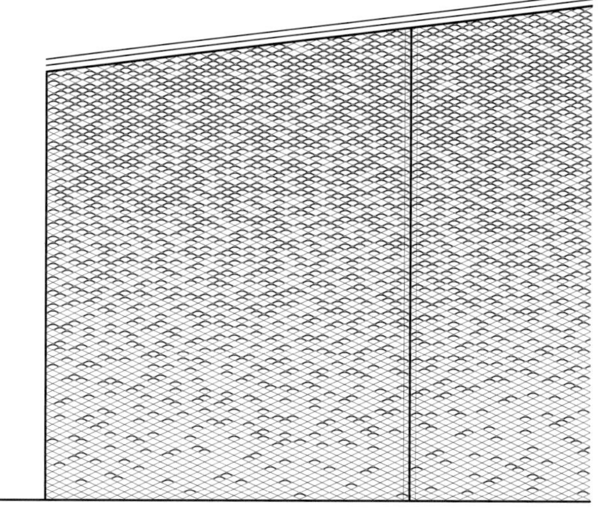

Elevation Diagram

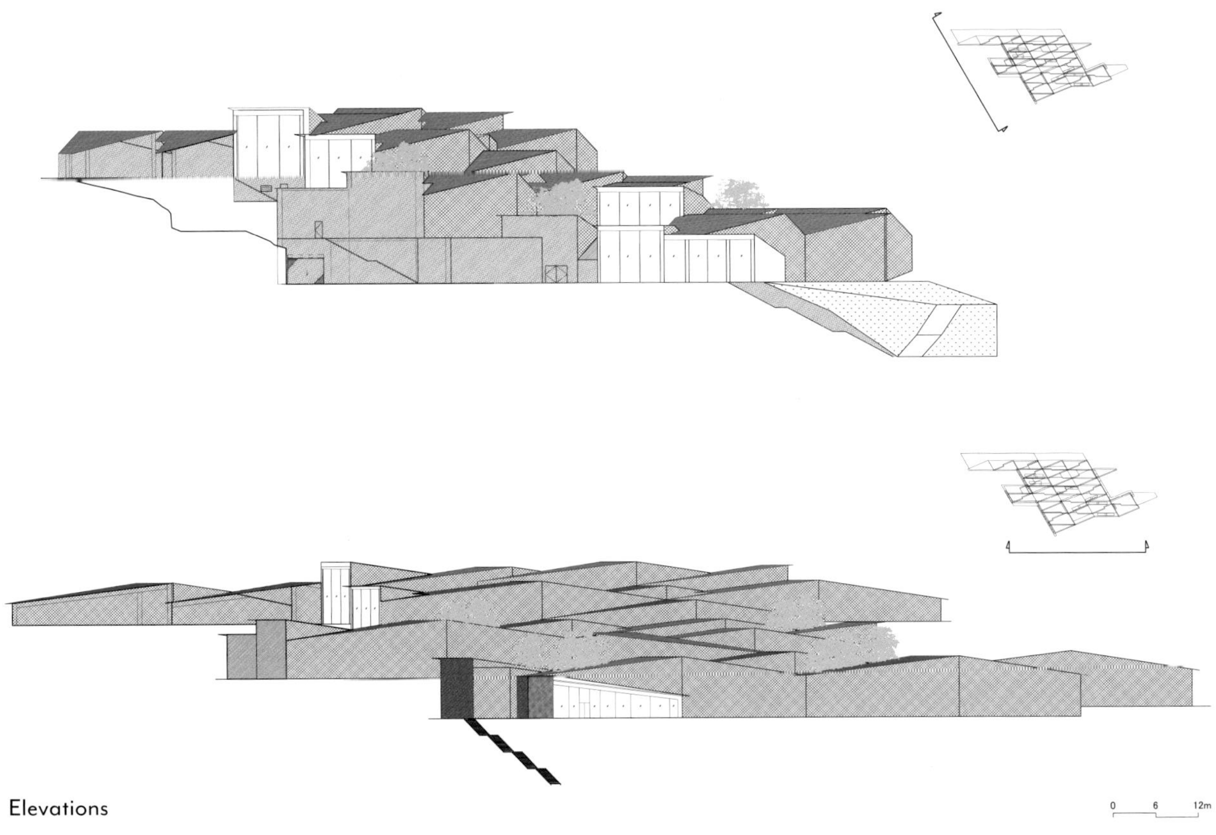

Elevations

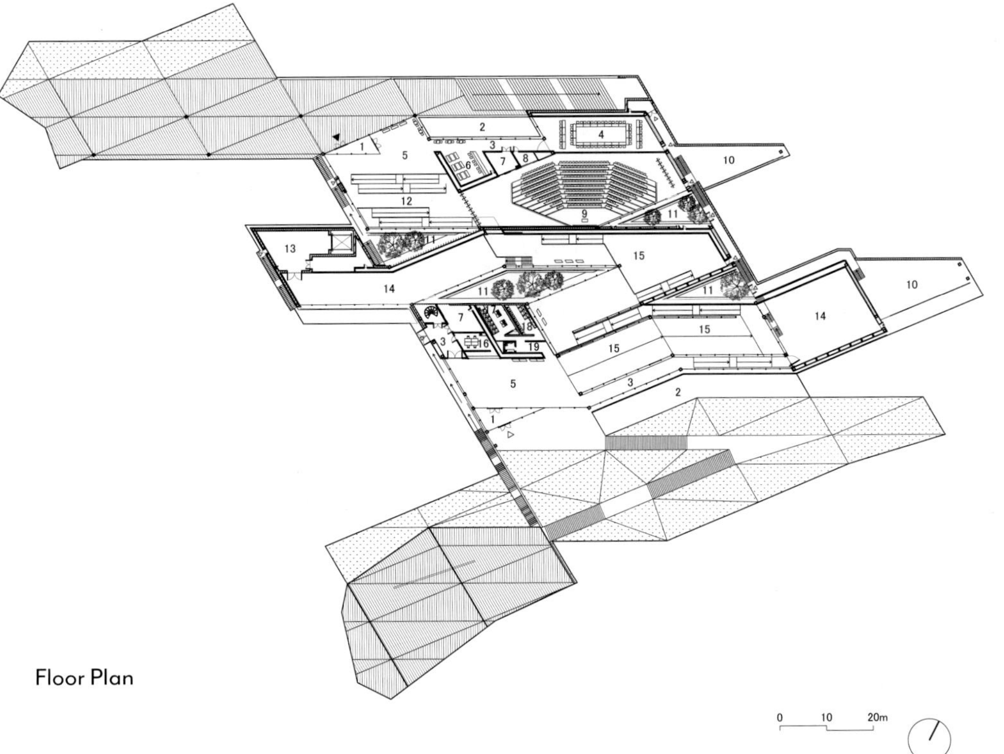

Floor Plan

1. Windbreak room
2. Water feature
3. Corridor
4. Conference room
5. Entrance hall
6. Cafe
7. Machinery room
8. Simulétneous interpretation room
9. Meeting room
10. Outdoor unit storage area
11. Courtyard
12. Hall
13. Front chamber
14. Special exhibition hall
15. Exhibition hall
16. Management office
17. Female toilet
18. Male toilet
19. Public toilet

MINERAL 6: V&A AT DUNDEE

Completion year: 2018
Location: Scotland, UK
Structure: RC/SRC (reinforced concrete / steel-reinforced concrete)
Building type: museum

The new building for the UK's Victoria & Albert Museum in Dundee, located on Scotland's northern waterfront, marks the first design museum in Scotland and serves as a cultural beacon aimed at promoting Scottish culture.

Situated on the banks of the river Tay, south of the Dundee River, the museum's structure extends over the water, embracing a design philosophy intended to harmonize with the natural environment and the surrounding landscape. Inspired by the rugged cliffs of Orkney Island in northern Scotland, the building's façade is composed of long slabs of precast concrete set at varying angles. This design choice creates a dynamic and nuanced appearance, achieved through advanced parametric design systems.

A significant architectural feature is the cave-like opening through the center of the building, which links the scenic river Tay with Union Street, the main thoroughfare in Dundee. Historically, Dundee was a thriving harbor city, but its connection to the river was obstructed in the twentieth century by the construction of warehouses. The removal of these structures as part of a broader urban redevelopment plan has reinstated the riverfront as a focal

For the exterior walls of the building, which project out over the river, a man-made architectural design seemed inappropriate. Instead, a naturally rough and powerful surface, reminiscent of the cliffs on Orkney Island, north of Dundee, was deemed more fitting. Inspired by the natural formation of cliffs, I aimed to mimic the accumulation of layers, using modern architectural materials. This approach reflects the randomness and beautiful rhythm formed over time through horizontal shapes.

To achieve this effect, bar-shaped precast concrete slabs with sharp edges and random angles were selected. Subtle irregularities were introduced along with gaps between the layers to enhance their aesthetic and structural qualities. The concrete was mixed with large aggregate to emulate the roughness of natural layers. Additionally, a solidifying delay additive was used to expose the top of the aggregate, providing the slabs with a textured surface.

point of city life, with the museum acting as a central symbol. The design incorporates a void reminiscent of the Torii gates in Shinto shrines, symbolizing a gateway that enhances the connection between the urban environment and nature.

Inside, the museum features randomly attached panels that contribute to creating a spacious and inviting atmosphere. The interior space expands upward, offering visitors a unique sense of openness uncommon in traditional museum foyers. This area also serves as a versatile venue for concerts and performances, positioning the V&A Dundee as a communal gathering place for the city.

When determining the overall volume of the building, ordinary 90-degree geometric angles were deliberately avoided to distance the structure from appearing man-made and to foster a sense of natural freedom. Furthermore, an effort was made to reconcile the existing axes on the site—the axis line of the adjacent RRS Discovery and the axis line of Union Street. By slightly twisting these axes, we effectively moved away from conventional geometry, further enhancing the building's integration with its natural surroundings.

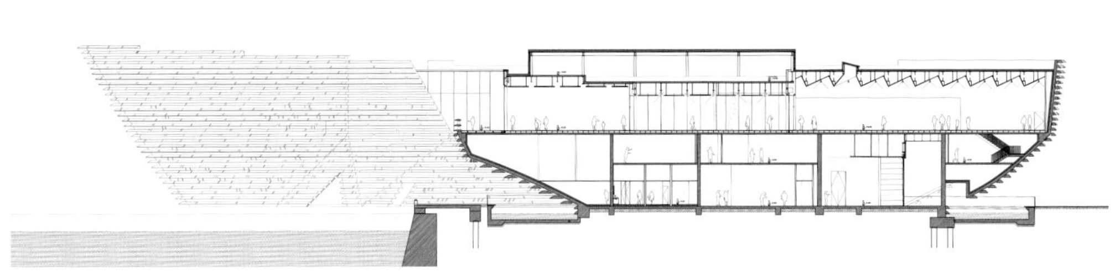

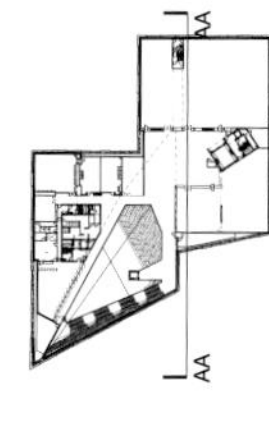

Section AA

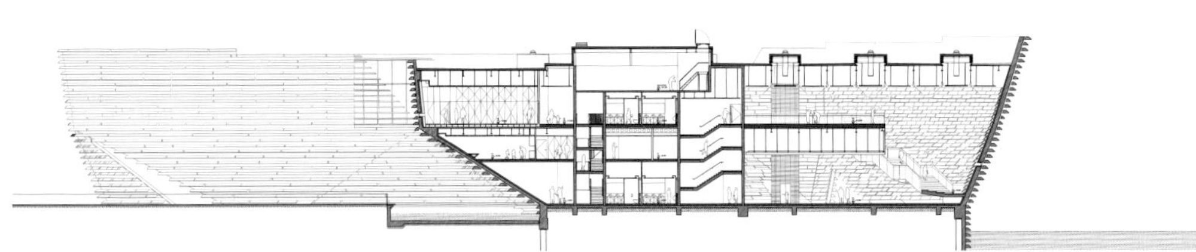

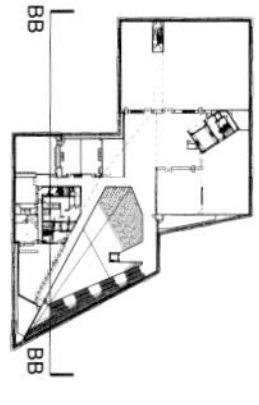

Section BB

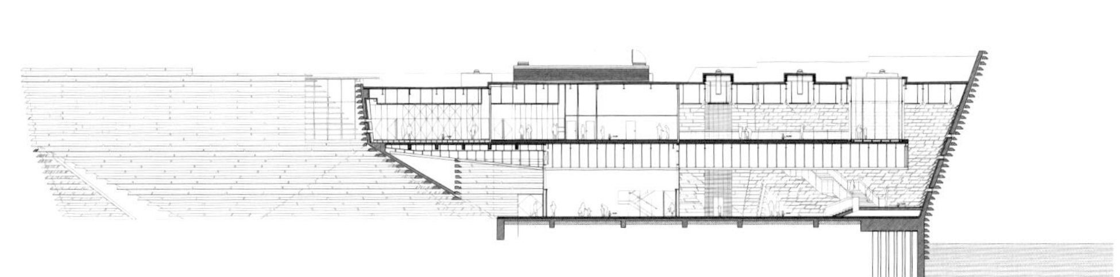

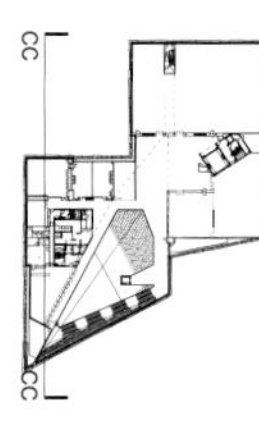

Section CC

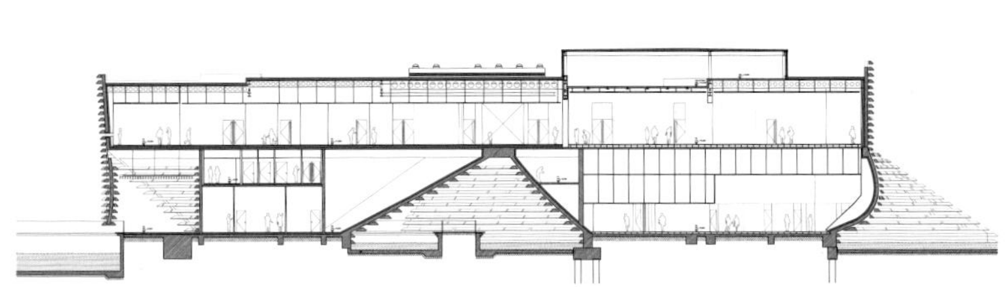

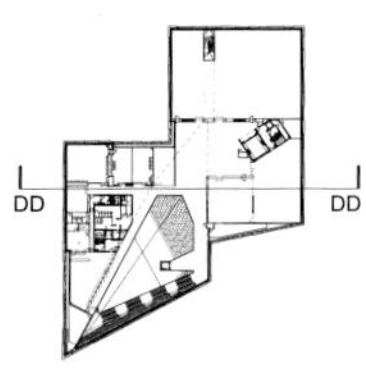

Section DD

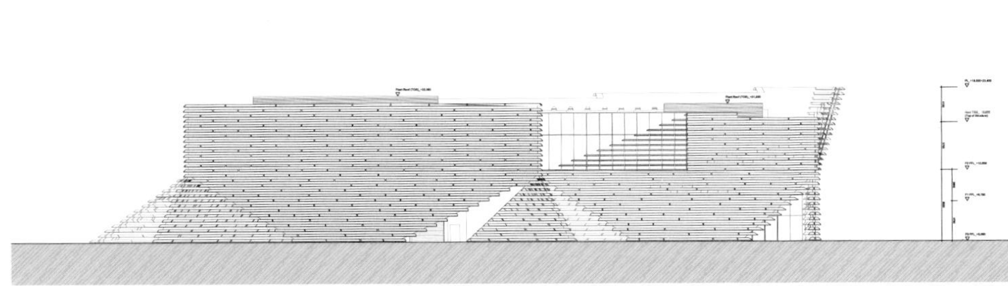
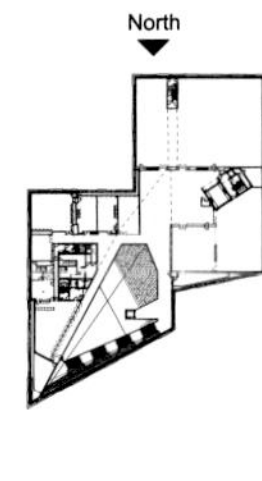

North Elevation

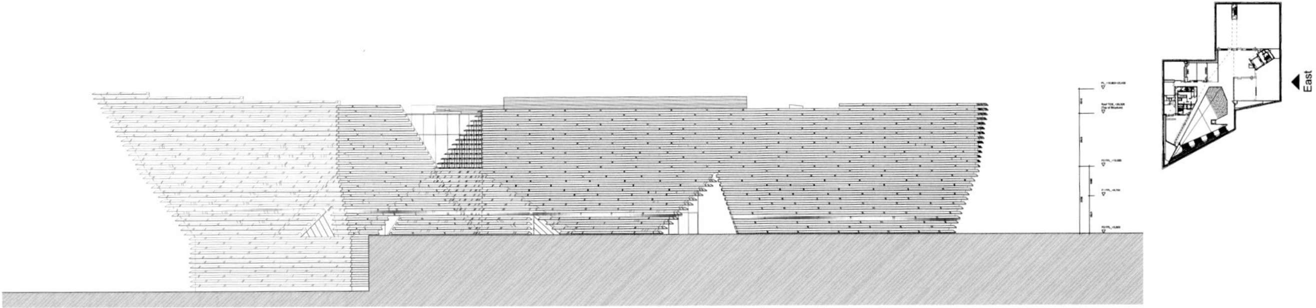

East Elevation

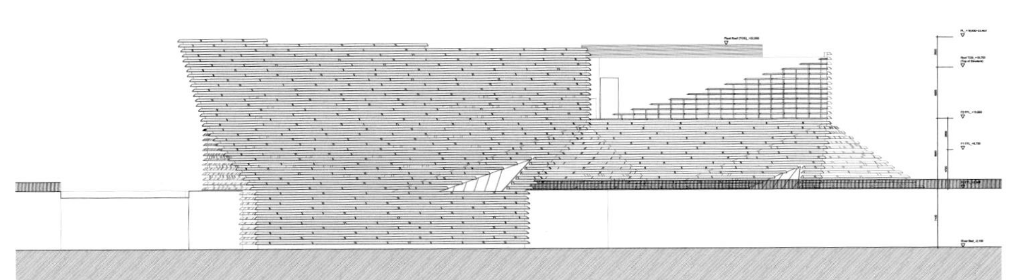
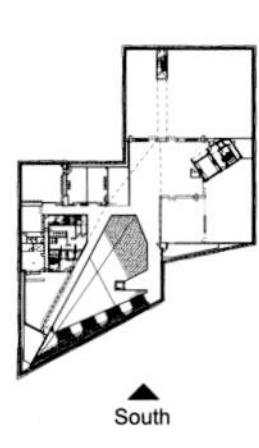

South Elevation

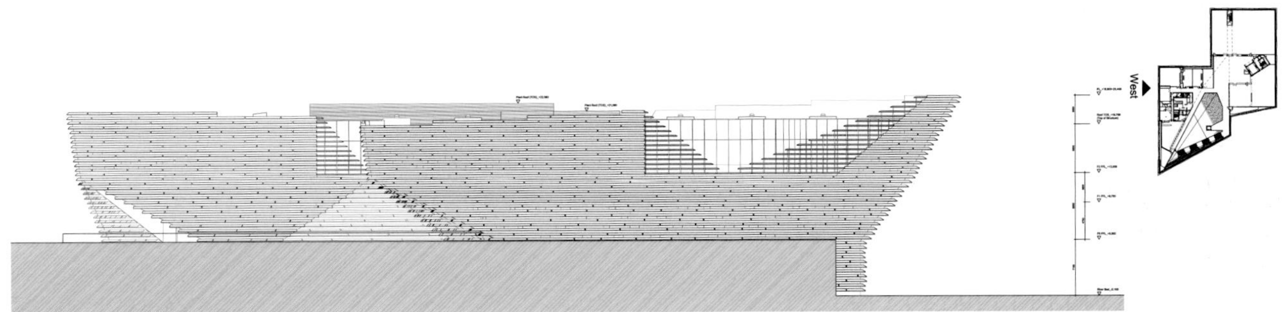

West Elevation

4.4m

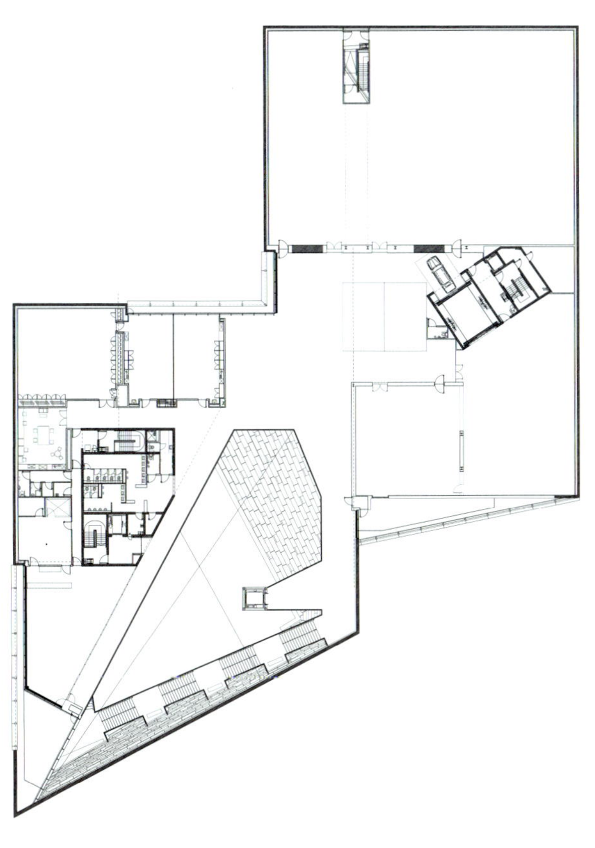

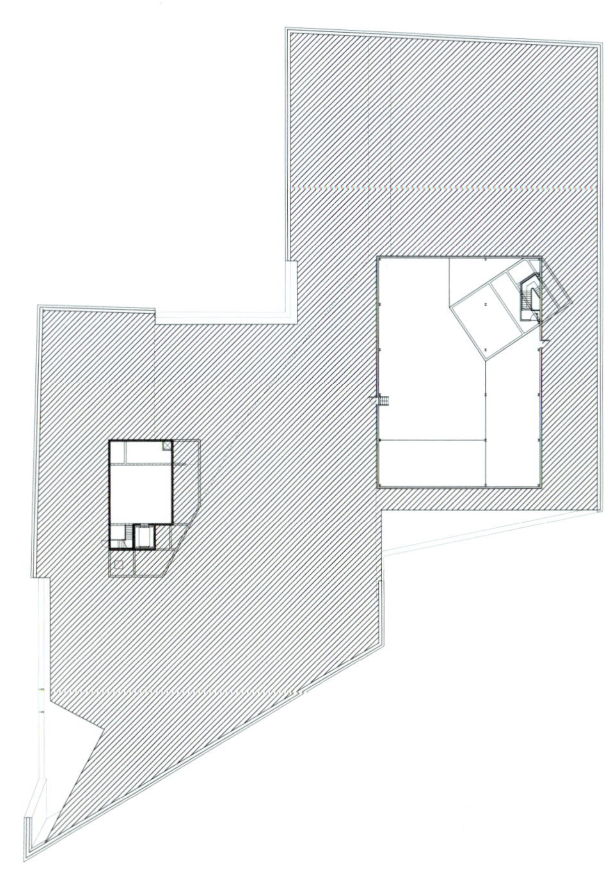

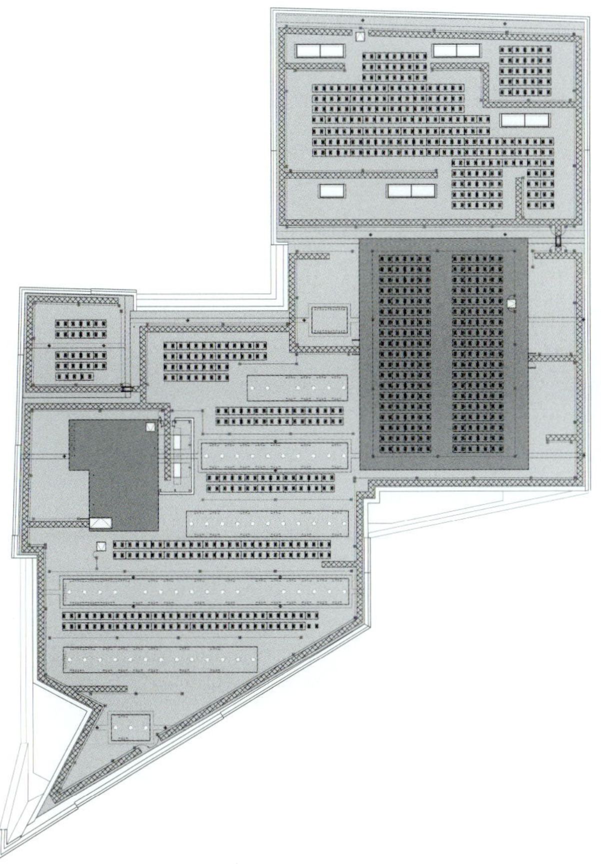

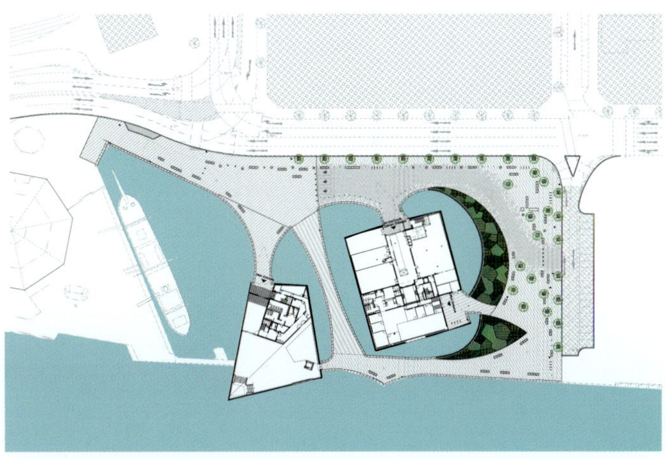

MINERAL 7: TOKOROZAWA SAKURA TOWN KADOKAWA CULTURE MUSEUM

Completion year: 2020
Location: Saitama, Japan
Structure: RC/SRC (reinforced concrete / steel-reinforced concrete)
Building type: museum

This multipurpose complex in Tokorozawa, situated on the Musashino plateau—a unique geological site formed by the collision of four crustal plates—blends an array of functions in an unprecedented manner. The facility integrates a digital-printing factory, a computer-controlled distribution warehouse, offices, an art gallery, a library, a museum, an anime-themed hotel, and venues dedicated to anime culture into a cohesive, cross-sectoral environment.

The Kadokawa Culture Museum, a key component of this complex, was constructed using twenty thousand 70 mm thick black-and-white granite slabs. The slabs are finished roughly, with adjacent sections intentionally misaligned to avoid the typical convex and concave surface matching. This design choice gives the impression that each stone slab has independently broken through the earth's surface, contributing to a sense of lightness and the illusion that the structure is floating.

Inside, the vast space is designed as a futuristic labyrinth that transcends traditional binary oppositions, mixing high culture, such as contemporary art, with low culture, such as anime. The bookshelves, crafted from structural plywood, are designed to

We initially contemplated using 30 mm thick stone slabs attached to concrete through conventional modern construction methods. However, we realized this would yield only a two-dimensional appearance, akin to texture mapping in 3-D rendering, and would not convey the impression of a colossal rock emerging from the plateau as we intended.

To achieve our vision, we opted for 70 mm thick granite slabs with a rough finish. We discovered that the outer wall of a sixty-one-face polyhedron, constructed with stone of this thickness, could not be adequately supported by a conventional soft-steel structure. To remedy this, we poured a concrete wall outside the steel frame, enhancing the structure's overall rigidity and improving its waterproof capabilities.

To preserve the raw, organic quality of the stone and maintain the impression that the structure was bursting forth from the ground, we introduced a novel architectural detail. Instead of aligning the edges, we designed visible gaps between the stones. This approach not only highlighted the natural texture of the granite but also reinforced the dynamic, eruptive character of our design.

mimic haze in the sky, creating a cellular, brain-like structure that fosters a three-dimensional interconnection among various genres and objects.

In the production and office wing, large stone seats resonate with the rough stone surfaces, aiming for a harmonious integration. The Musashino Reiwa Jinja Shrine, part of the complex, features an expanded aluminum fence with large openings and combines wave styles with traditional gables, reflecting a blend of modern and traditional architectural elements.

Furthermore, decorative architectural features representing female and male deities are juxtaposed and mixed, symbolizing an effort to create a new type of venue. This space is designed to be especially suited to the needs of the coronavirus age, surpassing traditional regional cultural facilities in scope and function.

In Europe, the traditional approach for handling rough-finish stone involves cutting the edges of each stone to align precisely with its neighbors at the joints, ensuring uniform thickness. However, this method compromises the natural roughness of the stone, giving it a decorative, classical appearance that we wanted to avoid.

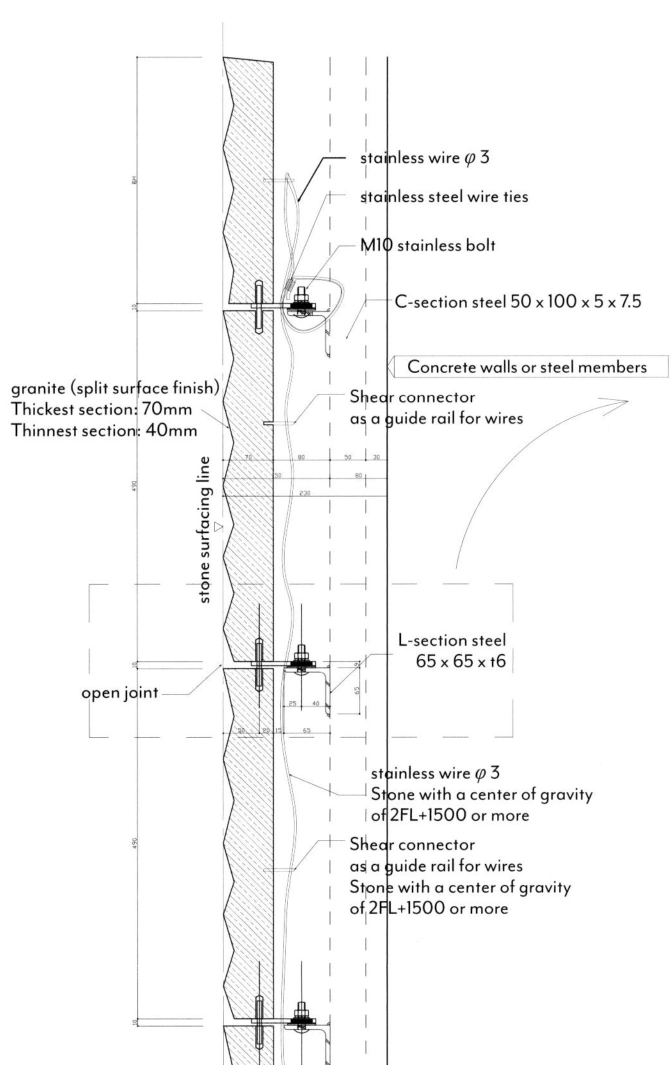

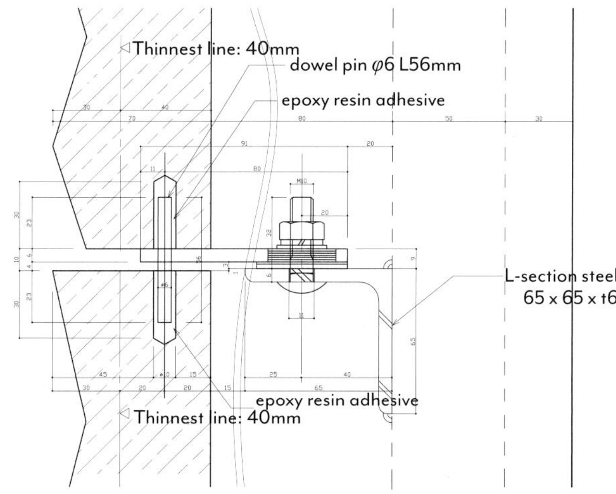

Sectional Detail

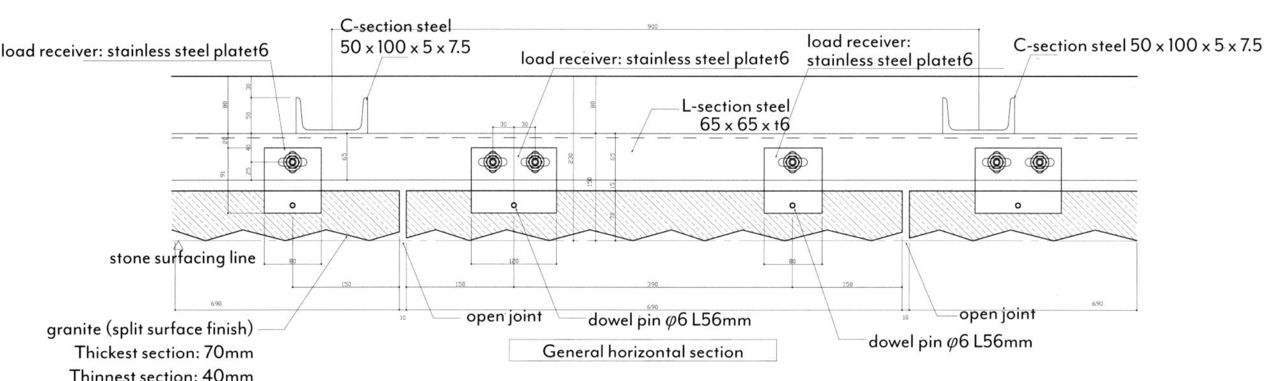

Outer Wall Details

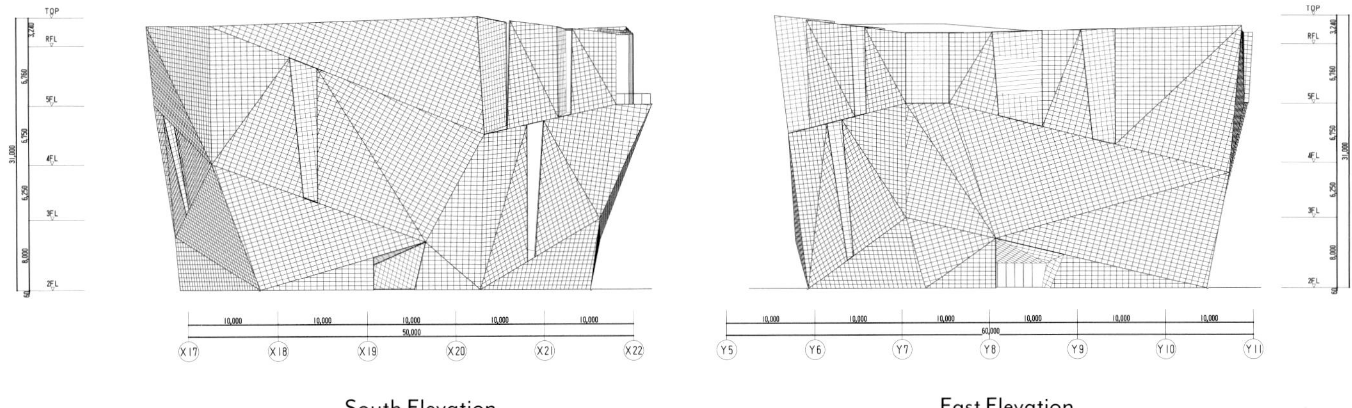

South Elevation

East Elevation

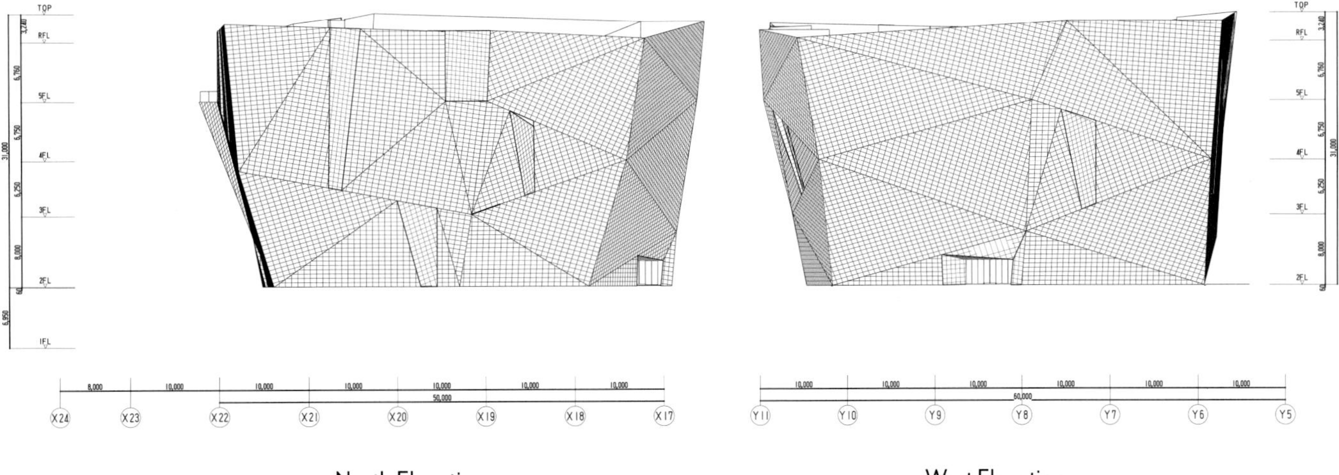

North Elevation

West Elevation

MINERAL 8: ISHIGAKI CITY HALL

Completion year: 2021
Location: Okinawa, Japan
Structure: RC (reinforced concrete), steel
Building type: city hall

The relocation of Ishigaki City Hall to higher ground was not just a response to its vulnerability in a tsunami inundation zone; it was also an opportunity to rejuvenate the traditional landscape of Ishigaki. This landscape is characterized by layers of red-tile stucco roofs set against the backdrop of lush greenery. Inspired by the settlement pattern of Ishigaki, where villages historically emerged at the intersections of rows of houses, our design strategically arranges various city hall functions along intersecting east–west and north–south axes. This layout fosters the creation of a street that is open and accessible to the community, facilitating a seamless integration with the surrounding environment.

The traditional roofing technique using plaster-coated tiles has been diminishing in Okinawa due to the plaster's susceptibility to damage. To address this, we revitalized the appearance of the traditional red-and-white tile pattern by applying a white glaze to create distinct borders on each tile. This modern intervention harnesses modern technology to preserve and celebrate the region's architectural heritage, ensuring that the iconic scenery of Ishigaki is maintained and enhanced for future generations.

The small-tiled roofs, which appear sporadically across the Japanese landscape, epitomize the characteristic scenery of village settlements. These roof segments reflect the modest scale, simplicity, diversity, and a certain uniformity of the houses within the villages, collectively presenting the impression of the village as a singular large house.

With this in mind, we envisioned Ishigaki City Hall not just as a municipal building but as a large "house" within this type of village setting. Our goal was to foster a sense of affection and familiarity with the city hall, akin to the way that residents feel about their own homes.

To achieve the effect of the roof appearing to float within the landscape, we painted the walls, pillars, and all elements other than the roof in a dark-beige tone. This color choice helps these elements blend seamlessly into the surrounding landscape, emphasizing the roof as the primary visual feature.

We particularly admired the beauty of the plaster-coated roof tiles used in Okinawa, regarded as among the most aesthetically pleasing across Japan. To reintroduce this traditional element in a durable and maintenance-efficient manner suitable for public buildings, we employed a special paint (glazing) technique. This modern adaptation allows us to preserve the visual heritage of Okinawan tiles while ensuring their practicality and longevity in a modern setting.

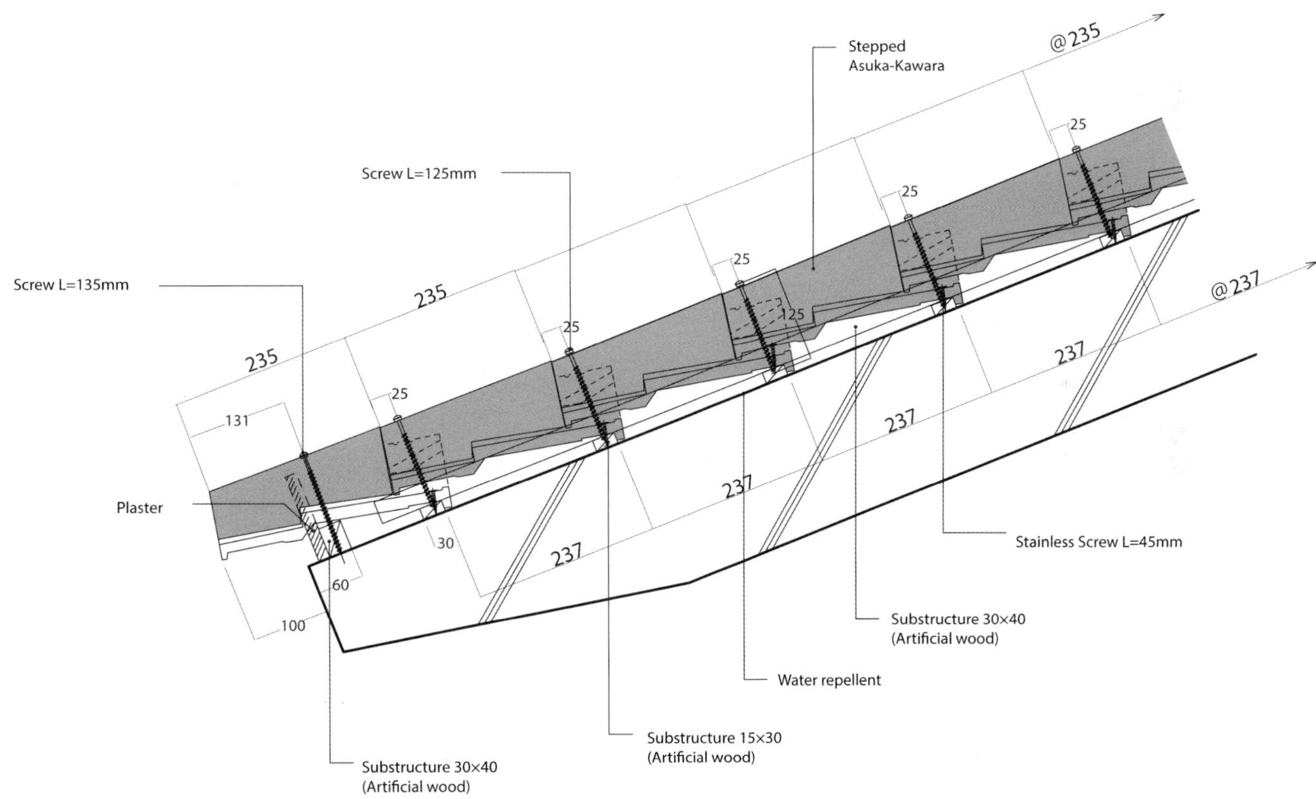

Roof Detail

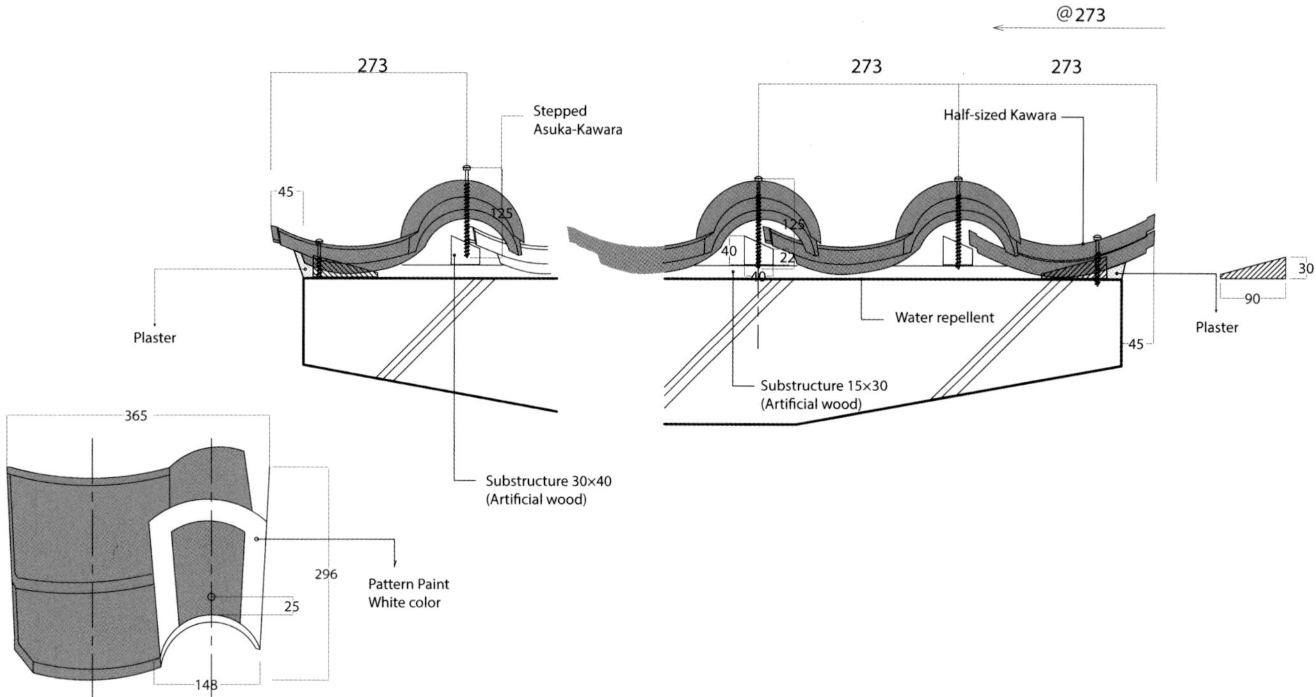

Roof Details: Traditional Tiles, *Kawara*

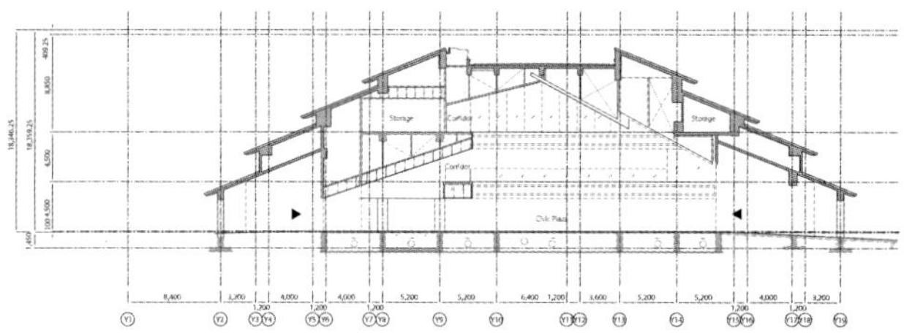

Section A

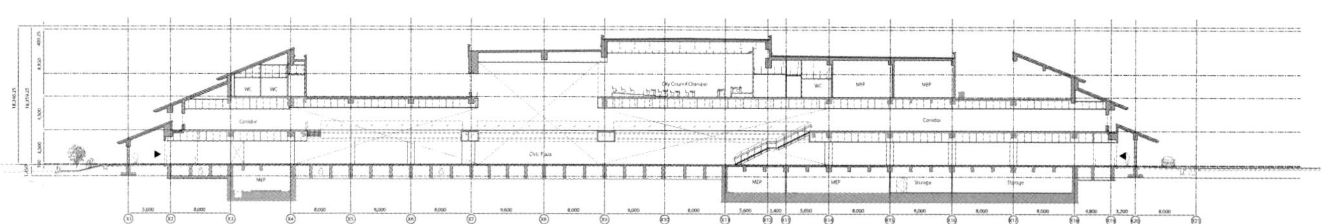

Section B

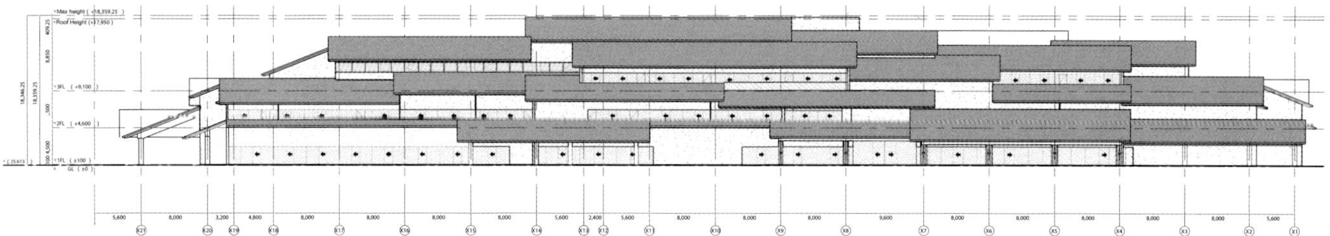

North Elevation

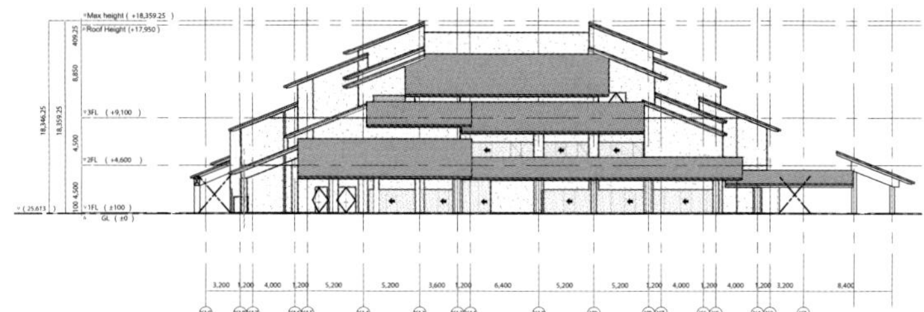

East Elevation

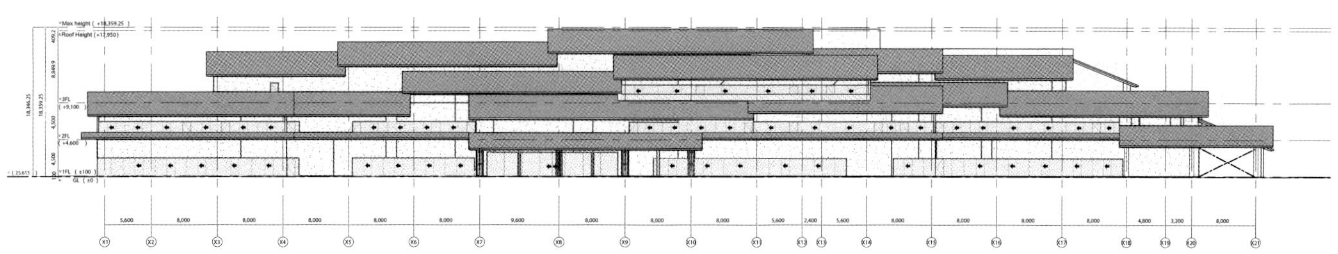

South Elevation

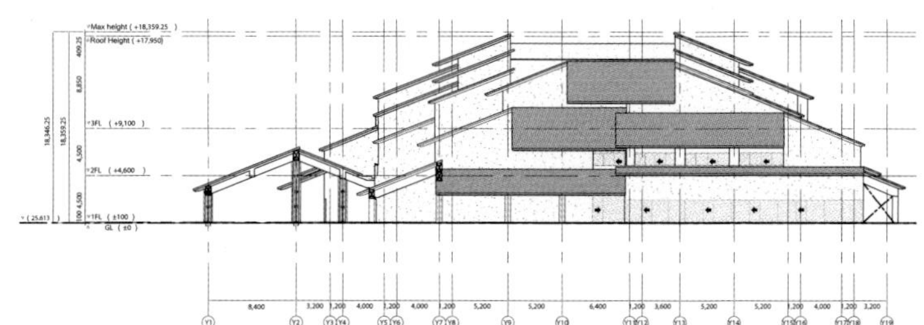

West Elevation

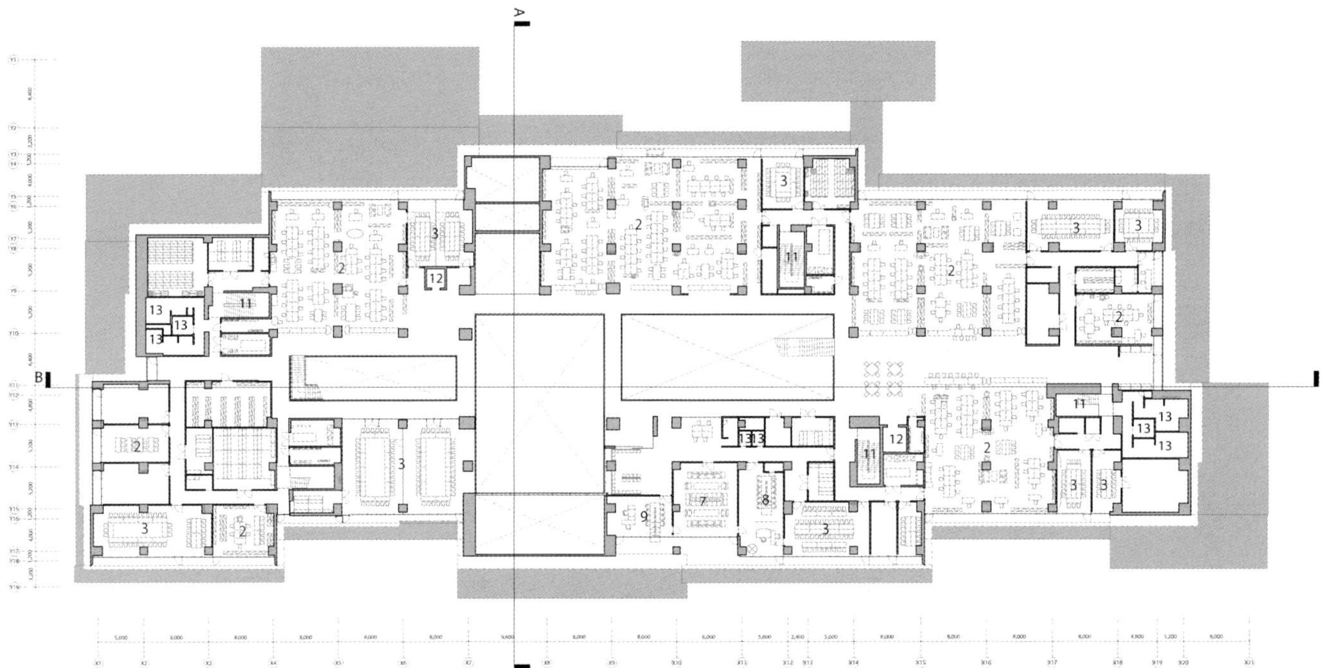

Second Floor

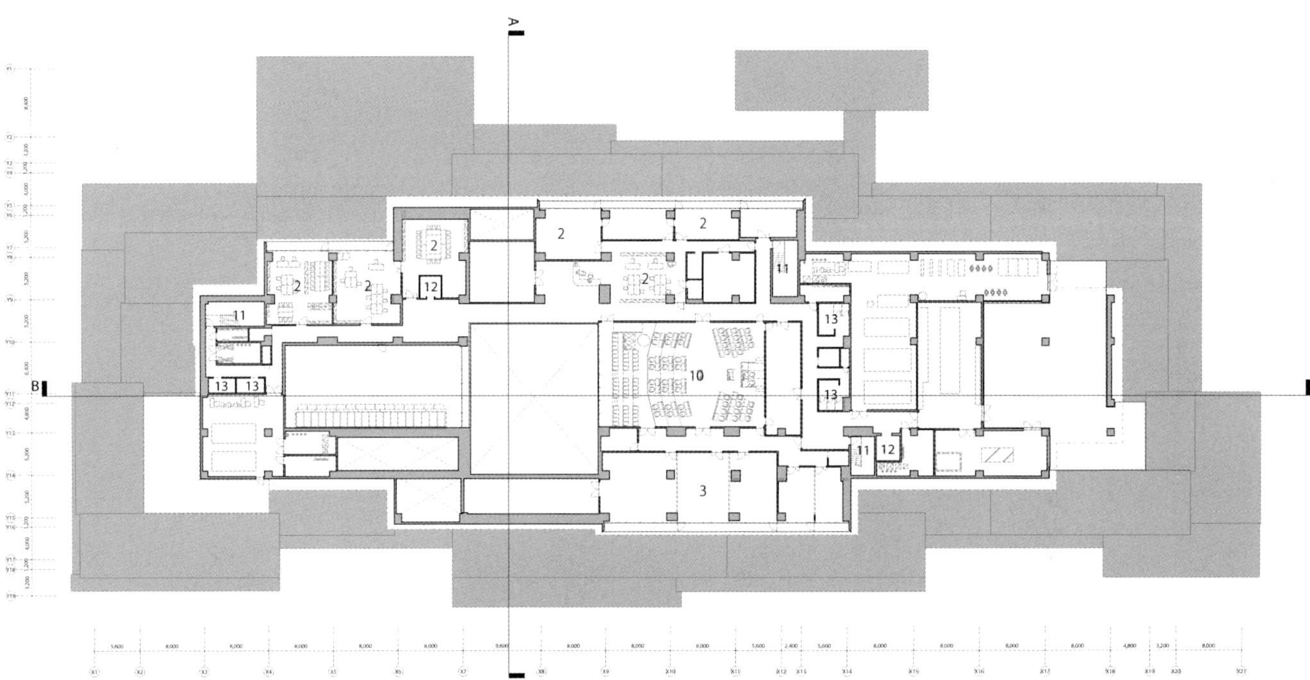

Third Floor

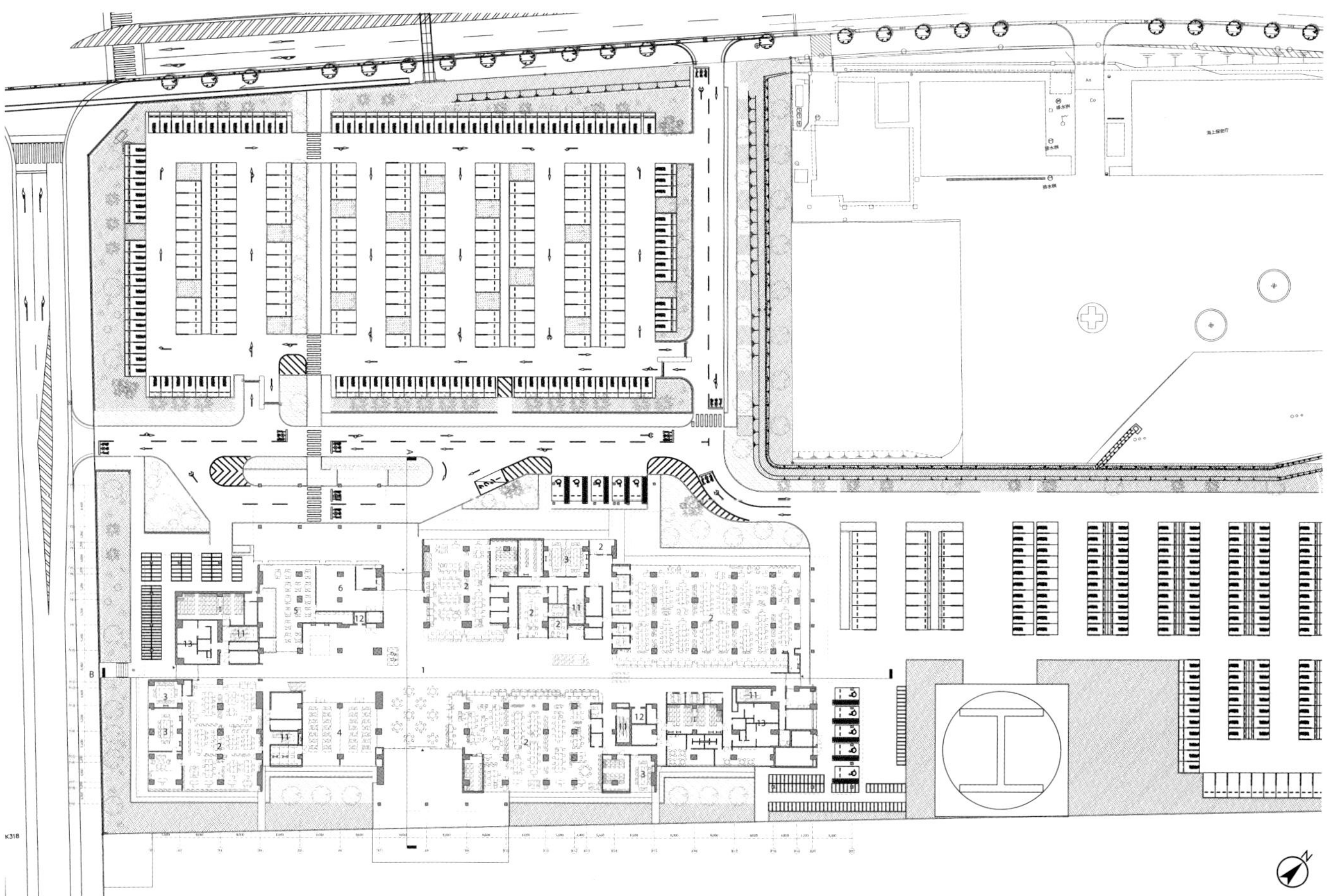

First Floor

1. Civic plaza
2. Office
3. Conference room
4. Community room
5. Cafeteria
6. Shop
7. Reception room
8. Mayor's office
9. Deputy mayor's office
10. City Council chamber
11. Stairs
12. EV
13. WC

CHAPTER 3 GREEN

From the time that I began to design buildings, I have wanted to erase structures by covering them with greenery. However, I do not want to bury buildings underground. Burying a building, while potentially allowing for green roofs, effectively severs the connection between the structure and nature, enclosing it within a concrete chamber—a method I find quite unsatisfactory. Similarly, the practice of greening vertical walls does not appeal to me; it often feels akin to merely applying a texture to a concrete box, a method that seems to disrespect the greenery itself.

Ultimately, I concluded that the most engaging design element is the garden outside a structure. This realization led to the formation of an in-house landscape design team. Led by Ryoko Mase, a seasoned expert with twenty years of experience at Iwaki Zoen, a premier garden-and-landscaping company in Japan, our team is deeply knowledgeable about trees, soil, and water.

Iwaki Zoen has a storied history, initiated in Tokyo by the nephew of Ogawa Jihei VII, a pivotal figure from the Meiji era who crafted the prototype of the modern Japanese garden. I hold a deep respect for their work, and the insights I've gained from the gardens created by Ogawa Jihei have been invaluable. He was known for his innovative introduction of large voids and axes into Japanese gardens, which help balance dense tree areas that might otherwise create a somber ambiance with expansive green-grass areas, ideal for outdoor gatherings and lightening the overall feel of the garden.

Moreover, Jihei elevated the southern end of the garden to facilitate water flow, utilizing this water axis to unify the garden's diverse elements. This technique, blending Western methods of creating voids and axes with the Japanese art of tree manipulation, led to the foundational design of the modern Japanese garden. His methods have provided me with numerous insights into how greenery can be thoughtfully incorporated into architectural and landscape designs, influencing my approach to effectively blending built environments with their natural surroundings.

GREEN 1: PORTLAND JAPANESE GARDEN CULTURAL VILLAGE

Completion year: 2017
Location: Oregon, USA
Structure: steel
Building type: cultural space

Portland Japanese Garden's new Cultural Village is a modest, human-scaled set of buildings arranged around a courtyard plaza, whose fourth side is the existing, untouched gardens from the 1960s. The project constitutes a village positioned along a journey from the city to the top of the hill, a form of modern monzenmachi wherein the pilgrimage pays homage to the spirit of nature.

There are four buildings, each with its own means of merging into the dramatic slopes of the terrain, in combination with the tall vertical lines of the Pacific Northwest conifers: the Ticketing Pavilion floating above gentle stepped ponds, the café hovering above the ravine, and the main Village House and Garden House.

Although the architecture is deferential to the landscape, the key device is the zigzagging roof—creating deep overhangs of soft metal and lush vegetation, and a porous boundary to encourage a direct relationship with the renowned Portland rain, and its temperamental sun—in a soft, indeterminate, and flexible border.

In collaboration with Sadafumi Uchiyama (landscape design), Hacker Architects, Walker Macy.

The design of the building strategically incorporates vegetation across the entire roof, making it feel as though it is an extension of a Japanese garden. The architectural plan was devised such that one side of the building faces a courtyard plaza, allowing its cross section to harmonize with the hill at the rear, while the opposite side is embedded into the hill, fostering a seamless integration of landscape and architecture.

To achieve a thin and lightweight roof, we utilized porous ceramic sheets, specifically a product called GreenBiz, which is made from recycled slag generated from home cloth dyeing. These sheets are only 32 mm thick, and plants are planted directly onto them, with their roots secured within the panel. This method significantly reduces the roof's weight and ensures that the edges are thin, allowing the roof to appear as if it merges seamlessly with its environment, enhancing the building's aesthetic harmony with the natural landscape.

When greening the roof, it was crucial to keep the soil layer as thin as possible. This approach was adopted to prevent the need for a thick soil base, which would not only add weight but also require a more robust supporting structure. Our concern was that a sturdier structure might compromise the translucency of the building, thereby diminishing the interplay between the building's internal and external environments and the continuity between nature and architecture. Additionally, a thick roof would be visibly bulky at the edges, projecting outward as a distinct object rather than blending with the natural surroundings.

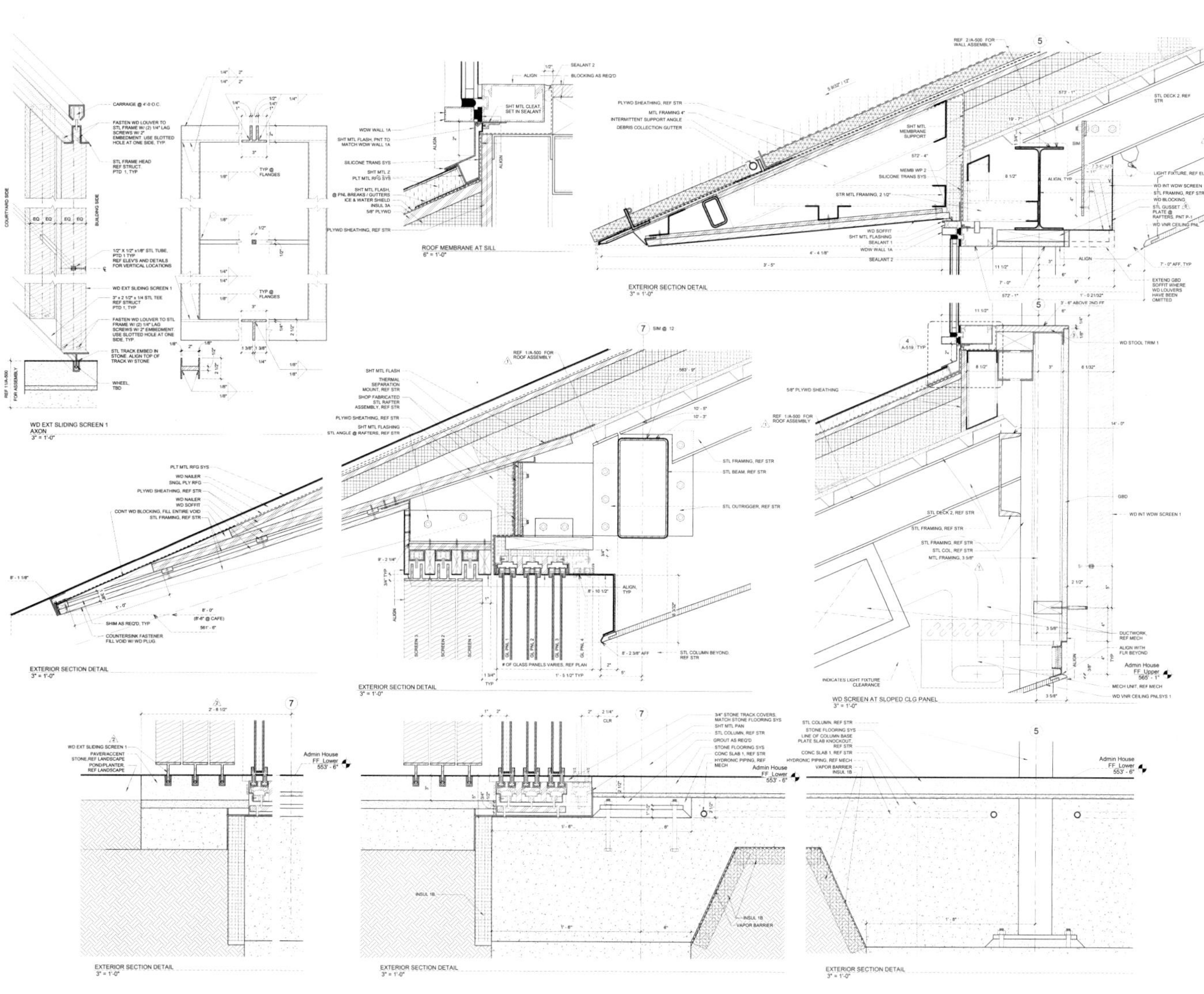
WD EXT SLIDING SCREEN 1
AXON
3" = 1'-0"
ROOF MEMBRANE AT SILL
6" = 1'-0"
EXTERIOR SECTION DETAIL
3" = 1'-0"
EXTERIOR SECTION DETAIL
3" = 1'-0"
EXTERIOR SECTION DETAIL
3" = 1'-0"
WD SCREEN AT SLOPED CLG PANEL
3" = 1'-0"
EXTERIOR SECTION DETAIL
3" = 1'-0"
EXTERIOR SECTION DETAIL
3" = 1'-0"
EXTERIOR SECTION DETAIL
3" = 1'-0"

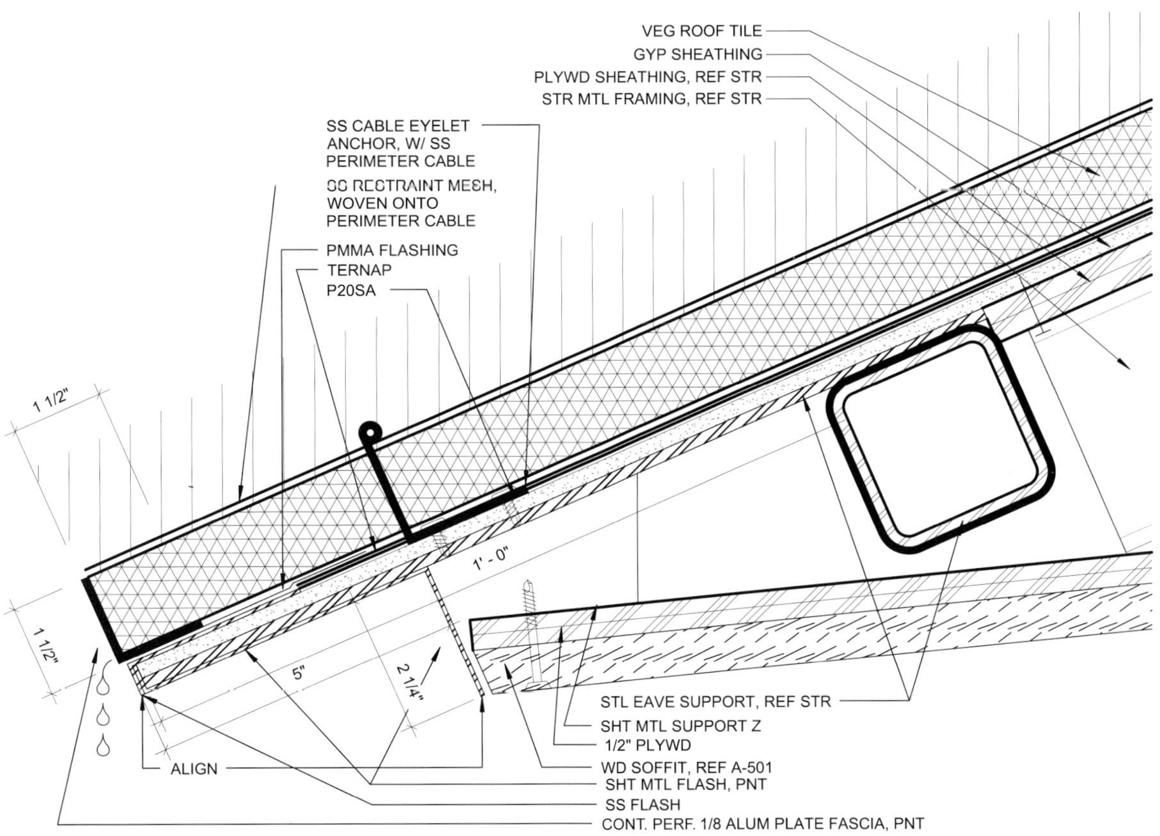

Enlarged Green Roof Edge

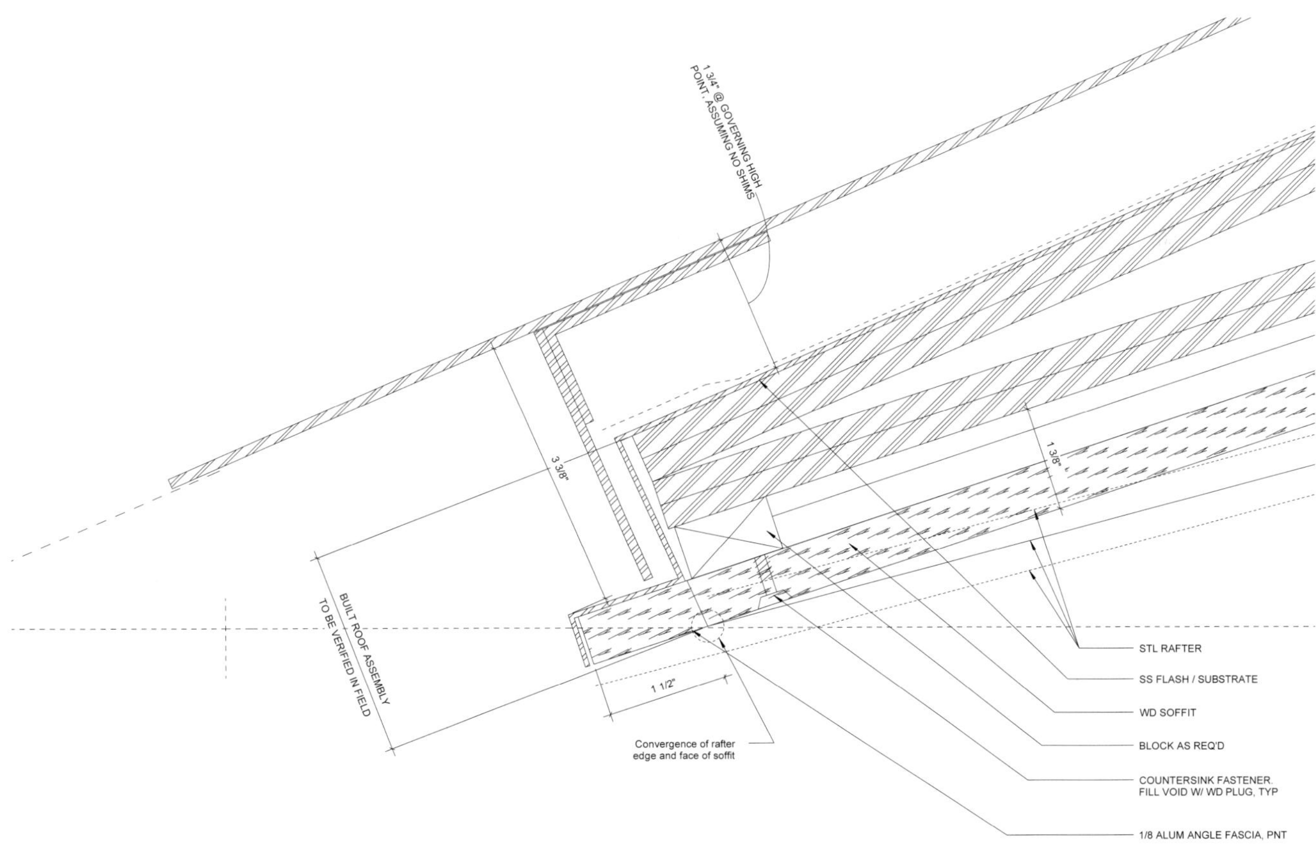

GREEN 2: TOKYO INSTITUTE OF TECHNOLOGY HISAO & HIROKO TAKI PLAZA

Completion year: 2020
Location: Tokyo, Japan
Structure: RC/SRC (reinforced concrete / steel-reinforced concrete)
Building type: educational

The site is located at the entrance of the Tokyo Institute of Technology's Ookayama Campus, and we designed a "platform" to support student activities. To preserve the view of the clock tower—a prominent landmark on the campus—most of the building is situated underground. Aboveground, the structure assumes a mound-like form, lush and seamlessly integrated with the surrounding landscape. The "roof," composed of stepped greenery and bleachers, harmonizes with the green, slanted wall of the adjacent library, together forming a green valley. This new green space invites life and activity, becoming a vibrant hub for students.

The boundary between the interior space and the exterior landscape is blurred by extending the stepped landscape into the building. This integration allows activities such as colearning and joint workshops to occur simultaneously on different levels. The space flows ambiguously, without clear divisions, stimulating the senses of the users both visually and physically.

To address the complex site conditions, we first established the overall sectional profile of the roof, followed by the design of the bleachers' strip-like steps fanning outward. This design process resulted in a roof silhouette that mimics a river delta spilling into the campus. By revealing the twisted structure that supports the roof, the interior space gains a sense of fluidity. Together, the exterior and interior landscapes create two architectural environments that resonate harmoniously with each other.

When designing the building's roof as a green hill, we aimed to use small particles to achieve a natural look, since many roof gardens built with concrete appear man-made and impersonal. We utilized thin deck boards made from recycled wood, each 25 mm thick, and showcased their thin edges with greenery sprouting from the gaps. This design provides a light and warm aesthetic, contrasting sharply with the more typical concrete roof garden.

We extended the deck boards as far out over the edge as possible to downplay the appearance of the vertical wall beneath them. This approach enhanced the hill-like image and grounded the design, moving away from architecture dominated by vertical elements.

We avoided using parallel and perpendicular angles in the deck's layout, opting instead for gently changing angles. We also varied the dimensions of the boards to break away from the authoritarian feel typically associated with classical grand staircases.

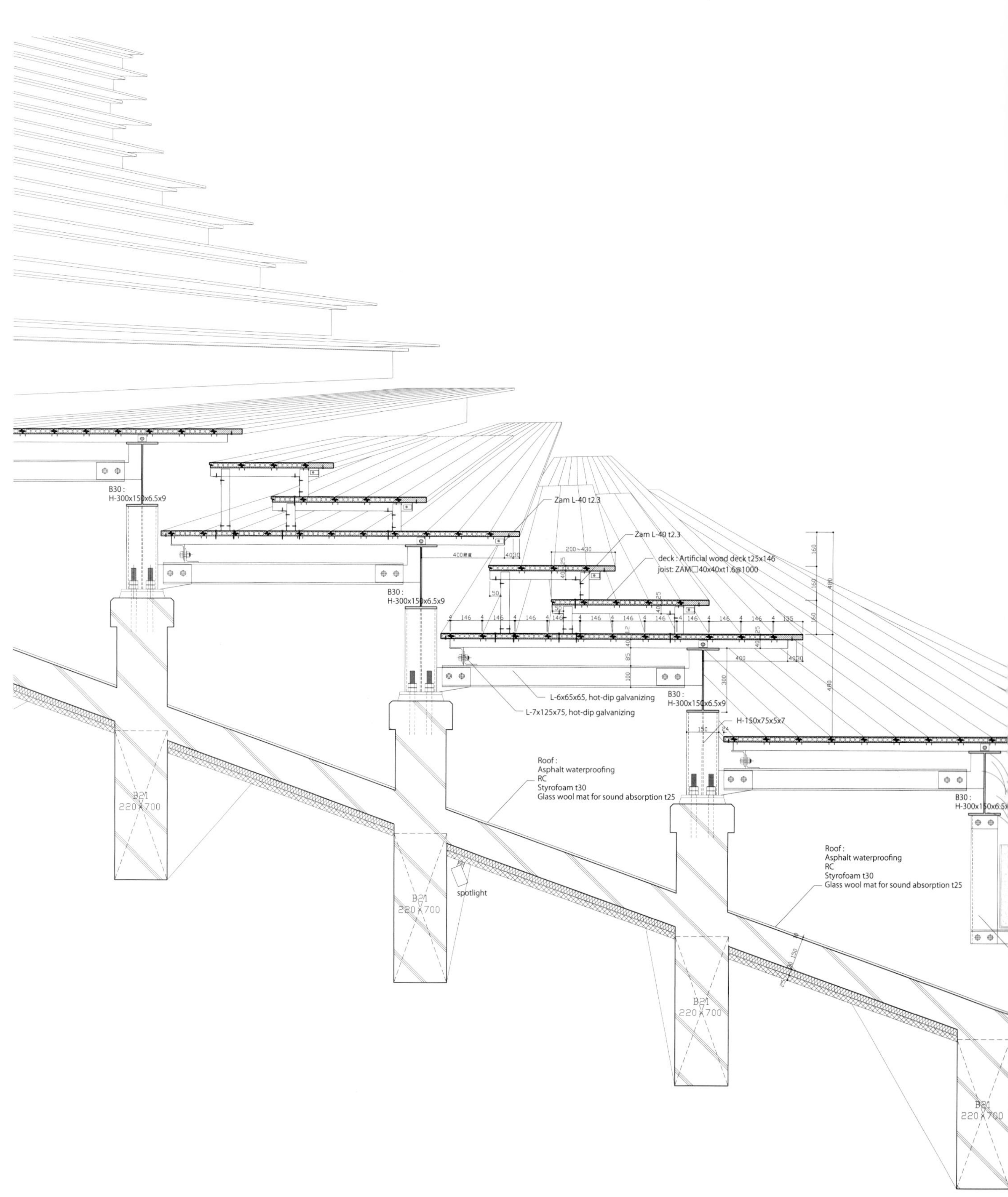
B30 :
H-300x150x6.5x9
Zam L-40 t2.3
Zam L-40 t2.3
deck : Artificial wood deck t25x146
joist: ZAM□40x40xt1.6@1000
L-6x65x65, hot-dip galvanizing
L-7x125x75, hot-dip galvanizing
H-150x75x5x7
Roof :
Asphalt waterproofing
RC
Styrofoam t30
Glass wool mat for sound absorption t25
B21
220 x 700
spotlight

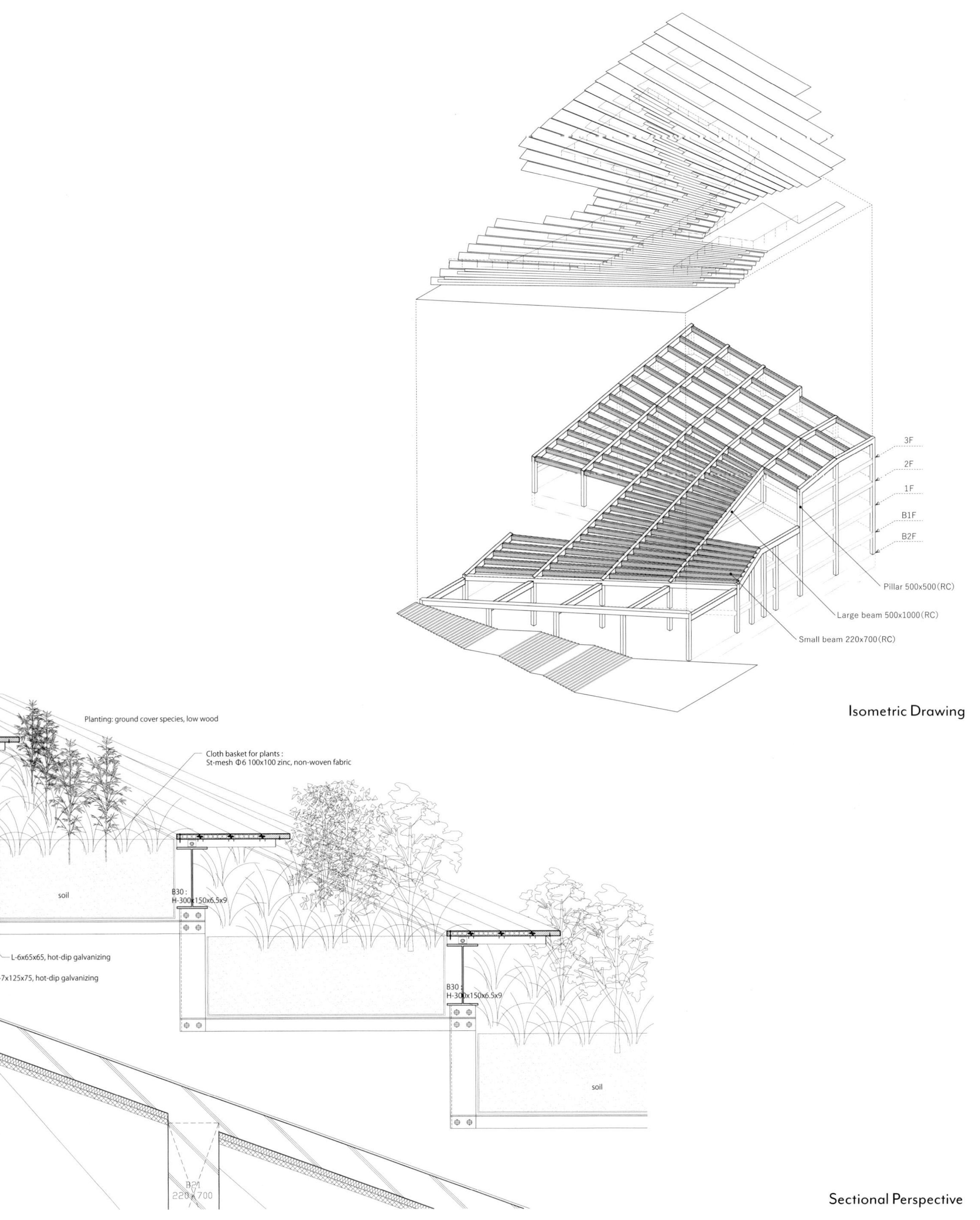

Isometric Drawing

Sectional Perspective

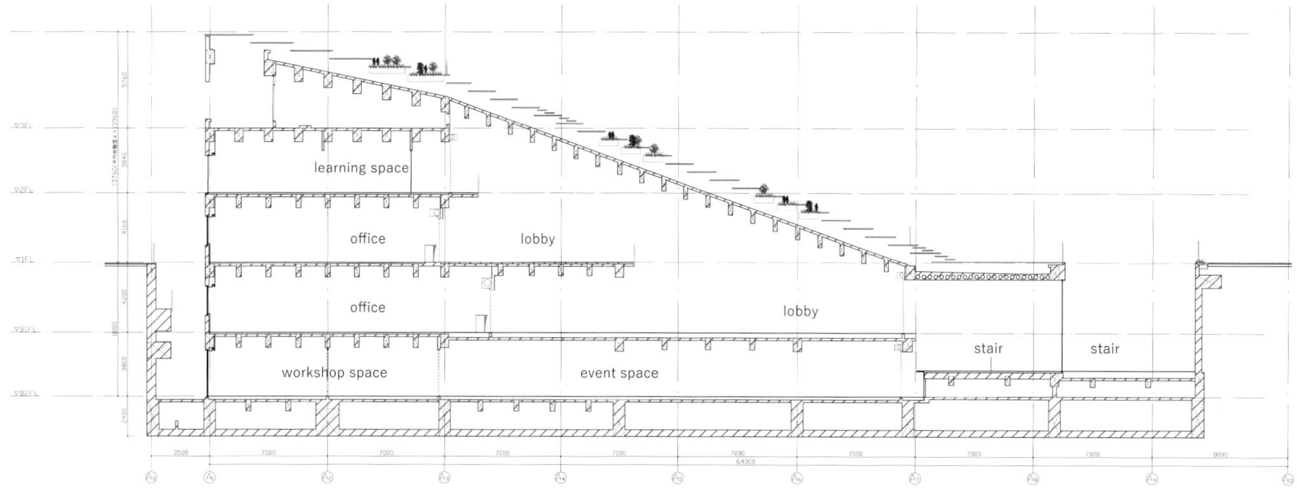

Section 1

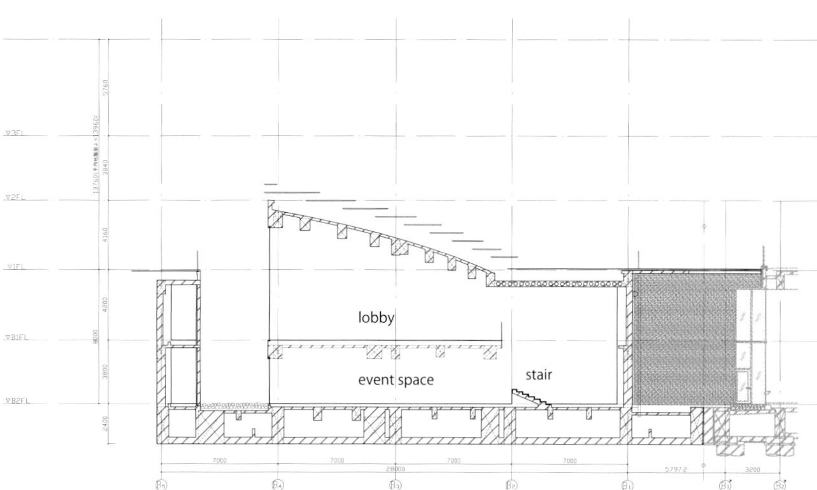

Section 2

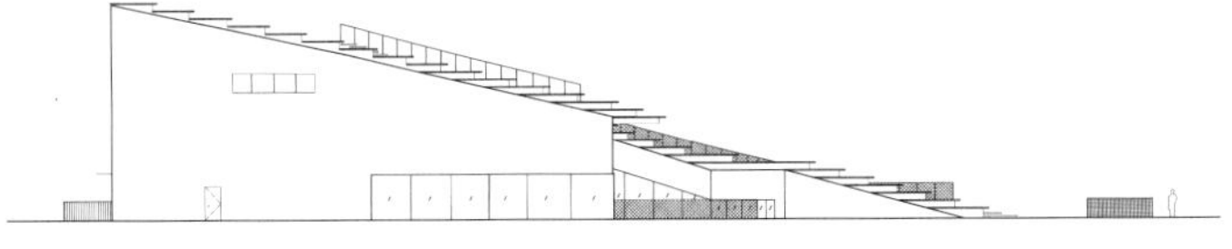

East Elevation

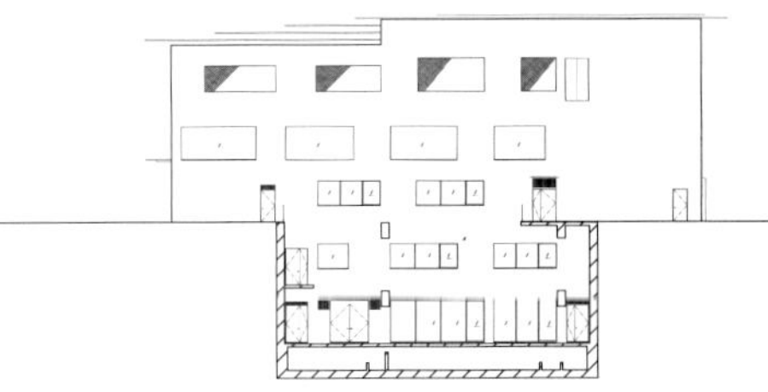

South Elevation

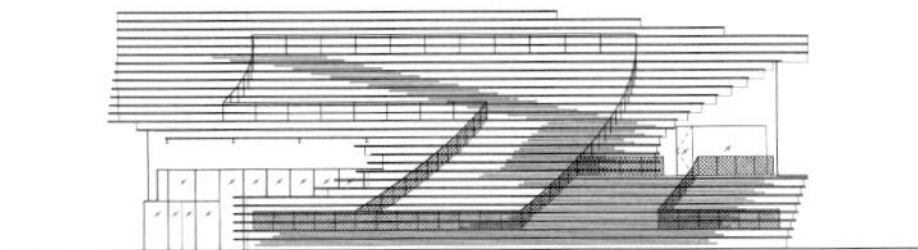

North Elevation

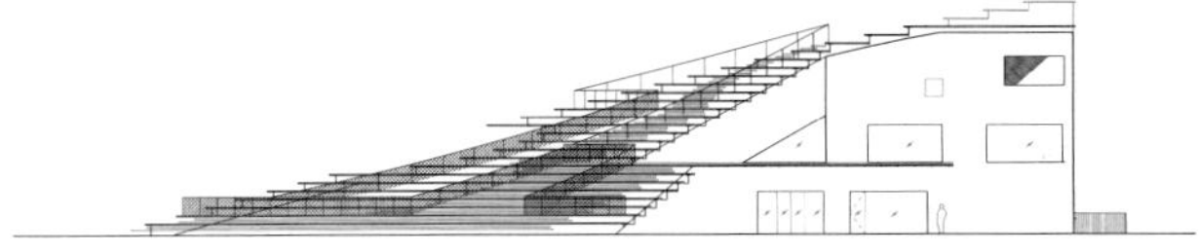

West Elevation

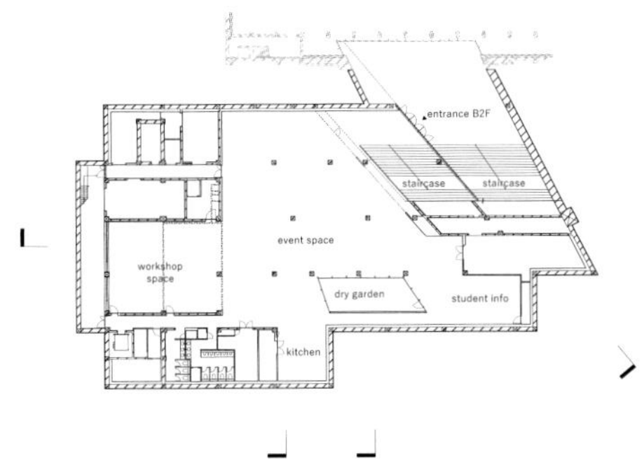

Basement 2 Floor

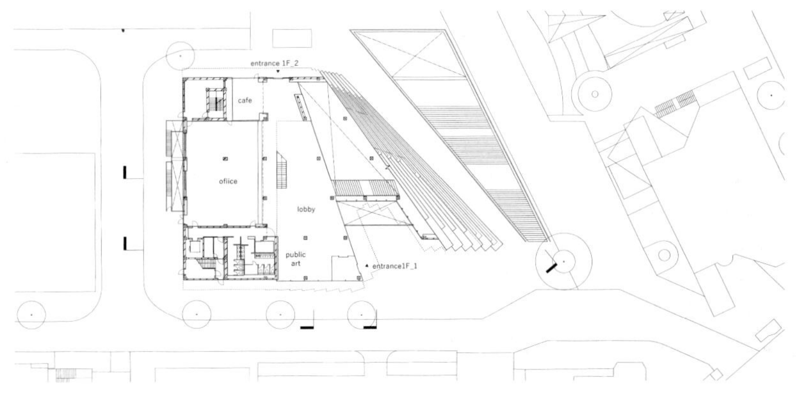

First Floor

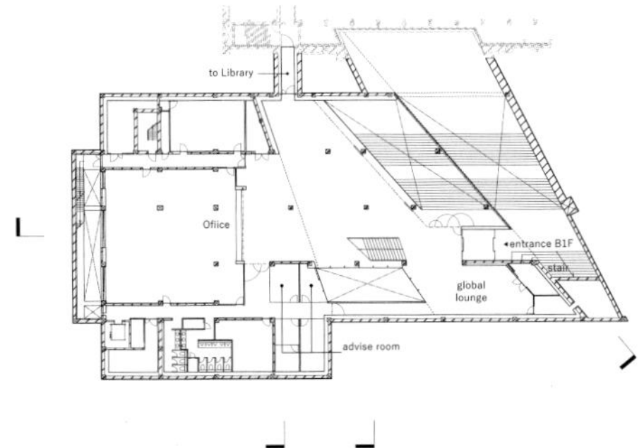

Basement 1 Floor

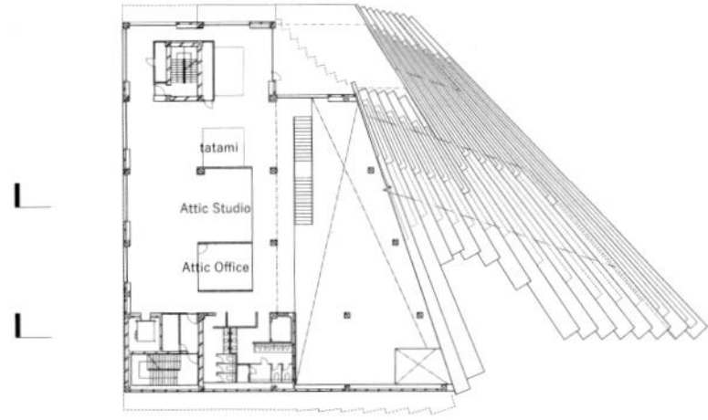

Second Floor

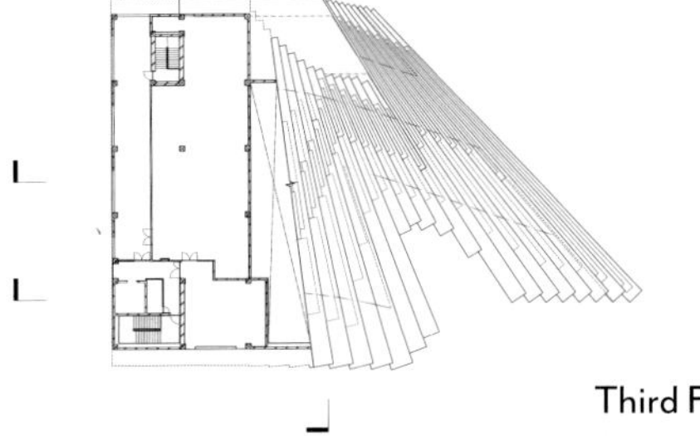

Third Floor

CHAPTER 4

THATCHING

I believe that thatched roofs connect Japanese houses to the earth, offering residents a sense of protection by the earth itself. These roofs, resembling grass fields, aesthetically link the building to the earth. More importantly, however, is the role of pampas grass, used in thatching, which is vital for the natural regeneration of forests in Japan.

Japan's landscape features many volcanoes, and much of its soil, composed of volcanic ash, is nutrient deficient, inhibiting tree growth. Initially, hardy pampas grass is planted in these barren areas to enrich the soil. Once improved, the land supports the growth of trees and crops. Thus, even though pampas grass is harvested for thatching, it plays a crucial role in supporting natural cycles in this volcanic country.

Above Japanese villages, forests serve as crucial resources, providing materials and energy for daily life. These supporting forests are known as "satoyama" (village mountains). Interestingly, it is estimated that nearly 40 percent of these satoyama were covered with pampas grass fields in the Meiji era before the introduction of Western-style architecture. This underscores the significance of pampas grass and thatched roofs in Japanese culture.

Thatched roofs in Japan have unique features that fascinate me, since they reflect the Japanese attitude toward this traditional roofing material. Unlike in Europe, where any part of the plant stalk might be used, in Japan the thick base of the stalk is pointed downward and trimmed with a sharp tool, giving the roof's edge a thick and defined appearance. This not only highlights the roof's robustness but also its grandeur. The roof, therefore, becomes a focal point of the house, with nature prominently represented through the soft pampas grass. This architectural detail embodies the ideology of worshiping nature in Japan.

THATCHING 1: COMMUNITY MARKET YUSUHARA

Completion year: 2010
Location: Kochi, Japan
Structure: RC/SRC (reinforced concrete / steel-reinforced concrete)
Building type: hospitality

Yusuhara Marche is a boutique hotel operated by the town of Yusuhara in Kochi Prefecture, which is known as "the town in the clouds." It has fifteen rooms centered on the atrium, which functions as a market for local produce. This allows people who visit the town to enjoy meals made with fresh ingredients beside the market.

A long time ago, there were rest houses called "Cha Do" with thatched roofs that served tea to the people traveling the path that went over the pass. Inspired by this tradition of hospitality, thatched sections were used for the exterior walls of this market. The thatched sections can be rotated up to provide ventilation.

To create this new exterior wall made of pampas grass, we collaborated with Yoshinori Kawakami, the sole thatching craftsman in Kochi Prefecture who resides in the town. His expertise was essential for developing the innovative crafting techniques required to utilize this traditional material in a new way. Without his participation, this project could not have been realized.

A flat roof was chosen for the three-story hotel due to the town's height restrictions. In Yusuhara, thatched roofs are commonly used for "Cha Do" rest houses and many other structures along the road. We decided to use thatched sections for the exterior walls as a symbolic architectural material in this region. Pampas grass, employed in thatching, offers excellent thermal insulation and helps regulate interior humidity, making it a promising material for sustainable contemporary architecture. Inside, no finish was applied to the pampas grass used on the exterior walls, leaving it exposed to allow people to experience its natural texture. *Photo by KKAA*

Roof: Solar photovoltaic system with galvanized steel plate 0.45mm
Polyethylene film 4.0mm
Asphalt-saturated and coated felt 1.0mm
Eaves: Galvanized steel plate 0.45mm
Polyethylene film 4.0mm
Asphalt-saturated and coated felt 1.0mm
Structural plywood 24.0mm
Top light: Wire-reinforced glass 6.8mm
Polycarbonate plate 2.0mm
Guestroom(302)
Bathroom(302)
Corridor
Guestroom(202)
Bathroom(202)
Corridor
Corridor
Community market
Ceiling: Japanese cedar strip 15.0mm oil stain
Ceiling: Silicate calcium board 10.0mm white paint
Wall: Wallpaper
Floor: Carpet tile
Floor: Porcelain tile
Wall: Concrete bed white paint
Traverse: Stainless mesh configuration
Cedar log(branch): 120-200mm L:4,000-6,300mm preservative-treated
Cedar log(trunk): 200-300mm L:5,500-6,000mm preservative-treated
Steel rod 16.0mm gray paint
Wall: Aluminum panel 3.0mm
Floor: Surface reinforcement mortar
Ceiling: Plaster board 12.5mm white paint
Wood louver: Japanese cedar 50*30@60mm preservative-treated
Rafter: Laminated wood(Japanese cedar)
Support pillar: Galvanized steel plate 25*300mm gray paint
Rotating shaft: Galvanized steel pin 18.0mm gray paint
Thatch unit: thatch 345mm thickness
Bamboo(vertical): approximately 40mm
Bamboo(horizontal): approximately 60mm
Wind-resistant beam: Galvanized wide flange beam 450*200*9*14mm gray paint

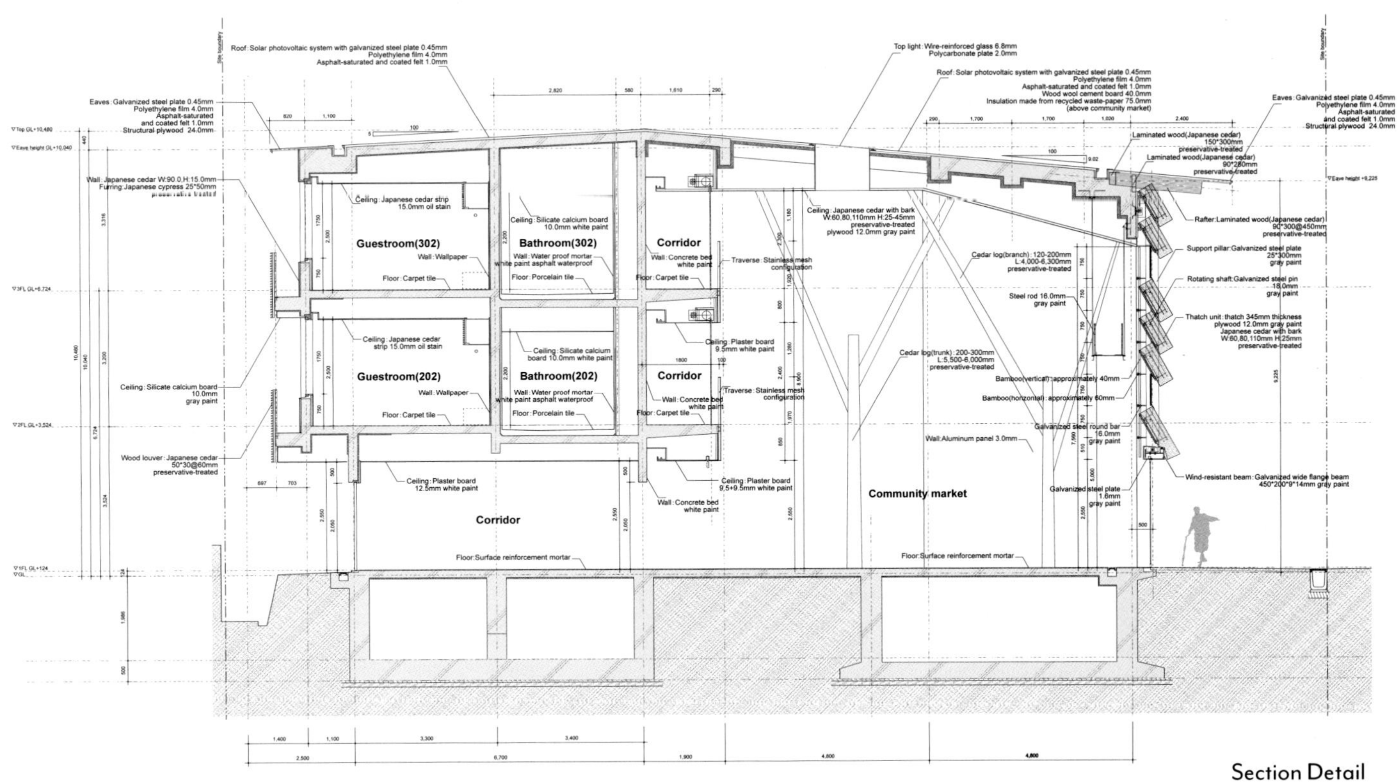

Section Detail

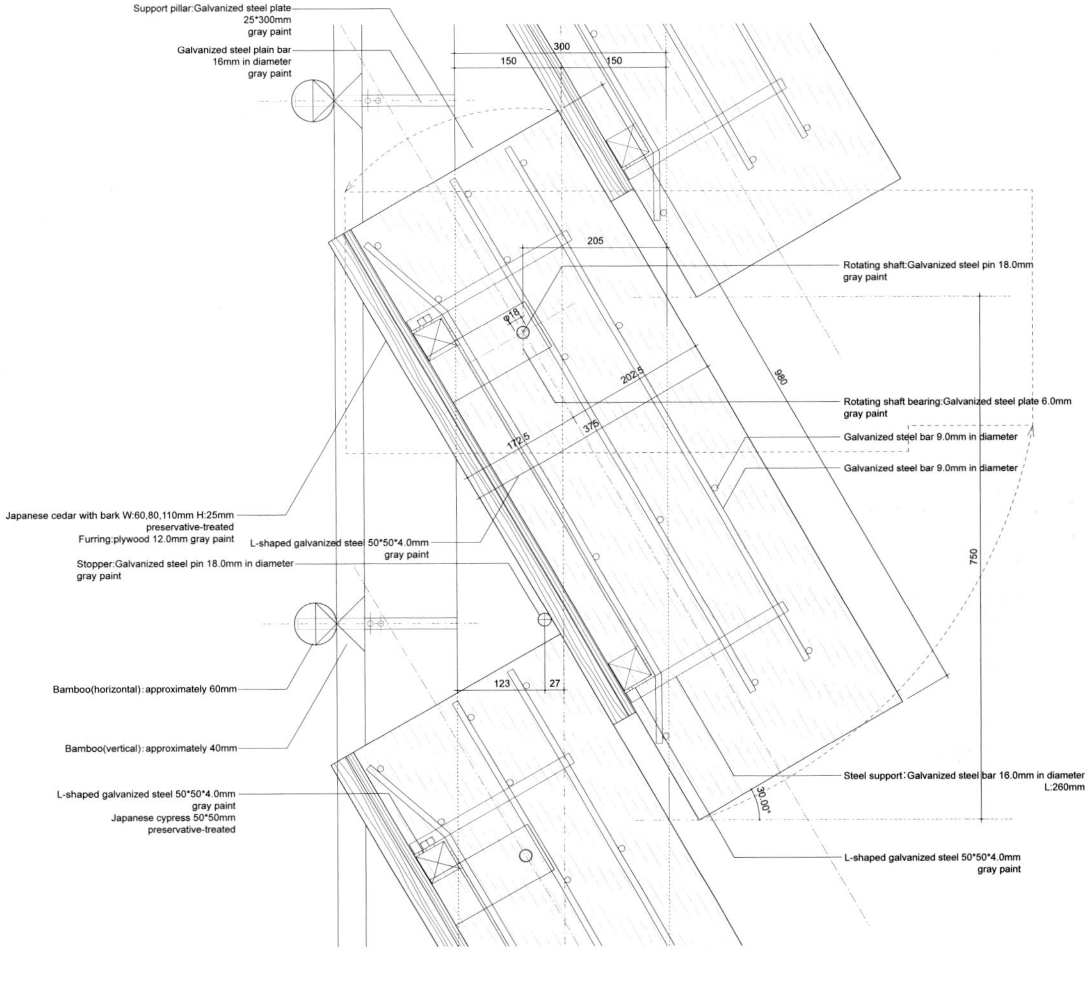

Support pillar: Galvanized steel plate
25*300mm
gray paint
Galvanized steel plain bar
16mm in diameter
gray paint
300
150
150
205
φ18
202.5
375
172.5
980
750
123
27
30.00°
Rotating shaft: Galvanized steel pin 18.0mm
gray paint
Rotating shaft bearing: Galvanized steel plate 6.0mm
gray paint
Galvanized steel bar 9.0mm in diameter
Galvanized steel bar 9.0mm in diameter
Japanese cedar with bark W:60,80,110mm H:25mm
preservative-treated
Furring: plywood 12.0mm gray paint
L-shaped galvanized steel 50*50*4.0mm
gray paint
Stopper: Galvanized steel pin 18.0mm in diameter
gray paint
Bamboo(horizontal): approximately 60mm
Bamboo(vertical): approximately 40mm
L-shaped galvanized steel 50*50*4.0mm
gray paint
Japanese cypress 50*50mm
preservative-treated
Steel support: Galvanized steel bar 16.0mm in diameter
L:260mm
L-shaped galvanized steel 50*50*4.0mm
gray paint

Thatched Wall Detail

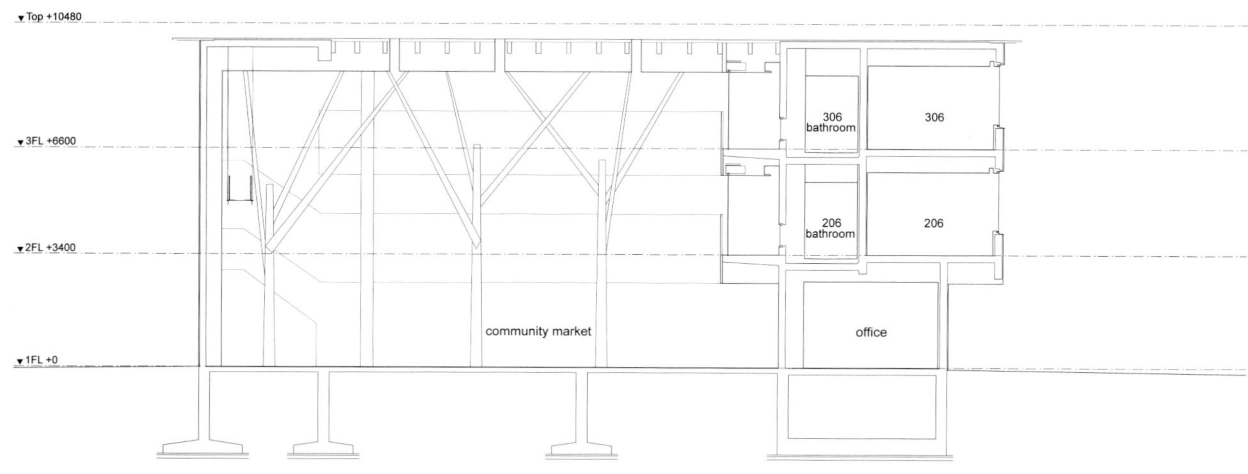

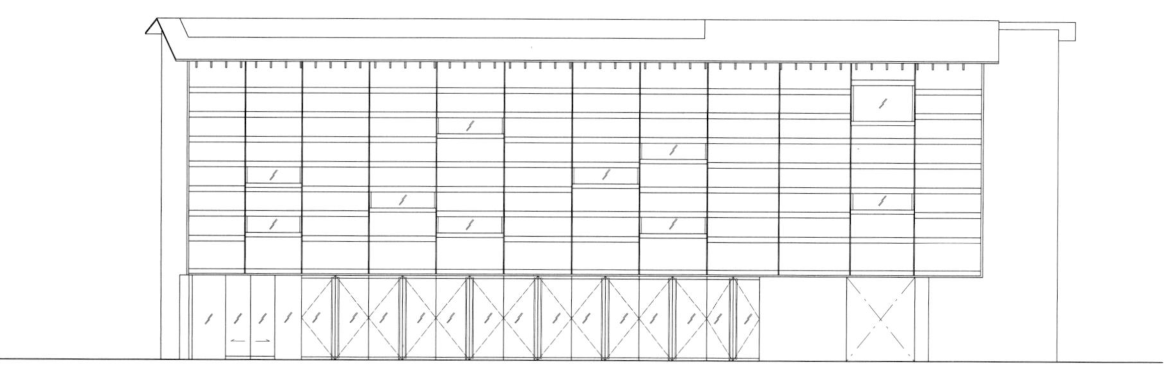

East Elevation

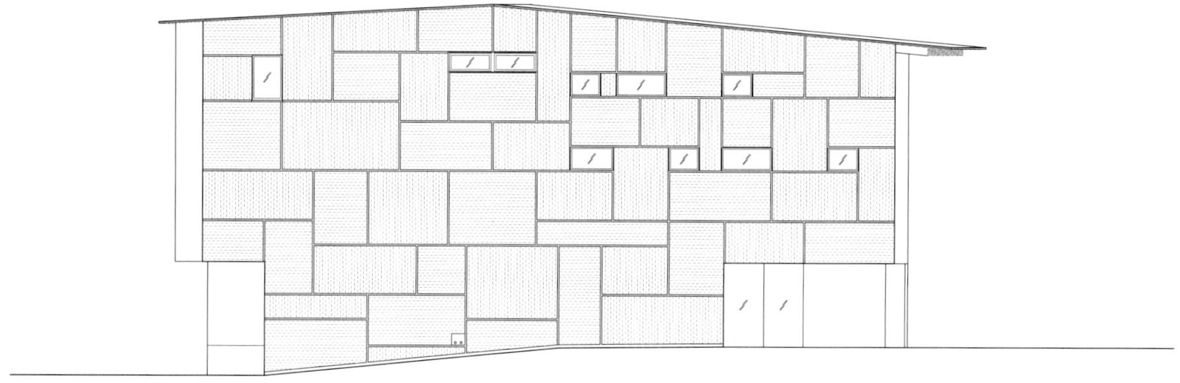

South Elevation

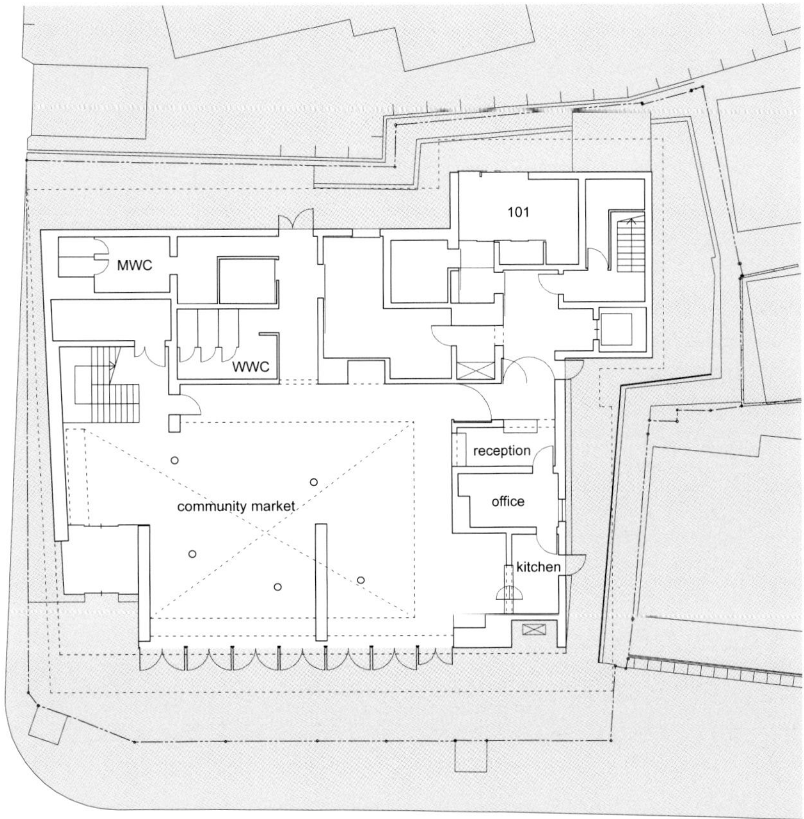

First Floor

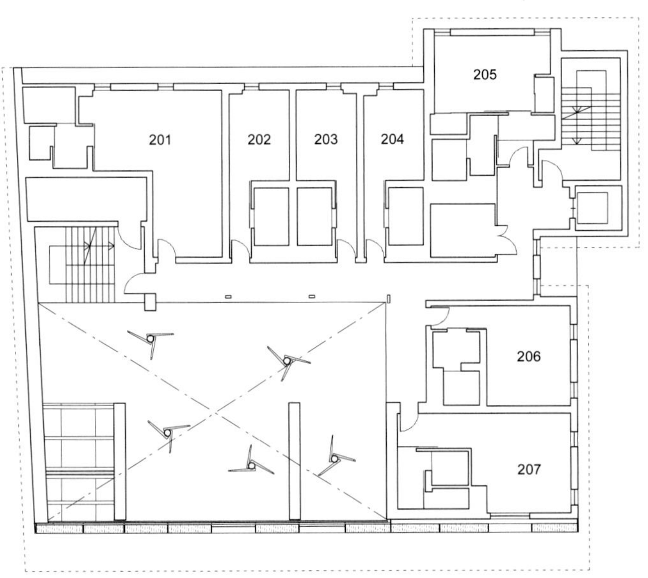

Second Floor

Third Floor

THATCHING 2: GREENABLE HIRUZEN

Completion year: 2021
Location: Okayama, Japan
Structure: wood
Building type: visitor center

A cycling center built on the grounds of GREENable HIRUZEN, a national park in Maniwa City, Okayama Prefecture, serves as a hub for cycling tourism. Local people gathered thatch, preparing bundles in various sizes ranging from 0.9 to 15 cm in diameter and 24 to 60 cm in length. With the assistance of thatch roofers from across Japan, we created a space that incorporates thatch in the ceilings and eaves, infusing it with the natural scent of thatch for a unique experience unlike typical thatched roofs.

There is a large miscanthus field (Kayaba) in Maniwa City where miscanthus (silver grass) that is used for thatched roofs is grown, and it has been protected as a portion of the diverse village mountain ecosystem. Silver grass has a warm texture and is used for counters and other furniture to transform the interior ambiance.

Historically, silver-grass grasslands, which were cultivated for thatch, played a significant role in the Japanese natural environment. Biodiversity was sustained through a series of activities such as burning the silver-grass fields, cultivating the thatch and its ecosystem, and harvesting the thatch.

The silver grass growing wild in the Hiruzen-Kogen Highlands possesses a unique texture that modern building materials lack. Thatch is not only soft but also a magical material that infuses architecture with life.

Cross-laminated timber (CLT) panels made at a factory in Maniwa City, which boasts the largest CLT production volume in Japan, were taken to Harumi in Tokyo and assembled. Subsequently, these panels were disassembled, transported to a green hill in Hiruzen, Maniwa, and reassembled. This process story illustrates the flexibility and ease of assembling this size of panel.

In the gift shop at the visitor center, 20 mm thick wooden members called lamina, typically used to configure CLT and laminated wood, are used to make cloudlike organic shapes. This application echoes a traditional Japanese technique called "kokera," which involves using thin wood boards for roofing and exterior walls. I view lamina as a modern interpretation of kokera. Incidentally, kokera is similar to shingle roofs in the West.

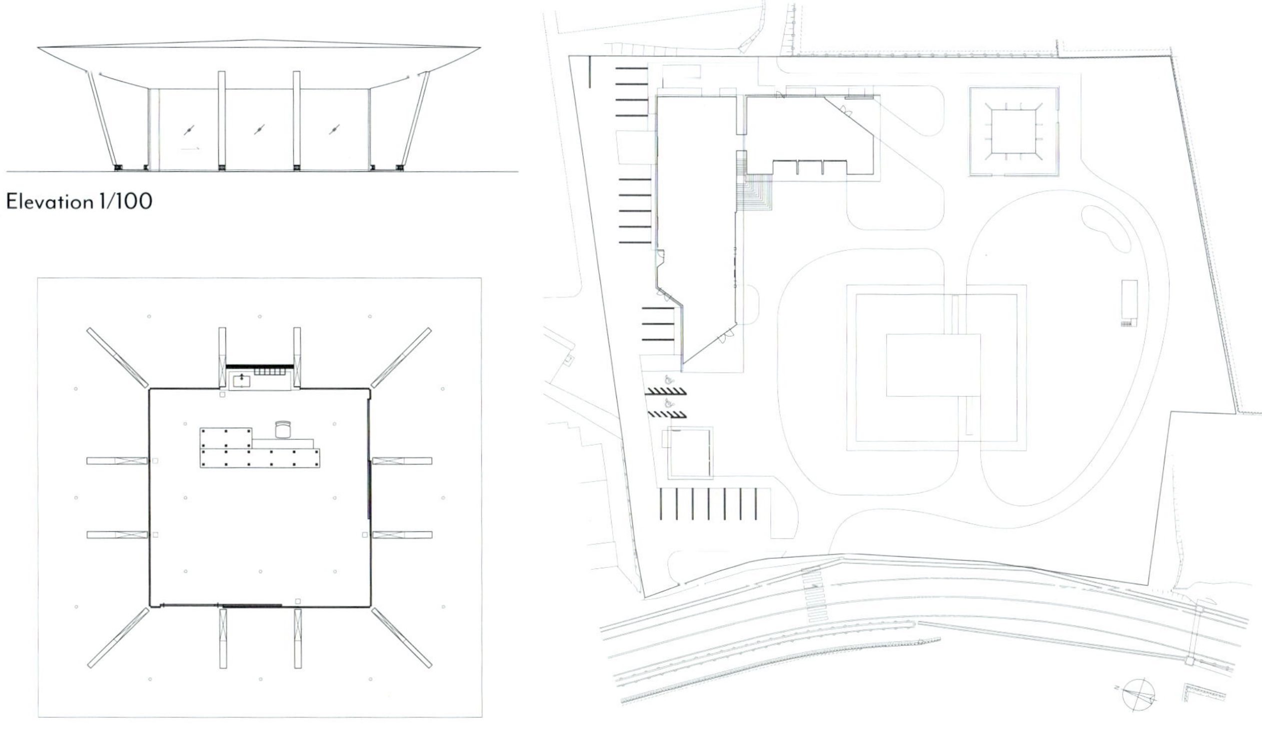
Elevation 1/100

Plan 1/100

Site Plan 1/500

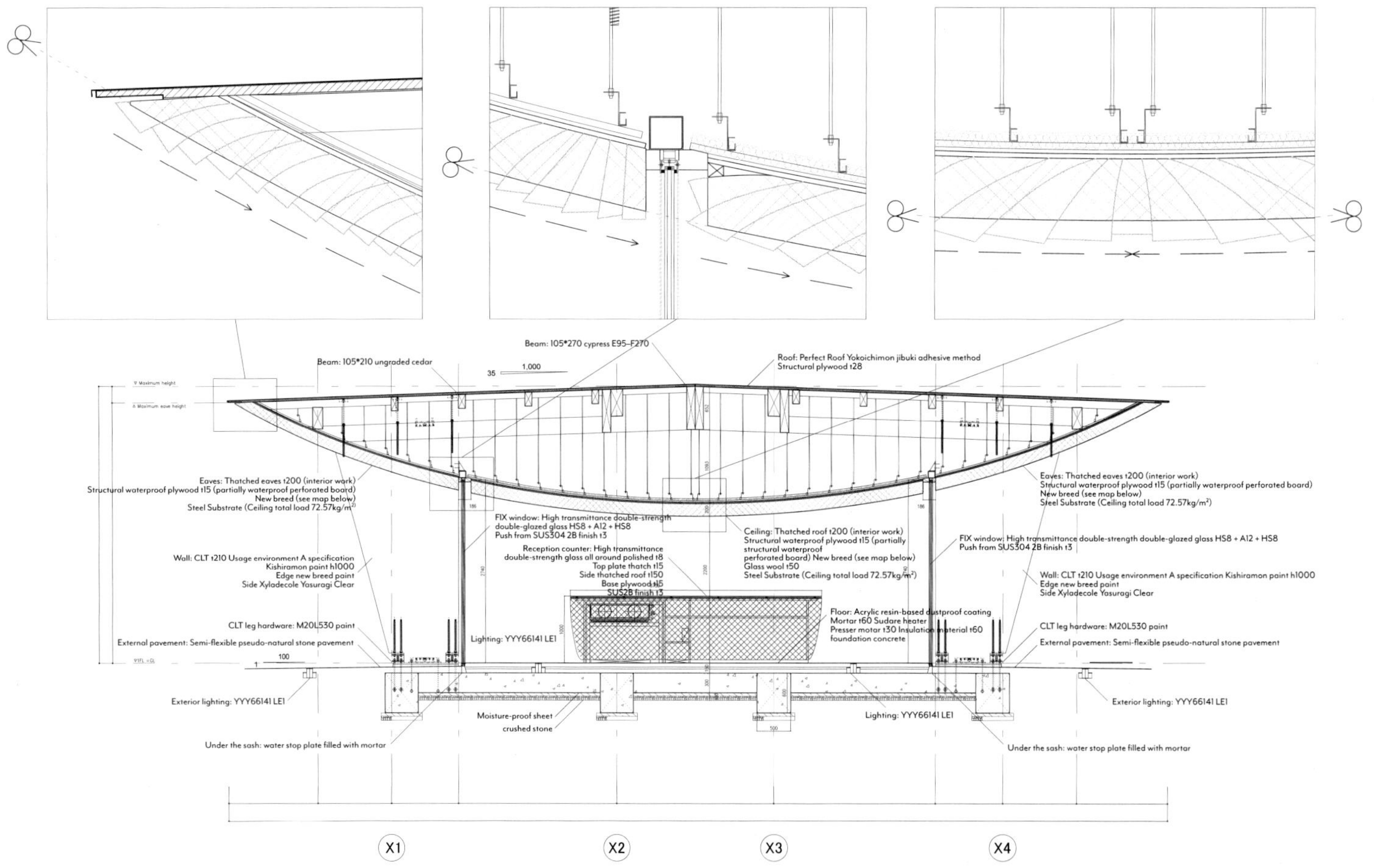

Beam: 105*270 cypress E95–F270
Roof: Perfect Roof Yokoichimon jibuki adhesive method
Structural plywood t28
Beam: 105*210 ungraded cedar
Eaves: Thatched eaves t200 (interior work)
Structural waterproof plywood t15 (partially waterproof perforated board)
New breed (see map below)
Steel Substrate (Ceiling total load 72.57kg/m²)
FIX window: High transmittance double-strength double-glazed glass HS8 + A12 + HS8
Push from SUS304 2B finish t3
Reception counter: High transmittance double-strength glass all around polished t8
Top plate thatch t15
Side thatched roof t150
Base plywood t15
SUS2B finish t3
Ceiling: Thatched roof t200 (interior work)
Structural waterproof plywood t15 (partially structural waterproof perforated board) New breed (see map below)
Glass wool t50
Steel Substrate (Ceiling total load 72.57kg/m²)
Wall: CLT t210 Usage environment A specification
Kishiramon paint h1000
Edge new breed paint
Side Xyladecole Yasuragi Clear
Floor: Acrylic resin-based dustproof coating
Mortar t60 Sudare heater
Presser motor t30 Insulation material t60
foundation concrete
CLT leg hardware: M20L530 paint
External pavement: Semi-flexible pseudo-natural stone pavement
Lighting: YYY66141 LE1
Exterior lighting: YYY66141 LE1
Moisture-proof sheet
crushed stone
Under the sash: water stop plate filled with mortar
X1
X2
X3
X4

Roof: Perfect Roof Yokoichimon jibuki adhesive method
Structural plywood t28 (tip only t18)
400
15
20
3
17
18
28
10
5
3
Edge of the eaves: Color steel plate
(GJE04 dark brown)
11
102
98
2
152
Eaves: Thatched eaves t150–200.
Structural waterproof plywood t15 (partially waterproof
perforated board). New breed (see map below).
Steel substrate (ceiling total load 72.57 kg/m²).

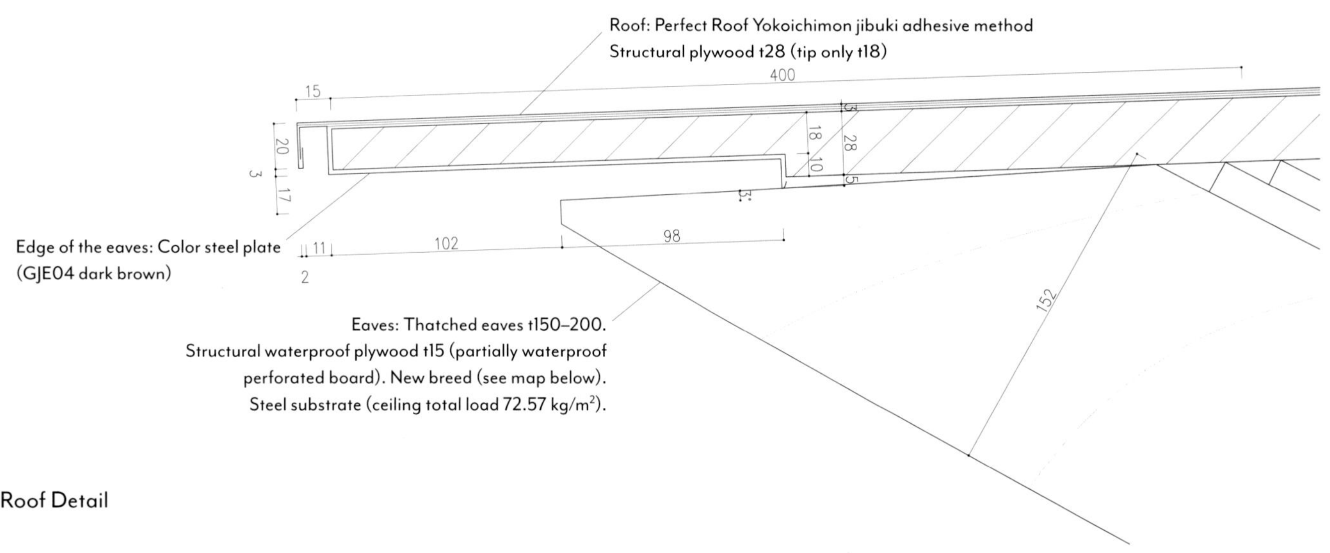

Roof Detail

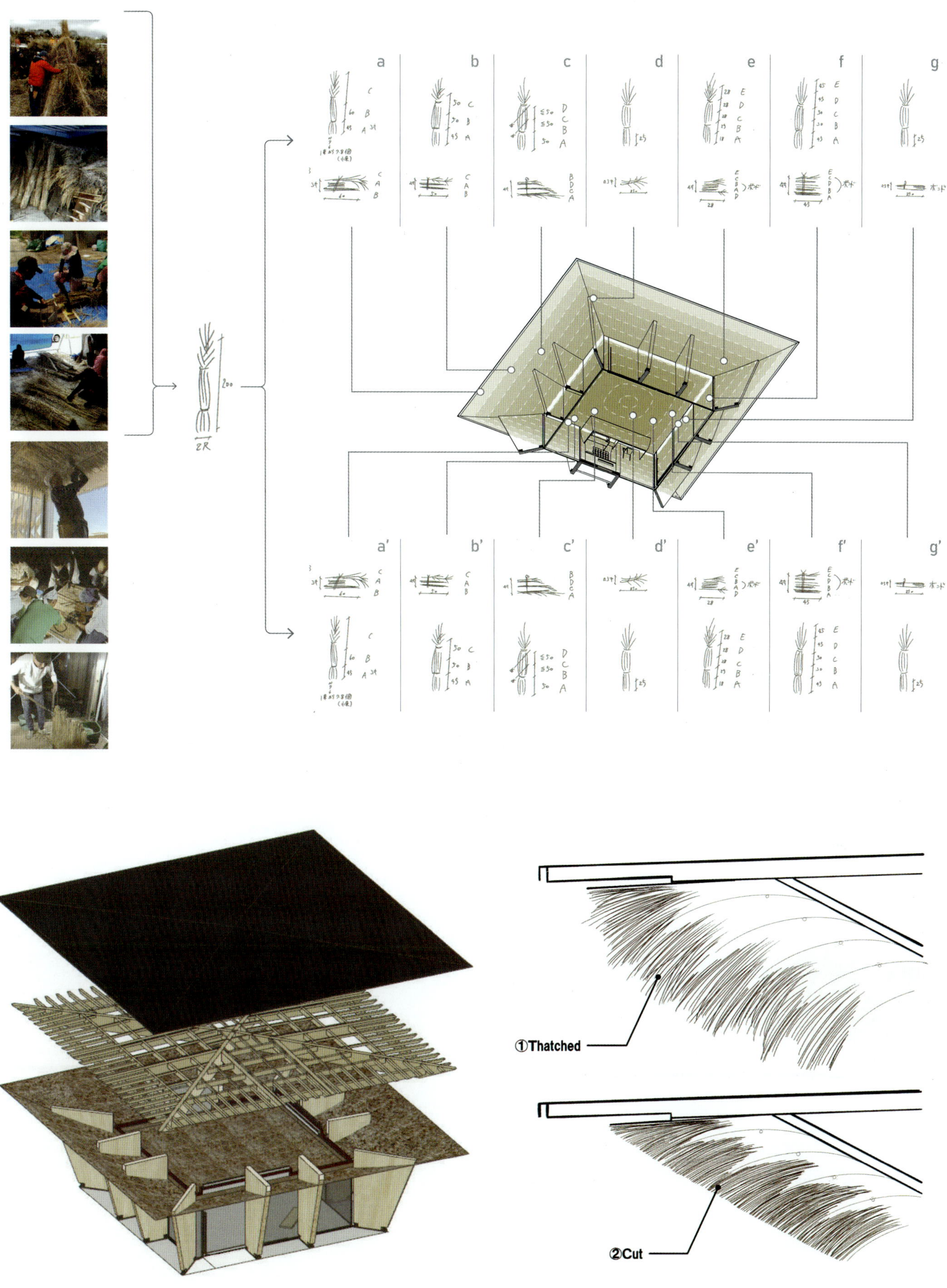

CLT Shed Assembly Hybrid Structure

CHAPTER 5

BAMBOO

There was a large bamboo grove behind the house where I grew up, and I often played in that grove. Various animals such as pheasants and snakes lived there, and we would dig up and eat the bamboo shoots when they came up in the spring, allowing us to experience the coming of spring with our entire body. Even more than this, the bamboo grove was filled with a special type of green light, creating a serene universe in stark contrast to the hustle and bustle of daily life.

This experience became the springboard for my strong interest in bamboo as a material. When I was first requested to design a structure in China, I really wanted to use bamboo to build a house. And I thought that I would like to create a space that resembled a bamboo grove, since I was using bamboo to build the structure. I guess I was thinking that I wanted to return to the paradise I experienced when I was a kid.

The geometry of bamboo is also something that is attractive to me. In addition, the fact that bamboo grows arbitrarily straight up toward the heavens without any curves or bends gives me a positive feeling.

However, the straight lines of bamboo are not like the dry, tasteless, and abstract lines drawn with a ruler, but are instead "living lines" with an organic rhythm like music created by knots and small branches.

I frequently incorporate bamboo both in the interiors and exteriors of buildings, guided by the idea that introducing "living lines" into structures—often perceived as rigid and lifeless—can vitalize them. In traditional Japanese architecture, bamboo is split to create semitransparent partitions and blinds that filter sunlight. These bamboo elements often play a central role in my designs. Furthermore, thin sticks produced by splitting bamboo are used in the manufacture of Japanese washi paper, a process that involves dissolving materials in water. This use underscores bamboo's significant connection to the delicacy and subtlety of materials.

BAMBOO 1: GREAT (BAMBOO) WALL

Completion year: 2002
Location: Beijing, China
Building type: hospitality

Our initial goal was to draw inspiration from the formality of the Great Wall. We were continually captivated by the way the Great Wall, never an isolated object, runs almost endlessly along the undulating ridgelines, fully integrated with its environment. This aspect challenged the traditional notion of "architecture" as an isolated object within its surroundings. Our intention, therefore, was to incorporate this characteristic of the Great Wall into residential design. This concept is why the structure is titled "WALL" rather than "HOUSE."

Regarding materials, we extensively used bamboo, a material of profound significance both in Chinese and Japanese cultures. Bamboo's variable density and diameter allow for diverse spatial partitions. Leveraging these traits, we positioned a bamboo "WALL"—a layer of bamboo set along the site's slope, echoing the Great Wall. Historically, the Great Wall divided two cultures; similarly, our BAMBOO WALL aims not just to partition but also to unify life and culture in various ways, just as the Great Wall did in essence.

The bamboo was initially heated to transition its color from green to yellow, and then a protective coating was applied. Additionally, the eaves were extended by 1.7 m to enhance the durability of the screens.

Moso bamboo from China, measuring 60 mm in diameter, was used to create screens with a pitch of 120 mm and a gap of 60 mm. These screens were utilized to construct various architectural elements, including the exterior and interior walls, ceilings, and floors.

Japanese housing projects have previously experimented with these "komagaeshi" bamboo screens. The bamboo delivered to the site in China varied in diameter and was often curved and twisted. However, these irregularities unexpectedly contributed to a softness in the screens, fostering an architecture that feels more natural and organic.

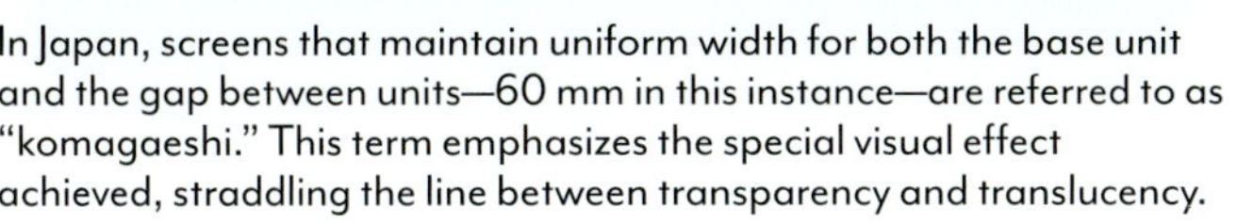

In Japan, screens that maintain uniform width for both the base unit and the gap between units—60 mm in this instance—are referred to as "komagaeshi." This term emphasizes the special visual effect achieved, straddling the line between transparency and translucency.

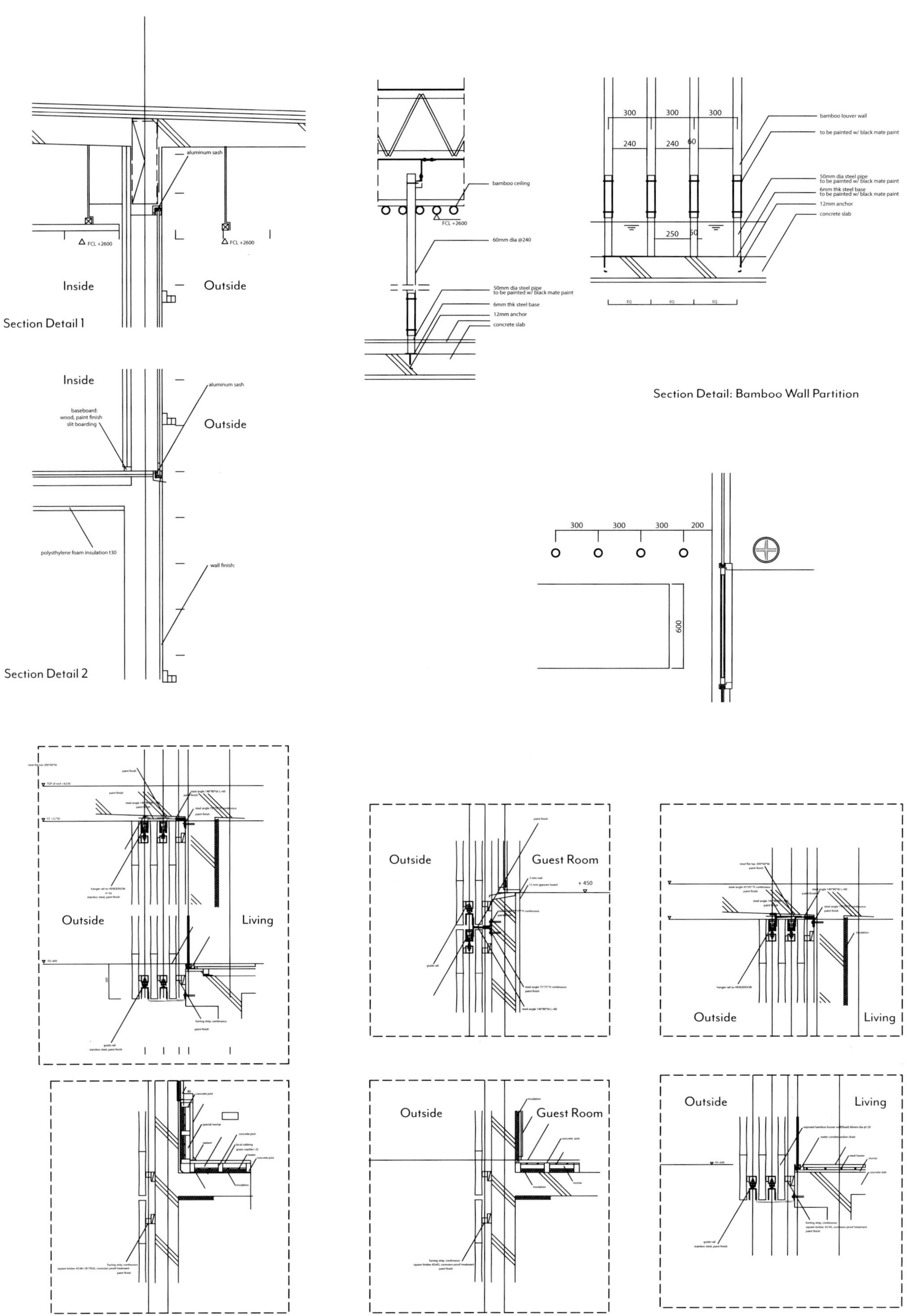
aluminum sash
FCL +2600
FCL +2600
Inside
Outside
Section Detail 1
Inside
aluminum sash
baseboard:
wood, paint finish
slit boarding
Outside
polysthylene foam insulation t30
wall finish:
Section Detail 2
bamboo ceiling
FCL +2600
60mm dia @240
50mm dia steel pipe
to be painted w/ black mate paint
6mm thk steel base
12mm anchor
concrete slab
300
300
300
240
240
60
250
50
bamboo louver wall
to be painted w/ black mate paint
50mm dia steel pipe
to be painted w/ black mate paint
6mm thk steel base
to be painted w/ black mate paint
12mm anchor
concrete slab
EQ
EQ
EQ
Section Detail: Bamboo Wall Partition
300
300
300
200
600
Outside
Living
Outside
Guest Room
+ 450
Outside
Living
Outside
Guest Room
Outside
Living

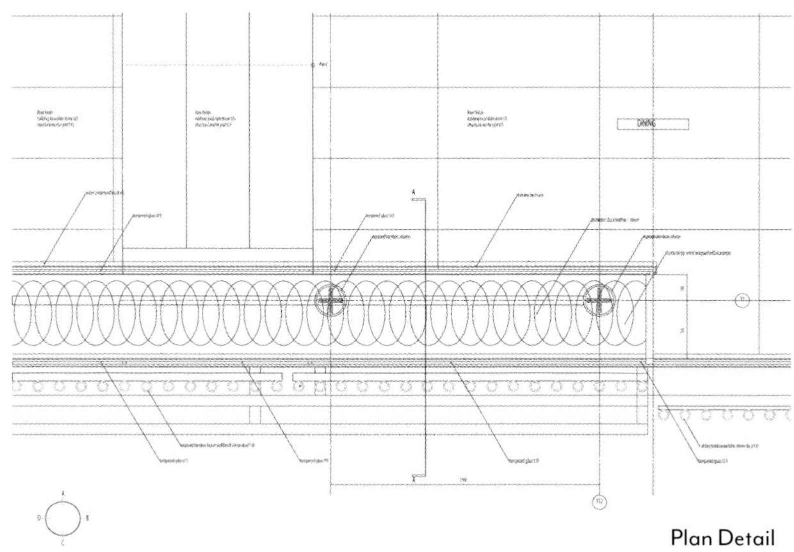

Plan Detail

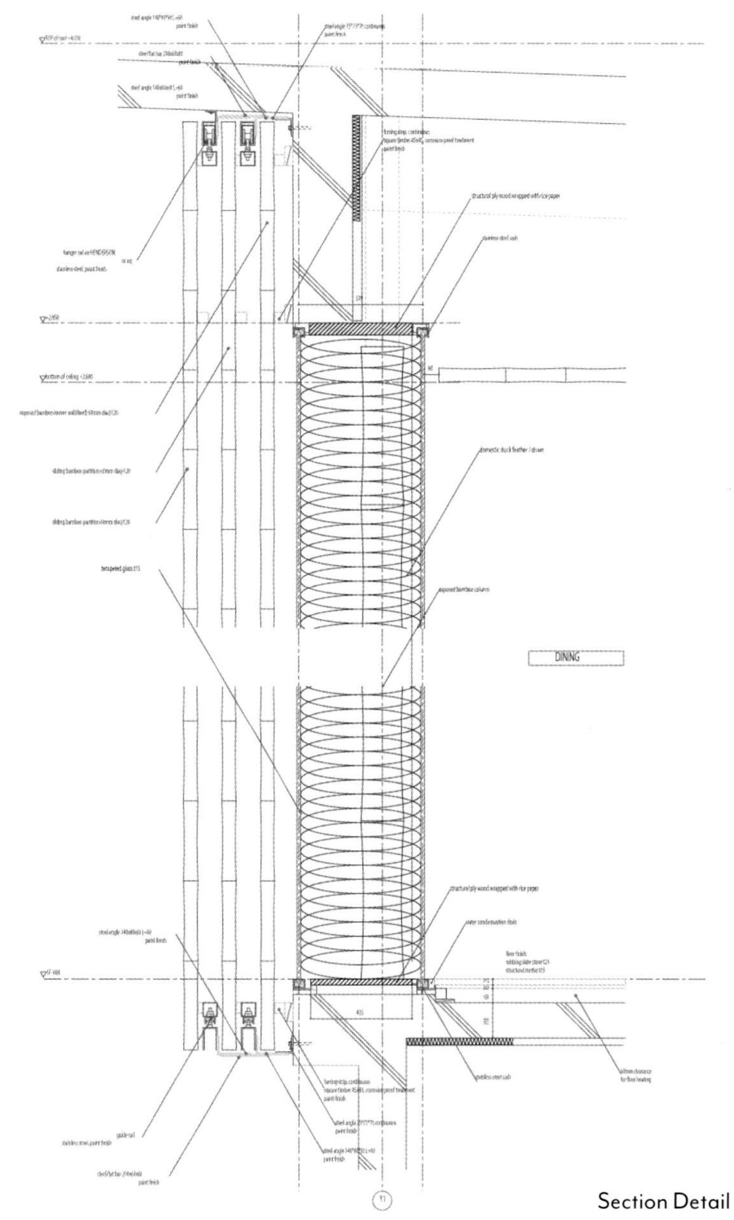

Section Detail

BAMBOO 2: TAKETA HISTORY AND CULTURE MUSEUM

Completion year: 2019
Location: Oita, Japan
Structure: RC/SRC (reinforced concrete / steel-reinforced concrete), steel
Building type: museum

This museum is located in the castle town of Taketa, renowned for the impregnable Bungo Okajo Castle. Rentaro Taki, born in Taketa, composed the folk song "Kojo No Tsuki" inspired by Okajo Castle. Designed along a water channel, the museum resembles a long fence, combining elements of a white building wall and a bamboo lattice. Inside, the smoked-bamboo lattice extends throughout, showcasing the history of this castle town and artworks by the literati painter Chikuden Tanomura, who hailed from the Oka domain (clan). Situated on a slope behind the museum, the historical residence of Chikuden Tanomura, known as "Chikuden-sou," is accessible via an elevator covered by a lattice. This design integrates the museum seamlessly with the town's historical context.

"Bamboo," or "take," which lends its name to the city of Taketa, was chosen as the primary material for two cultural facilities that were completed simultaneously. The city is surrounded by abundant bamboo, and the exquisite bamboo craftsmanship by Taketa artisans, flourishing since the Edo period, is renowned worldwide as a symbol of their artisan culture.

For the screens, smoked bamboo with a diameter of approximately 80 mm was arranged at a pitch of 160 mm. This construction method, known as "koma gaeshi," creates screens with gaps equal to the diameter of the bamboo. This ancient technique achieves a delicate balance between opaqueness and transparency.

In the History and Culture Museum, smoked bamboo, which is darker than ordinary bamboo, has been used to create a façade that harmonizes with the historic streets of the castle town. The smoking process not only darkens the bamboo but also enhances its durability.

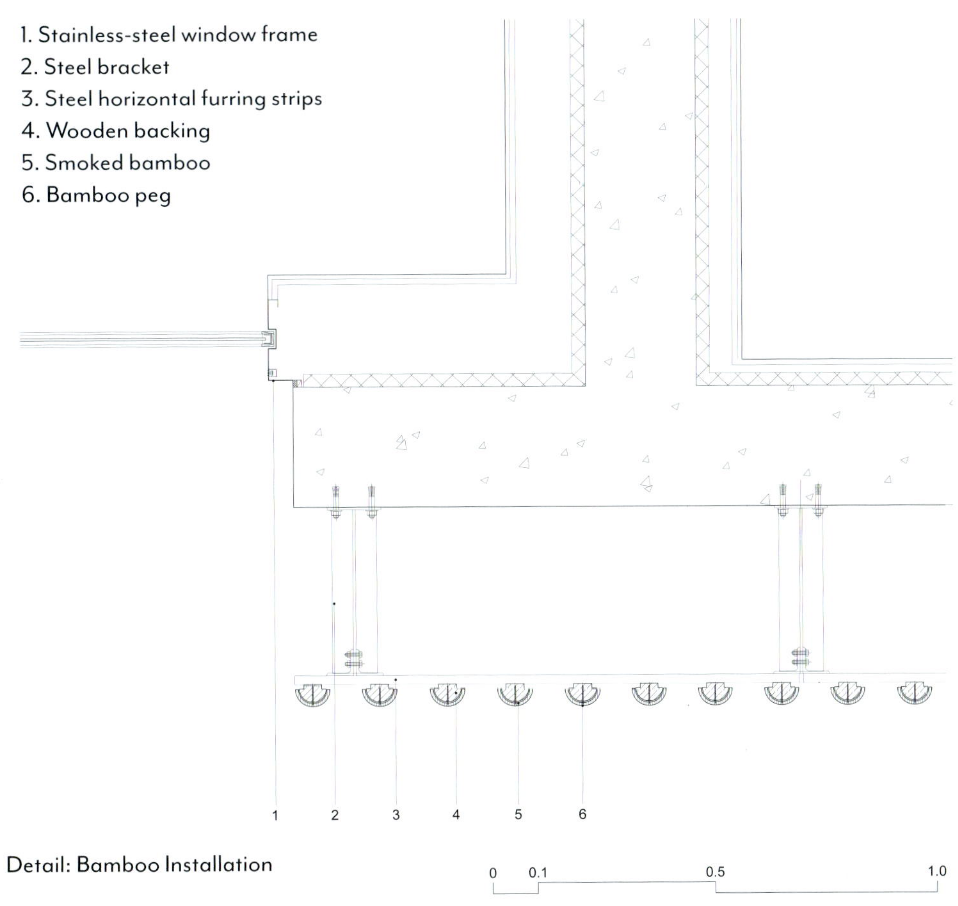

Detail: Bamboo Installation

BAMBOO 3: TAKETA CASTLE TOWN PLAZA

Completion year: 2020
Location: Oita, Japan
Structure: steel, wood
Building type: cultural space

This community center in the middle of Taketa is designed using burnt cedar and bamboo. With its central location, it functions as a node for the walking network in this castle town.

The building is designed as an outdoor stage facing a square. The proscenium, which is a three-dimensional assembly of bamboo, not only serves as a backdrop for events but also symbolizes the new character of Taketa, where modernity and history exist in harmony.

The "komagaeshi" style is used for the façade, but there is a gap of 150 mm between bamboo pieces, with a pitch of 230 mm in order to provide space for lighting fixtures to be installed.

The Castle Town Plaza has a ladder-shaped structure made from bamboo with a diameter of 60 mm. The framework for the structure was made by welding steel pipes with a diameter of 40 mm, which was covered from both sides by splitting bamboo that is about 60 mm in diameter. The bamboo is suspended with wire at a pitch of approximately 200 mm.

The ladder-shaped structure functions as a proscenium arch that frames the stage area where various community events are held.

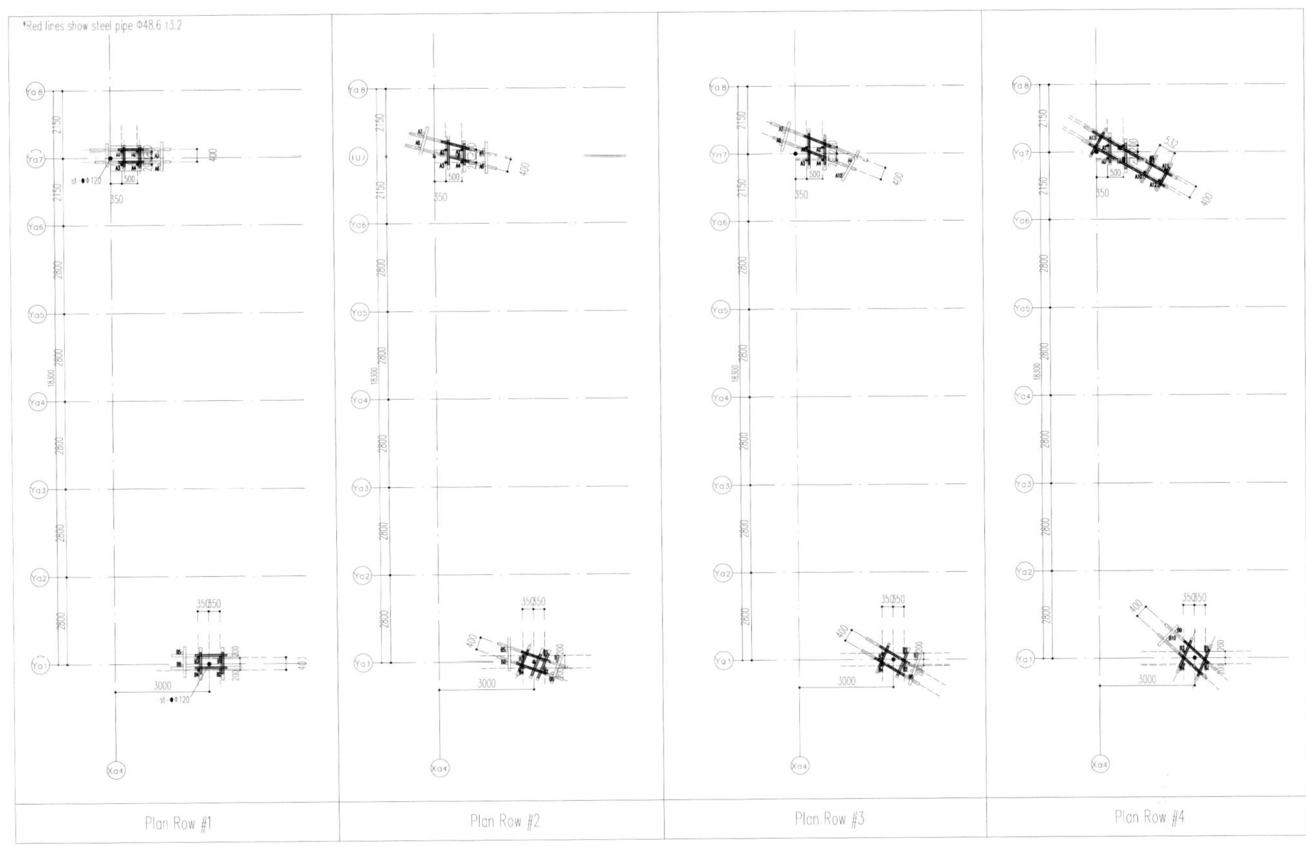
*Red lines show steel pipe Φ48.6 t3.2
Plan Row #1
Plan Row #2
Plan Row #3
Plan Row #4

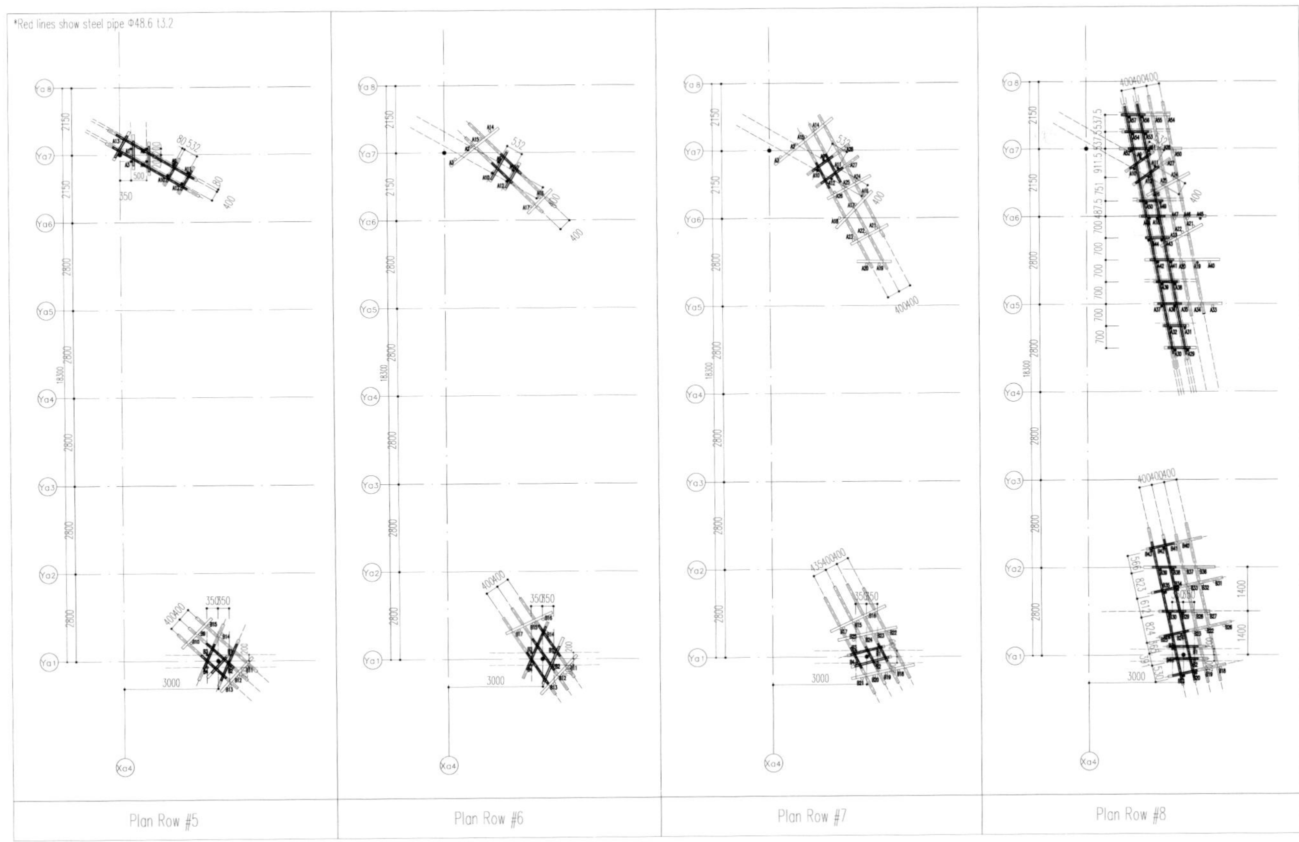
*Red lines show steel pipe Φ48.6 t3.2
Plan Row #5
Plan Row #6
Plan Row #7
Plan Row #8

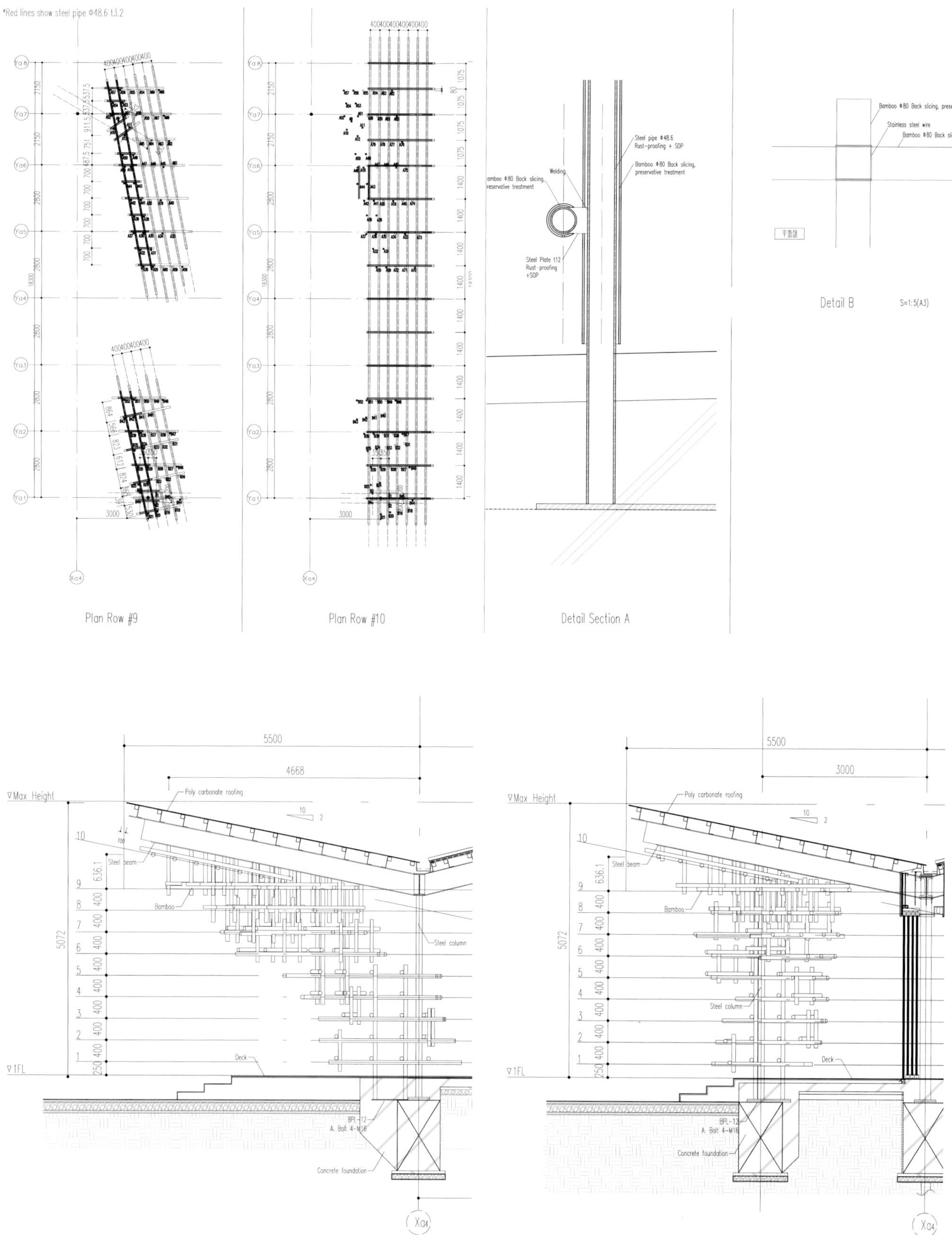

Elevation A

Elevation B

A
Ya8
Ya7
Ya6
Ya5
Ya4
Ya3
Ya2
Ya1
Xa4
2150
2150
2800
2800
18300
2800
2800
2800
B
3000

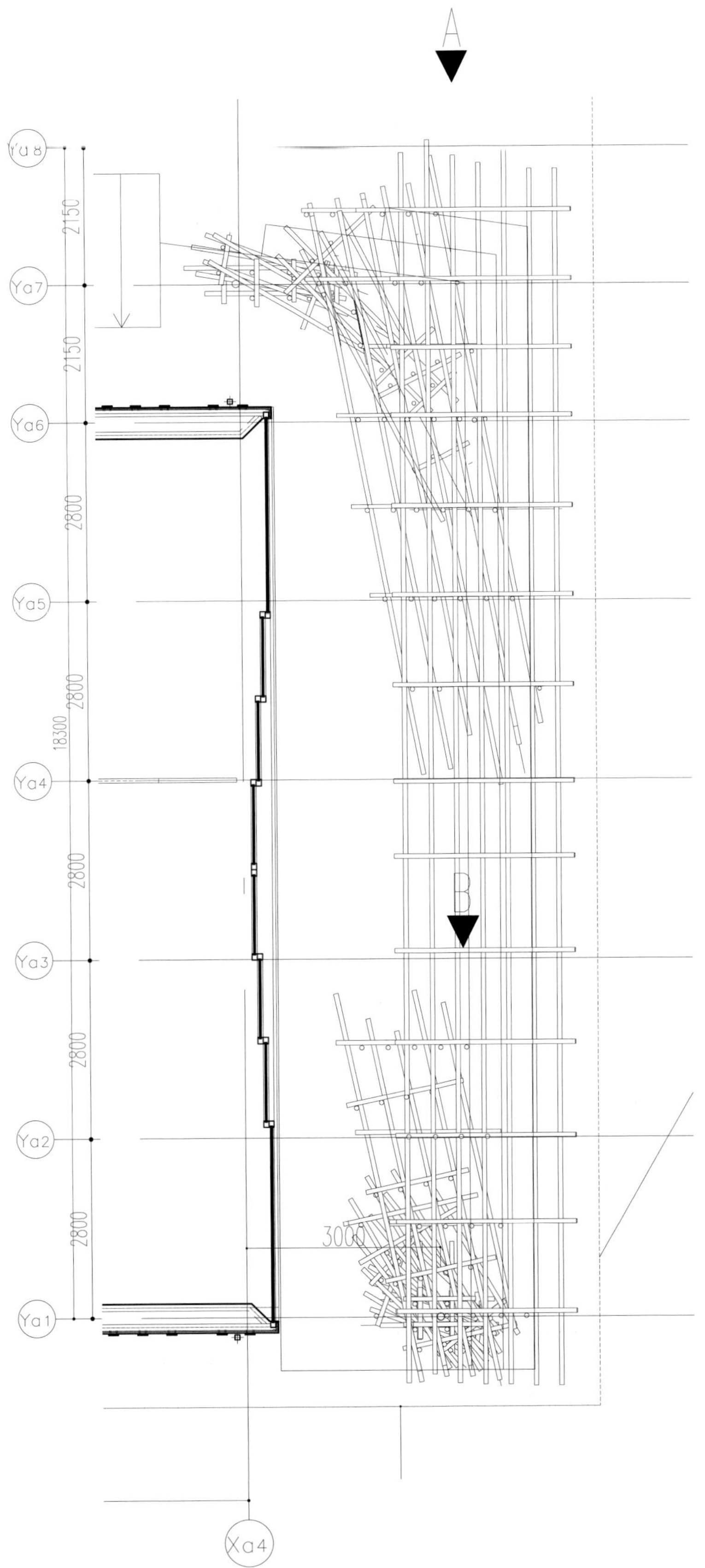

Plan

CHAPTER 6 WOOD

Historically, buildings in Japan were constructed entirely of wood, which also formed the basis for all civil engineering structures, such as bridges. This gave the cities a warm texture and a natural limit in scale, resulting in an intimate, human-scaled urban environment.

Wood's softness and workability allowed for expansions or modifications after construction. A notable innovation from the Kamakura period is the "wagoya"—a type of wooden space frame roof structure. This design enabled the roof to act as a single rigid component. As long as the roof could connect to the supporting members below, the pillars and partitions could be adjusted freely. This flexible system, unique in the world, offered an advanced level of architectural freedom that surpassed even the universal space concepts of twentieth-century modernist architecture, allowing for movable partitions beyond regularly spaced pillars. Structures built in this way in Japan could be dynamically altered postconstruction to accommodate varying functions and lifestyle changes.

However, the shift from wood to concrete was precipitated by two major twentieth-century disasters: the Great Kanto earthquake and World War II. These events led to a perception of wooden structures as outdated, and the ensuing widespread use of concrete and steel transformed not only Japanese architecture and cities but also the culture and lifestyle of the people, losing the gentleness, flexibility, and delicacy that were the essence of Japanese culture.

In an effort to revive this lost cultural heritage, I have been advocating for a return to wood in Japanese architecture. It was recognized in 1990 not only that using wood captures carbon dioxide, helping combat global warming, but that sustainably managing forests through planned cutting and replanting also enhances forest conditions and helps prevent the increasingly frequent floods. This realization rekindled interest in wooden structures in Japan from the late 1990s onward.

The interest in wood is not confined to Japan. With global warming and extreme weather becoming critical worldwide, there is a growing global interest in wooden structures. This has spurred international research into improving wood's fire resistance and preservation.

Since 2000, our efforts to reintegrate wood into building practices in Japan have gained international attention, leading to opportunities to design wooden structures globally. A key focus of our work has been the recognition that wood, like all living things, thrives best in its native environment. Just because wood is inexpensive does not mean it likes to be transported to a different location. We must not forget to try to feel like trees during the design process, choosing to use wood in a manner that is suited to the respective location. It's essential to respect this compatibility between wood and its natural habitat during the design process, ensuring that wood is used in ways that are appropriate for each specific location.

WOOD 1: NAKAGAWAMACHI BATO HIROSHIGE MUSEUM

Completion year: 2000
Location: Tochigi, Japan
Structure: RC (reinforced concrete), steel
Building type: museum

Works of art by the Japanese ukiyo-e-artist Ando Hiroshige (Utagawa Hiroshige), who was strongly influenced by impressionists, are on display at this art museum. I wanted to create a building that represented the unique spatial configuration created in his woodblock prints, and attempted to create three-dimensional space that expresses his overlapping layers. This method uses transparent layers, which is in contrast with the use of perspective to create three-dimensional space in Western paintings and had a large impact on the architecture of Frank Lloyd Wright.

We decided to use wood louvers made from Japanese cedar, which is a local specialty, to create a structure that incorporates this superimposition method. These cedar planks can be used as roofing material after they undergo fire-retardant and preservative treatment. The louvers block the rays of the sun, and the long-extended eaves, with a unique cross section, achieve high environmental performance.

In addition to cedar, local stone, Japanese paper made by local craftsmen, and other materials available in the region were used extensively to stimulate the regional economy to revitalize local circulation and regional communities that did not depend on Tokyo before the advent of modern industrial society.

Thin cedar louvers with a cross section of 30 by 60 mm were arranged at a pitch of 150 mm, enveloping both the exterior and interior spaces of the building. From the entrance to the approach, three layers of modules with identical dimensions but different finishes were organized, enhancing the experience as visitors progress toward the back, moving from one layer to the next.

The first layer retains the natural color of the cedar, protected only by a clear coat. The second layer, matching the first in dimensions, is wrapped in Japanese paper. In the third layer, the entire screen—mirroring the dimensions of the first—is also wrapped in Japanese paper, casting the silhouette of the cedar louvers onto the paper at the back. This gradual integration of the same louvers into the soft texture of Japanese paper diminishes the wood's tactile presence, drawing visitors step by step into the deeper parts of the museum and ushering them into an almost ethereal realm.

Our plan involved doubling the 150 mm unit for the pitch of the louvers across all spaces. The floor stones are set to a width of 300 mm, which is twice the base unit of 150 mm, creating a rhythm of delicate lines that resonate throughout the spaces.

wooden louver:30x60x@=120
furnishing base of wooden louver :FB-6x200
sheet stud
: SUS-304-2.0t(@=720x900)
continous suspention rod:galvanized steel plate t=0.4
verge cantilever metal attachment : 35x35x3.2tx@=465
sheet stud
@=720
sheet stud
@=720
St-L-35x35x3.2t(continous)
St-PL-1.0t(zincing steel plate)
water drip
continous suspention rod : galvanized steel plate t=0.4
shade holding base:30x30x2.3t
shade holding base : C-100x50x20x2.3t
furring strips:C-75x45x15x2.3tx@=455
window breaking shutter
asphalt roofing 940
hard wooden concrete plate t=18
external wall:harper's strong roof@=360
(fluoride steel platet=0.6)
insulation
insulation: extruded polyethylen foam plate t=30
C,T steel
H steel
asphalt roofing 940
extruded polyethylen foam plate
+hard wooden concrete plate t=30+18
(complex plate) place concrete

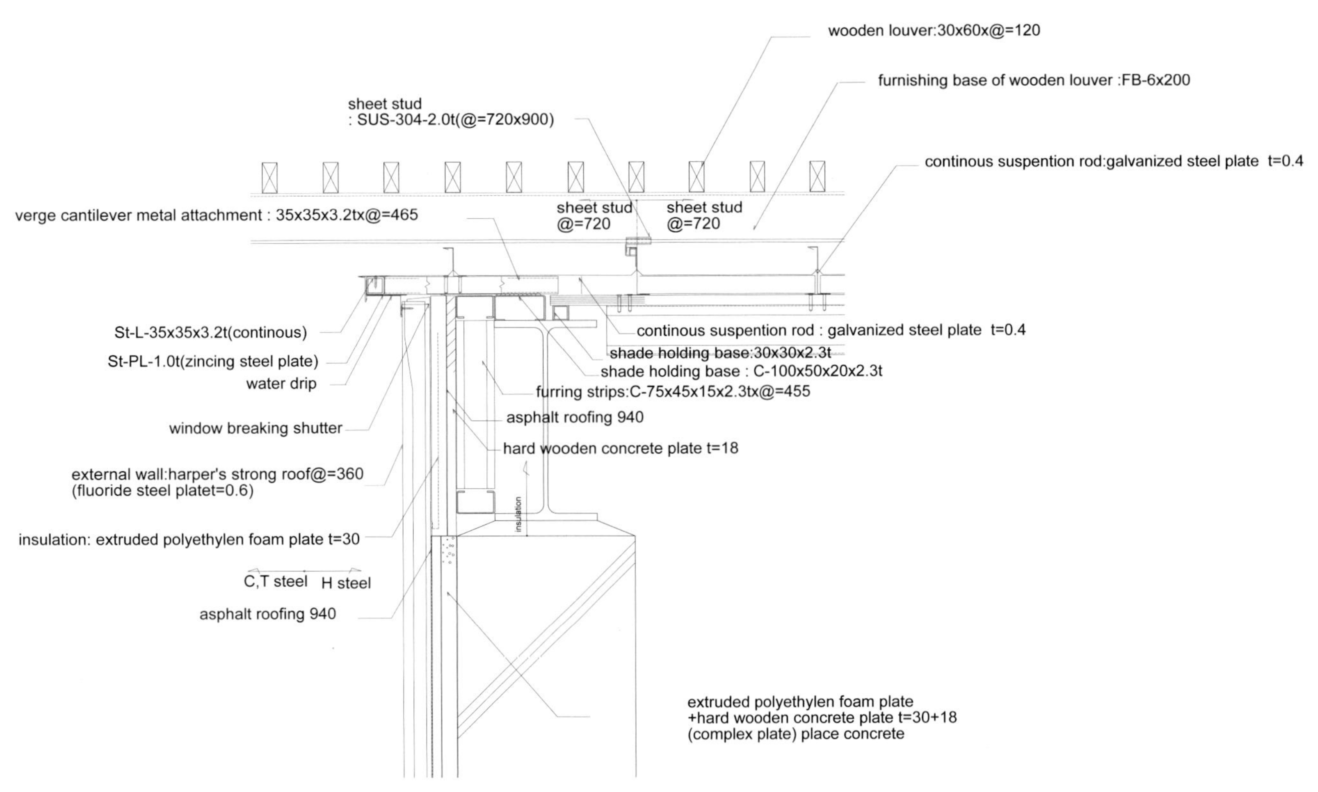

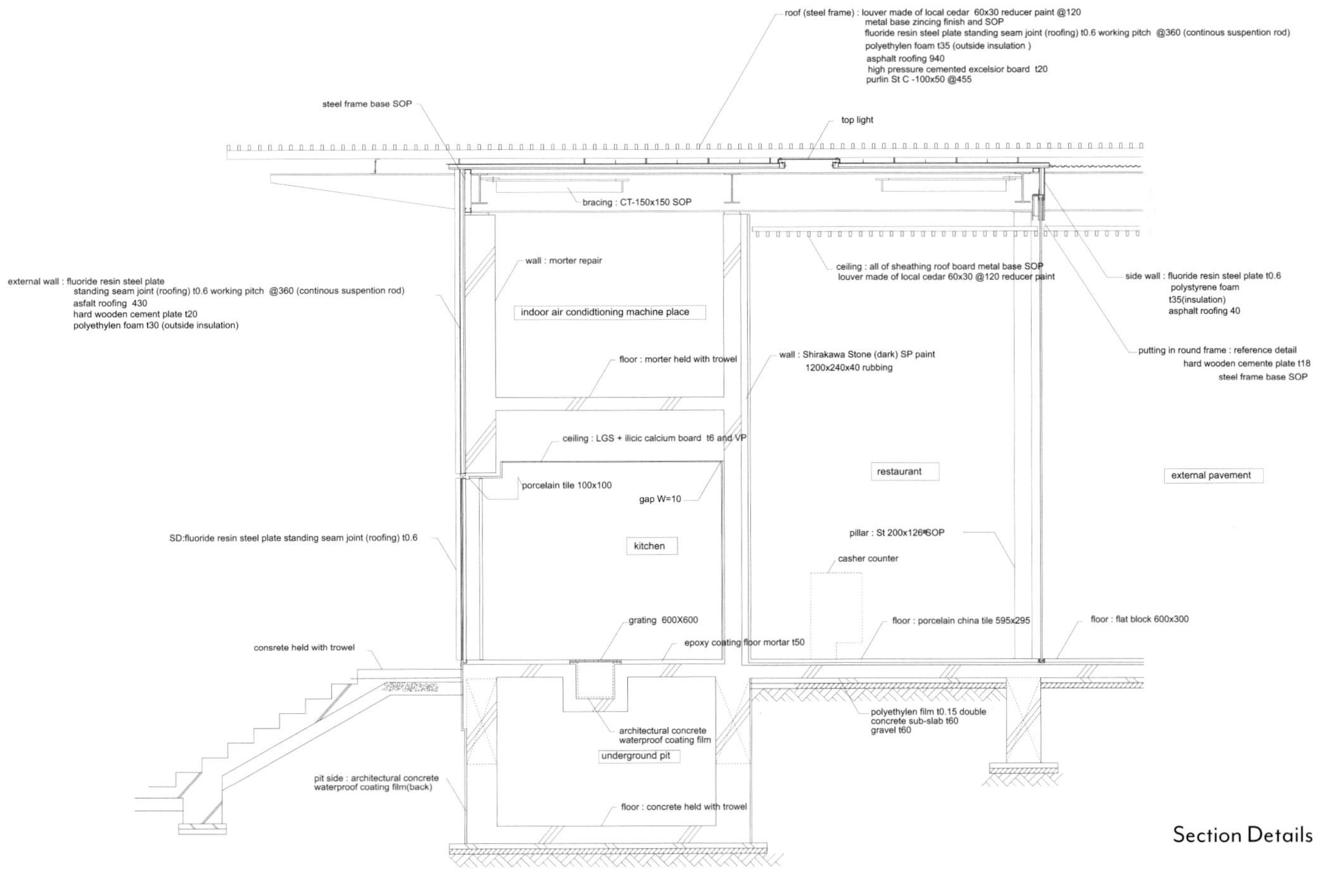

roof (steel frame) : louver made of local cedar 60x30 reducer paint @120
metal base zincing finish and SOP
fluoride resin steel plate standing seam joint (roofing) t0.6 working pitch @360 (continous suspention rod)
polyethylen foam t35 (outside insulation)
asphalt roofing 940
high pressure cemented excelsior board t20
purlin St C -100x50 @455
steel frame base SOP
top light
bracing : CT-150x150 SOP
wall : morter repair
ceiling : all of sheathing roof board metal base SOP
louver made of local cedar 60x30 @120 reducer paint
side wall : fluoride resin steel plate t0.6
polystyrene foam
t35(insulation)
asphalt roofing 40
external wall : fluoride resin steel plate
standing seam joint (roofing) t0.6 working pitch @360 (continous suspention rod)
asfalt roofing 430
hard wooden cement plate t20
polyethylen foam t30 (outside insulation)
indoor air condidtioning machine place
floor : morter held with trowel
wall : Shirakawa Stone (dark) SP paint
1200x240x40 rubbing
putting in round frame : reference detail
hard wooden cemente plate t18
steel frame base SOP
ceiling : LGS + ilicic calcium board t6 and VP
restaurant
external pavement
porcelain tile 100x100
gap W=10
pillar : St 200x126*SOP
SD:fluoride resin steel plate standing seam joint (roofing) t0.6
kitchen
casher counter
grating 600X600
epoxy coating floor mortar t50
floor : porcelain china tile 595x295
floor : flat block 600x300
consrete held with trowel
architectural concrete
waterproof coating film
polyethylen film t0.15 double
concrete sub-slab t60
gravel t60
underground pit
pit side : architectural concrete
waterproof coating film(back)
floor : concrete held with trowel

Section Details

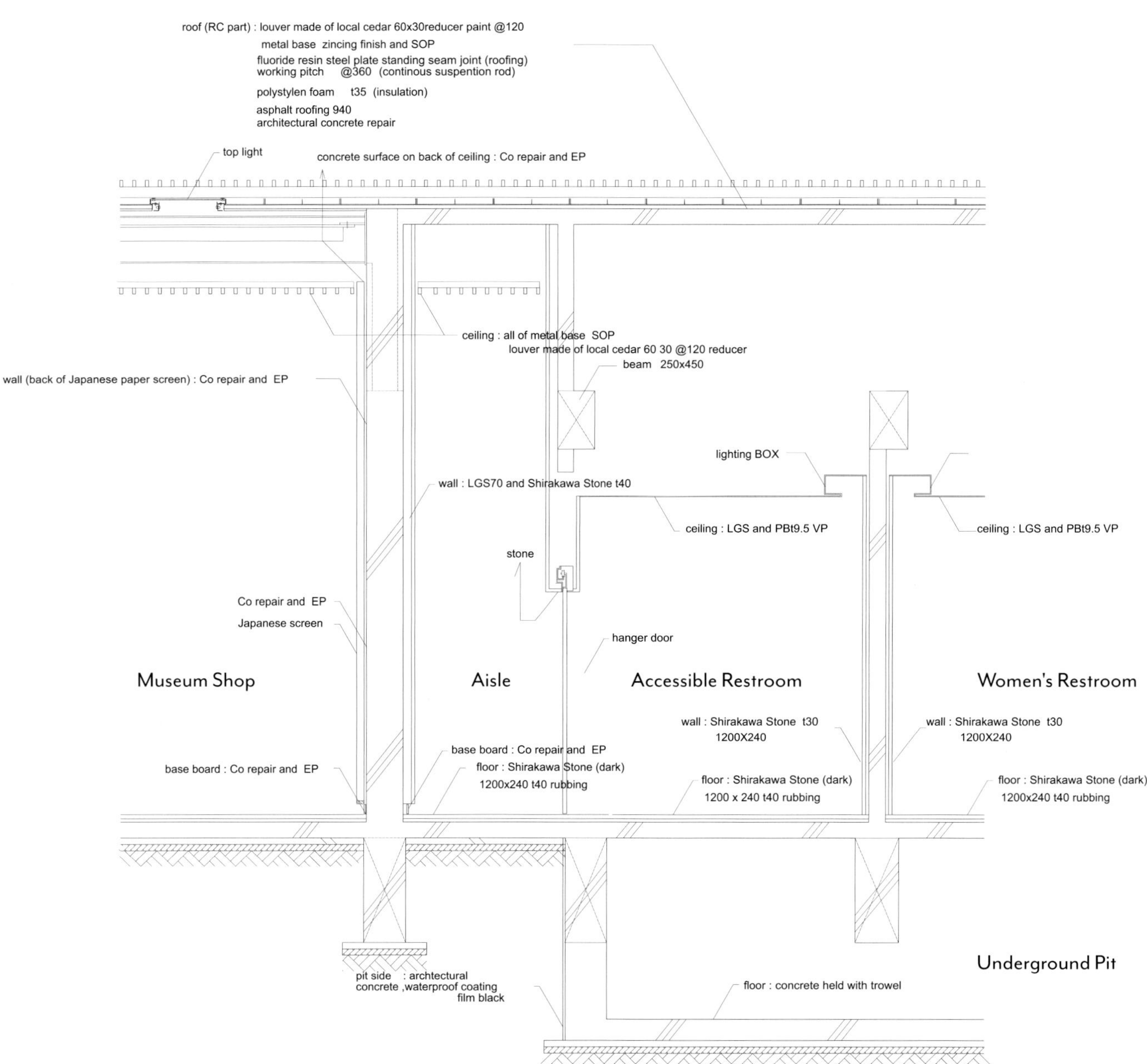

Section Detail

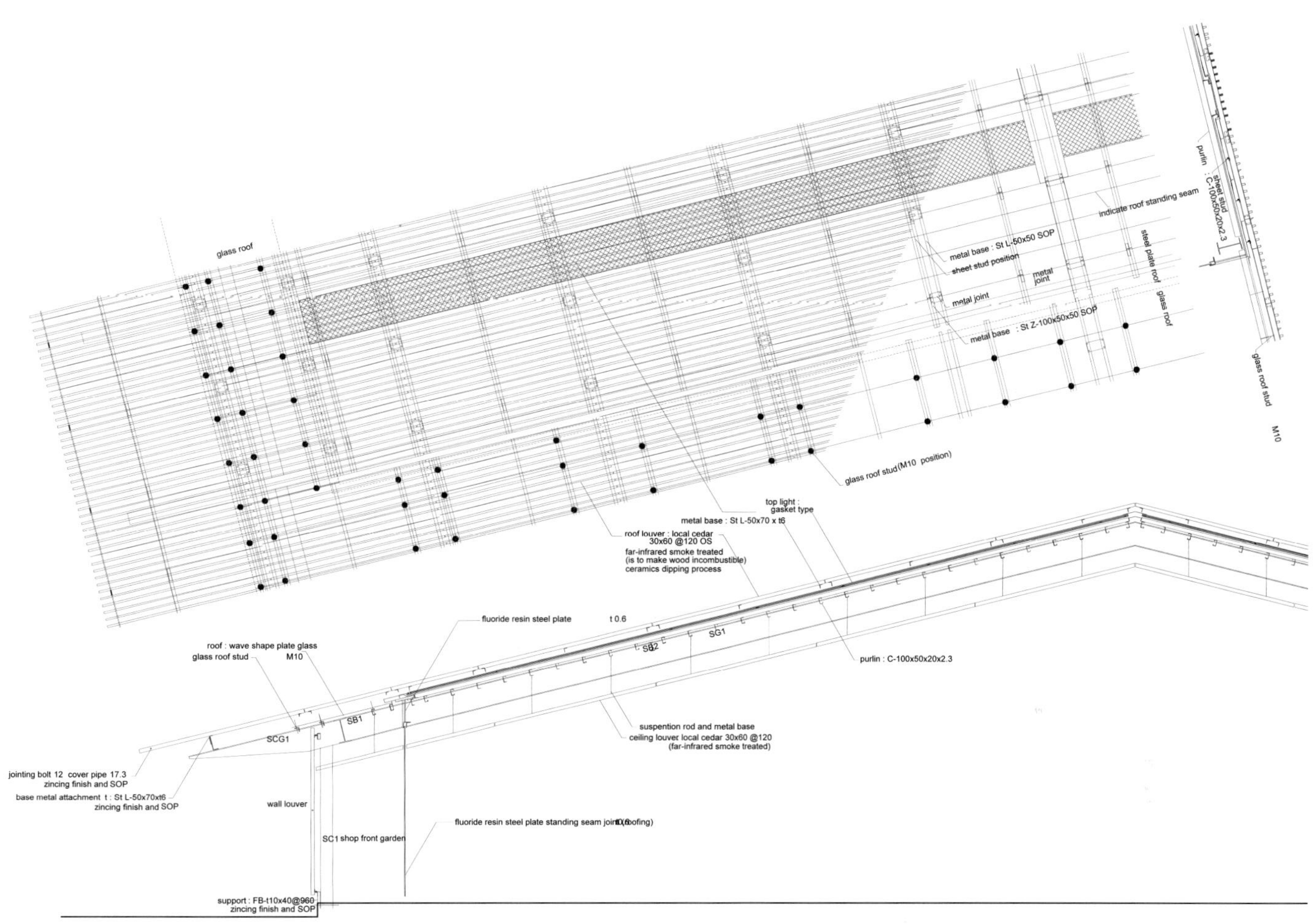

Section/Plan Details

WOOD 2: YUSUHARA WOODEN BRIDGE MUSEUM

Completion year: 2010
Location: Kochi, Japan
Structure: wood
Building type: gallery

We adopted a unique cantilever bridge design for this structure, a traditional technique that has been forgotten in Japan. The structure is created by using laminated wooden members with small sections and gradually extending the bridge girder a little at a time from both ends by using many overlapping members. The only remaining structure of this type in Japan where wooden planks are used instead of a steel structure is the "Sarubashi" in Yamanashi Prefecture.

To adapt the structure to the site, a bridge pier is provided in the center to receive the vertical load, and the load on both sides was balanced, making it a bridge structure that should be called a "balancing toy bridge." A roof that has the opposite shape of the bridge structure covers the studio and gallery that are provided on both sides at the top of the slope.

Rather than using the large-section laminated wood typically employed for new, expansive wooden spans in Europe, we aimed to achieve a broad-span wooden structure by assembling laminated wooden members with smaller cross sections of 180 × 300 mm. Historically, various spans in Japanese wooden structures were constructed using small-diameter logs with cross sections of 150 × 150 mm or less. This system not only facilitates the effective use of lumber from thinning operations but also supports the sustainable management of forests in Japan.

The overall structure incorporates the "Tokiyo" system, a technique of overlapping wooden members from traditional Japanese temple architecture. This method fills the structure with a tangible presence and a sense of abstractness akin to "wood masonry," a quality unattainable with standard framework structures. The laminated wooden members themselves possess both presence and abstractness reminiscent of wood masonry. By connecting these members, we aimed to expand their dimensions and create a nonhierarchical architecture that integrates physical properties, technology, information, and history.

This represented an attempt to create new public architecture capable of bridging a wide range of issues, including the rejuvenation of regional culture, urban design, structural technology and materials, and traditional expression.

Furthermore, from an aesthetic perspective, the use of small-diameter logs has defined traditional Japanese architectural spaces, characterized by their delicacy and transparency. Essentially, small-diameter logs form the foundation of Japanese architecture, significant both for resource circulation and aesthetic considerations. In essence, Japanese wooden architecture is built on what might be termed a "small system" in every sense of the word.

For this project in Yusuhara, a town of six hundred people, the laminated lumber produced at the local small-scale mill—with a cross section of 150 × 300 mm—perfectly aligns with the town's self-sustaining economic system. This approach underpins the design of this bridge and is integral to the human-scaled design that characterizes it.

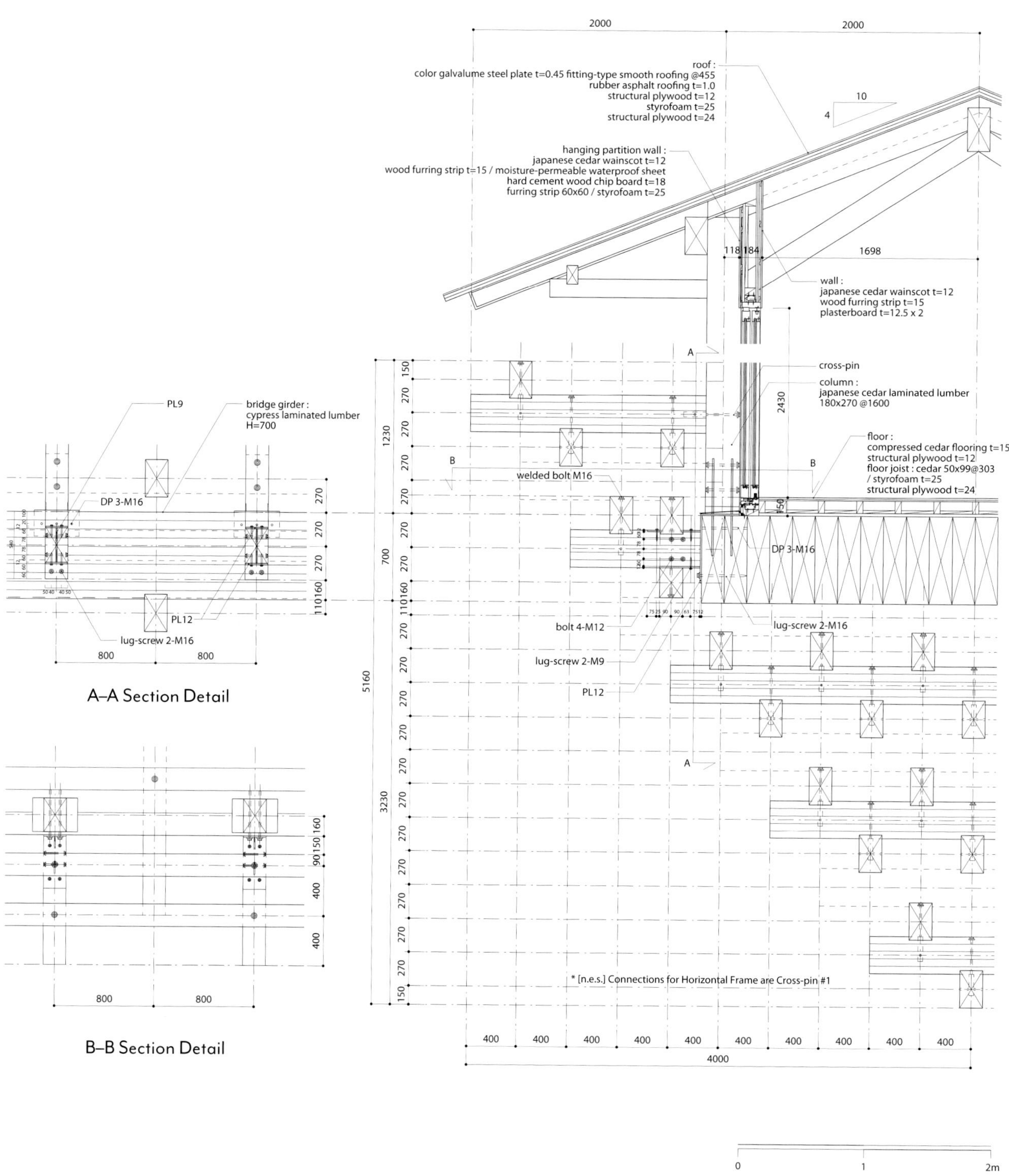

Detail: Bridge Wood Framing

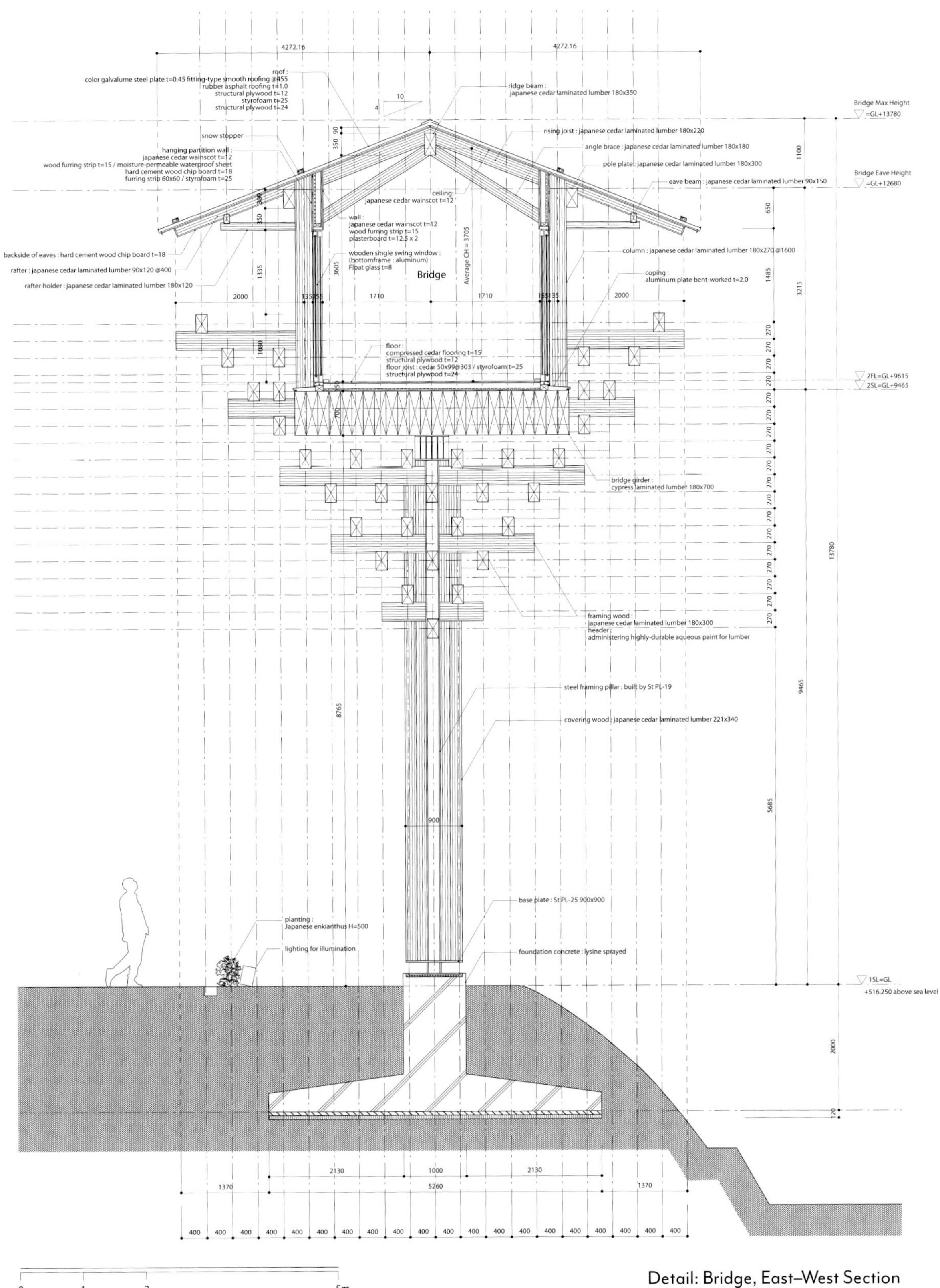

Detail: Bridge, East–West Section

WOOD 3: GC PROSTHO MUSEUM RESEARCH CENTER

Completion year: 2010
Location: Aichi, Japan
Structure: RC/SRC (reinforced concrete / steel-reinforced concrete), wood
Building type: museum

Design of this structure consisted of taking on the challenge of creating a medium-scale wooden structure built by combining small sections of wooden members (6 × 6 cm) based on a traditional wooden toy from the Hida Takayama region in Japan. No glue was used to build the structure. The wood grid supports the structure and also serves as display space for the items exhibited in the museum. The structure protrudes out on the upper part of the structure to protect the wooden members from rain, and white paint is used to protect the wooden members on the edges.

The foundation of traditional wooden architecture in Japan involves skillfully combining slender wooden members with a cross section of 150 × 150 mm or smaller, creating a frame structure with strong seismic resistance. In this project, we utilized wooden members with a cross section of 60 × 60 mm, which is less than half that of the traditional 150 mm, to construct a 10 m tall, three-story wooden structure arranged in a 500 × 500 mm Cartesian grid. The use of these slender 60 mm square members provides a delicate expression and a unique transparency not found in typical wooden architecture.

For this project, furniture such as chairs and tables using 60 mm square wooden members were also designed. The chairs, named GC chairs after the project, have been marketed and sold.

A traditional method involves combining members in the x, y, and z directions at joints, where a portion of the cross section is removed. These special joints, requiring advanced techniques, are known as chidori joints in Hida Takayama—a region renowned for its high level of woodworking technology—and are also referred to as shiho-gumi (judicial joints).

This type of joint technology in Japan, which eschews metal, has developed to a degree unmatched anywhere else in the world. One reason for this is the need to avoid metal corrosion due to the rainy climate. Moreover, the structural system's ability to absorb seismic forces by providing a certain softness in the wood is particularly suited to a country prone to earthquakes.

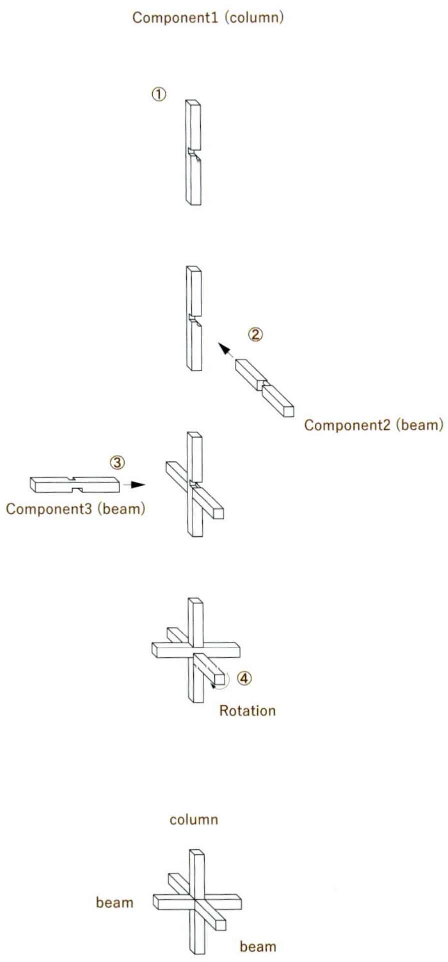

Component1 (column)
①
②
Component2 (beam)
③
Component3 (beam)
④
Rotation
column
beam
beam

Assembly Drawing

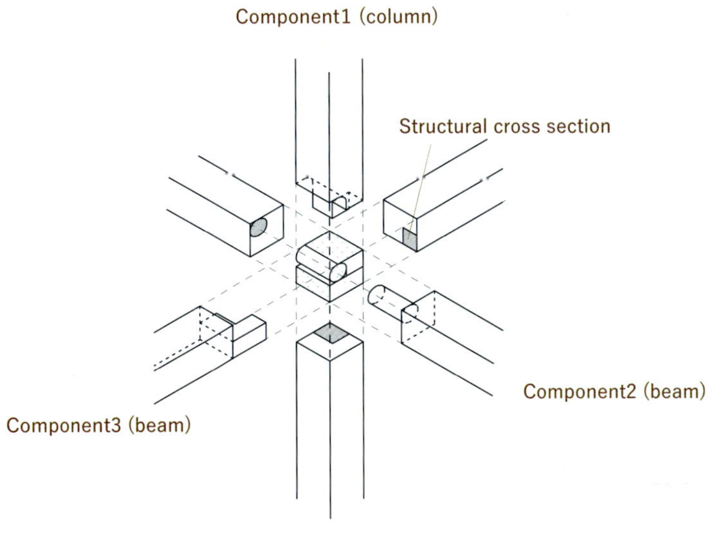

Component1 (column)
Structural cross section
Component2 (beam)
Component3 (beam)

Joint of Parts: Exploded View

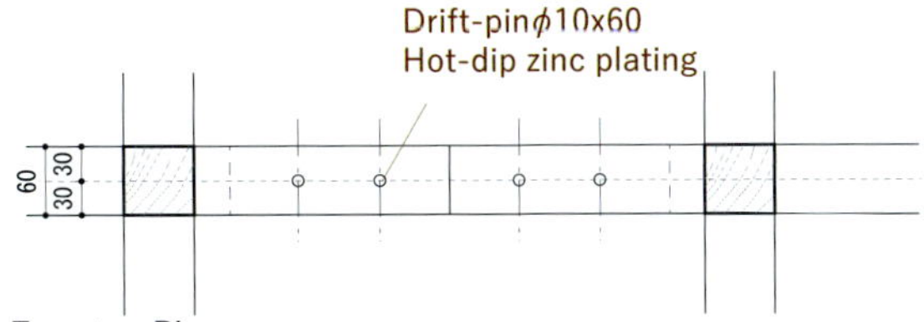

Drift-pinϕ10x60
Hot-dip zinc plating
60
30
30

Framing Plan

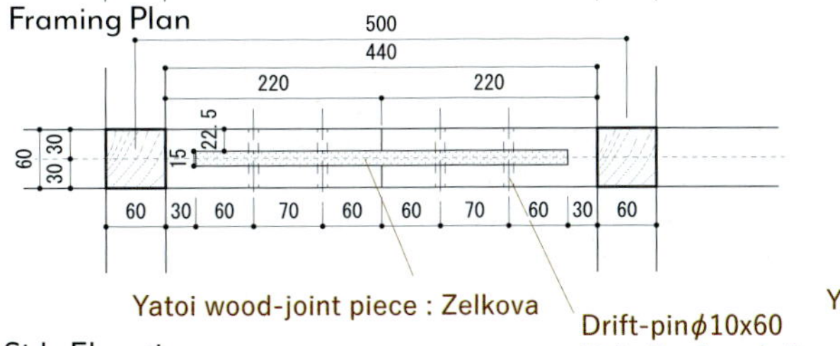

500
440
220
220
22.5
15
60
30
30
60
30
60
70
60
60
70
60
30
60
Yatoi wood-joint piece : Zelkova
Drift-pinϕ10x60
Hot-dip zinc plating

Side Elevation

Drift-pinϕ10x60
Hot-dip zinc plating
60
10
22.5
15
22.5
30
30
Yatoi wood-joint piece : Zelkova

Section

Joint

2000
2000
3000
proecessing
Yatoi wood-joint piece
proecessing
Joined with yatoi wood-joint piece

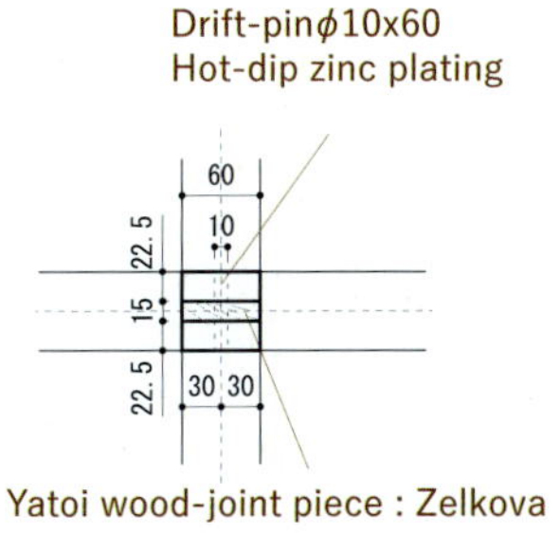

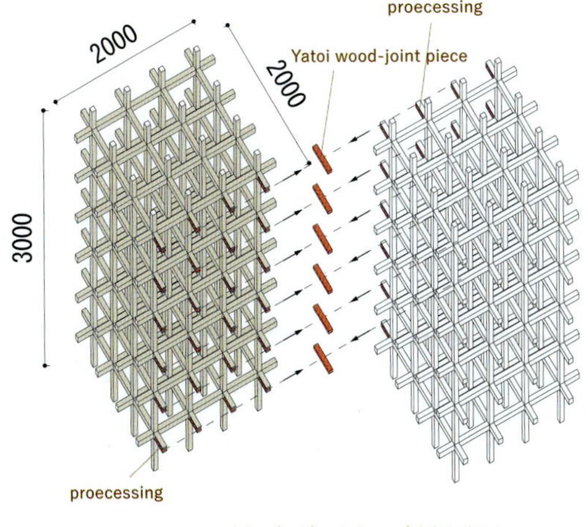

Unit Drawing 1/100

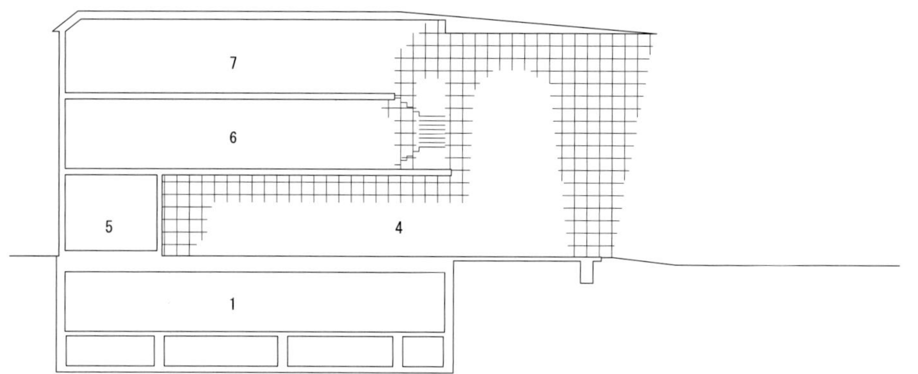

1. Communal space
2. Archive
3. Dry area
4. Gallery
5. Electrical
6. Bureau
7. Laboratory

Section

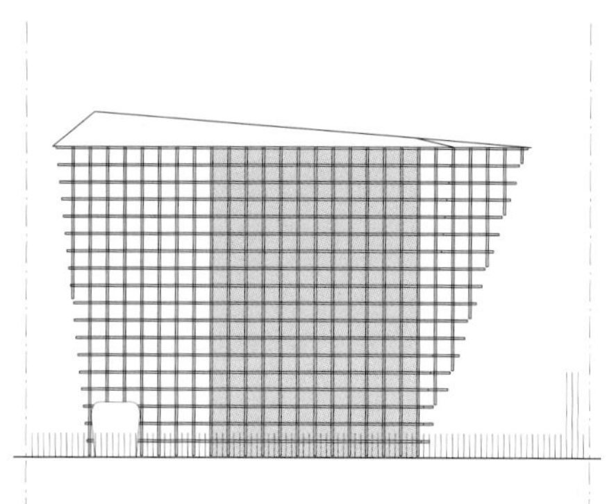

Elevation

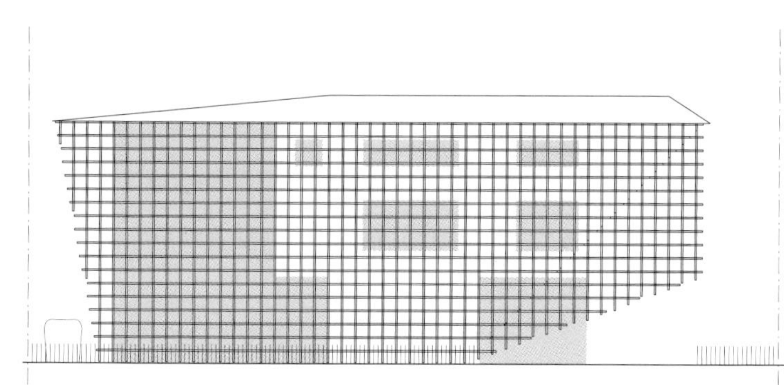

Elevation

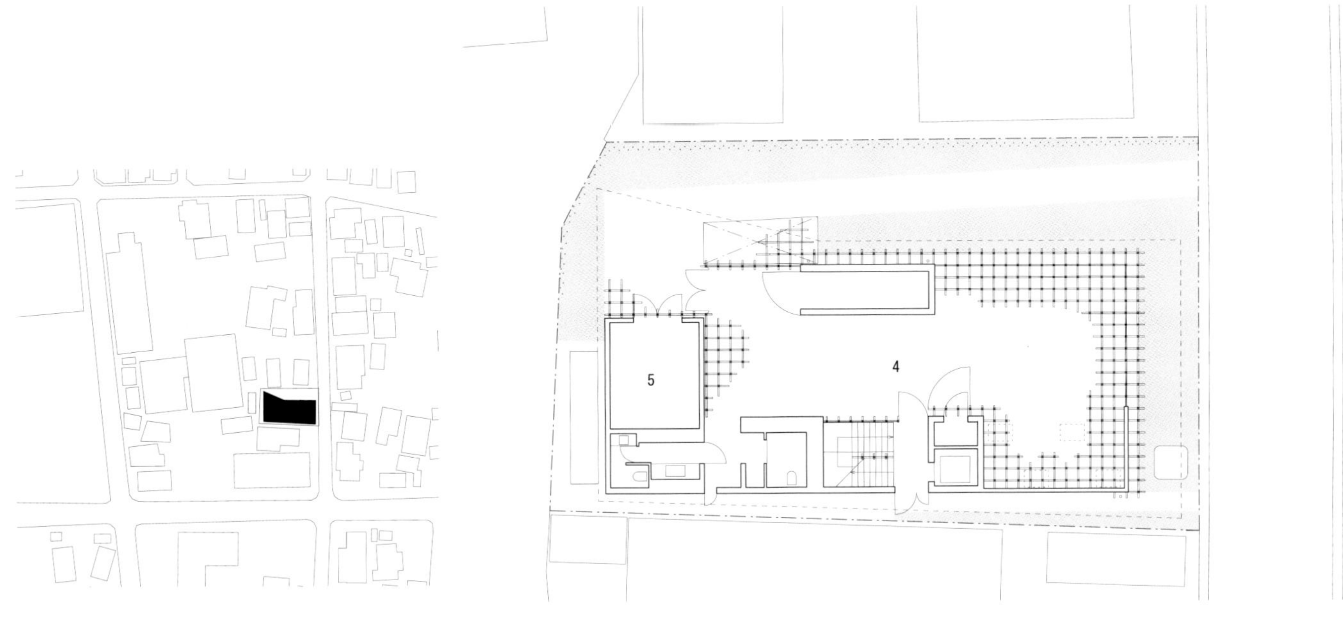

First Floor

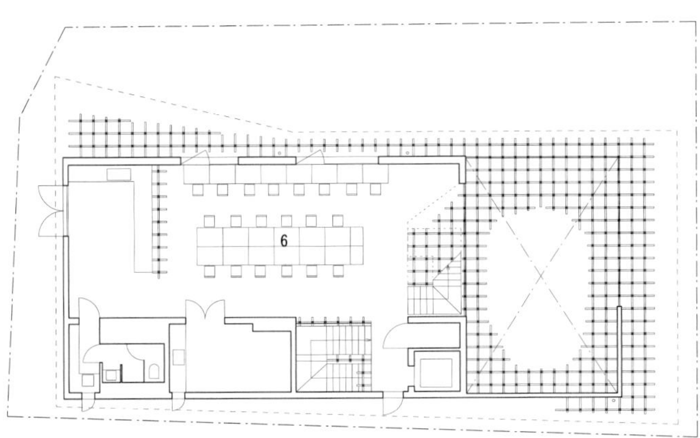

Second Floor

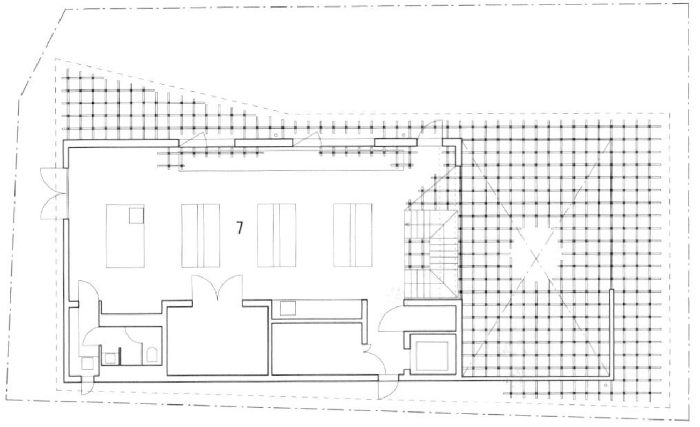

Third Floor

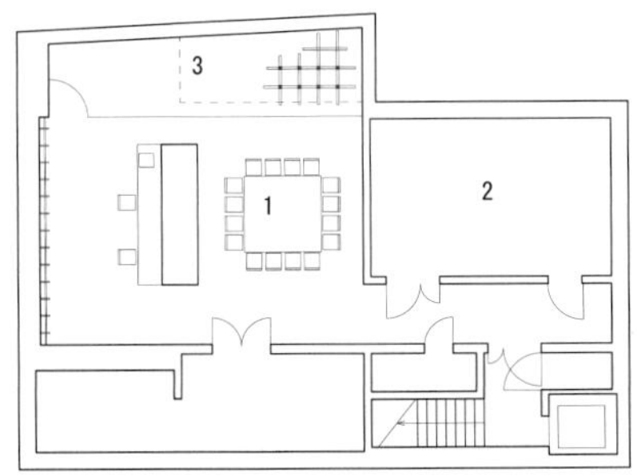

Basement Floor

1. Communal space
2. Archive
3. Dry area
4. Gallery
5. Electrical
6. Bureau
7. Laboratory

WOOD 4: STARBUCKS COFFEE AT DAZAIFU TENMANGU OMOTESANDO

Completion year: 2011
Location: Fukuoka, Japan
Structure: RC/SRC (reinforced concrete / steel-reinforced concrete)
Building type: café

This Starbucks Coffee shop is located on the main approach to the Dazaifu Tenmangu Shrine in Omotesando. The site is uniquely long and narrow, measuring 7.5 m in width and approximately 40 m in depth. In response, small pieces of wood were intricately woven together to create an organic space that flows like light and wind.

The interior is enveloped by an X-shaped wooden framework, constructed using about two thousand cedar pieces ranging in length from 1.3 to 4 m with a 6 cm cross section, totaling 4 km in length. The members were assembled diagonally to enhance structural support. Dowels were inserted at the joints once the overall structure was assembled, to add stiffness. The fusion of modern wooden-construction technology with the historic site of Dazaifu has resulted in a distinctive space that sets this Starbucks apart from others.

For the GC Prostho Museum, 60 mm square wooden members were used to create a Cartesian grid in which the members cross at right angles. However, for the Dazaifu project the narrow entrance required a different approach. Here, diagonal members were woven together to facilitate the flow of people into the depths of the thin, long space, and open edges were used for the wooden members, representing a challenge to create a space frame that is very free and open. A new type of cut was made for the joints where four diagonal members meet, differing from traditional joints. Stainless-steel dowels were incorporated to develop a structural system that efficiently transfers forces between members.

The entire space is composed of bar-shaped 60 mm square wooden members, and even the lighting fixtures were designed using bar-shaped 60 mm square acrylic members. Additionally, the same angles used for the diagonal structural members were applied to the customer sofas, aiming to design the overall space with a rhythmic harmony akin to composing music with a certain rhythm.

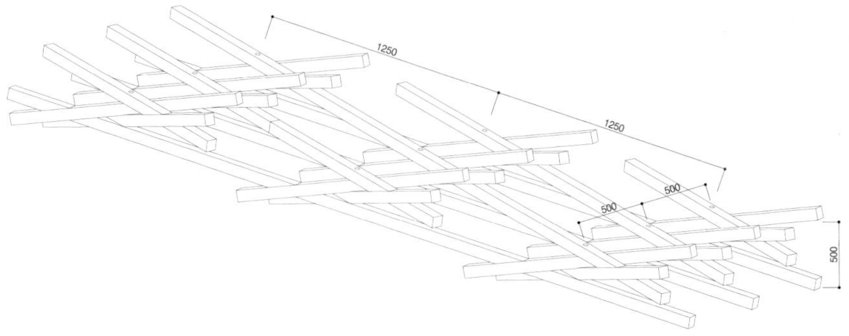

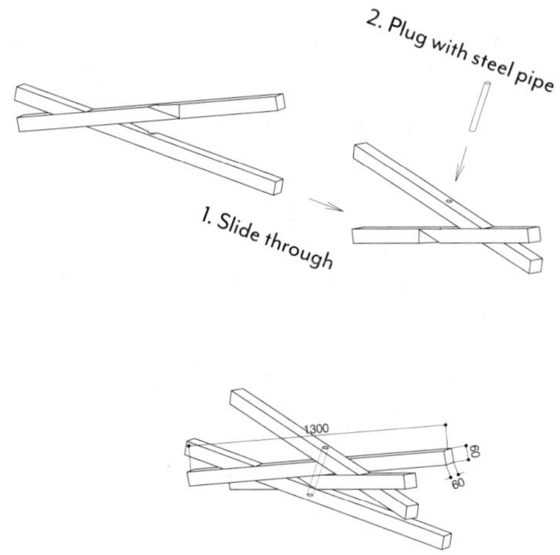

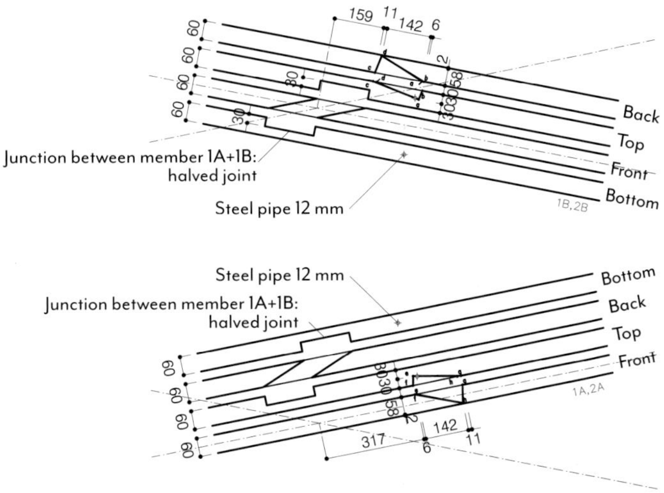

2. Plug with steel pipe

1. Slide through

Junction between member 1A+1B: halved joint

Steel pipe 12 mm

Back

Top

Front

Bottom

Steel pipe 12 mm

Junction between member 1A+1B: halved joint

Bottom

Back

Top

Front

Details: X-shaped wood framework

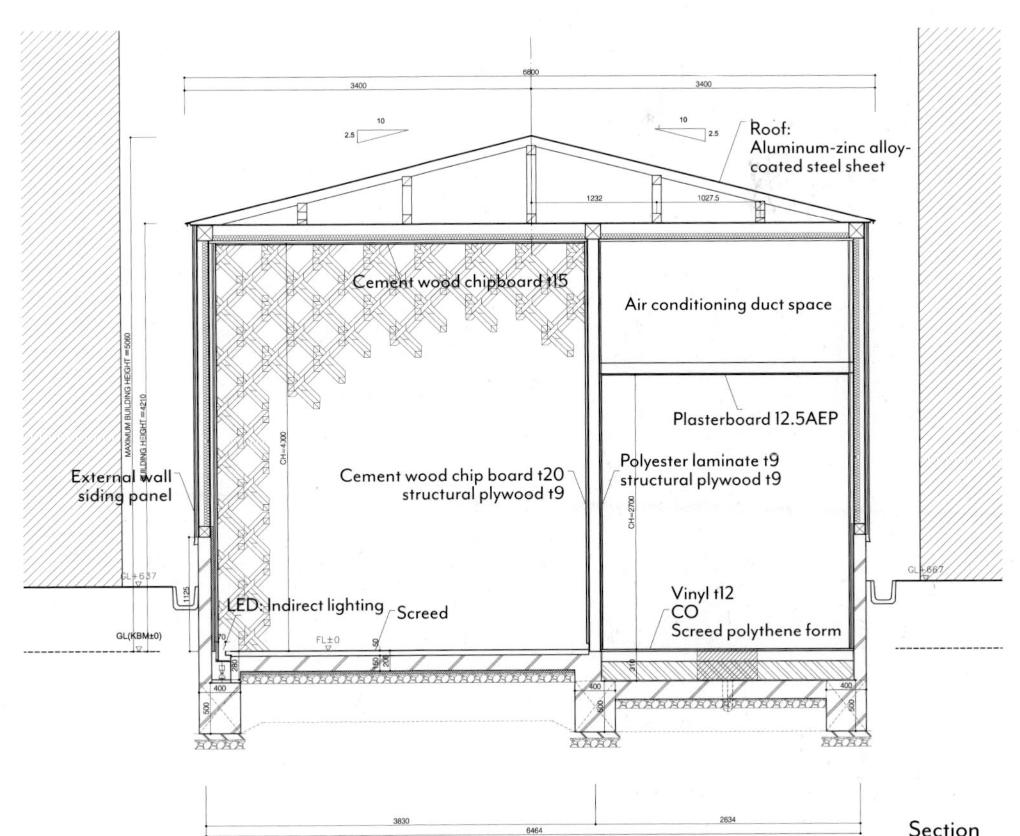

Section

WOOD 5: ASAKUSA CULTURE TOURIST INFORMATION CENTER

Completion year: 2012
Location: Tokyo, Japan
Structure: steel
Building type: information center

On a compact corner site of just 326 square meters across from the Kaminari-mon Gate, the building was designed to accommodate multiple programs, including a tourist information center, a conference room, a multipurpose hall, and an exhibition space.

The center vertically extends the vibrant atmosphere of Asakusa's neighborhood, stacking roofs that cover various activities beneath them, thereby creating a "new section" not found in traditional layered architecture. Equipment is housed in the diagonally shaped spaces that form between the roof and the floor, allowing us to maintain a large air volume despite the building's moderate height compared to other high- and medium-rise structures. Moreover, the roofs do more than just cover the building; they divide the structure into seven single-story units and define the function of each floor.

Each floor has been designed to counteract the verticality typical of high-rise buildings, aiming to evoke the image of humble, stacked, single-story wooden houses. This effect is achieved by prominent horizontal eaves that separate each level, with each floor's façade characterized by varying pitches and rhythms in the vertical louvers.

Sensoji Temple, located directly opposite the building, has been a focal point for the common people since the Edo period. The low-rise shopping street called Nakamise, in front of the main temple, continues to this day. The goal of this project was to construct a 24 m high midrise building that maintains the intimate scale and texture reminiscent of Nakamise.

The first and second floors feature an atrium and indoor stairs, enhancing the perception of the dual roof slopes. On the sixth floor, the slanted roof design facilitates the installation of a terraced floor, transforming the entire room into a theater. Since the roof angles toward Kaminari-mon and the heights vary from floor to floor, each level interacts differently with the outside, imparting a distinct character to each space.

The entire exterior wall is clad with cedar wood screen units featuring a wedge-shaped cross section that has been treated for fire resistance. These screens help control sunlight, reducing energy consumption in conjunction with the horizontal eaves installed on each floor.

The top floor features a café with a covered terrace in front, designed to reflect the Edo-period emphasis on living in semi-outdoor spaces under roofs. This setting aims to re-create the lifestyle characteristic of that era.

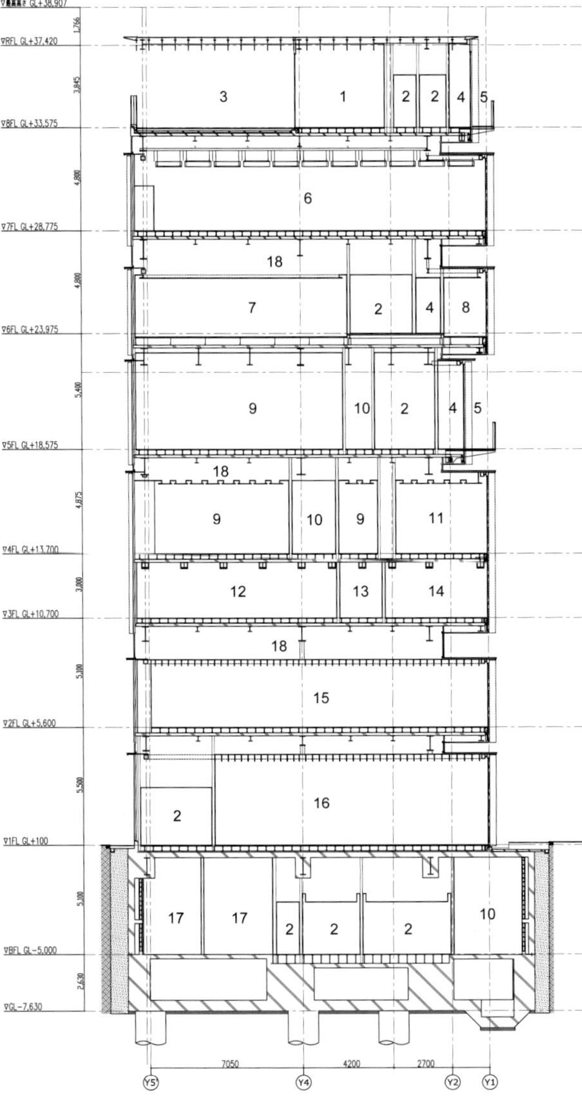

AA' Section

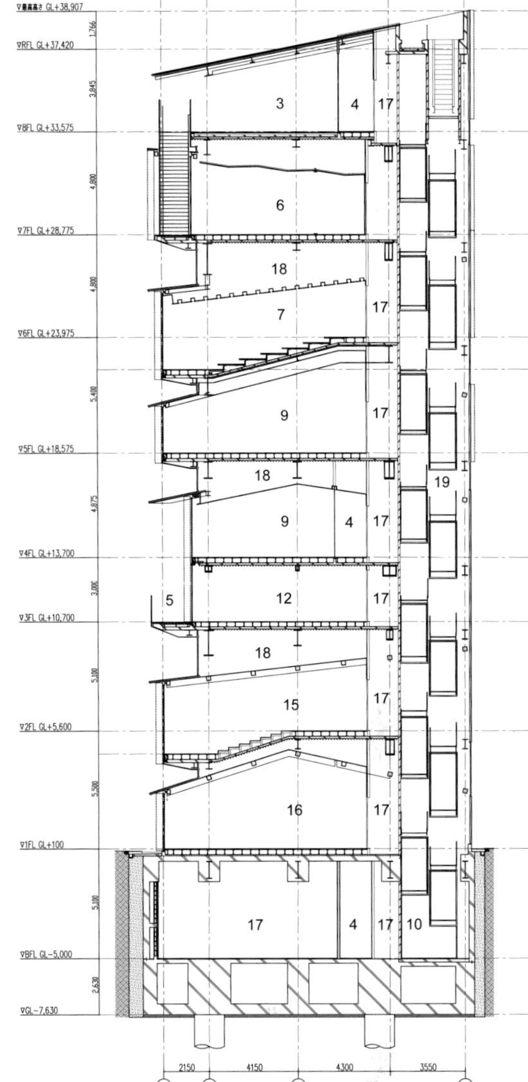

BB' Section

1. Café
2. Toilet
3. Viewing terrace
4. Corridor
5. Terrace
6. Exhibition space
7. Multi-purpose room
8. Lounge
9. Conference room
10. Storage
11. Seminar room
12. Office
13. Coat room
14. Group tourist support
15. Tourist information
16. Information lobby
17. Machine room
18. Machine space
19. Stairs
20. EV hall
21. Locker room
22. Windbreak room
23. Nursing room
24. Foreign exchange
25. Break room

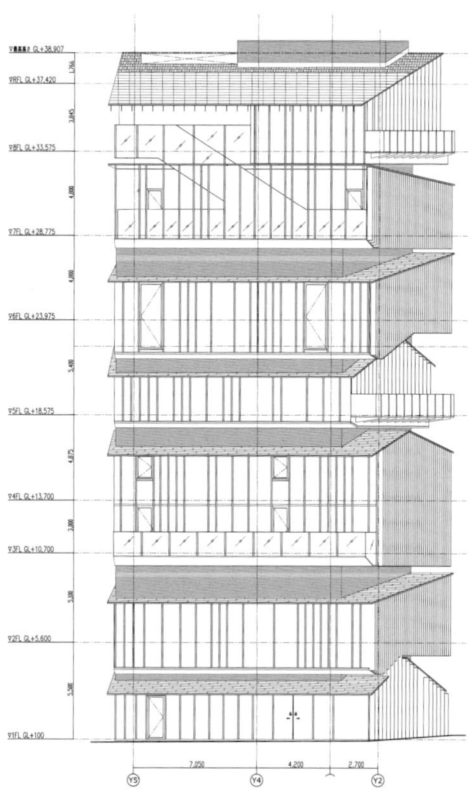

North Elevation

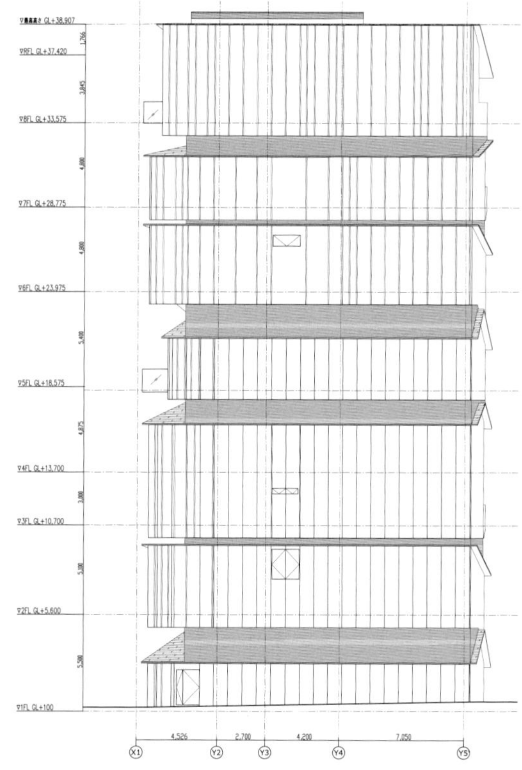

South Elevation

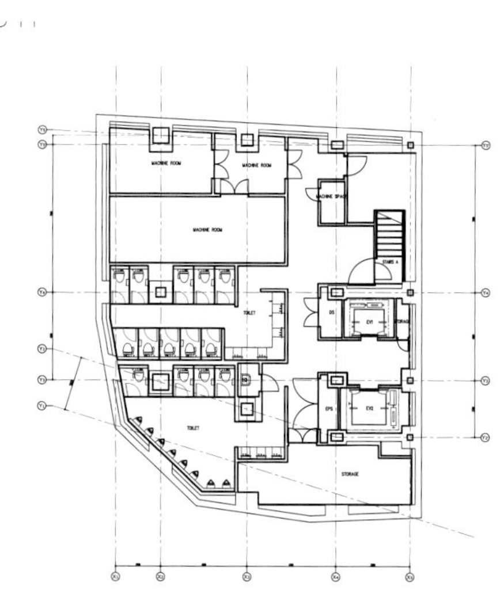

Basement Floor

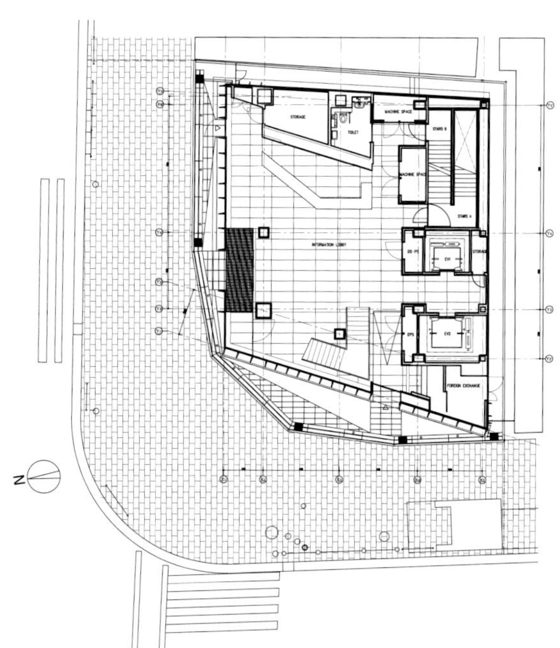

First Floor

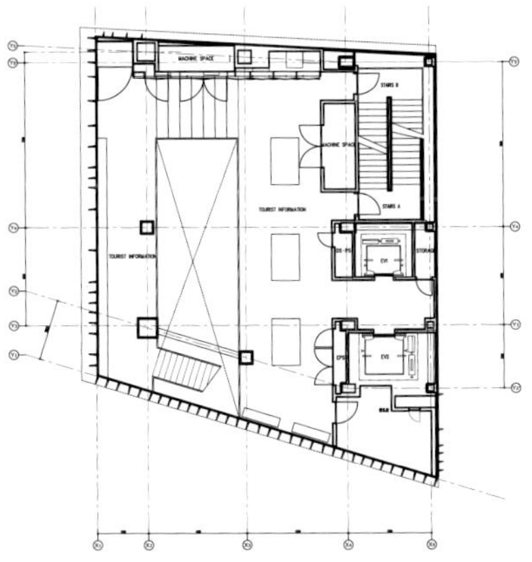

Second Floor

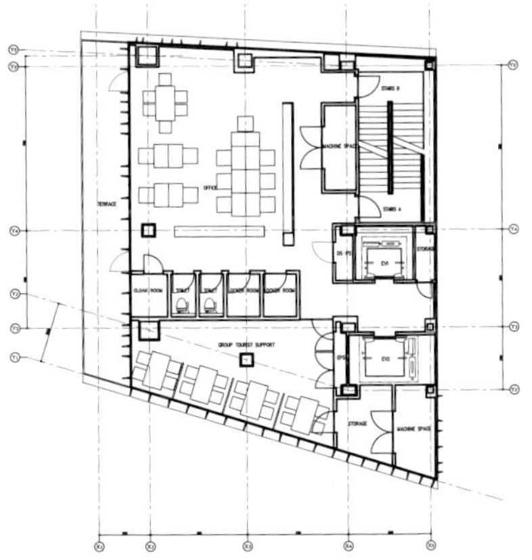

Third Floor

Fourth Floor

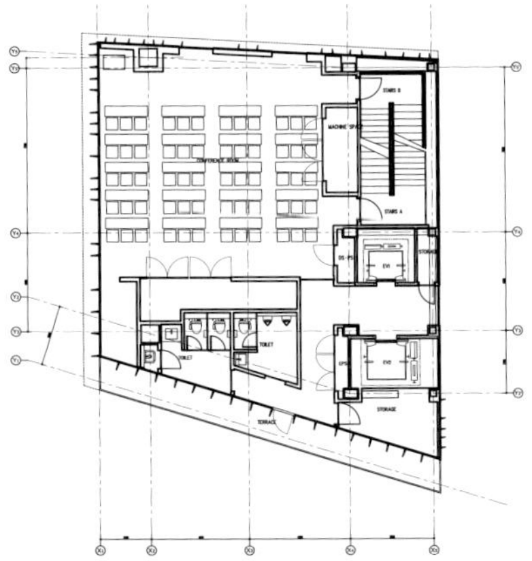

Fifth Floor

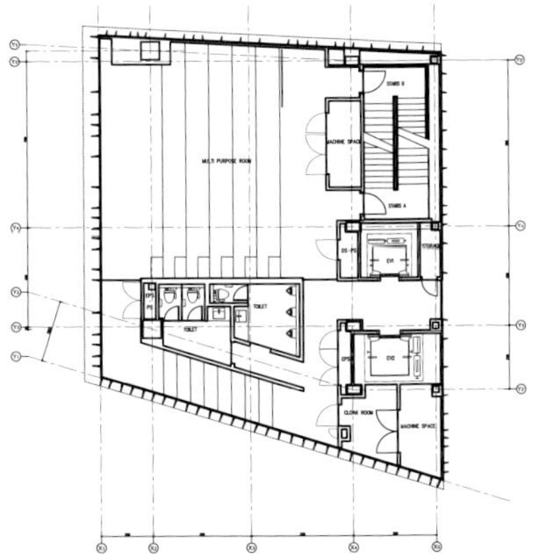

Sixth Floor

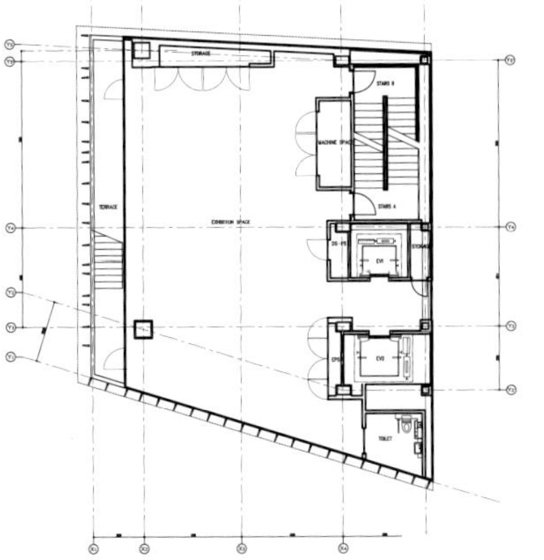

Seventh Floor

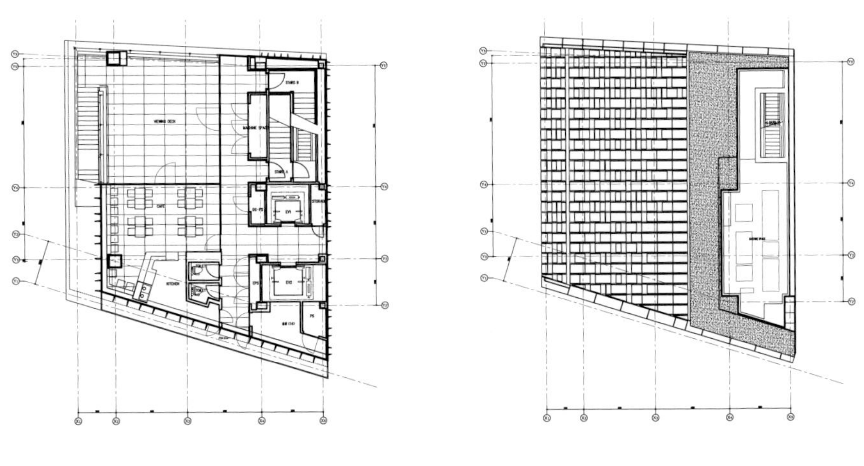

Eighth Floor

Roof

WOOD 6: SUNNY HILLS JAPAN

Completion year: 2013
Location: Tokyo, Japan
Structure: RC/SRC (reinforced concrete / steel-reinforced concrete)
Building type: retail

We utilized a traditional Japanese wood joint system called "jigoku gumi" to craft a space that feels as soft and warm as a forest or cloud. This 3-D structural system allowed us to reduce the cross section of each wooden member to just 60 × 60 mm, akin to thin branches. These same slender wooden members that structure the space might also be used to taste pineapple cake made from selected ingredients.

Exposing the complex structure at the top of the three-story building creates the appearance of an organic forest, offering a delightful surprise to passersby. This striking structure, emerging in the midst of the city, presents a very interesting and unexpected architectural feature.

The diagonal frame structure from the Starbucks Dazaifu project was expanded into three dimensions, enabling the construction of an 11.4 m high, three-story wooden structure using thin wooden members with a 60 × 60 mm cross section. The "jigoku gumi" system, traditionally used in crafting furniture, joinery, and small products due to its complex, strength-enhancing design, which achieves rigidity by overlapping three layers, served as the basis for combining the diagonal members. The adaptation of this intricate woodworking technique to a building was made possible through advanced 3-D CAD analysis and seamless data exchange with the structural engineer, Jun Sato.

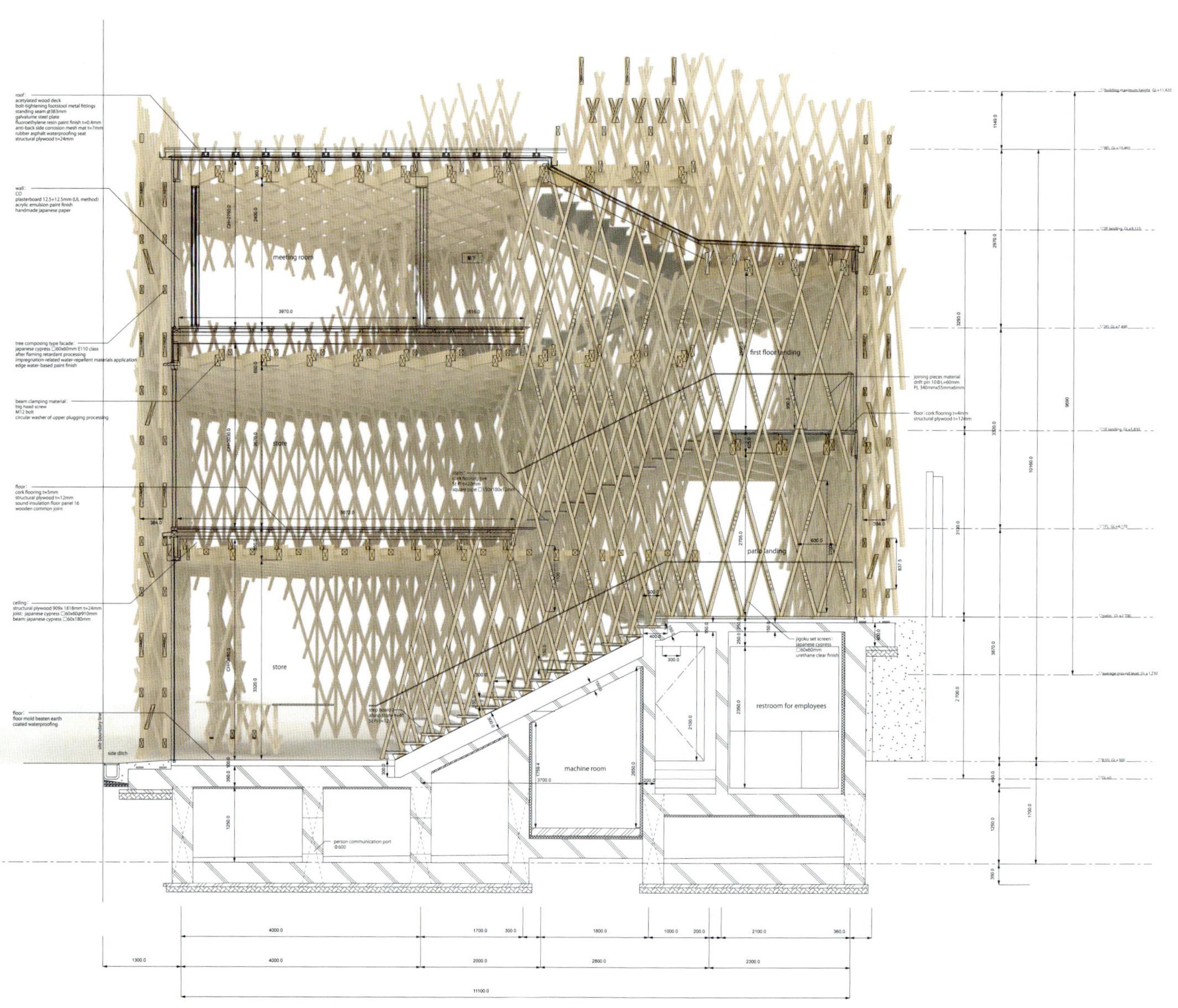

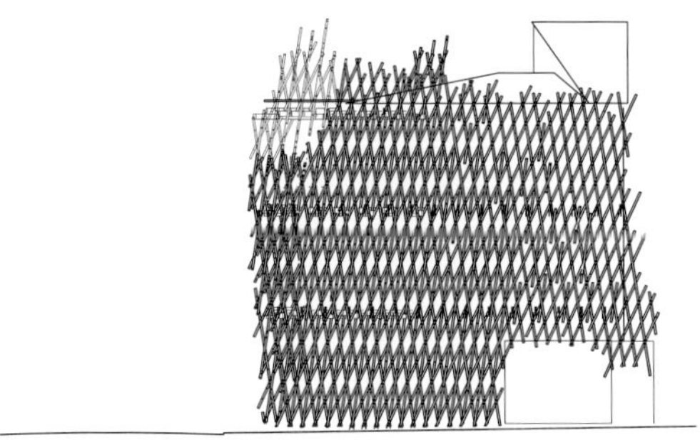

North Elevation

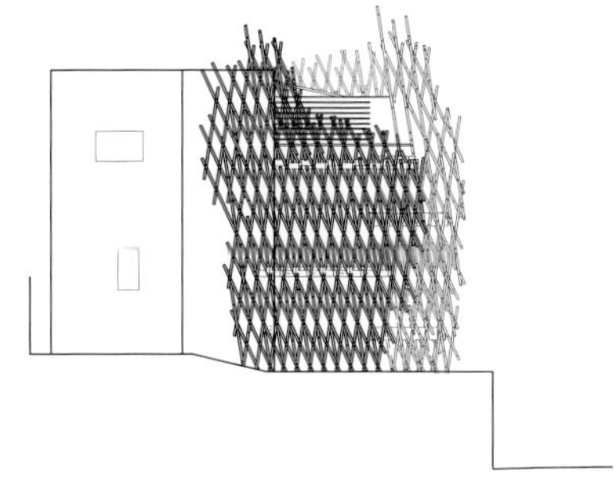

South Elevation

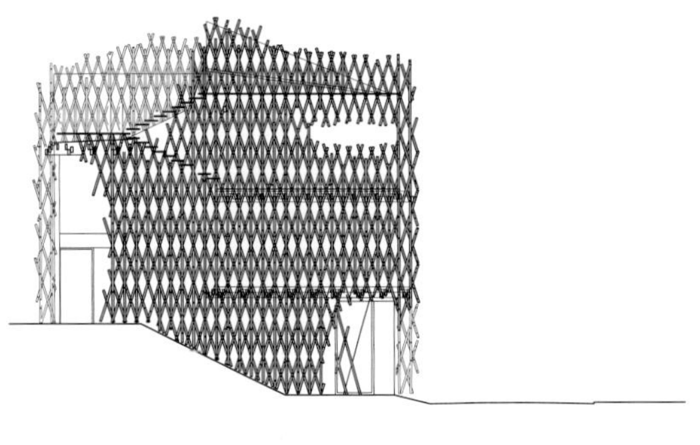

East Elevation

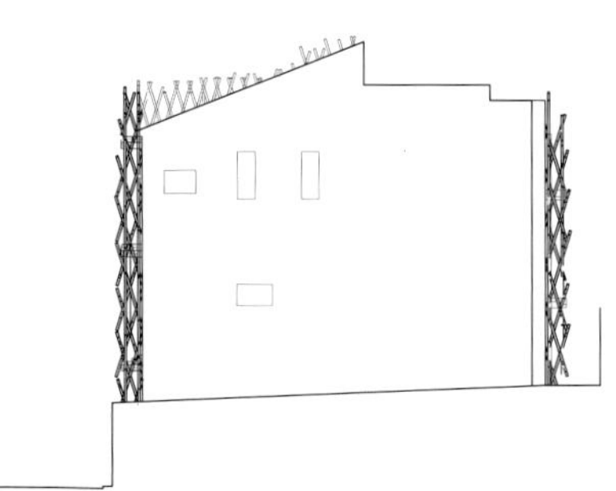

West Elevation

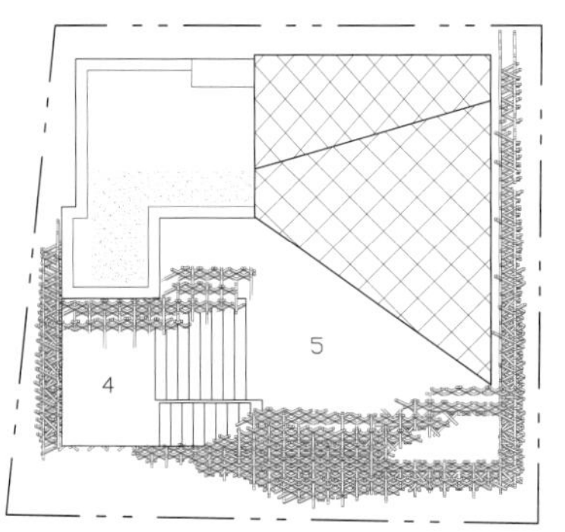

Roof Floor

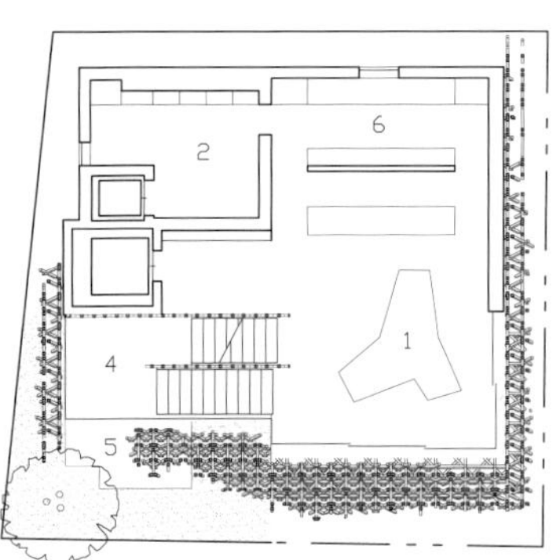

First Floor

1. Store
2. Storage
3. Parking
4. Stair landing
5. Terrace
6. Pantry
7. Meeting room
8. Restroom
9. Office

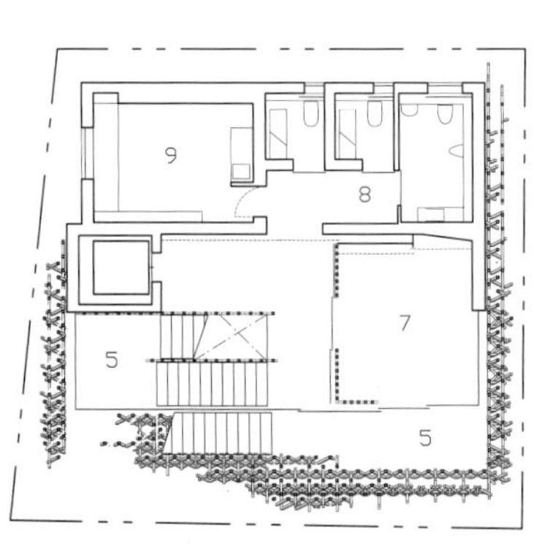

Second Floor

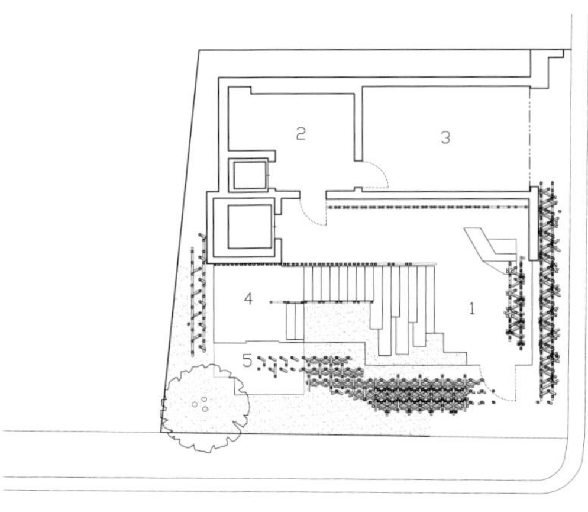

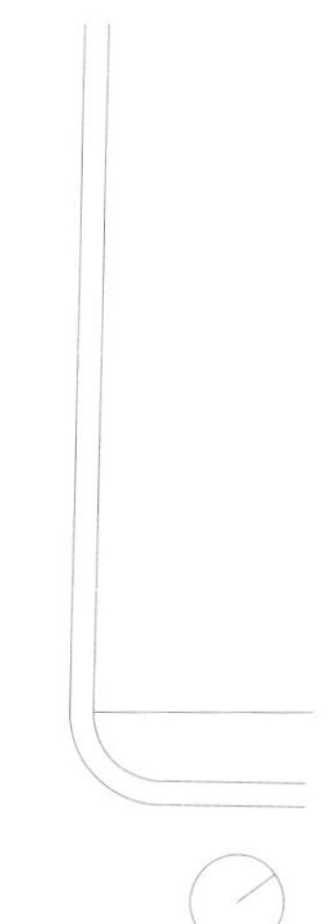

Ground Floor

WOOD 7: UNIVERSITY OF TOKYO, UBIQUITOUS-COMPUTING RESEARCH BUILDING

Completion year: 2014
Location: Tokyo, Japan
Structure: steel
Building type: educational

This building was constructed for the university's new field of research on ubiquitous computing. Our aim was to break away from the conventional image of campuses that consist of hard materials such as concrete, metal, or stone, and instead to design a soft building made with wood and earth. Here, scalelike panels of natural materials (wood and earth) gently undulate to form a smooth and organic façade.

At the center of the building comes an organ-like aperture covered with a soft membrane. It joins the lane in the front and the Japanese garden (part of the university president's guesthouse) at the back. The opening also generates a gentle and organic flow of light and wind in the campus, which is otherwise dominated by the strict grid arrangement.

In this project, which stands on the University of Tokyo campus, we attempted to create the accumulation of random lines in the scratch tiles with wooden planks.

The plan for the University of Tokyo campus created by Yoshikazu Uchida after it was destroyed by the Great Kanto earthquake (1923) fully utilized the scratched face tile that Frank Lloyd Wright used for the Imperial Hotel (1923). Wright had scratches made with a comb in the surface of the hard tiles, to give them a softness that is in harmony with the scenery in Japan. Furthermore, the mosaic façade created by Yoshikazu Uchida, which mixed various shades, resulted in the discovery of an organic sensation of unity that is created by the flocculating shadows made by the scratches.

The individual units, which were made by combining planks, were attached to the building in a manner that resembles fish scales. This fish-scale detail gently follows the twisting shape of the overall building. Overlaying panels in a fish-scale-shaped form is often used for traditional architecture in Japan, and we frequently try to resurrect this detail. Fish scales represent a great invention for the exterior skin of living things.

The exterior wall, which was made by combining wooden planks with various widths and gaps, also projects softness and warmth in harmony with the polychrome scratched face tiles. The randomness of the units was controlled by a computer, in an effort to optimize work and reduce costs.

Daiwahouse Nobuo Ishibashi hall
staircase
plaza
cafe
gallery
gallery
▽Penthouse
▽TOP
▽RFL
▽3FL
▽2FL
▽1FL(GL+90)
△GL
▽B1FL
▽B2FL
▽base
roof : asphalt waterproof
crest table : aluminum board non-stick
exterior wall : lightweight cement board ricin staining

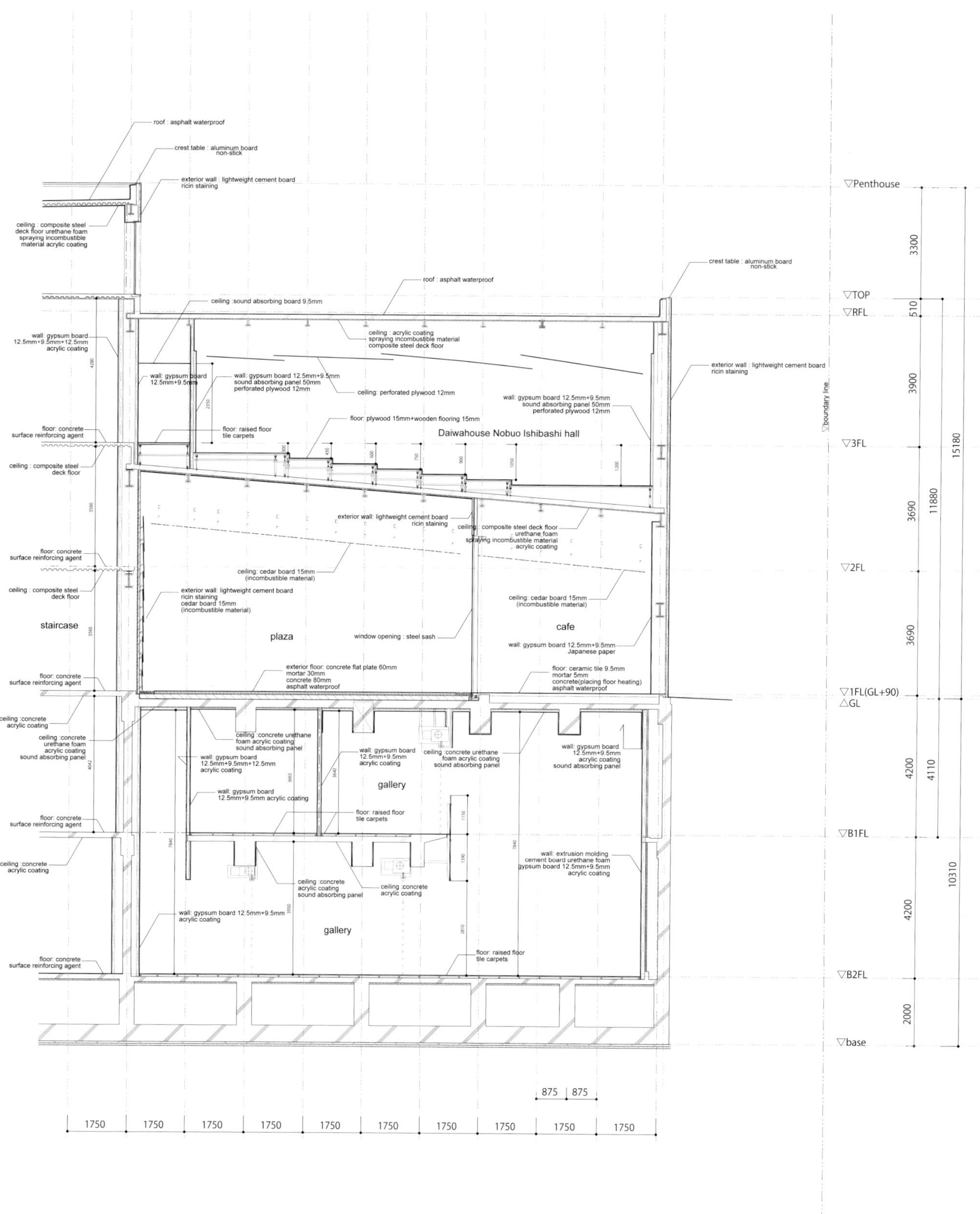

Section

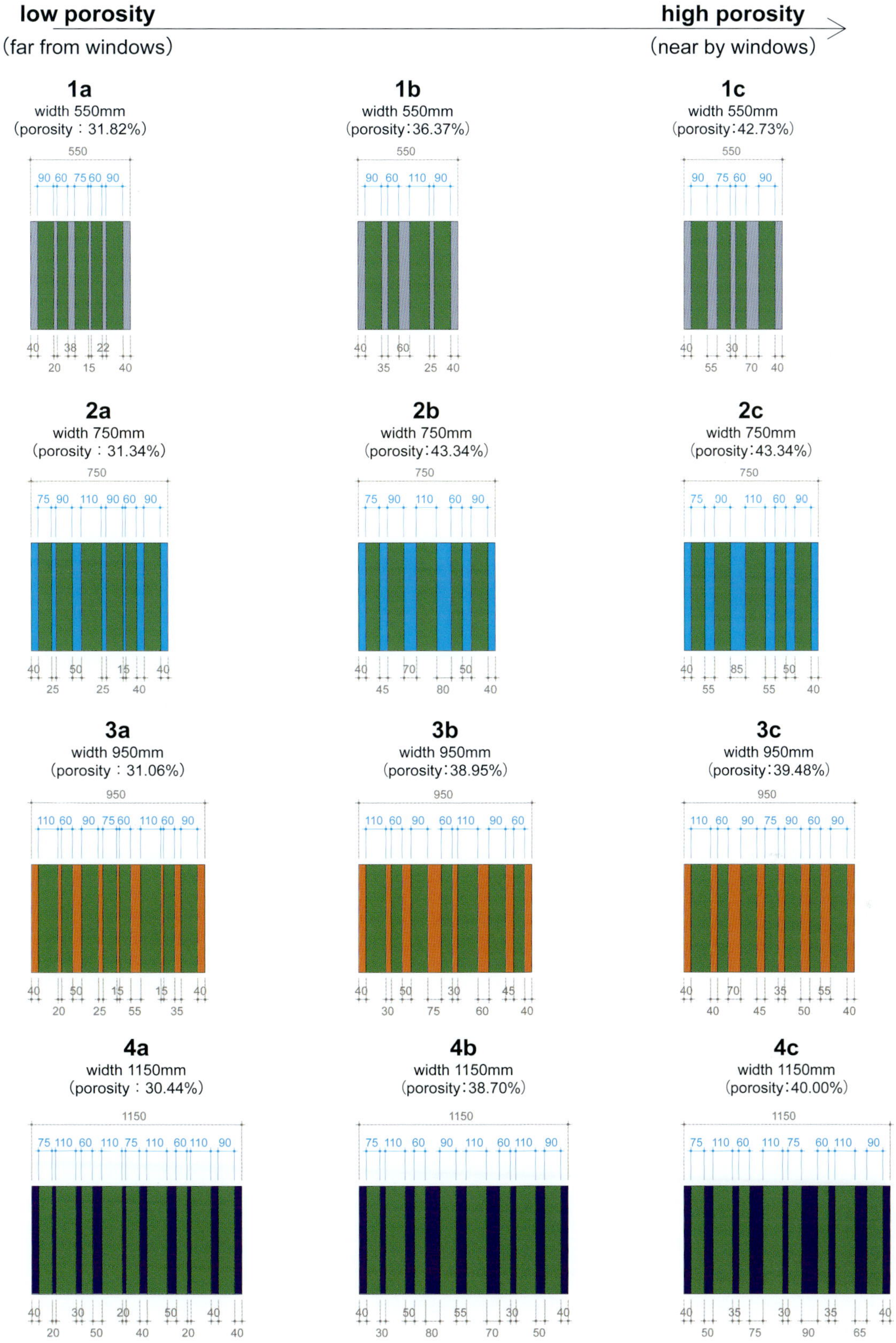

low porosity (far from windows) → **high porosity** (near by windows)

1a
width 550mm
(porosity : 31.82%)

1b
width 550mm
(porosity:36.37%)

1c
width 550mm
(porosity:42.73%)

2a
width 750mm
(porosity : 31.34%)

2b
width 750mm
(porosity:43.34%)

2c
width 750mm
(porosity:43.34%)

3a
width 950mm
(porosity : 31.06%)

3b
width 950mm
(porosity:38.95%)

3c
width 950mm
(porosity:39.48%)

4a
width 1150mm
(porosity : 30.44%)

4b
width 1150mm
(porosity:38.70%)

4c
width 1150mm
(porosity:40.00%)

※ Red dimension lines indicate width of cedar boards.
※ Gray dimension lines indicate width of vacancy.

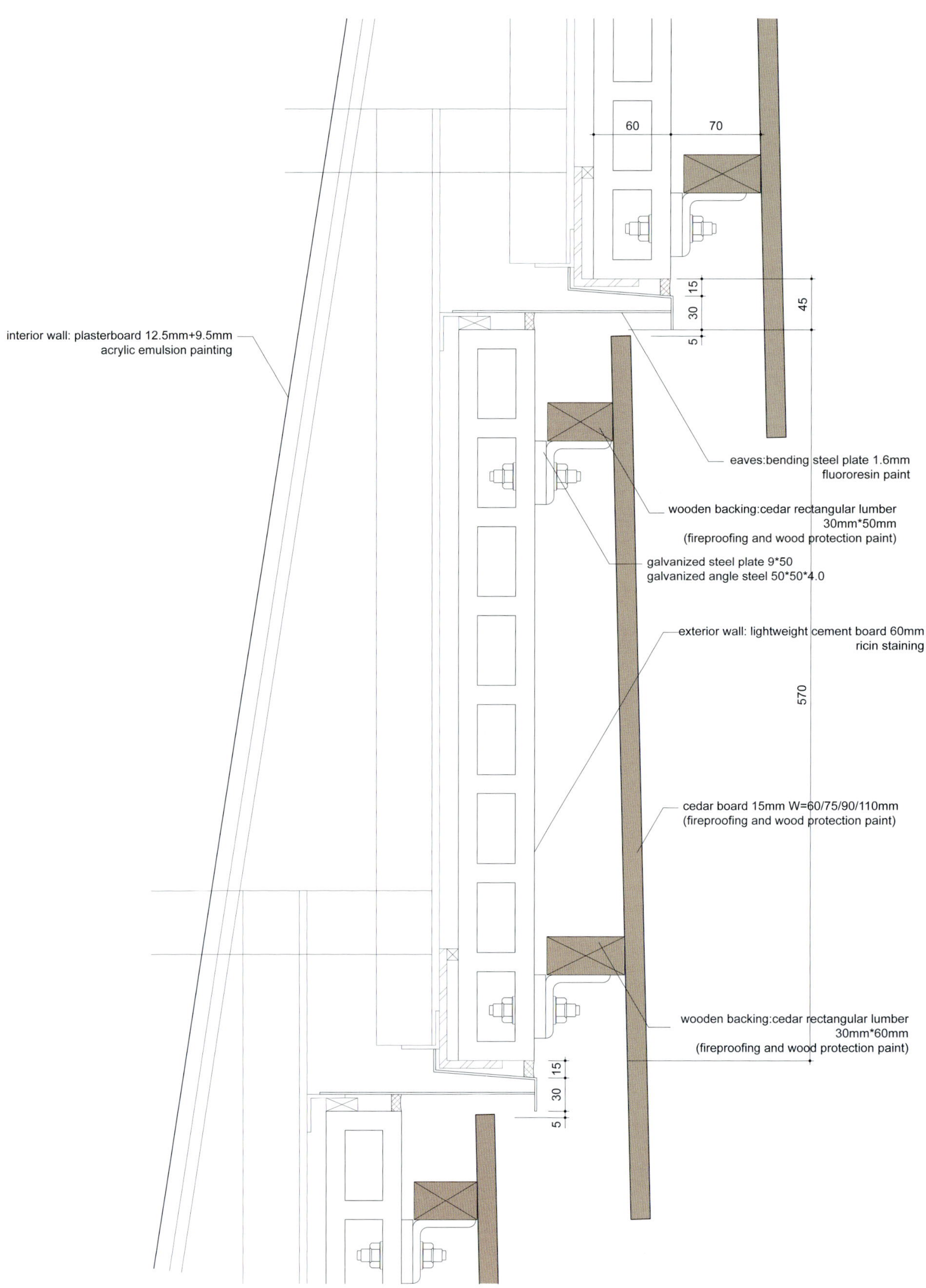

Section Detail: Cedar Board

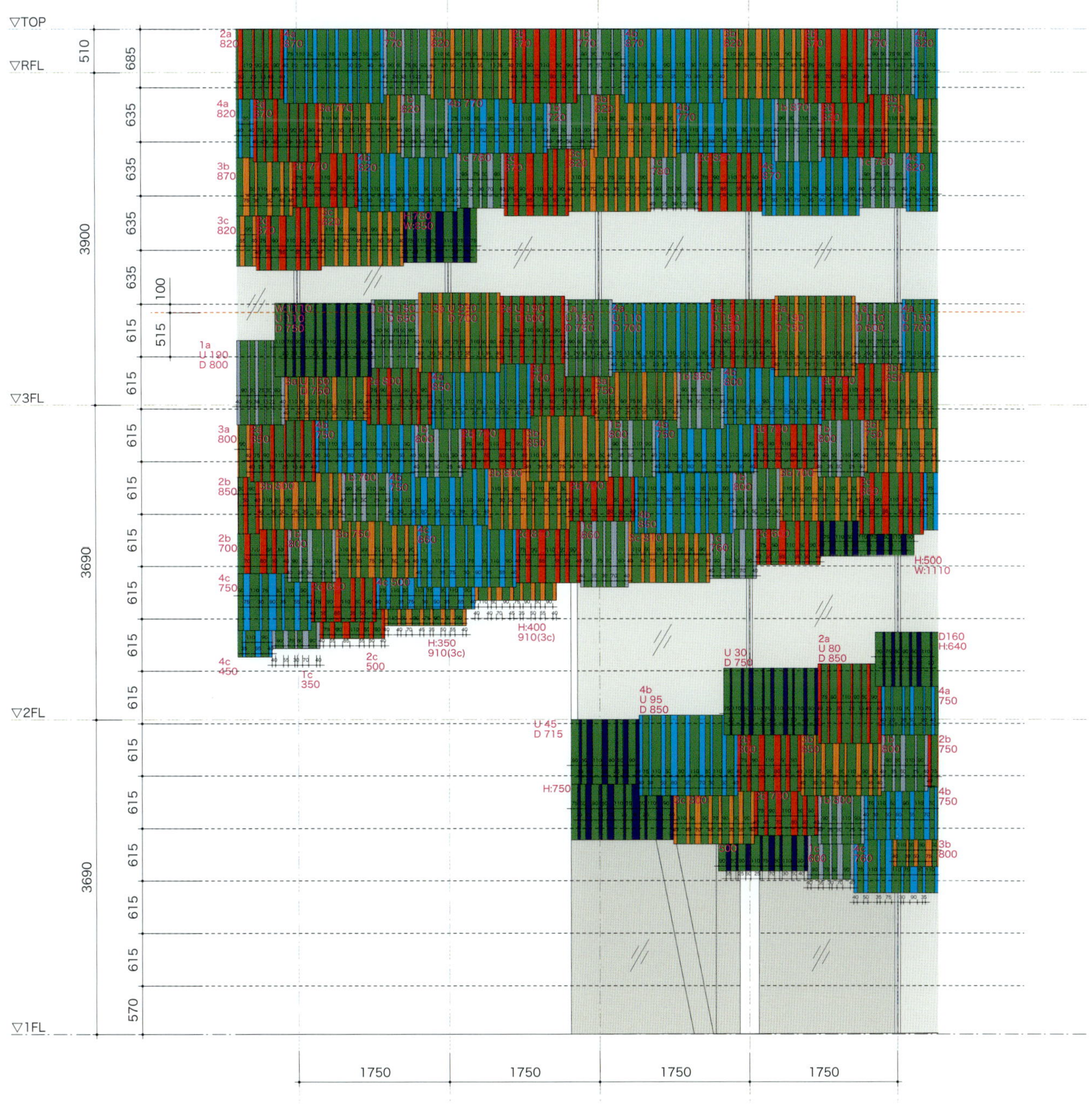

※ 'D' indicates height of downside of broken line.

※ 'U' indicates height of upside of broken line.

※ Green units are exceptions of 12 provisions patterns.
They are adjustment units of edge.

WOOD 8: COEDA HOUSE

Completion year: 2017
Location: Shizuoka, Japan
Structure: wood, steel
Building type: café

Randomly stacking 8 cm square cedar boards, we made a huge treelike structure. Reinforcing with a carbon fiber rod (with a tensile strength seven times that of iron), it becomes possible to have a single trunk with large branches while still diminishing movement during earthquakes. The site lies on a cliff overlooking the Pacific Ocean, and due to the treelike form we were able to eliminate columns at the perimeter, which would otherwise obscure the landscape.

First, members with a 100 × 100 mm cross section were cut, using an electric saw. Then, an electric planer was used to gradually plane the four sides until the final 80 × 80 mm cross-section members, free from warpage and twist, were achieved. This careful process prevented twisting in these 8 m long, extremely slender 80 × 80 mm members.

The innovative method of using carbon fiber to suspend the clip bar at the leading end was developed by Norihiko Ejiri, a leading expert in the seismic reinforcement of national-treasure wooden structures. Ejiri has employed carbon fiber to reinforce notable structures such as Kiyomizu Temple in Kyoto and Zenkoji Temple in Nagano. Steel, with its high specific gravity and heaviness, is generally unsuitable for reinforcing wooden structures. By using carbon fiber, which is significantly lighter than steel and possesses several times its strength, Norihiko Ejiri pioneered a new approach to reinforcing traditional structures in Japan. This novel method, initially developed for existing structures, was applied to a newly built wooden structure in this project.

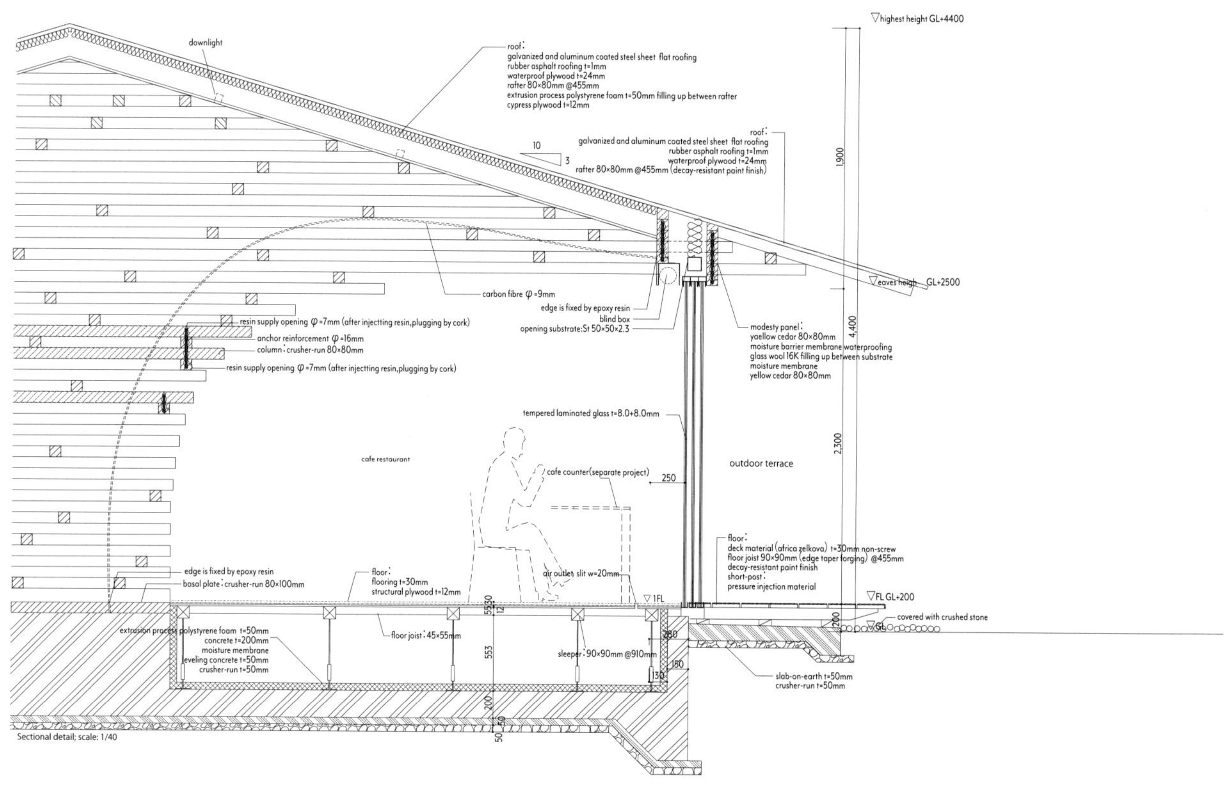

Sectional detail; scale: 1/40

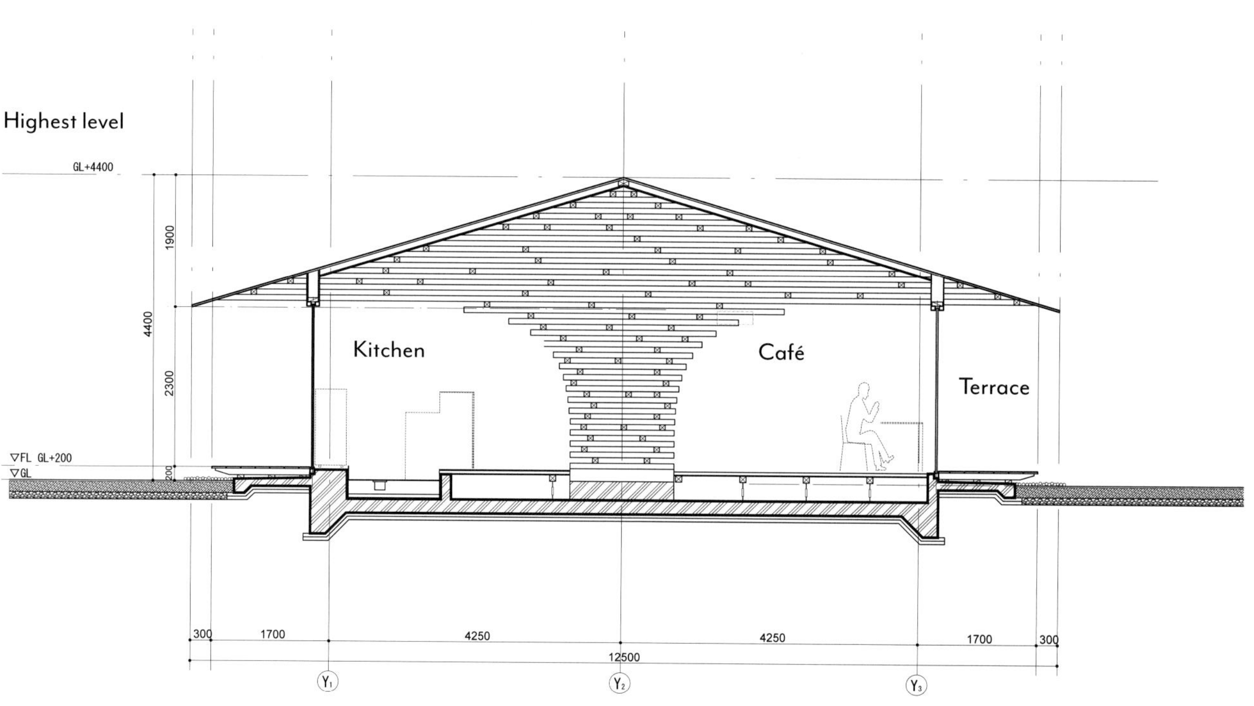

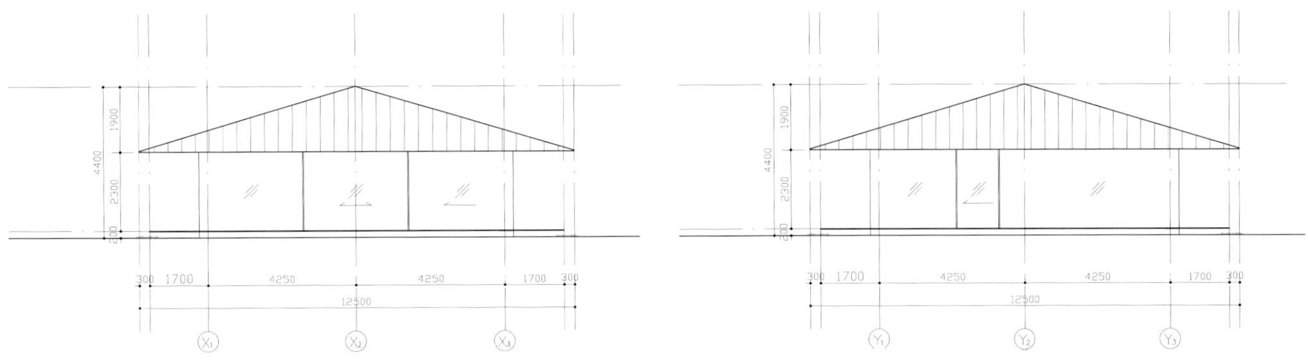

Elevations

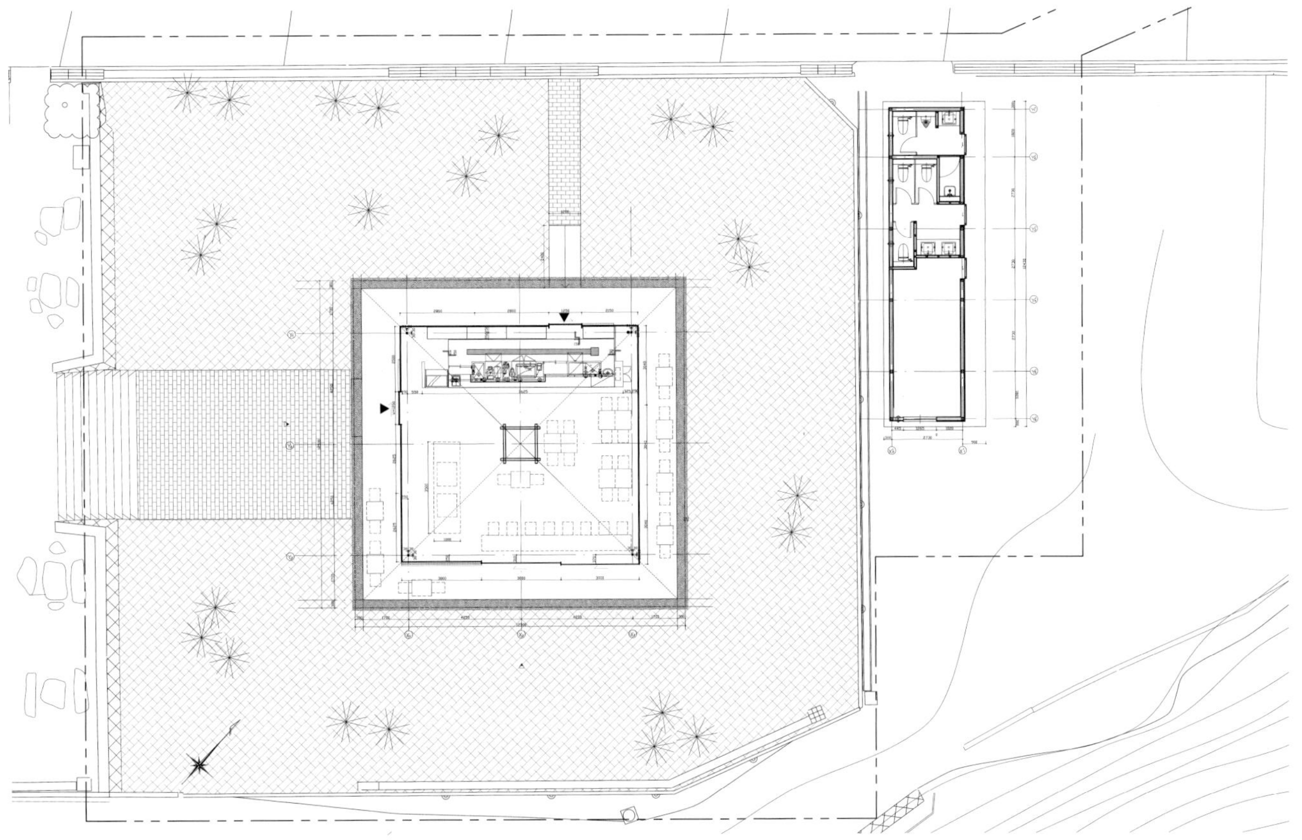

Plan

WOOD 9: JAPAN NATIONAL STADIUM

Completion year: 2019
Location: Tokyo, Japan
Structure: steel, RC/SRC (reinforced concrete / steel-reinforced concrete)
Building type: stadium

This large stadium was designed as a collection of small-diameter pieces of wood. The façade consists of overlapping, multilayered eaves. The underside of each eave is covered with small-diameter wood louvers, in an effort to express the tradition of beautiful eaves in Japanese architecture in an appropriately modern manner.

Square cedar lumber measuring 105 mm, the most common size in Japan, was split into three 50 mm pieces to create these louvers. The frequency and density of the louvers were varied to give a human scale to the eave.

The roof has a truss structure that combines steel beams and laminated lumber with a medium cross section, utilizing the axial stiffness of wood to minimize deformation of the roof trusses due to wind or earthquakes.

In the West, large wooden structures often utilize laminated lumber with substantial cross sections, such as beams 1 m in height. In contrast, we embraced the challenge of using laminated lumber with smaller cross sections and thin planks to create a large-scale wooden structure that embodies a uniquely Japanese, human-scaled modesty.

For the roof, cruciform-cross-section beams were crafted from steel plates, and laminated lumber with a 300 × 300 mm cross section was inserted from all sides to achieve a hybrid steel-and-wood structure. Typically in such mixed structures, the prominence of steel beams and their strong visual impact can diminish the wood's presence. However, in this design the wood conceals the steel plates, enhancing the wood's visual impact and imparting a softer, warmer feel.

Additionally, the use of a mixed wood-and-steel structure reduces the overall load, decreasing foundational costs and minimizing the increase in total costs associated with using wood. Moreover, constructing most of the foundation from precast concrete, manufactured off-site, shortened the construction period and reduced carbon dioxide emissions. Conventionally, South Sea wood is used for molds in on-site concrete pouring, leading to environmental concerns due to the destruction of South Sea forests. We addressed these issues by maximizing the use of factory-produced precast concrete to lessen the environmental impact.

The stadium's design includes a donut-shaped half that allows sunlight to nourish the natural grass on the field. The center along the longitudinal axis is narrowed by 3 m, creating a gentle arch that enhances seismic performance. This arch not only looks like a large wave but also forms an organically soft shape that harmonizes with the surrounding forest of the outer gardens of Meiji Shrine.

Transparent solar panels, resembling clear glass, cover the transparent portion of the donut-shaped roof. The energy generated by these panels is used to irrigate the plants integrated into the building's balconies. The plant boxes are crafted from brown fabric made with basalt, whose warm tones complement the cedar used on the exterior walls, enhancing the overall aesthetic harmony.

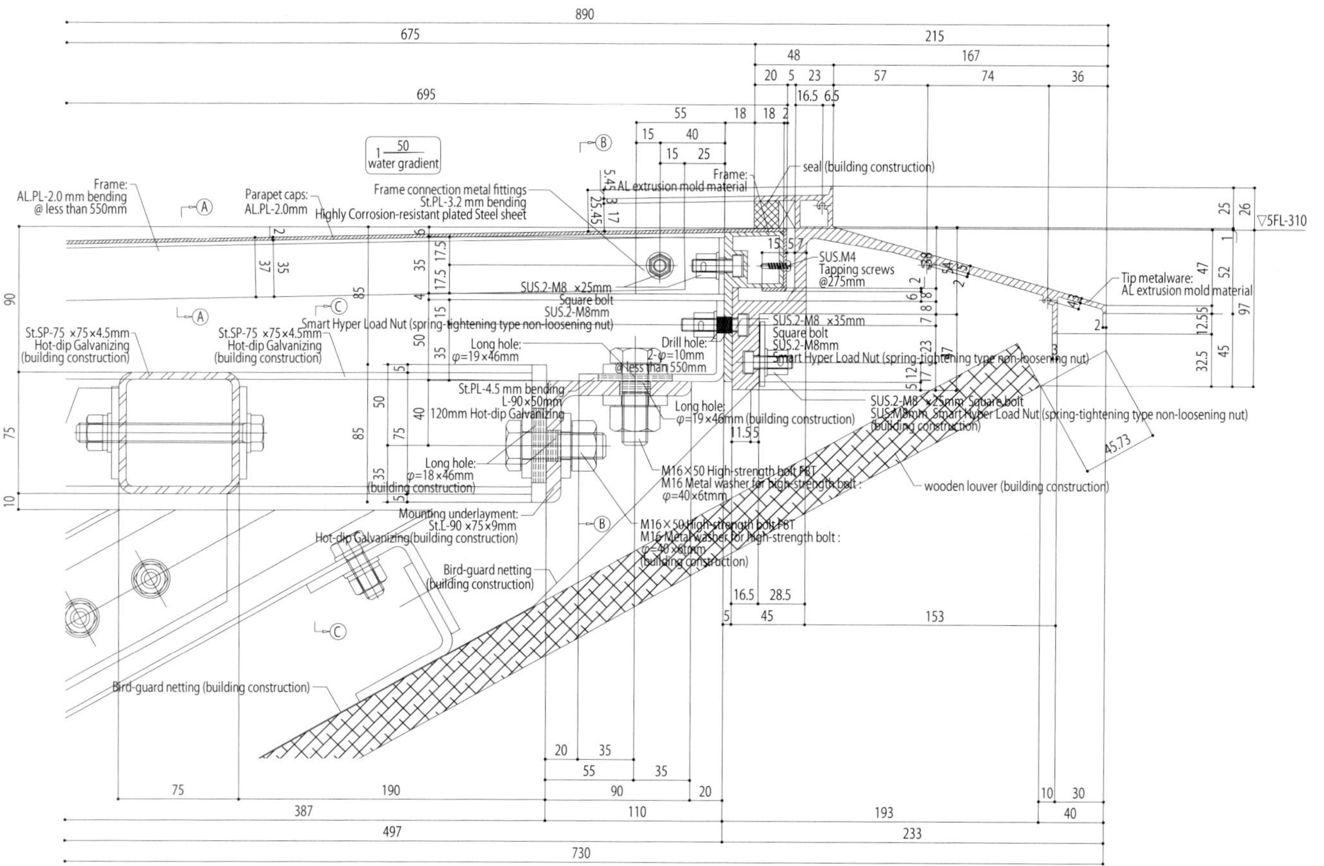

Sectional Detail of Eaves

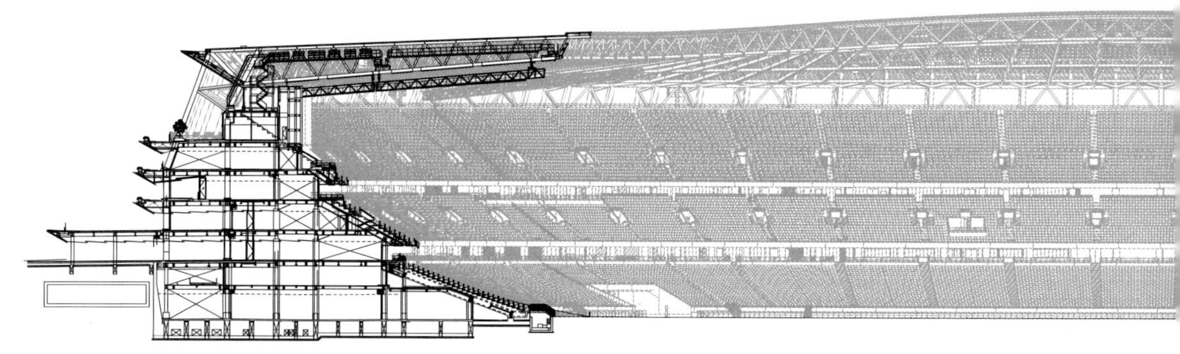

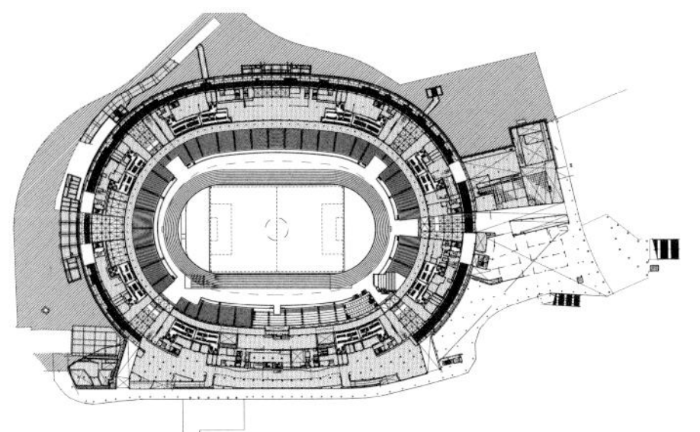

Basement 1 Floor

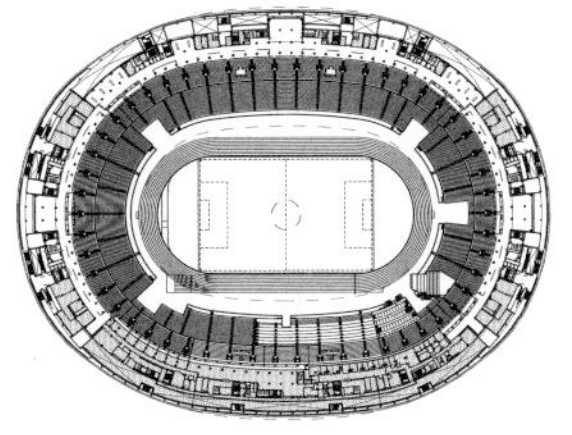

Third Floor

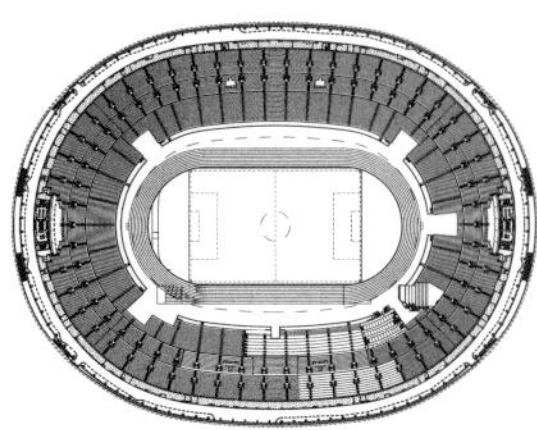

Fifth Floor

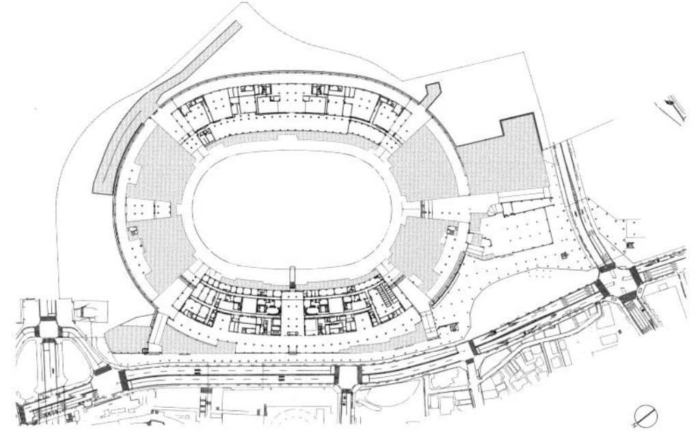

Basement 2 Floor

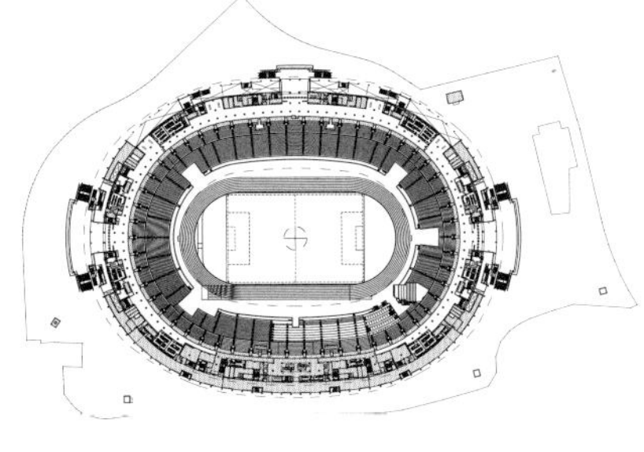

Second Floor

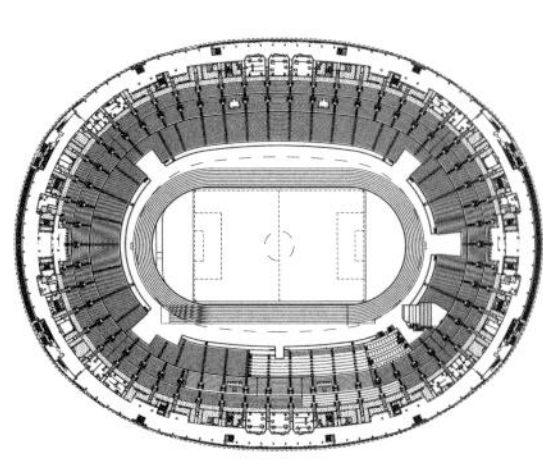

Fourth Floor

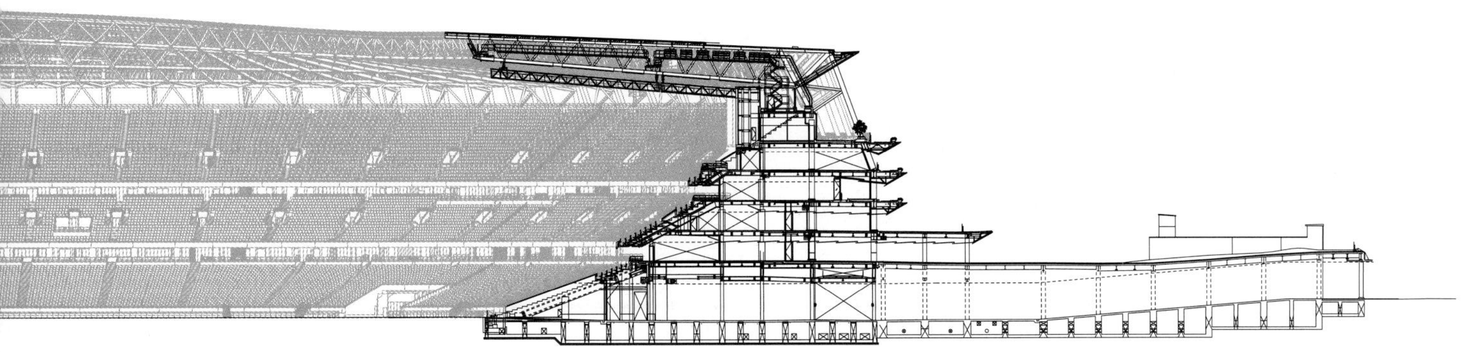

WOOD 10: THE EXCHANGE

Completion year: 2019
Location: Sydney, Australia
Structure: RC/SRC (reinforced concrete / steel-reinforced concrete), steel
Building type: commercial

This "wooden community center" is located in Darling Harbour, at the heart of Sydney's downtown district. The goal for this community center was to create a soft, warm, low-rise structure that integrates with the square, providing a contrast to the surrounding high-rise multidwelling buildings.

On the ground floor, food trucks are arranged randomly behind glass screens that open, blending seamlessly with the vibrant street community outside. The wooden, spiral-shaped façade extends into the square, transforming into a pergola that offers shade. The upper floors house a childcare center, library, restaurants, and other community necessities. Each floor is staggered to ensure unique views and varied terrace layouts.

The use of New Zealand pine that has undergone acetylation—a special preservation process—with a thickness of 30 mm and varying widths of 95, 120, 145, and 195 mm, allowed for the creation of a wooden façade with a soft impression. This material can be bent into gentle curves without the need for heat treatment.

The bent-pine material was assembled into panels measuring approximately 4.1 m and 4.7 m at a factory, then attached to flat steel bars on-site. The joints between the panels are almost imperceptible, contributing to a seamless visual continuity across the façade.

iag
DARLING
SQUARE
LIBRARY

The building is enveloped in a wooden screen made of "threads" wrapped around it in an irregular pattern, giving it a distinct appearance different from the neighboring high-rises. The bent accoya softwood members are placed randomly, overlapping in a way that conceals the joints on-site.

This design creates an interior space that resembles a silkworm cocoon, and a façade that looks like a bird's nest, offering an oasis amid the urban landscape.

We took on the challenge of integrating the wooden façade with the building, driven by the conviction that a primary urban issue is the disconnection of buildings from squares and other public spaces. The façade's orientation shifts from vertical to horizontal as it gently twists, eventually transforming into a pergola. This tail of the structure, resembling a large living entity, extends over the square, fostering a sense of unity between the softly enveloped building and the square.

Exploded Axon. | Façade System

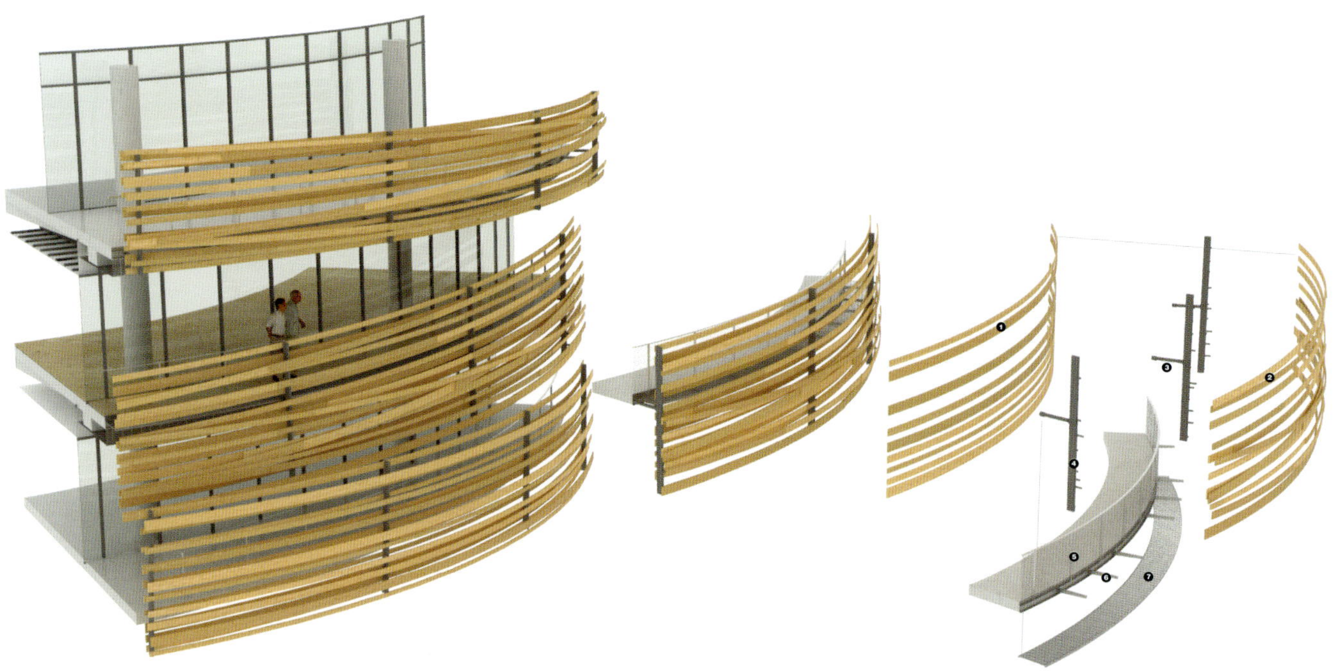

1. Inner skin: Wood stripes
2. Outer skin: Wood stripes
3. Facade system: Bracket support
4. Facade: Vertical support system
5. Handrail: Metal net
6. Grating: Bracket support
7. Grating: For maintenance access

North Elevation
South Elevation
East Elevation
West Elevation

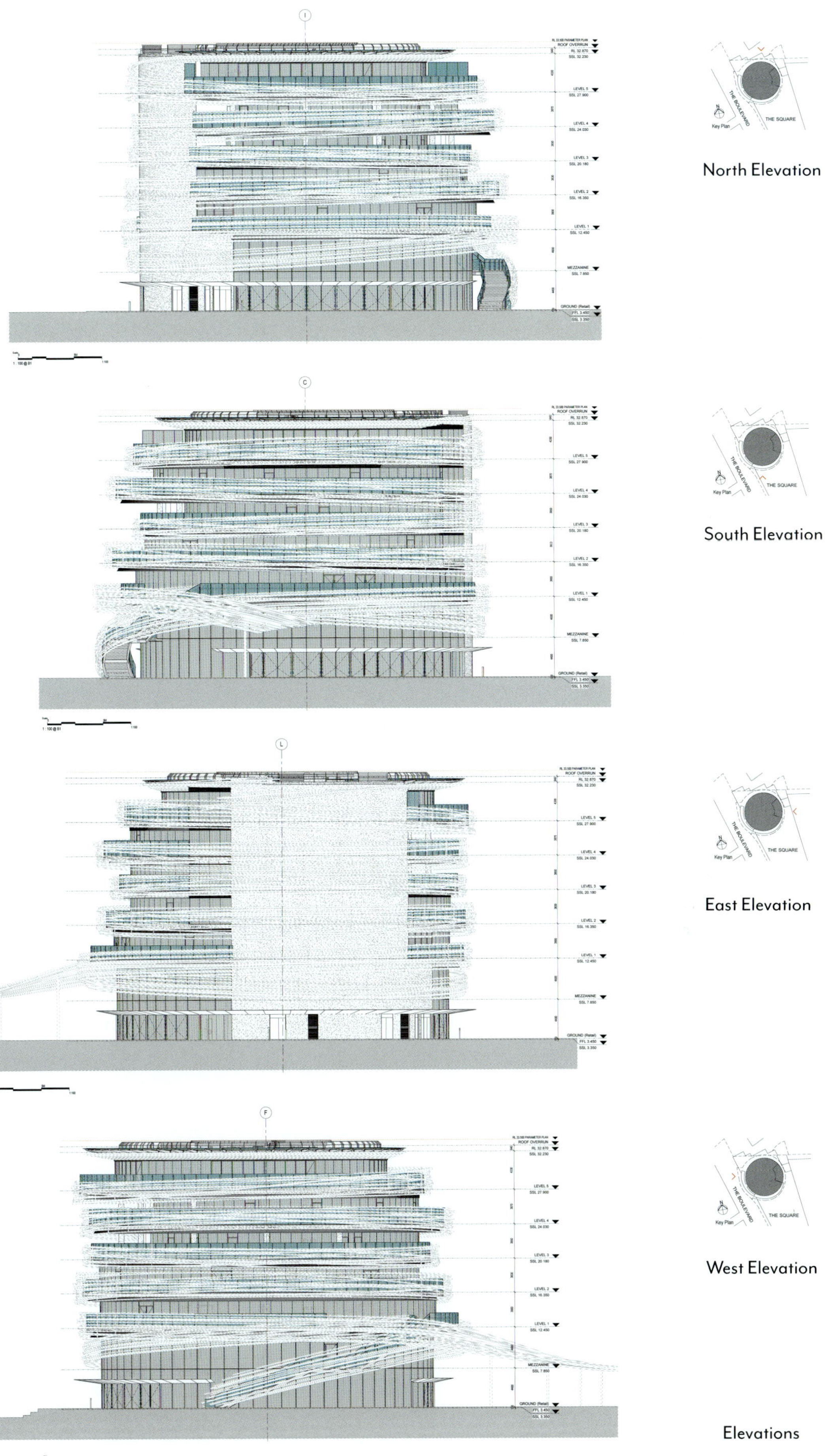

Elevations

WOOD 11: NAKABASHI

Completion year: 2020
Location: Miyagi, Japan
Structure: RC/SRC (reinforced concrete / steel-reinforced concrete), steel
Building type: bridge

Nakabashi is a footbridge symbolizing the restoration efforts in Minami Sanriku, a project we have been involved with since 2013. We designed the bridge as a place of prayer, linking the bustling Minami Sanriku Sun Sun Shopping Village with the Reconstruction Prayer Park, located at the former site of the disaster prevention office building.

The bridge serves multiple connective purposes. Crossing from the former disaster prevention office, one arrives at the Kaminoyma-Hachiman Shrine. In Japanese shrine architecture, bridges are traditionally seen as transitional spaces that separate and connect the ordinary world to the sacred realm. Nakabashi features a gentle arch, reminiscent of a typical "taiko" shrine bridge. Additionally, the bridge's arch is mirrored to form a lenticular truss structure, spanning 80 m. This design allows the upper chord to arch upward, offering a footpath with ocean views, while the mirrored lower chord dips close to the river's surface, integrating two distinct perspectives and experiences.

The bridge's primary structure is made of steel, with wood used both as a finishing material and as a supplemental structural element to minimize oscillation, enhancing the long-span structure's soft and warm character. All the wood employed is cedar from the local forests of Minami Sanriku, referred to as beauty cedar due to the attractive color of its surface. Approximately 50 cubic meters of this wood were used in the construction.

Tall wooden columns along the path to the lower footbridge span the gap between the upper and lower arches, a feature that local people have come to refer to as senbon-torii ("torii" shrine gates).

The integration of wooden elements with the steel structure not only prevents structural deformation but also enhances the bridge's warm, natural ambiance, befitting an "ocean town footbridge." Here, wood and steel are not just connected; they are interdependent, contributing to the structural integrity and aesthetic of the bridge.

The load capacity of the footbridge was set at 350 kg/m^2, supported by 37 mm thick deck boards designed to withstand this load. The edges of these boards were cut but left unfinished to expose their texture, creating a sense of floating lightness. For the floor joists, we used highly durable wood reinforced with long glass fiber plastic foam, known as marine lumber. These joists measure 90 × 90 mm, and a reduced pitch of 600 mm was chosen to further reduce floor oscillation.

The wooden columns, known as senbon-torii ("torii" shrine gates), rising from the deck are composed of a steel-and-wood composite. They play a crucial role in controlling the overall oscillation of the bridge.

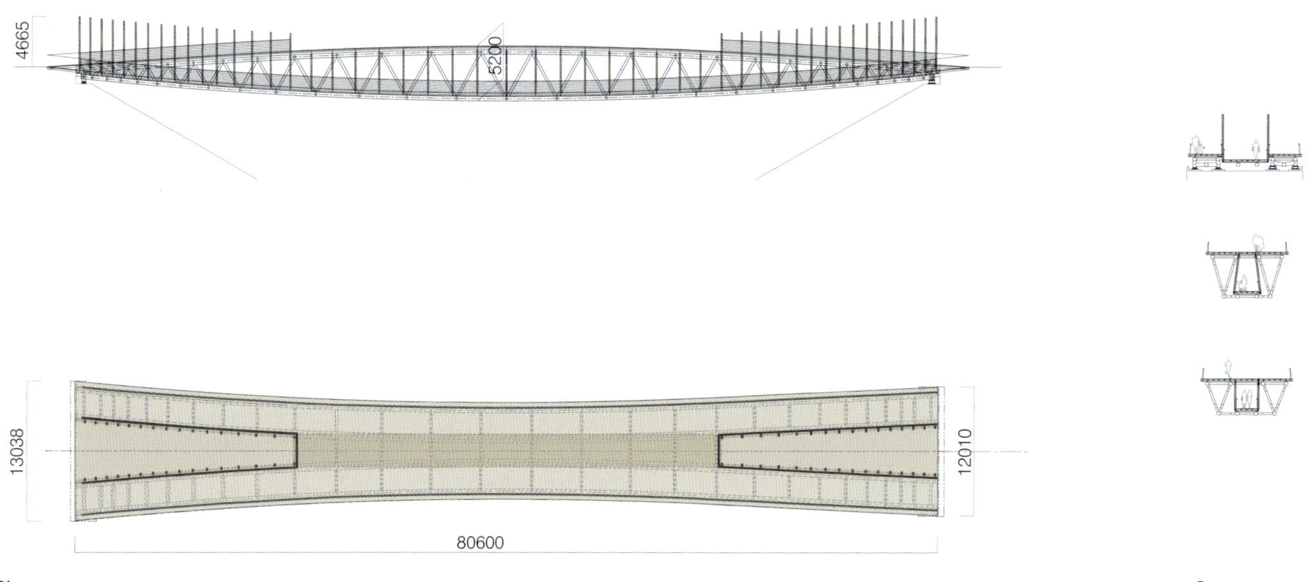

Plan

Sections

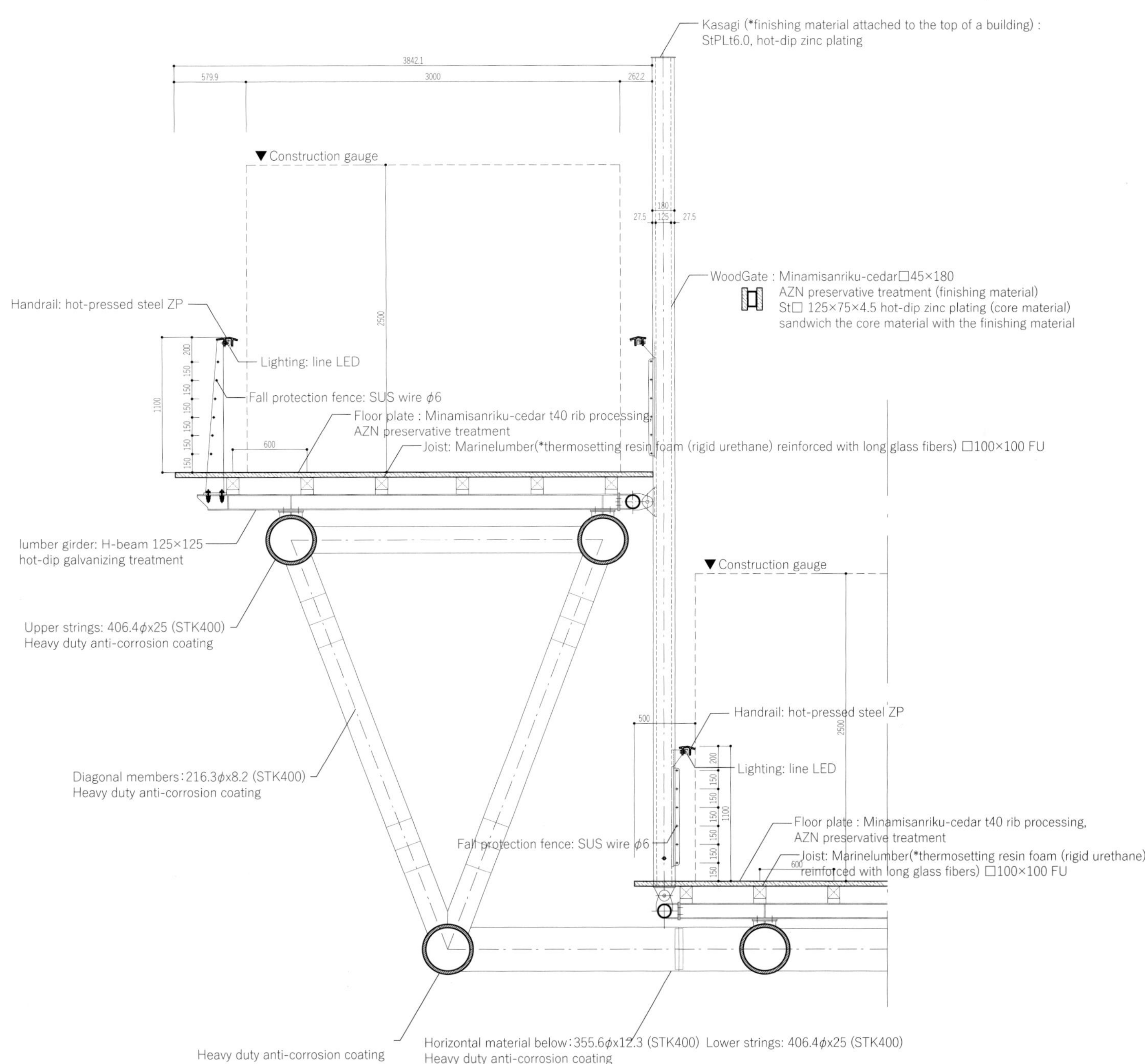

Section Detail

WOOD 12: THE WASEDA INTERNATIONAL HOUSE OF LITERATURE (THE HARUKI MURAKAMI LIBRARY)

Completion year: 2021
Location: Tokyo, Japan
Structure: RC/SRC (reinforced concrete / steel-reinforced concrete)
Building type: library

We renovated the Waseda University Campus Building #4 into the new Haruki Murakami Library by integrating a "wooden tunnel" that penetrates through the existing structure. This tunnel transcends time and space, echoing the tunnels in Murakami's novels that connect different dimensions into a tangible architectural form.

To highlight the new addition, we neutralized the original building by repainting the exterior walls white, which accentuates the three-dimensional wooden screen canopy. This canopy not only marks the entrance to the tunnel but also symbolizes the threshold between dimensions. The wooden tunnel itself, a vertical incision through the existing slab, functions simultaneously as a bookshelf, theater, and lecture hall.

While the twentieth century favored concrete, with its "hard" and "cold" qualities, we envisioned a tunnel for this library that offers protection and nurtures dreams, utilizing wood for its delicate and soft properties.

To achieve this lightness, the wood was shaved down to a thickness of 12 mm, allowing it to be bent into curves without heating. This process determined the overall shape. However, the design required twisting the wooden planks to connect the front and side eaves seamlessly, ensuring continuity between the main entrance and the café. The planks, oriented in different directions, were meticulously shaped to appear as if they are smoothly connected through a series of soft curves.

The wooden eaves added to the entrance were designed to be as light and transparent as possible while retaining the warm texture of wood, aiming to capture the literary world of Haruki Murakami, which hovers between dreams and reality.

For the supporting steel framework, the focus was on minimizing thickness to avoid loading the existing structure. The vertical load is supported by an independent foundation, with only horizontal steady strain transferred to the existing structure. This was achieved using a combination of unusually thin 60 mm and 40 mm diameter steel members, facilitating a design that typically poses significant challenges.

Large steps running through the central interior space, created by opening holes in two existing slabs, are covered with thin planks bent to conform to the space, evoking Murakami's recurring tunnel motif. To achieve the necessary thinness, 15 mm thick stainless-steel flat bars were bent and sandwiched between layers of 15 mm thick oak veneer on both sides, resulting in a final thickness of 25 mm. This construction creates the illusion that the structure is floating.

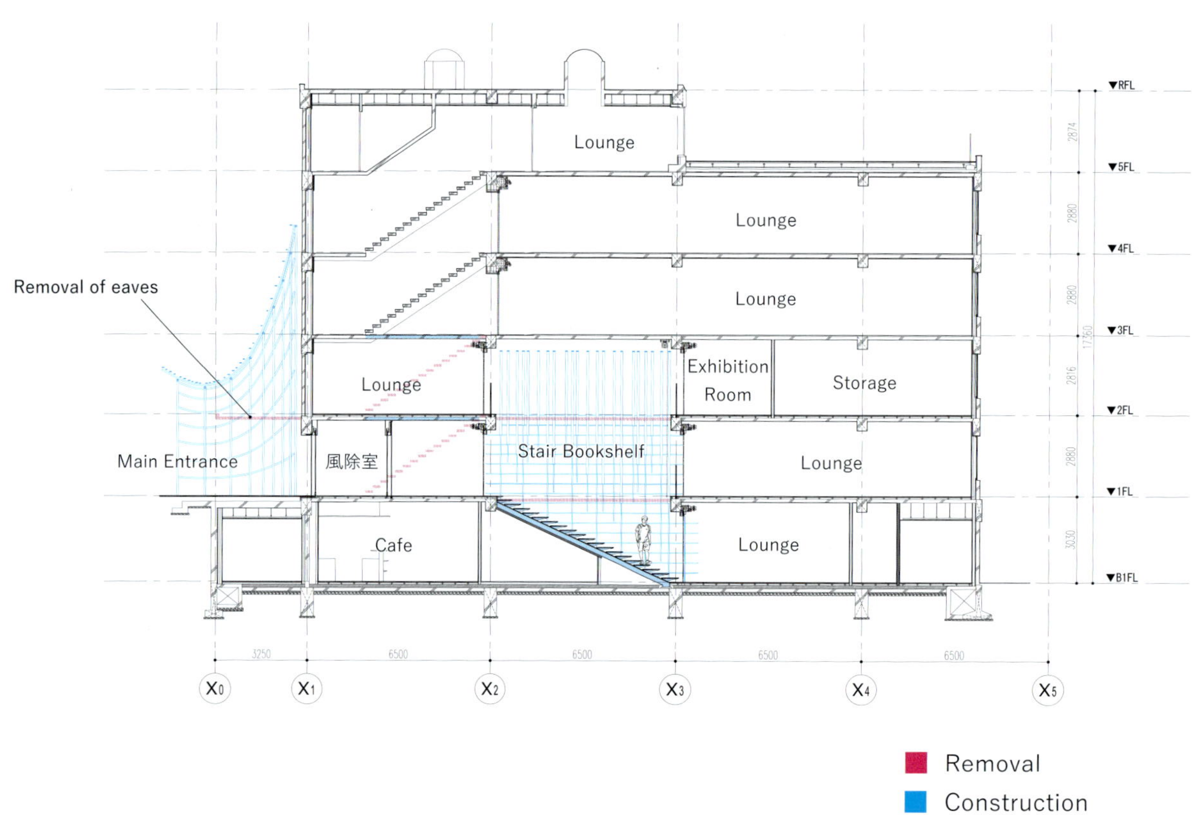

Lounge
Lounge
Lounge
Removal of eaves
Lounge
Exhibition Room
Storage
Main Entrance
風除室
Stair Bookshelf
Lounge
Cafe
Lounge
RFL
5FL
4FL
3FL
2FL
1FL
B1FL
X0
X1
X2
X3
X4
X5
Removal
Construction

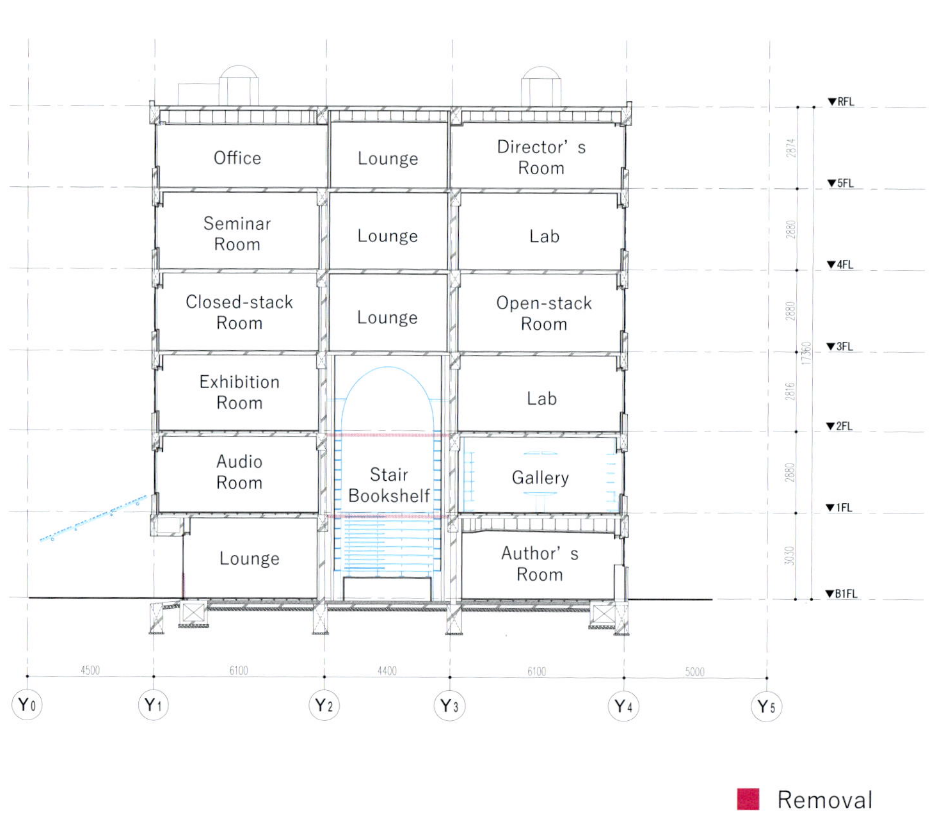

Office
Lounge
Director' s Room
Seminar Room
Lounge
Lab
Closed-stack Room
Lounge
Open-stack Room
Exhibition Room
Lab
Audio Room
Stair Bookshelf
Gallery
Lounge
Author' s Room
RFL
5FL
4FL
3FL
2FL
1FL
B1FL
Y0
Y1
Y2
Y3
Y4
Y5
Removal
Construction

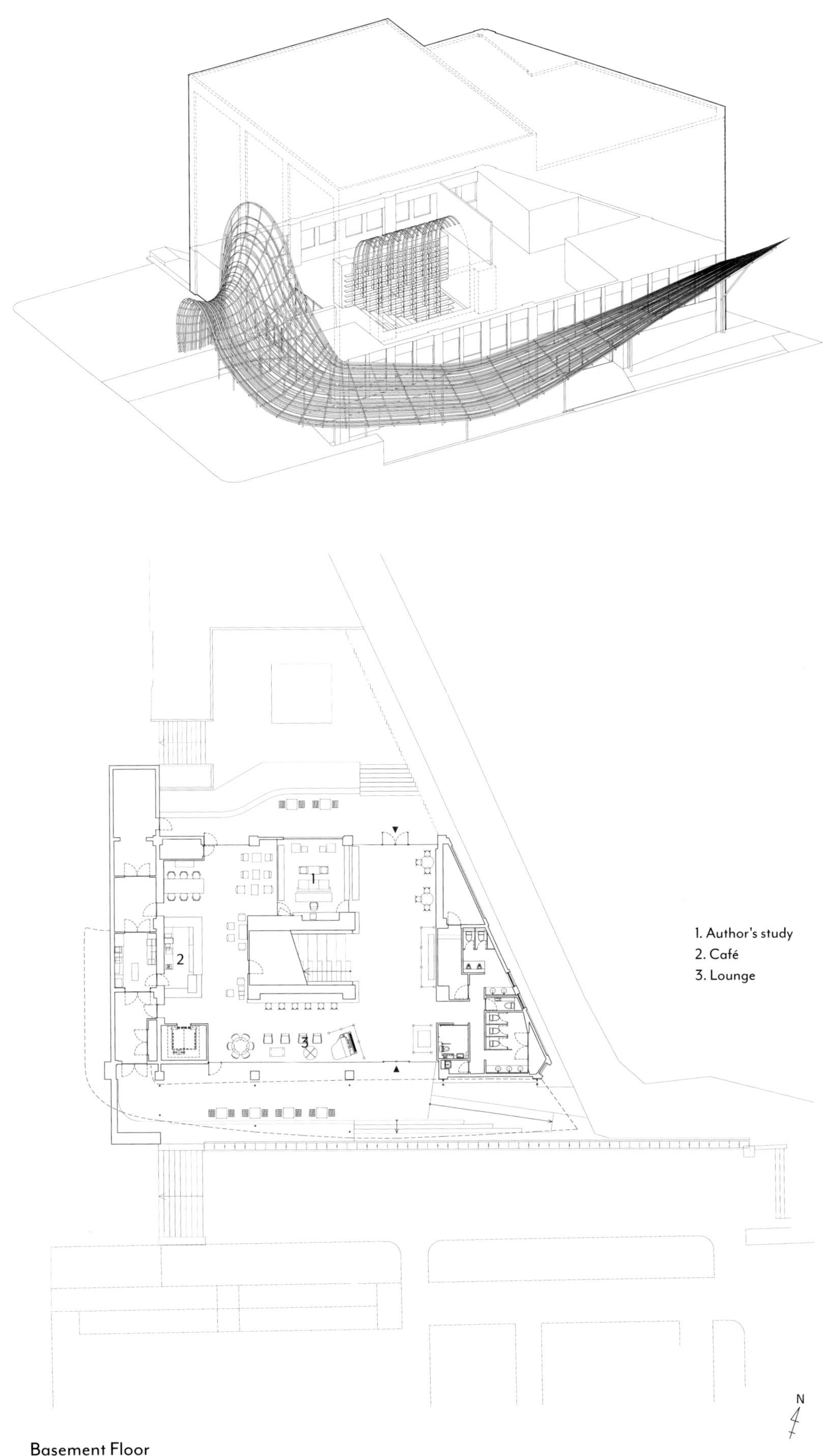

Basement Floor

1. Gallery
2. Bookshelf stairway
3. Information
4. Audio room
1
2
3
4
N
First Floor

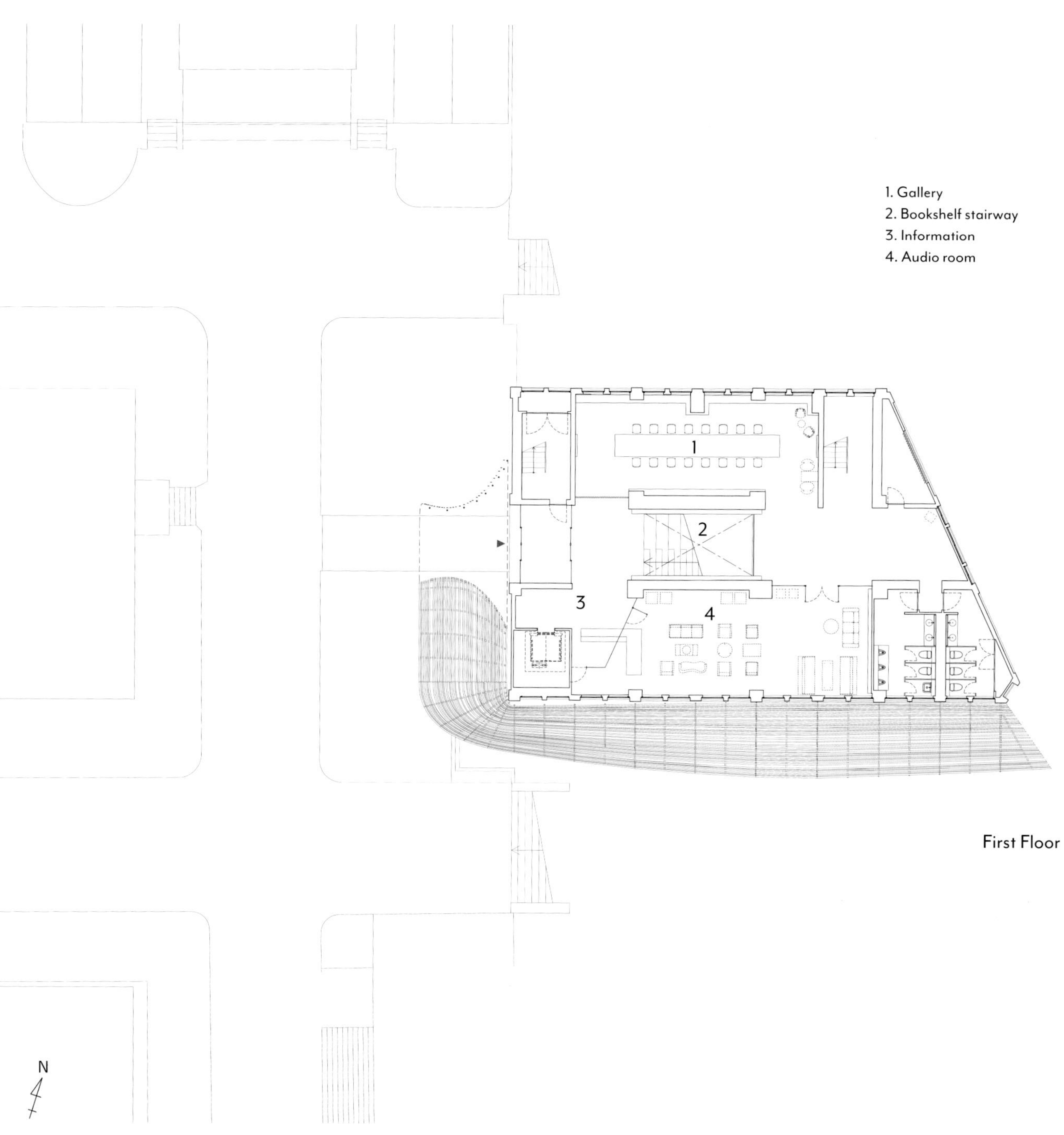

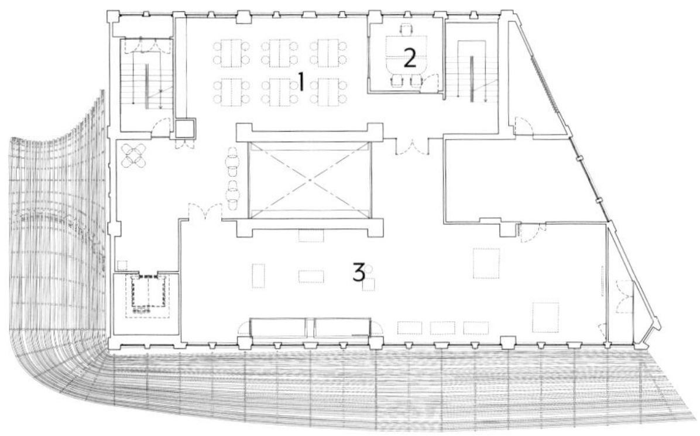

Second Floor

Fourth Floor

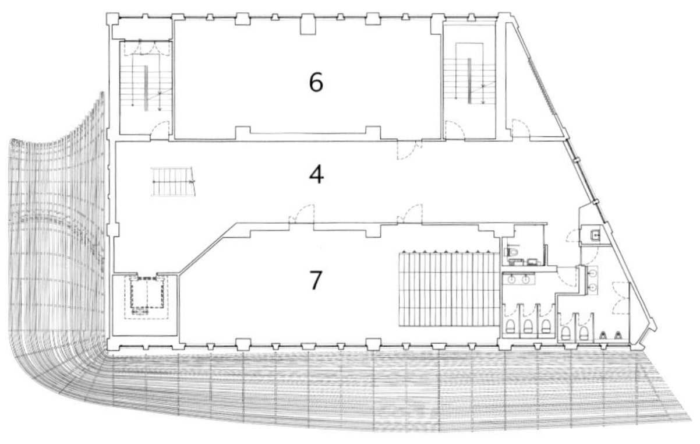

Third Floor

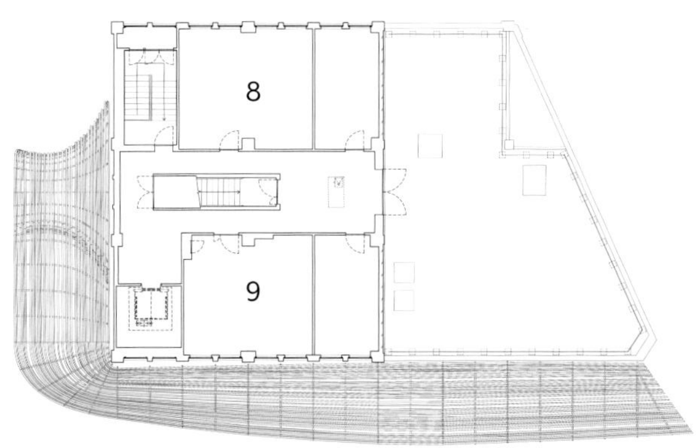

Fifth Floor

1. Lab
2. Studio
3. Exhibition room
4. Lounge
5. Seminar room
6. Open-stack room
7. Closed-stack room
8. Director's room
9. Office

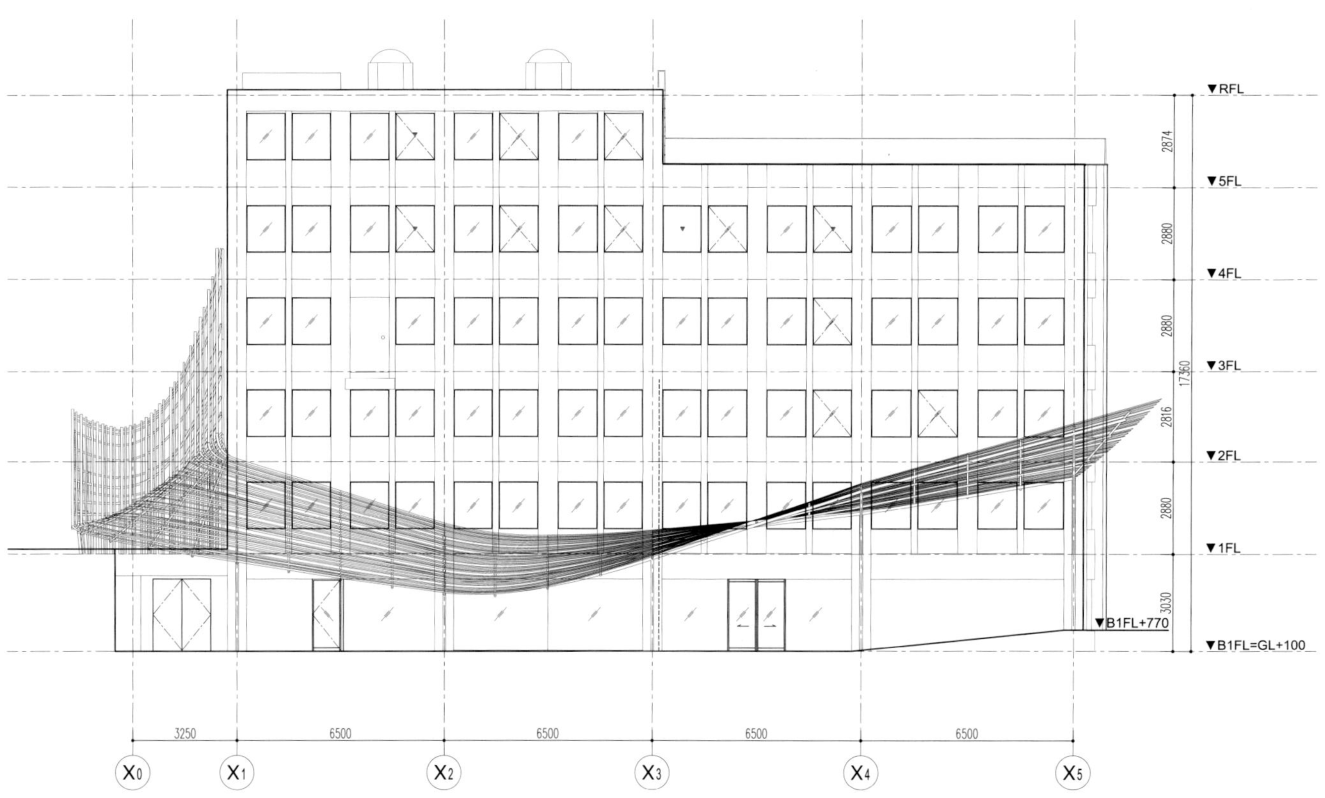

South Elevation

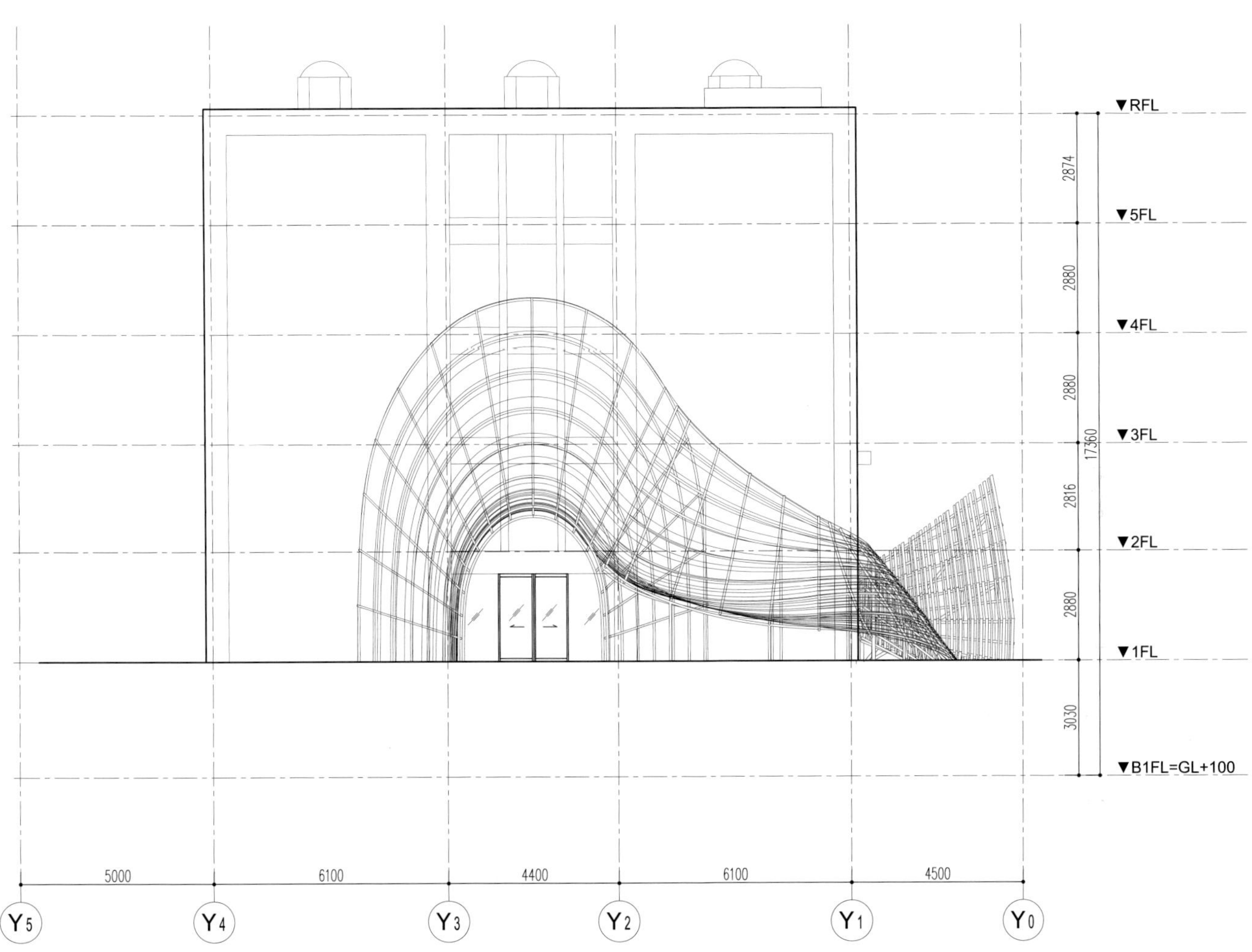

West Elevation

WOOD 13: ALBERT KAHN MUSEUM

Completion year: 2022
Location: Boulogne Billancourt, France
Structure: RC/SRC (reinforced concrete / steel-reinforced concrete)
Building type: museum

Located on the south side of the Bois de Boulogne in western Paris, this art museum was founded by Albert Kahn (1860–1940), a trading merchant who meticulously documented his global travels. Kahn amassed a remarkable collection comprising 72,000 color photographs and 183,000 m of film. These items, especially those capturing life in Asia, form the core of the museum's collection and hold significant historical and ethnographic value due to Kahn's keen interest in Japan and other Asian regions.

Kahn's dream was to re-create gardens from the five continents, with the Japanese garden, crafted by gardeners he brought from Japan, being a particularly notable feature. The museum's display space extends in a linear sequence from the paths through this garden.

The façade facing the garden is adorned with fine wooden horizontal louvers featuring a diamond-shaped cross section, chosen to complement the delicate design of the Japanese garden, where pebbles are a focal element. Unlike typical louvers with a rectangular cross section, these diamond-shaped louvers enhance the façade with sharp, distinct lines. Additionally, the mounting angle of the louvers has been adjusted, creating dynamically changing shadows that add depth and texture to the structure.

An innovative screen made of aluminum and wood bridges the gap between the path and the external environment, weaving horizontally and vertically to manage the interaction between the two. In this way, Kahn's vision of merging the garden with the display space is realized, harmonizing the environment with the architecture.

The building's façade facing the city is primarily aluminum, while the side facing the garden is predominantly wood. These materials sometimes blend in a gradational fashion, providing the structure with a "biological skin" that sensitively adjusts to and interacts with varying environments.

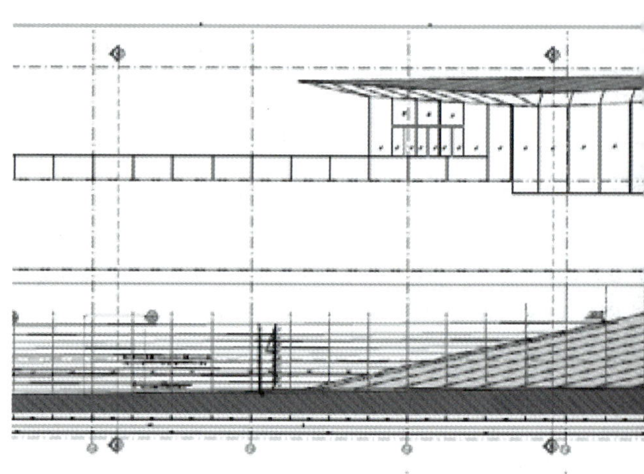

While screens made from fine bamboo sticks are commonly used in spaces adjacent to Japanese gardens, our design approach has facilitated the creation of an organic screen that captures a similar soft aesthetic. The louvers are affixed to the façade by using fine stainless-steel wires, a method selected to maintain the subtlety of the diamond-shaped louvers. This installation technique helps prevent the hardware from overshadowing the delicate louvers, unlike more-traditional mounting methods that use a base frame.

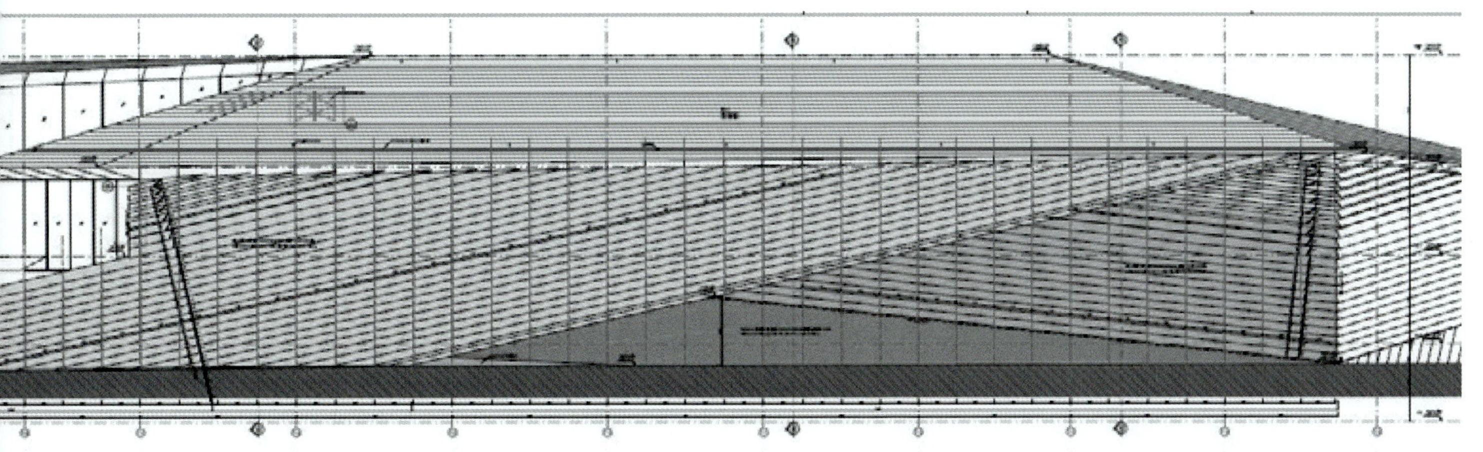

South Facade: Anodized Aluminum

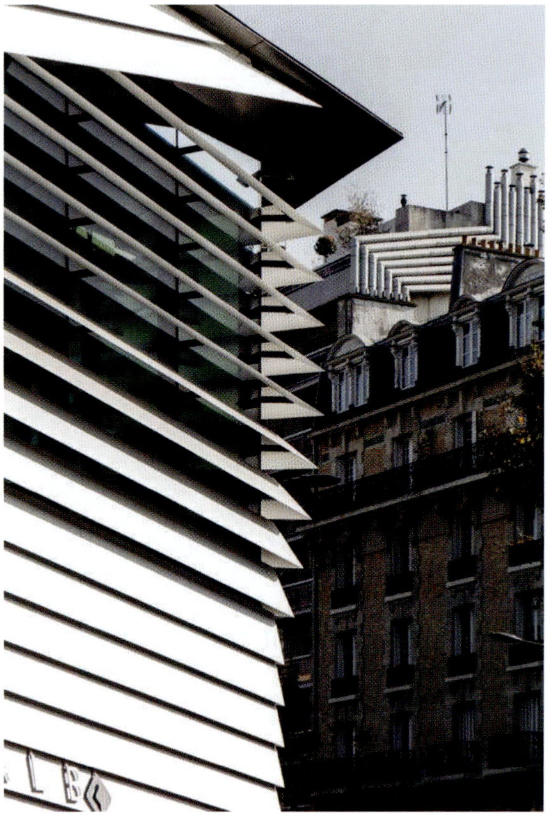

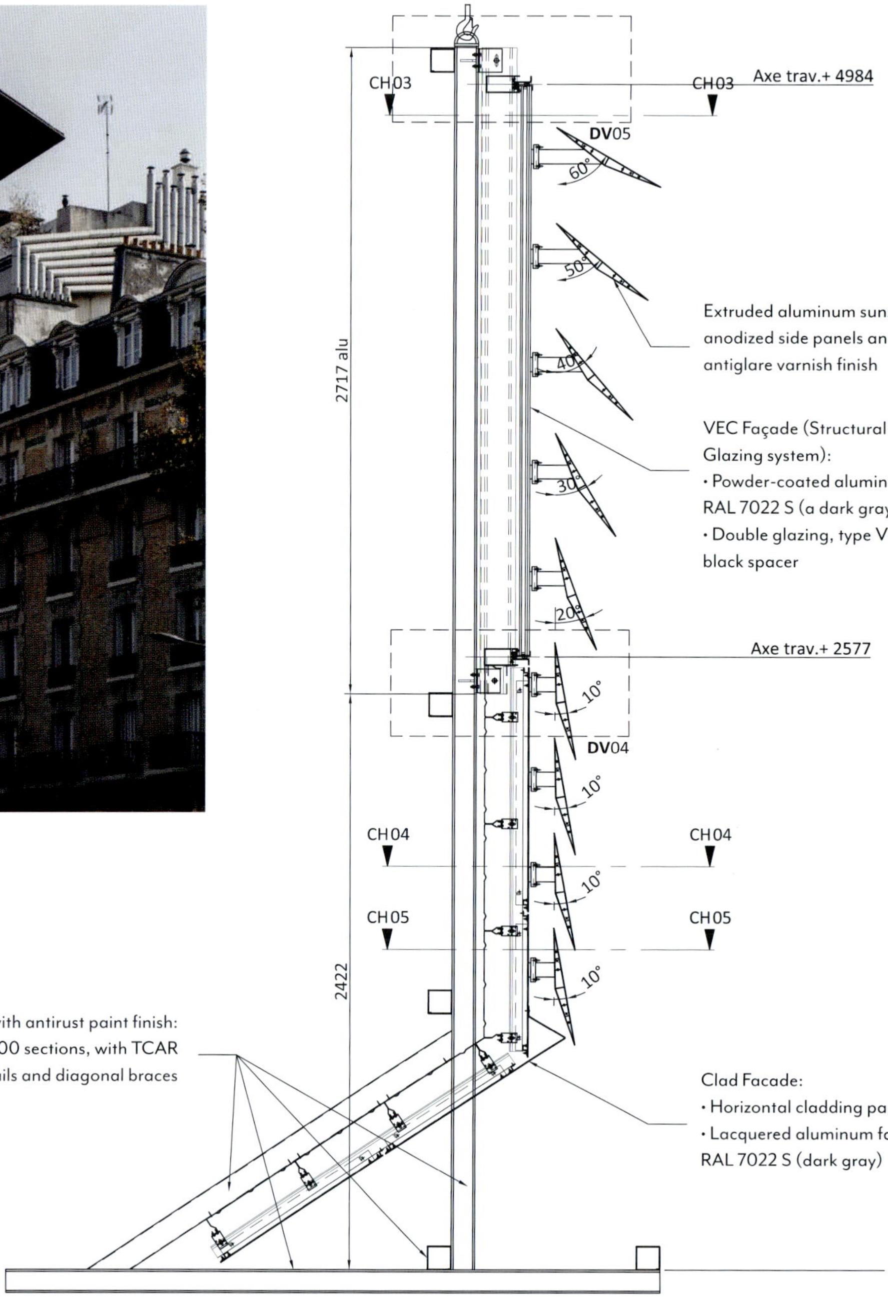

CH03
CH03
Axe trav.+ 4984
DV05
60°
50°
40°
30°
20°
2717 alu
Extruded aluminum sunshade with brushed anodized side panels and a transparent antiglare varnish finish
VEC Façade (Structural Silicone Glazing system):
• Powder-coated aluminum frame, RAL 7022 S (a dark gray shade)
• Double glazing, type VV-01, with black spacer
Axe trav.+ 2577
10°
DV04
10°
CH04
CH04
10°
CH05
CH05
10°
2422
Steel support frame with antirust paint finish:
• Frame made of HEA 100 sections, with TCAR 100x100x3 horizontal rails and diagonal braces
Clad Facade:
• Horizontal cladding panels
• Lacquered aluminum façade panels, RAL 7022 S (dark gray)
Theoretical level + 0

10 mm thick plate (knife plate) supporting the sunshade,
• bolted onto a preinstalled I-shaped element, with Ø6 unthreaded stainless-steel studs welded together, to be lacquered
Extruded aluminum sunshade
Brushed anodized finish
Clear antigraffiti varnish coating (colorless)
245
36
500
40
500
40
10 mm thick I-shaped element fixed to the stair nosing or aluminum rail
• Welded M6 studs
• M6 hex socket head cap screws
Entire assembly in stainless steel to be lacquered
Aluminum side panels, 20/10 thickness (2 mm) fixed onto the sunshade alveolar mounts, brushed anodized finish
• Stainless steel countersunk sheet metal screws, 4.8x22 mm

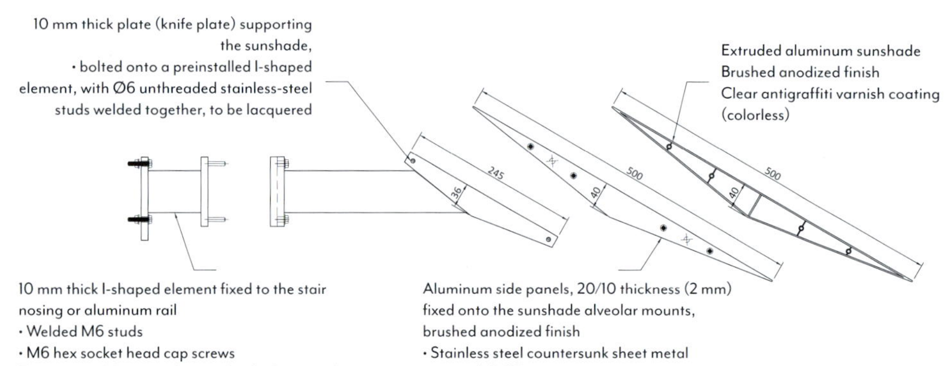

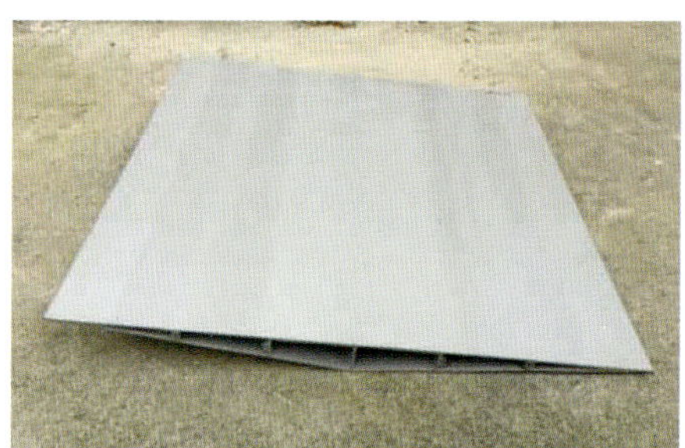

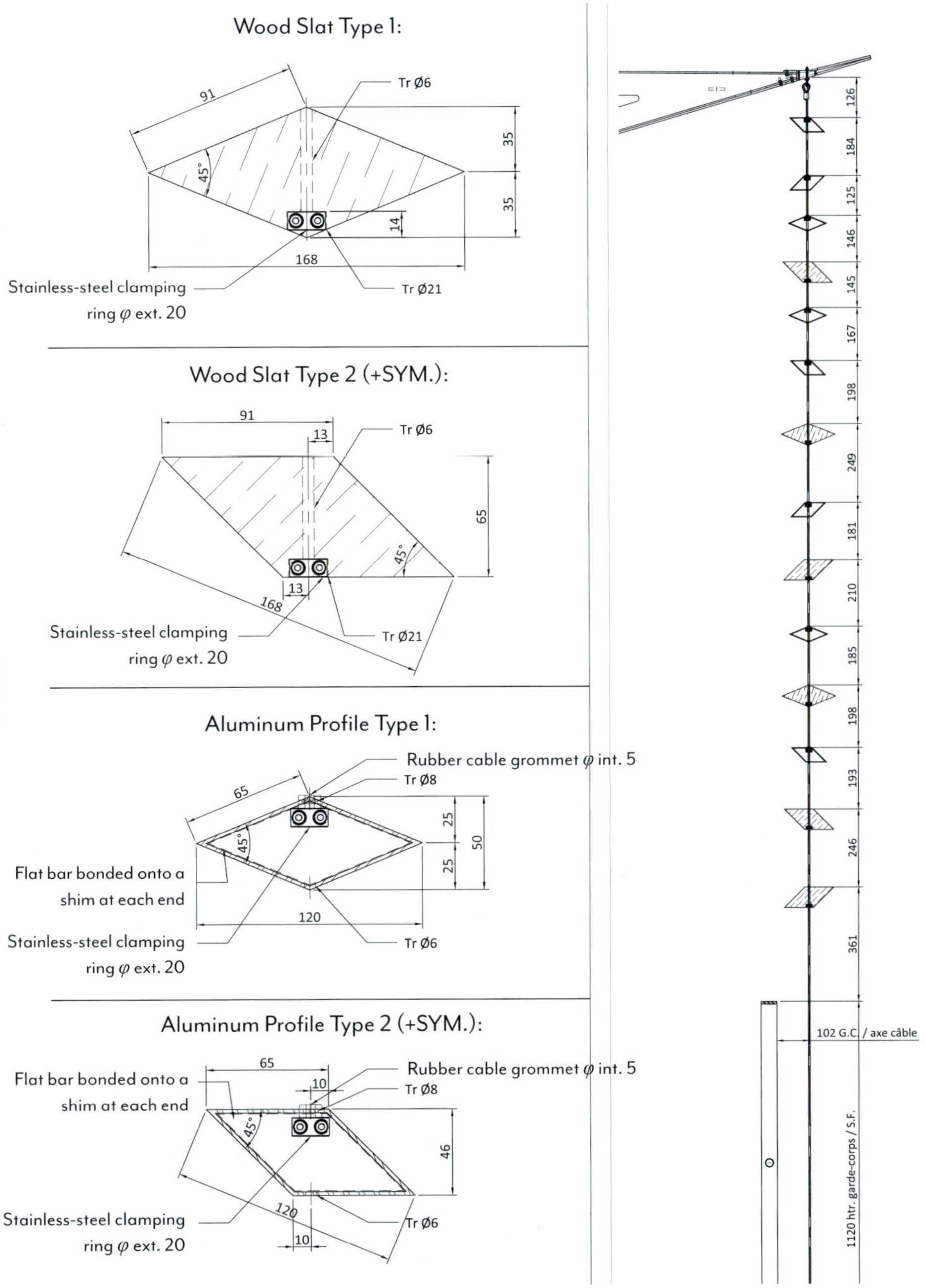

Wood Slat Type 1:

91
Tr Ø6
35
45°
35
14
168
Stainless-steel clamping ring φ ext. 20
Tr Ø21

Wood Slat Type 2 (+SYM.):

91
13
Tr Ø6
65
45°
13
168
Stainless-steel clamping ring φ ext. 20
Tr Ø21

Aluminum Profile Type 1:

Rubber cable grommet φ int. 5
Tr Ø8
65
25
50
45°
25
Flat bar bonded onto a shim at each end
120
Stainless-steel clamping ring φ ext. 20
Tr Ø6

Aluminum Profile Type 2 (+SYM.):

65
Flat bar bonded onto a shim at each end
Rubber cable grommet φ int. 5
10
Tr Ø8
45°
46
Stainless-steel clamping ring φ ext. 20
120
10
Tr Ø6

126
184
125
146
145
167
198
249
181
210
185
198
193
246
361
102 G.C. / axe câble
1120 htr. garde-corps / S.F.

Section D–D North Facade

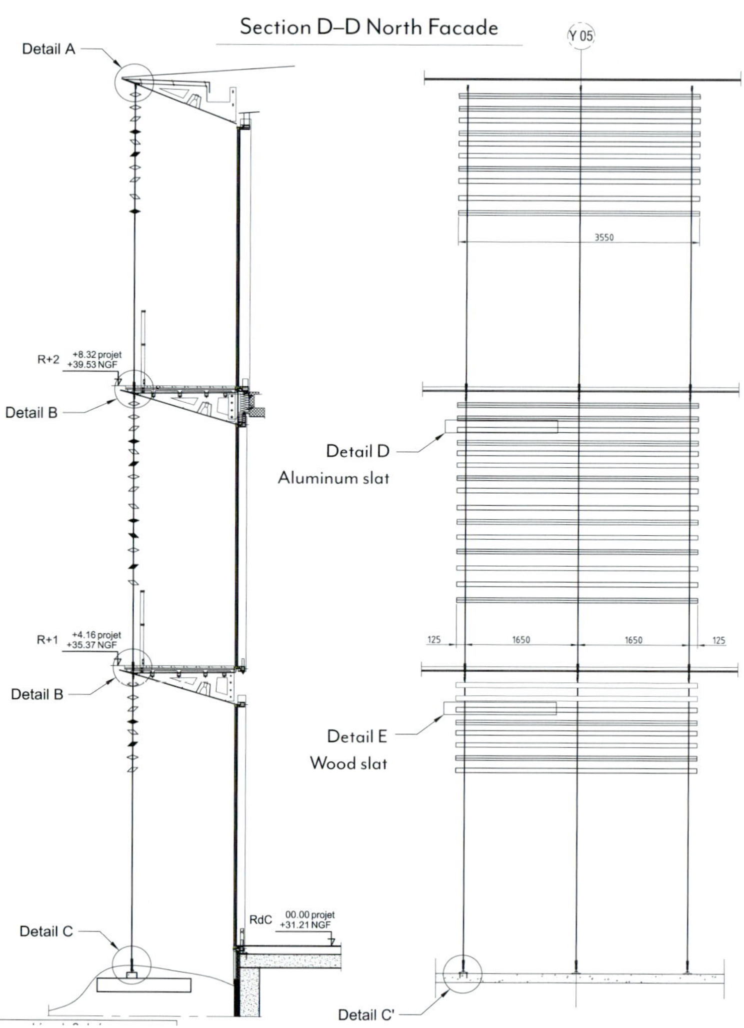

Detail D: Aluminum Slat

91

84

91

45°

Tr φ9 for φ8 cable or Tr φ6 for φ5 cable

Edge of sudare with anodized finish

150

150

1

1

Steel retaining piece with galvanized finish

3

2

2

3

Stainless steel clamping ring

Trou Ø28

Aluminum extrusion is anodized, including its end faces

φ8 stainless-steel cable for long spans or φ5 for shorter runs

Detail E: Wood Slat

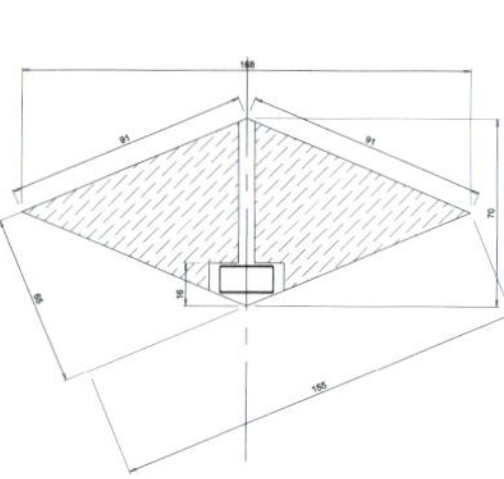

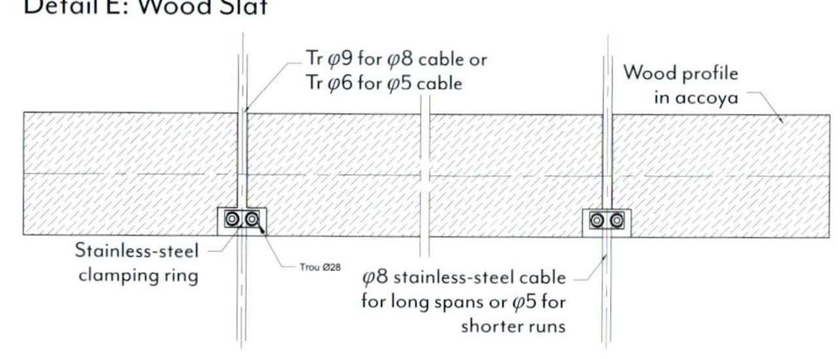

Indoor Ceiling Detail

Section View

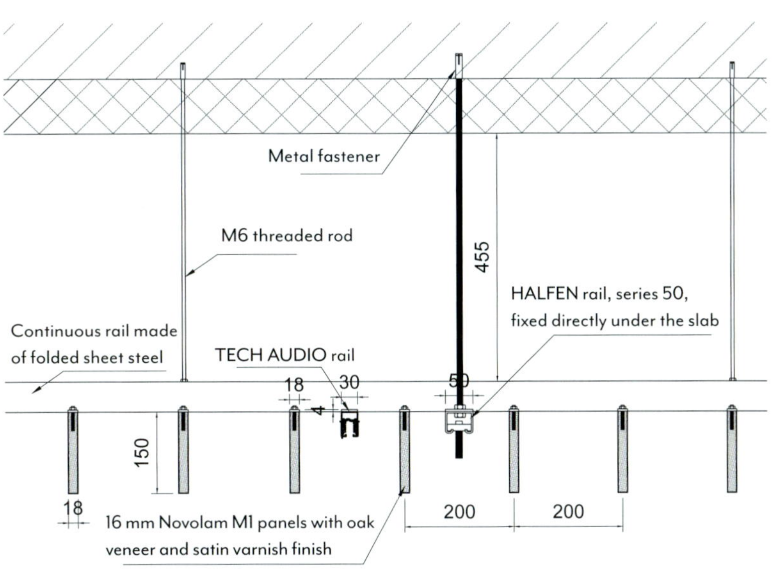

Slat Detail

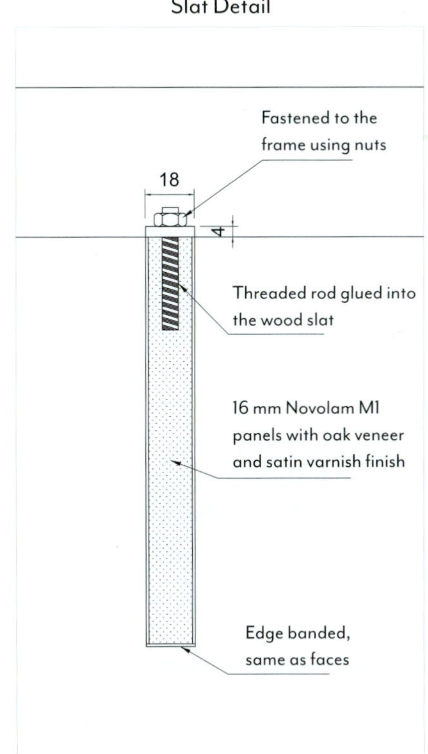

Auditorium: Bamboo Ceiling
40/50/60 mm Diameters

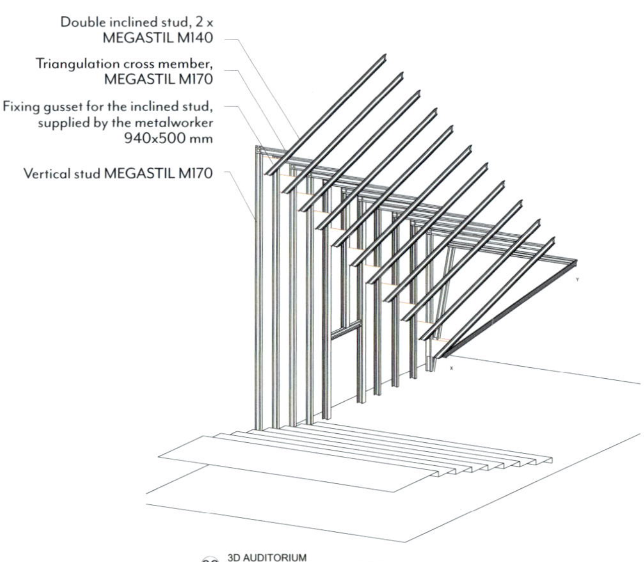

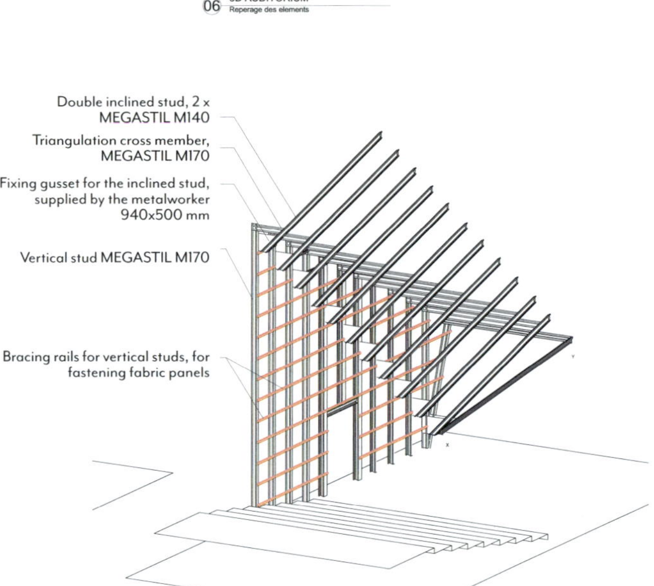

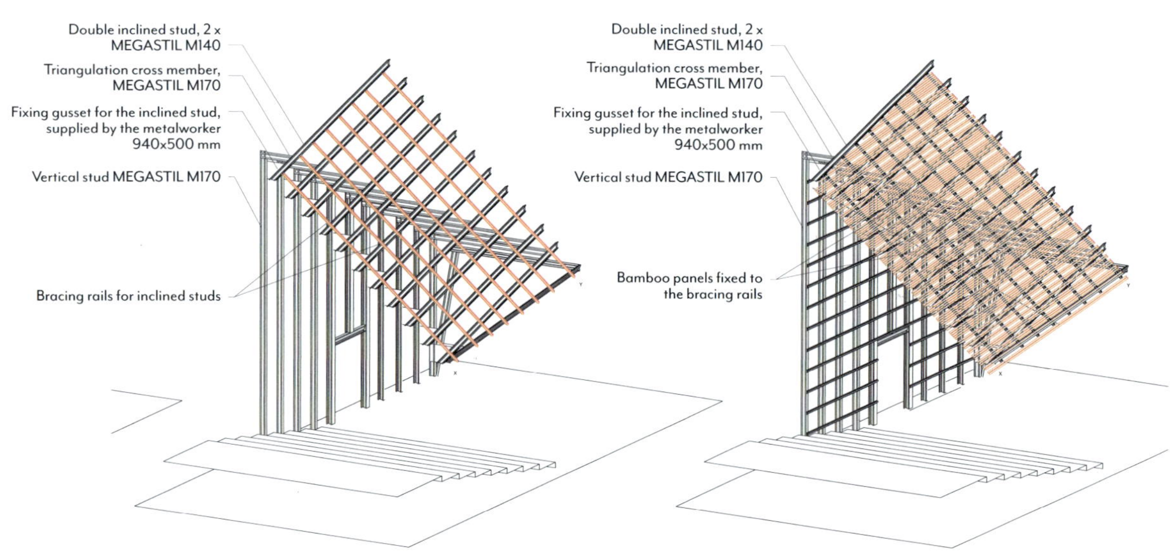

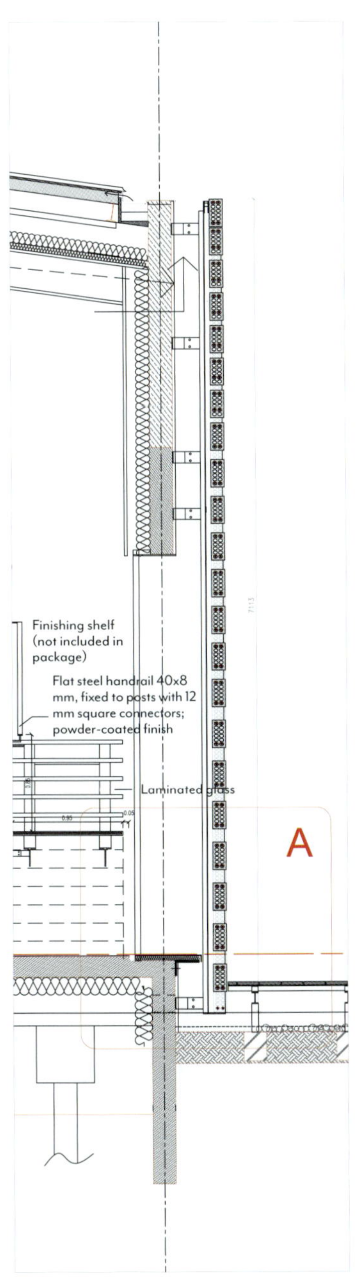

Section BB

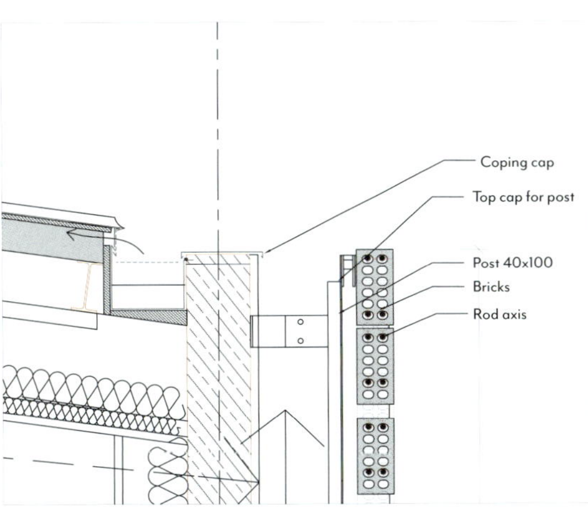

Detail B

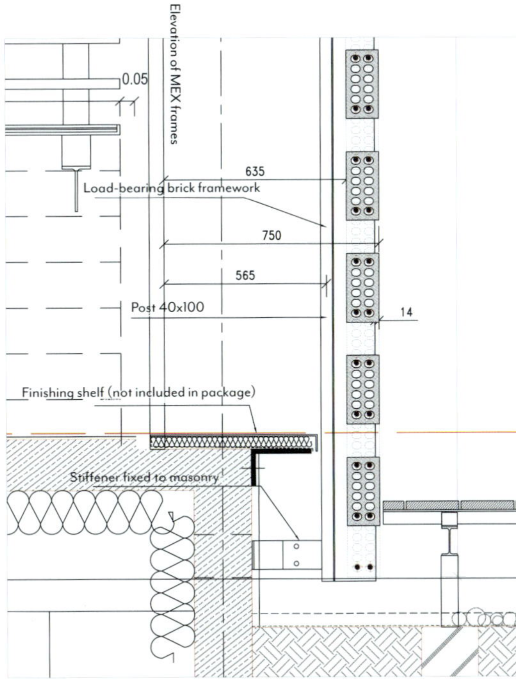
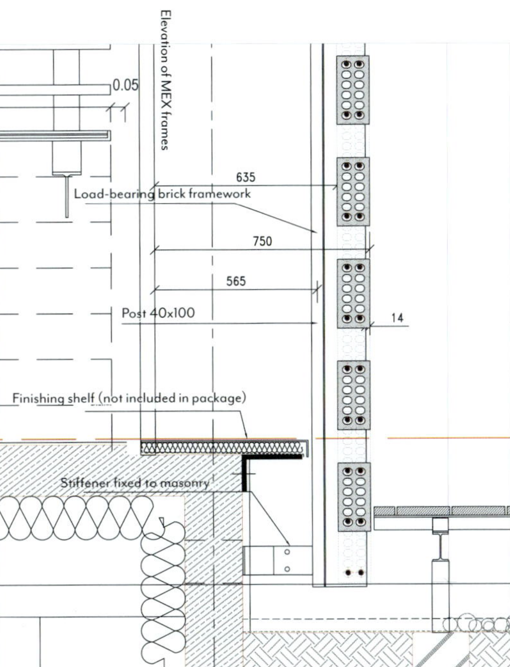

Detail A

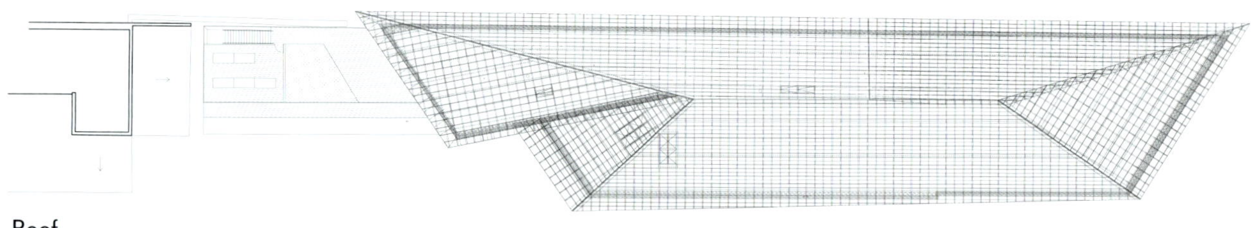
Roof

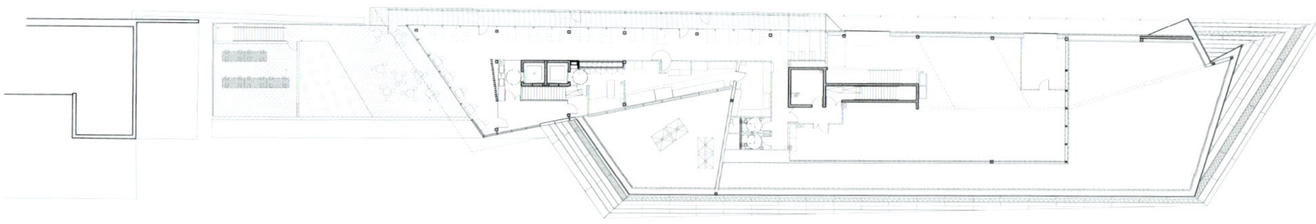
Third Floor

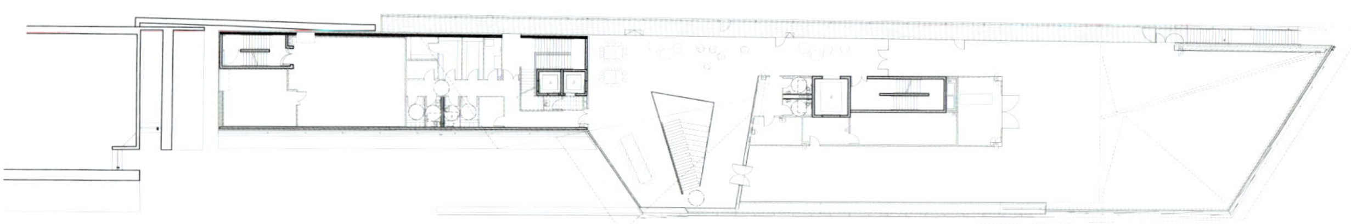
Second Floor

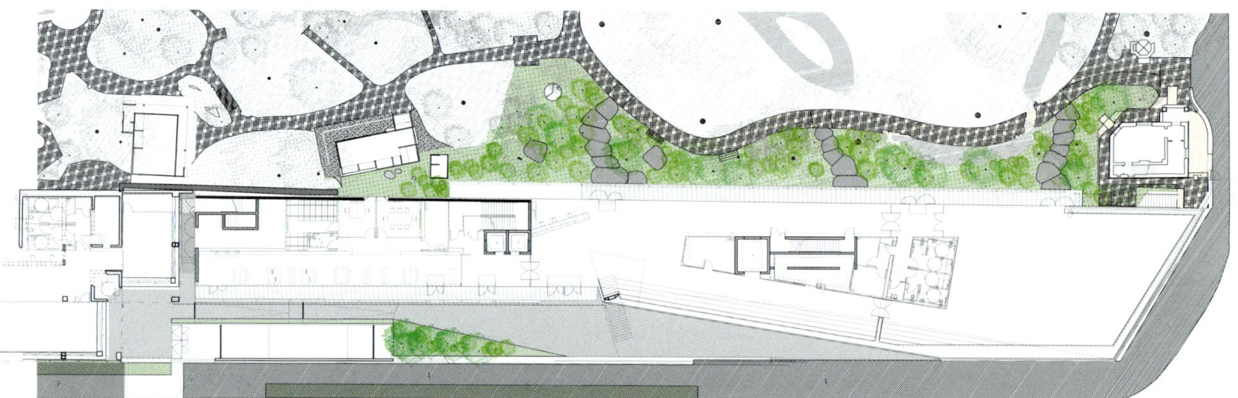
First Floor

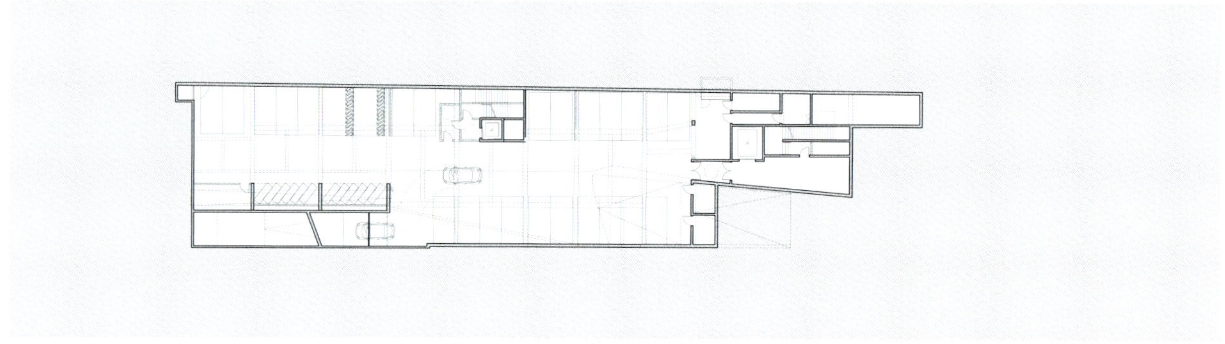
Basement Floor

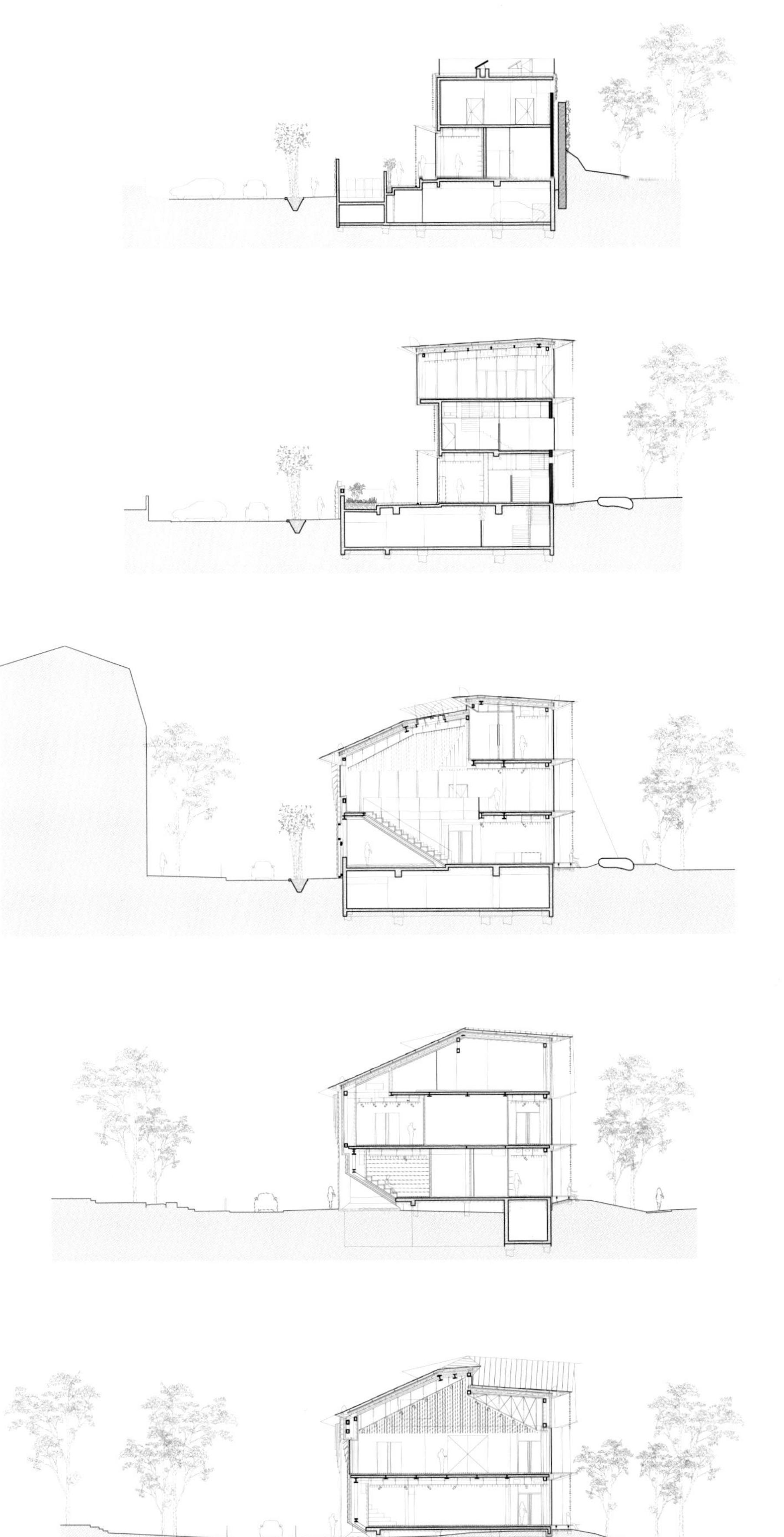

Sections

WOOD 14: KUSUGIBASHI

Completion year: 2022
Location: Yamaguchi, Japan
Structure: RC/SRC (reinforced concrete / steel-reinforced concrete)
Building type: bridge

This bridge in Osogoe, Shuto Town, Iwakuni City, which was destroyed during the Western Japan flood in July 2018, has been reconstructed as a wooden bridge. This new structure has become a symbol of resilience and renewal for the community. Notably, Asahi-Shuzo, the producer of the renowned Japanese sake "Dassai," is located on both sides of the bridge. The brewery contributed to the reconstruction by covering the cost of the wooden components through donations.

In designing the bridge, considerations were made for the potential risk of future disasters. To address this, a reinforced-concrete (RC) frame was integrated with cypress balustrades measuring 105 square units—a common size in Japanese wooden construction. This design choice not only ensures durability but also pays homage to traditional carpentry techniques, imbuing the bridge with a nostalgic and human-scaled dimension. The arrangement of the cypress members forms a gentle curve that mirrors the surrounding mountainous landscape, seamlessly integrating the structure into its natural environment.

This bridge represents a fusion of Japan's esteemed carpentry craftsmanship with modern computational design technologies. The result is a structure with a uniquely soft and human expression, distinct from traditional civil engineering projects. It stands as a testament to the community's ability to blend heritage and innovation in the face of adversity.

Significant curves were introduced at the edges of the bridge where it meets the road, extending the wooden elements to foster a seamless integration between the bridge and road, rather than creating a division. This approach helps the bridge naturally blend into the surrounding scenery.

The volume of the bridge's form was manipulated by extending the wooden balustrades both upward and downward in the central portion, while tapering them at the ends. This design choice inverts the typical arch structure configuration, which usually features a smaller volume at the center and larger at the edges. Here, the opposite is true, enhancing the bridge's ability to blend into and seemingly disappear into nature, thereby smoothing its connection with the surrounding environment.

To counteract the inherently robust appearance of the necessary reinforced-concrete structure, which is crucial for flood protection, wood was incorporated to soften the bridge's aesthetic. This design strategy aimed to give the bridge as soft an impression as possible.

Three types of wooden balustrades were utilized: those that hide the lower structure of the bridge, those that hide the concrete from the inside, and those that obscure the concrete from the outside. By arranging the wooden members in a slanting orientation, a vertical appearance was avoided. Despite each wooden member being straight, their tilted arrangement imparts a soft and delicate image to the bridge.

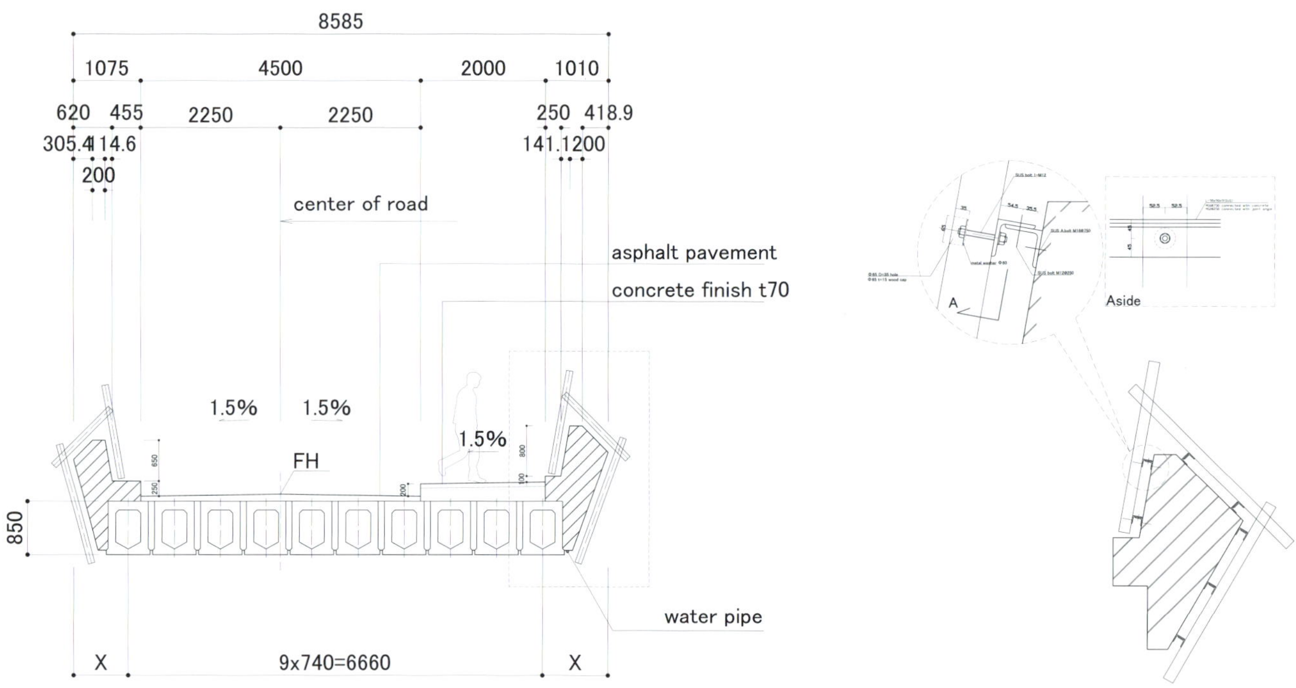

Section

Detail

1. Handrail: Wood (Hinoki)
2. Handrail Base: CO+ water allocated coating (specified color)
3. Handrail: SUS FB-50x12, SUS wire φ 4@220, H100mm
4. Sidewalk: CO+Mt, brush finish+surface strengthening agents
5. Guardrail

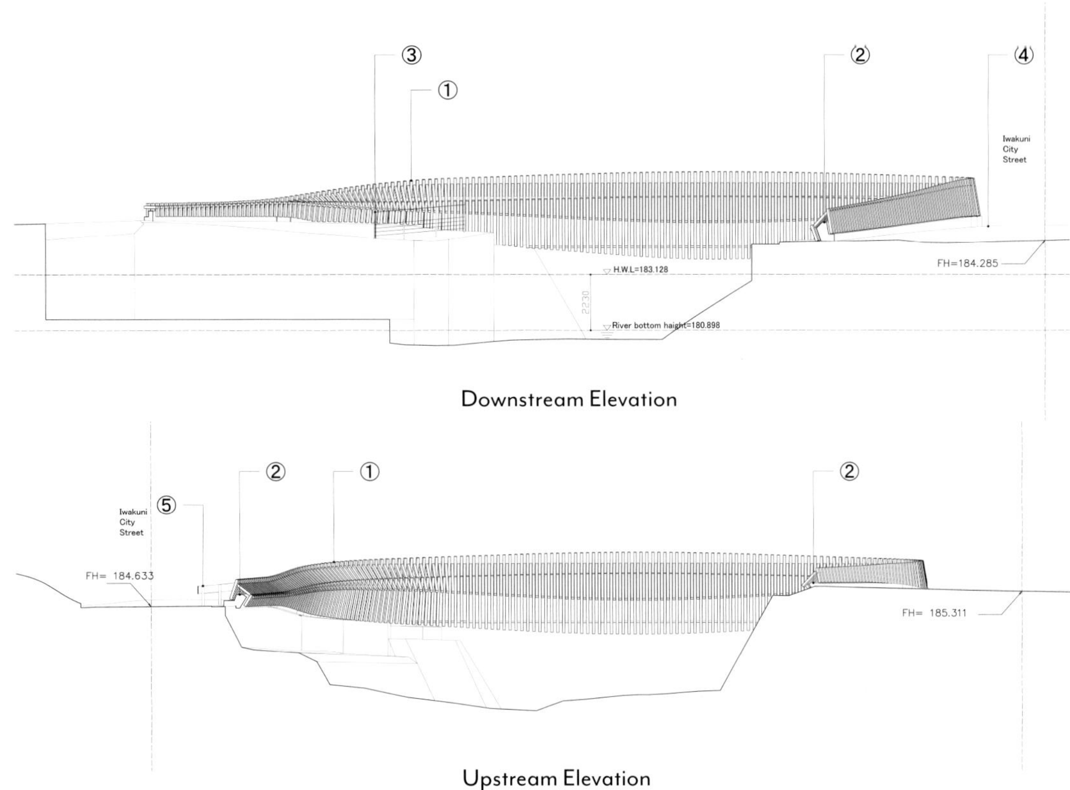

Downstream Elevation

Upstream Elevation

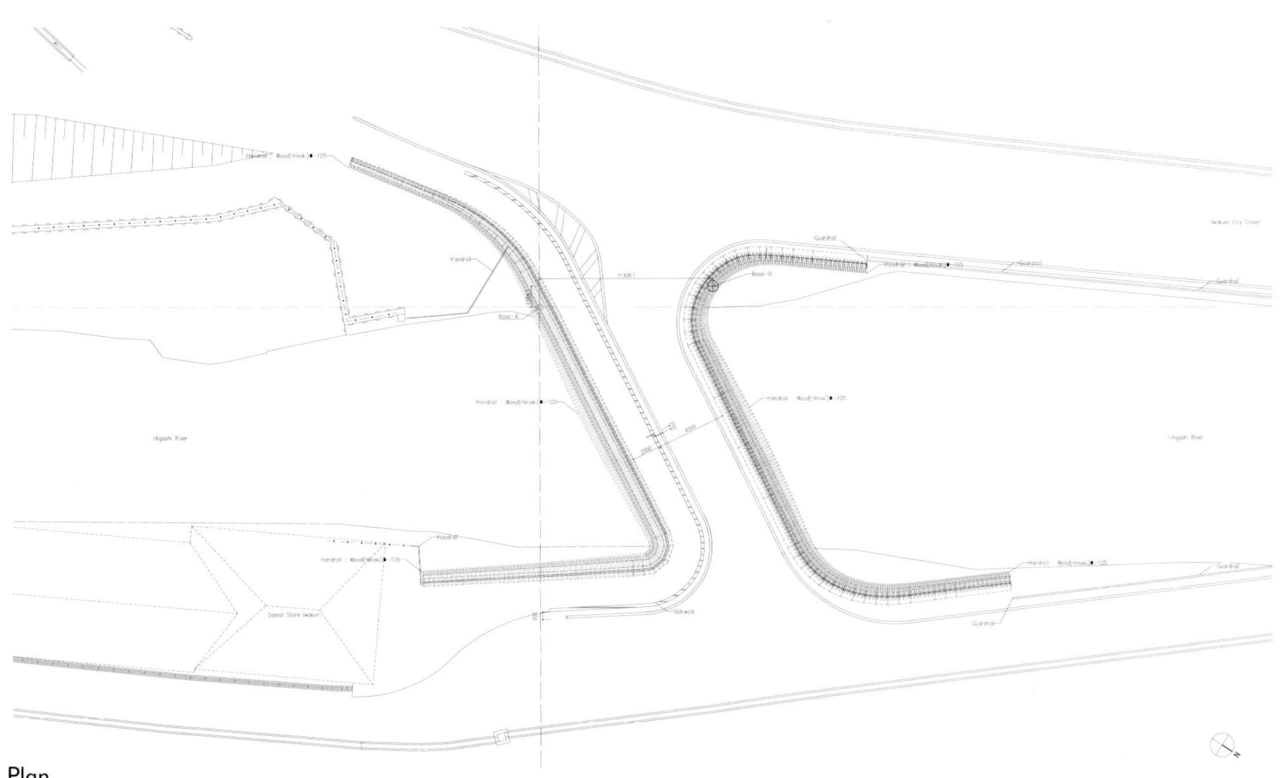

Plan

WOOD 15: TOTTORI TAKAHAMA CAFÉ

Completion year: 2022
Location: Tottori, Japan
Structure: RC (reinforced concrete)
Building type: café

The observatory/café we designed, overlooking the Tottori Sand Dunes, employs a hybrid structure that combines the robustness of reinforced concrete with the aesthetic and environmental benefits of cross-laminated timber (CLT). The building is envisioned as a "staircase to the sky," with its CLT exterior offering a warm texture that harmonizes beautifully with the natural landscape of the surrounding sand dunes.

As an homage to Tottori, which is well known for folk crafts, or "mingei," the interior design of the observatory/café integrates local craftsmanship. The chairs are crafted from CLT, and light pendants are fashioned from washi paper sprinkled with local sand.

The bathroom sinks in the café are produced by Nakai-gama, a renowned Tottori pottery workshop. These sinks feature a striking glaze combination of green and black.

For the exterior walls and roof of the observatory/café, asphalt roofing was chosen to enhance the waterproofing capabilities and protect the integrity of the cross-laminated timber (CLT), which serves as the primary structural material. Over the asphalt layer, a 30 mm thick laminar covering was applied to provide additional protection. Additional header laminae were applied to prevent the cross sections of two layers from being exposed and appearing cumbersome as a means of showing the overall composition of the CLT.

Local Chizu cedar from Tottori was selected for the CLT. Chizu cedar is cultivated through meticulous forestry practices, which include repeated improvement cutting and thinning. These techniques are tailored to the specific climatic conditions of the mountainous regions in Tottori, where there are stark temperature differences and dense planting. The result of this careful cultivation is a dense wood grain and a characteristic vivid reddish hue, which creates a beautiful contrast with the sand dunes.

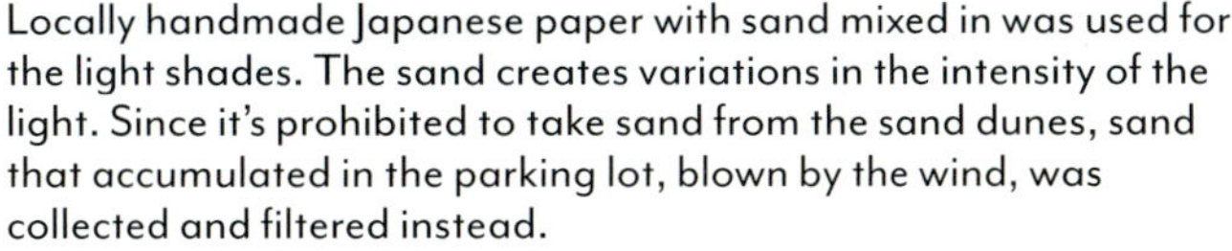

Locally handmade Japanese paper with sand mixed in was used for the light shades. The sand creates variations in the intensity of the light. Since it's prohibited to take sand from the sand dunes, sand that accumulated in the parking lot, blown by the wind, was collected and filtered instead.

10
10
10
3
terrace
Tottori Sand Dune View
machine room
cafe
cafe
5150
13000
4800
2950
1260
2400
3800
2580
2800
5650
2700
5400
2350

Section

Lamina
Water proof
CLT
Wood panel
RC
Lamina
CLT
Water proof
Lamina
HS t12

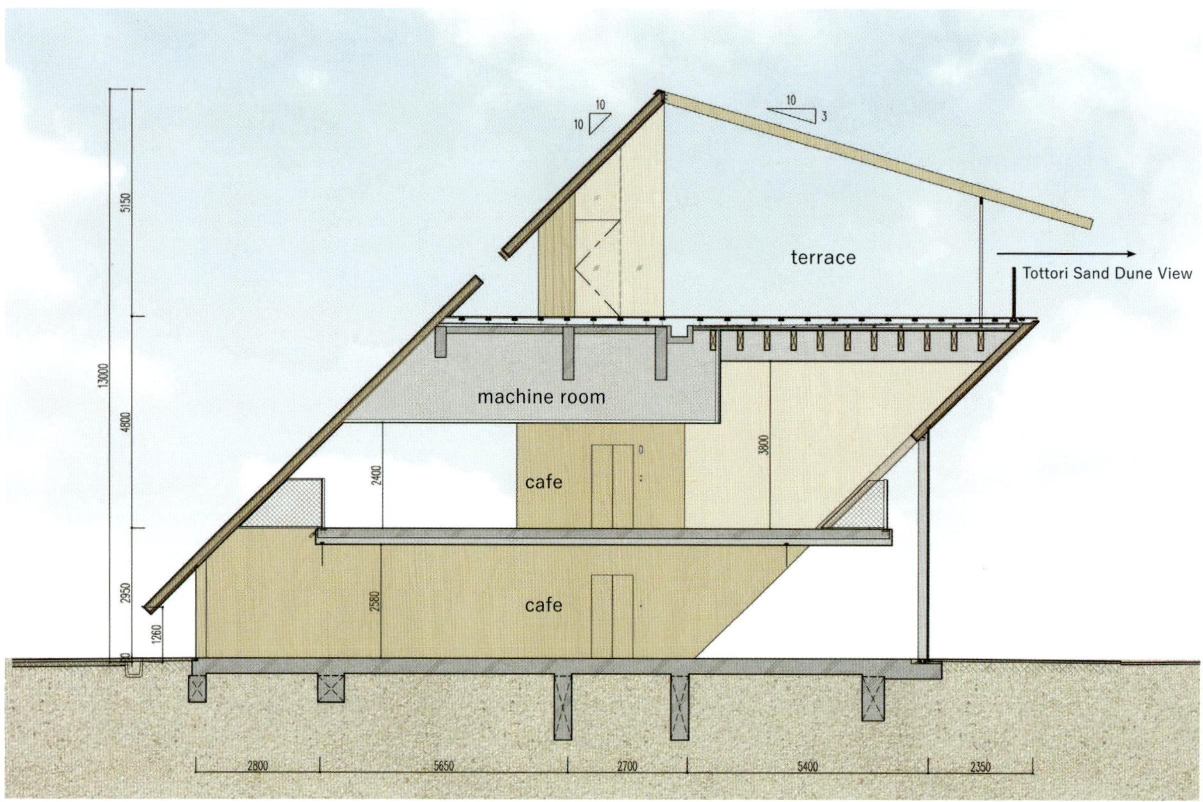

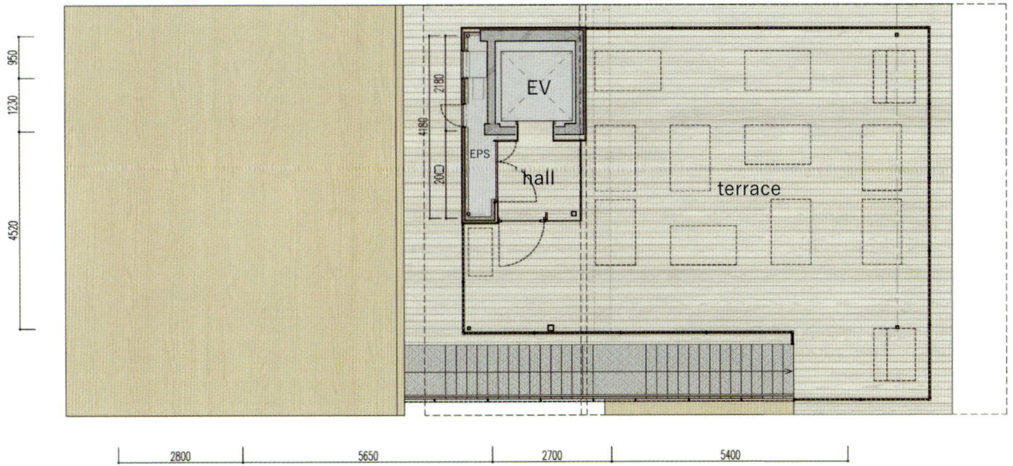

Roof

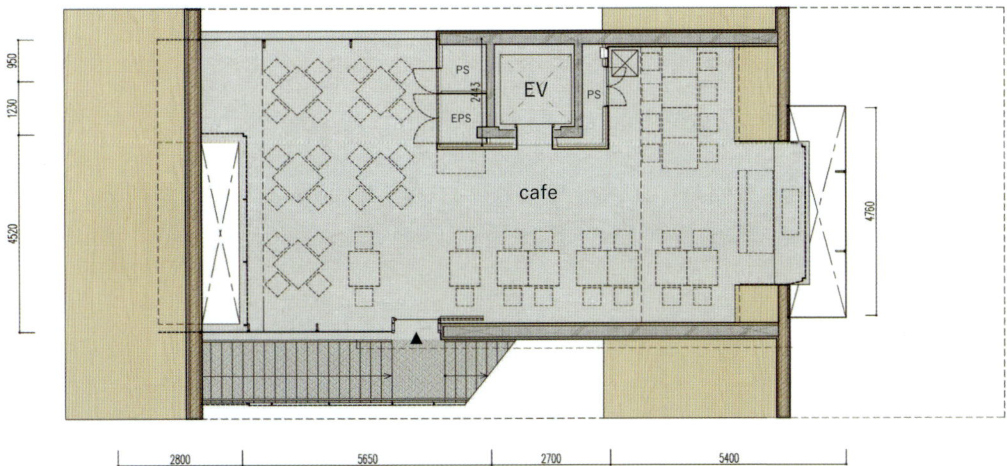

Second Floor

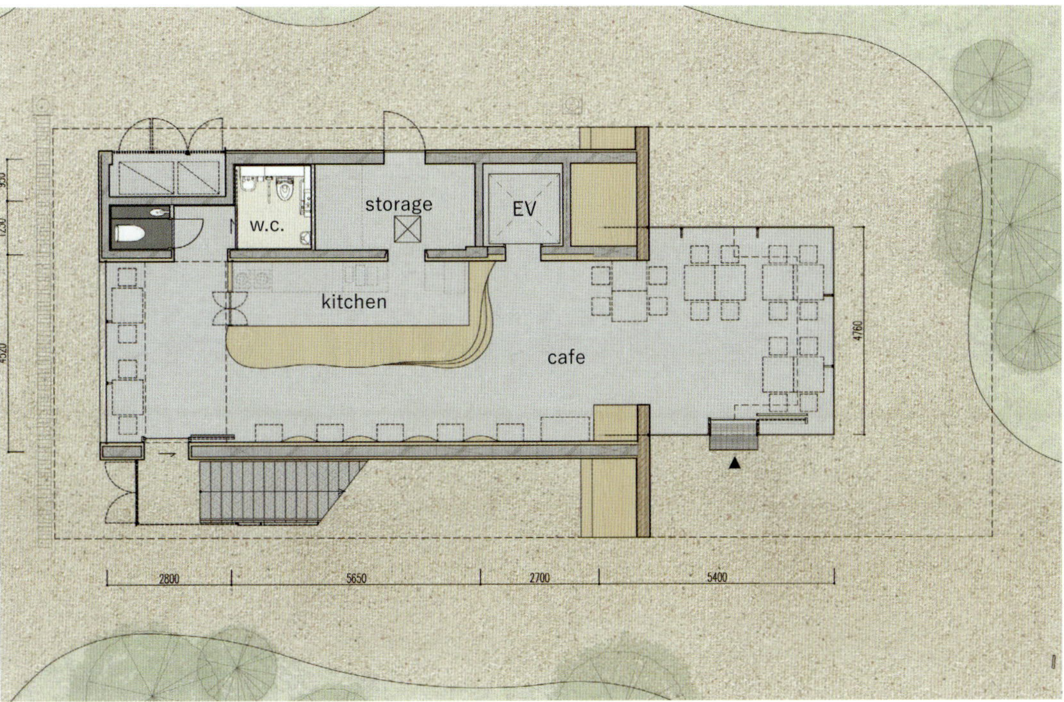

First Floor

WOOD 16: SANA MANE SAUNA SAZAE

Completion year: 2022
Location: Kagawa, Japan
Structure: wood
Building type: sauna

The organic wooden sauna "Sazae" is located at the center of the glamping facility known as Sana Mane, near the small inlet of Naoshima. Constructing this sauna involved a significant challenge: wood masonry made by stacking 150 layers of CNC-processed, 28 mm thick plywood. The walls of the solid-wood sauna have an average thickness of 450 mm, essential for effective heat insulation and retention.

The exterior of the sauna features numerous folds, resembling a shell, which cast striking shadows on the surface. Inside, the pleats are gently shaped to conform to the body, enhancing comfort for users. Light enters solely through an oculus, contributing to a meditative experience within the sauna.

Despite the complex spiral-pleated geometry, which required 1,500 plywood sheets, the entire design and plywood paneling were meticulously controlled by using 3-D CAD and programming.

This sauna is unique; despite its high ceiling, temperature and humidity levels are maintained at optimum levels. This is achieved through careful environmental simulations and the design of a forced-ventilation airflow system, distinguishing it from typical saunas.

Japanese larch plywood, available in thicknesses of 28 mm and 12 mm, was precision-cut using a numeric-control (NC) cutter. The plywood was then assembled into 158 overlapping steps, using dowels and glue to form the organic shape of the structure. This structure is frameless, relying entirely on the masonry-like stability provided by the laminated layers.

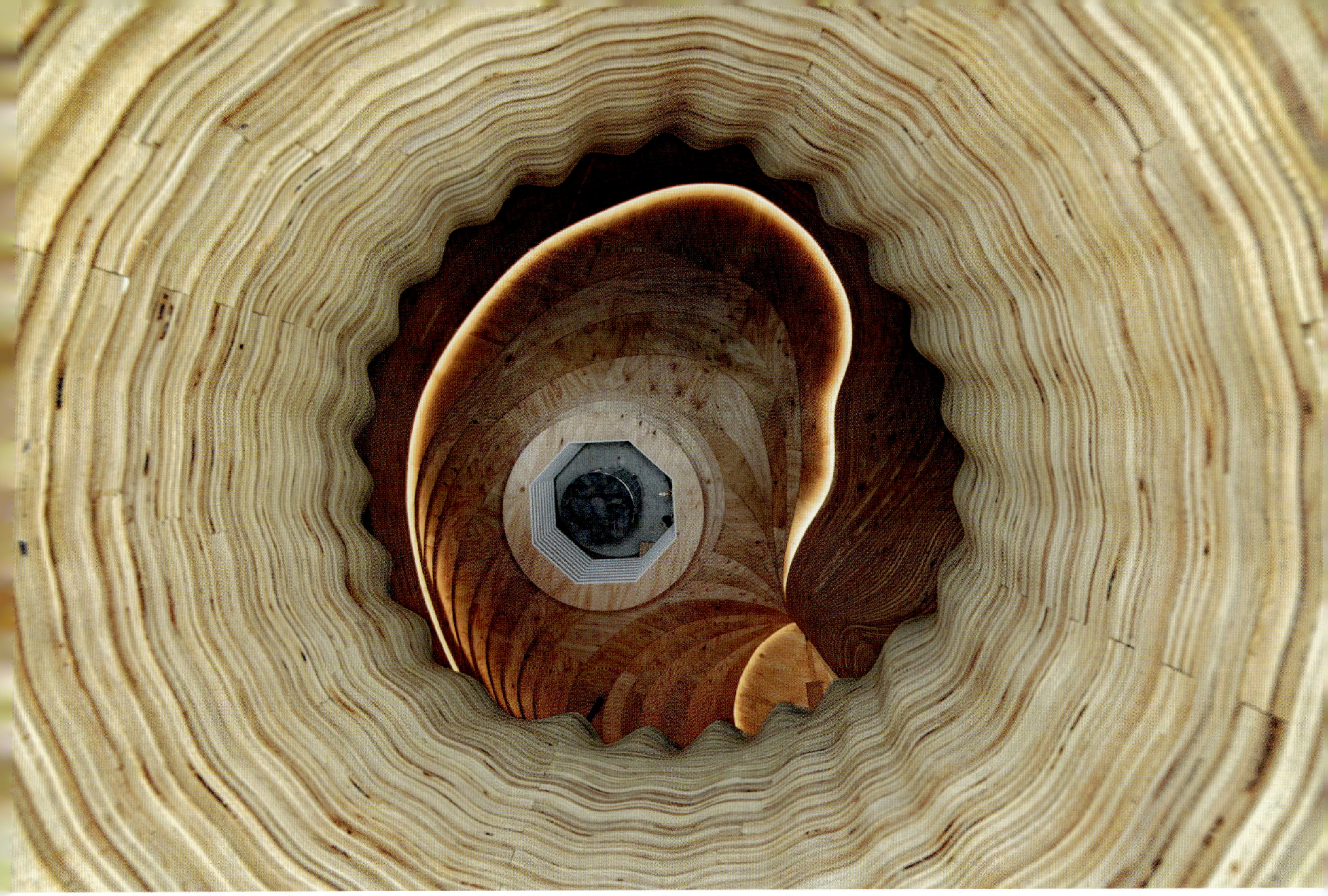

Each plywood piece was cut with the NC cutter from standard 900 × 1,800 mm sheets. Strategic tiling was employed to minimize waste, which helped control overall costs.

The exterior curvature employs clothoid curves, which gradually change, giving the structure and entrance a spiraling, upward-inward shape reminiscent of a turban seashell.

On the outside, small pleat-shaped walls help diminish the perceived scale of the building, creating an object that resembles a light sensor, subtly changing over time.

For the bench and floor—surfaces that come into direct contact with the body—thin (12 mm thick) plywood was used. This allows for the creation of delicate curves, resulting in a soft and gentle cross section that comfortably conforms to the human body.

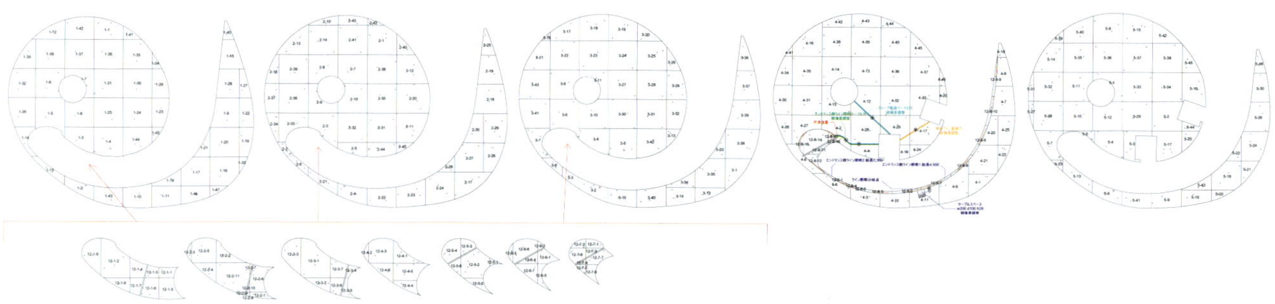

12 mm Entrance Steps

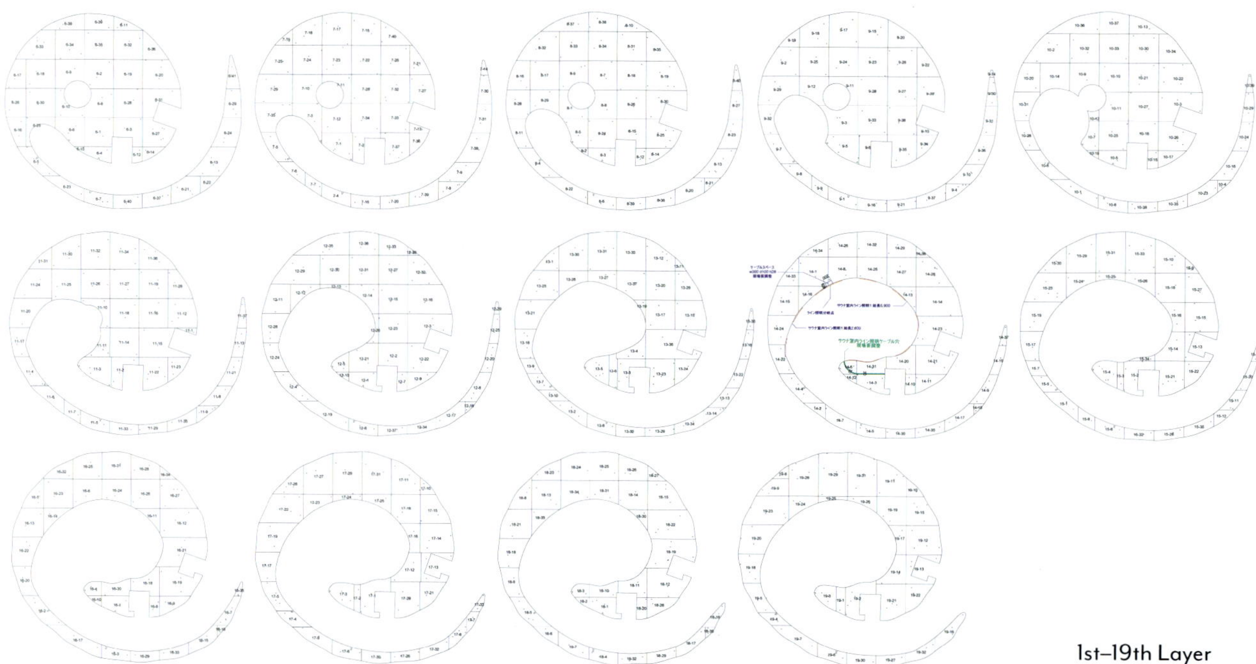

1st–19th Layer

20th–46th Layer

1st–19th Layer

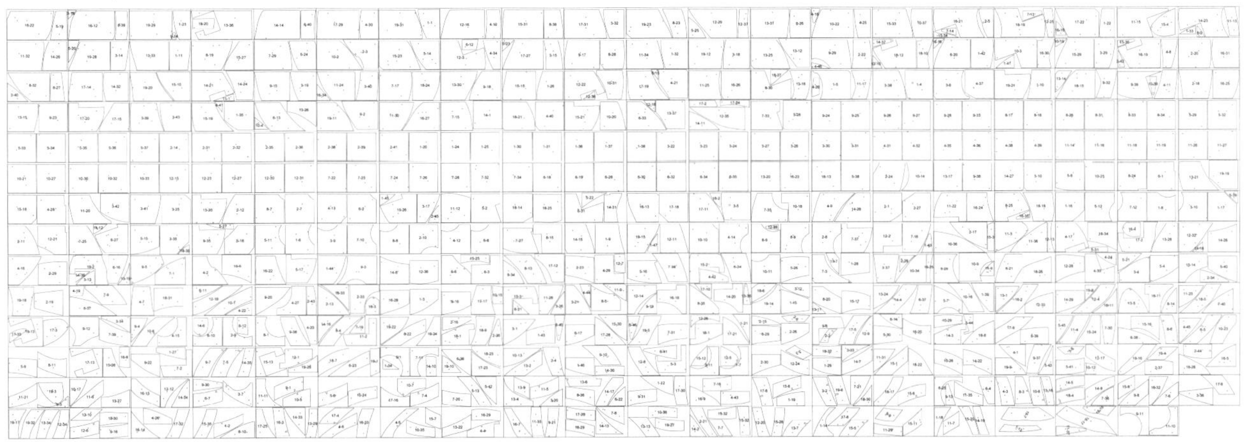

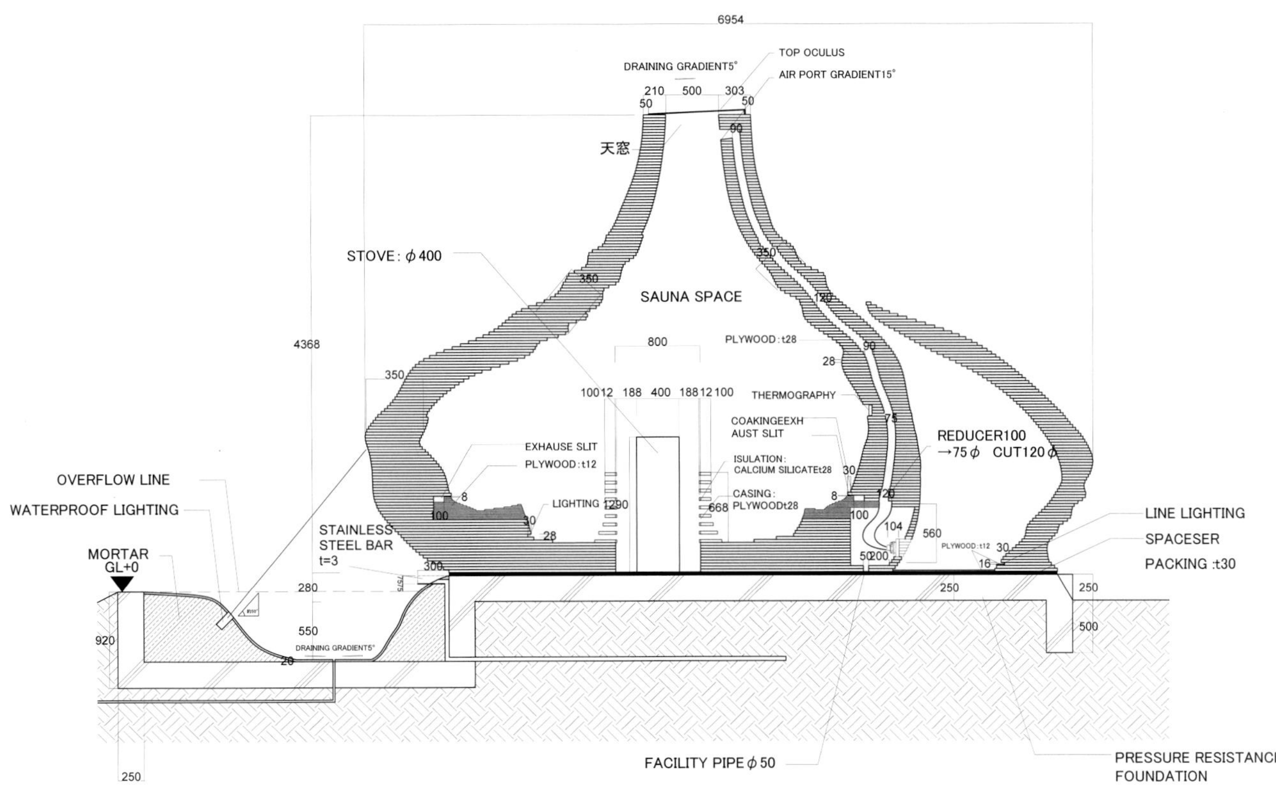

A–A' Section

WOOD 17: MINAMISANRIKU 311 MEMORIAL

Completion year: 2022
Location: Miyagi, Japan
Structure: steel
Building type: museum

Since 2013, I have been involved in the reconstruction of Minamisanriku, a town severely impacted by the Great East Japan earthquake on March 11, 2011. My role was to create a master plan for the elevated man-made ground, raised 10 m, on the basis of three key concepts: (1) reconnecting the town with the sea, (2) reconnecting the mountains and shrine, and (3) creating a walkable and enjoyable street.

As part of this plan, we designed three core facilities: the Sun Sun Shopping Village (2017), the Nakabashi Bridge (2020), and the 3.11 Memorial (2022). The 3.11 Memorial, marking the culmination of the reconstruction efforts, serves as a central hub linking the ocean, mountains, and town (street). It also aims to bridge memories of the past with hopes for the future.

The memorial building is designed to function as a portal, drawing people in along the east–west axis from the ocean, through the shopping street, and toward the mountains; and along the north–south axis from the Disaster Memorial Park, across the Nakabashi Bridge, to the Kaminoyama Hachimangu Shrine. Its appearance is reminiscent of a sacred torii gate.

The exterior of this symbolic gate is clad in louvers made from Minamisanriku cedar. These louvers are arranged radially from a vanishing point, creating a perspective effect that draws the viewer into a visual "hole."

Inside the memorial, various items and artworks convey the memories of the disaster. This includes Memorial by Christian Boltanski, inspired by the events, and a collection of works by young artists from the Tokyo University of Arts, who personally experienced the disaster.

Solid Minamisanriku cedar from the local area was used for the louvers, which add a rhythmic quality to the outer wall and ceiling, provide perspective, and help draw people into the memorial, which is designed as a "hole." The louvers on the outer wall are 30 mm thick and 220 mm wide, with their ends diagonally cut to an aspect measurement of 10 mm. This design helps divide light and shadows through the narrow line effect.

For the ceiling, louvers are 40 mm thick and either 210 or 410 mm wide. Both types of louvers are radially mounted at 2-degree increments, fundamentally centered on the vanishing point. This arrangement enhances the visual effect of being drawn into the space, reinforcing the architectural intent of guiding visitors toward the memorial.

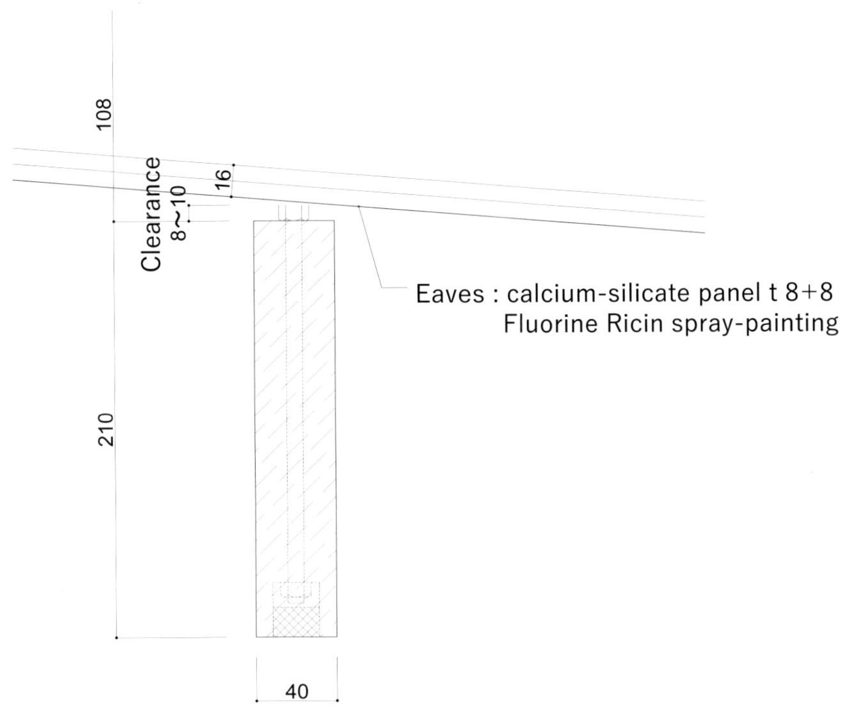

Detail: Ceiling Wood Louver

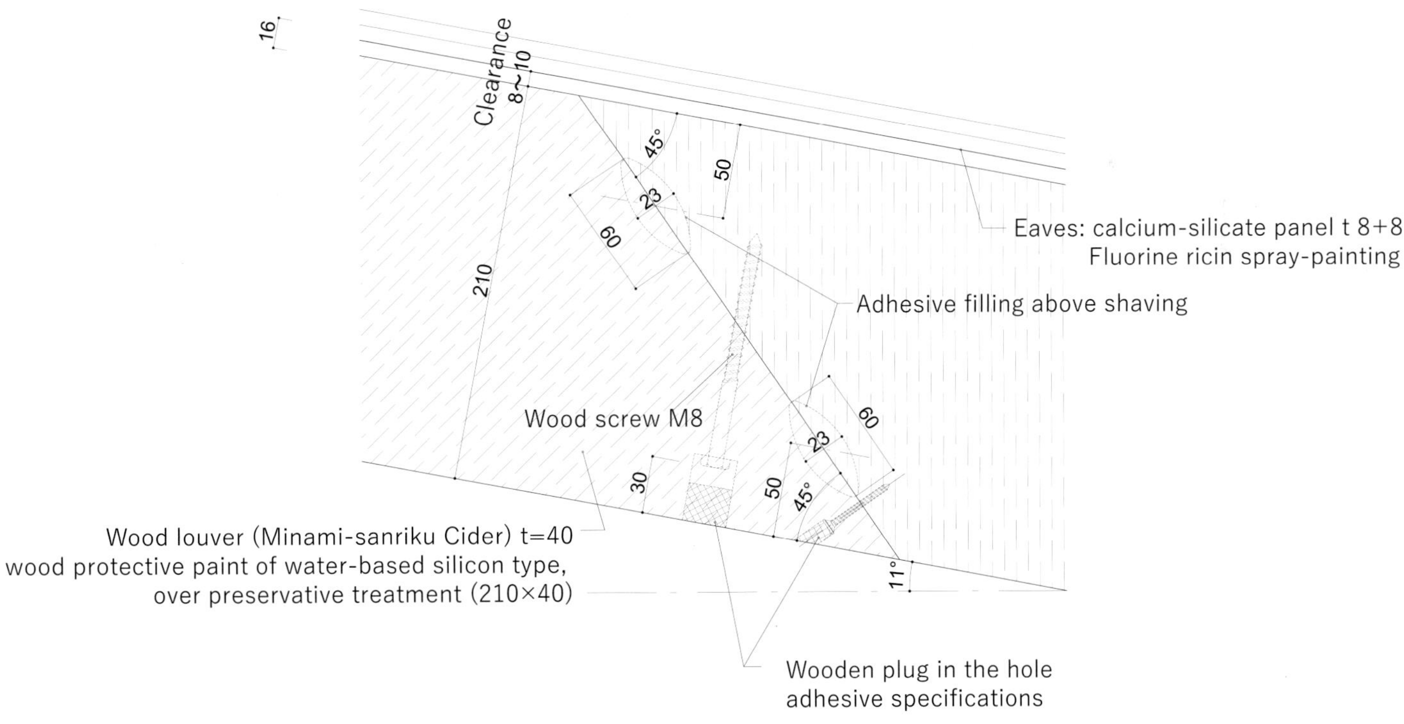

Joint Details / Elevation Diagram

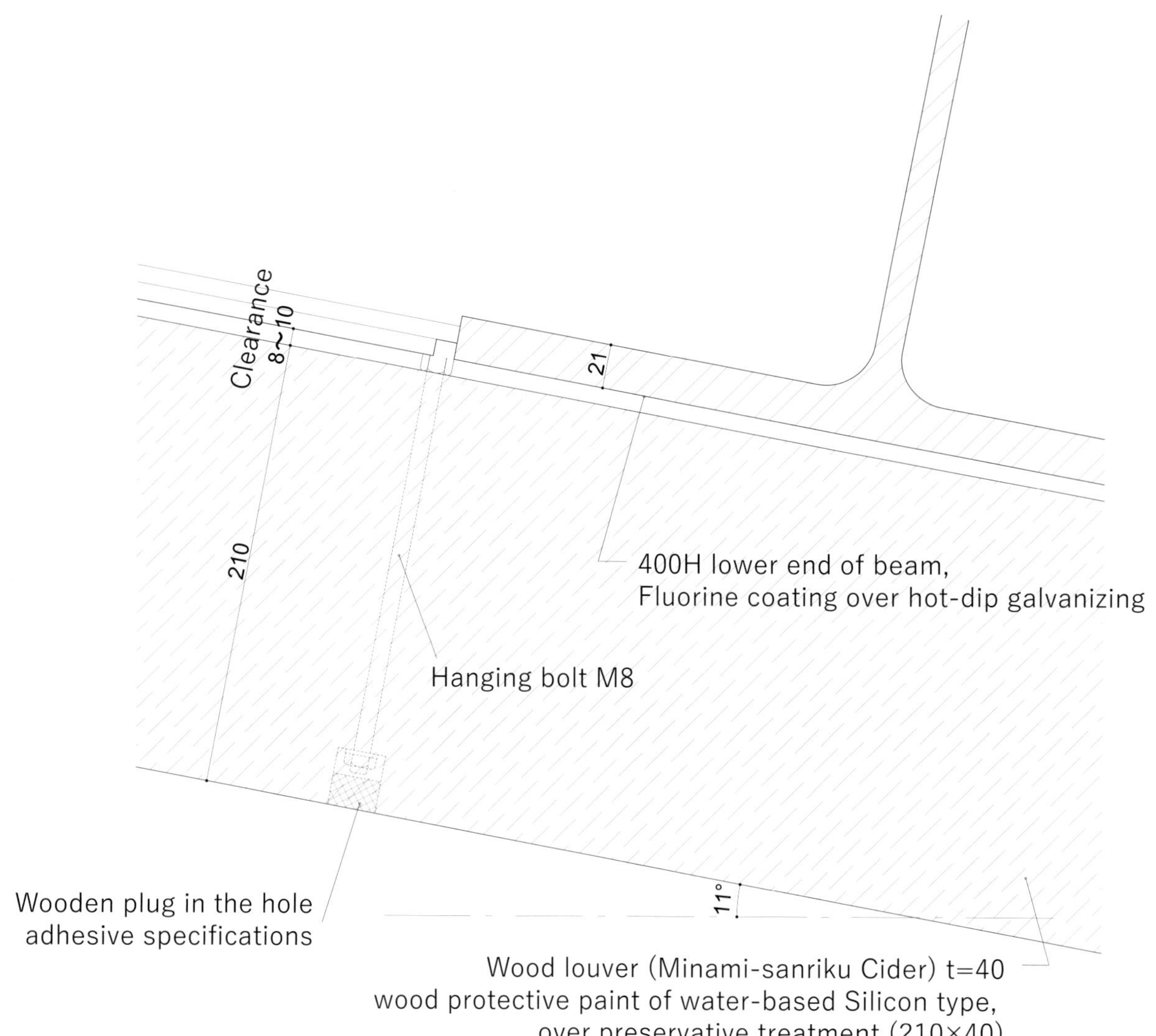

Detail: Ceiling Wood Louver

wood louver (Minami-sanriku Cider) t=40
wood protective paint of water-based silicon type,
over preservative treatment (210×40)
Showing multi-layered glass surface
Stiffening material
L-65x65x8
(7.66kg/m)
(Hot-dip Galvanizing, Fluorine coating)

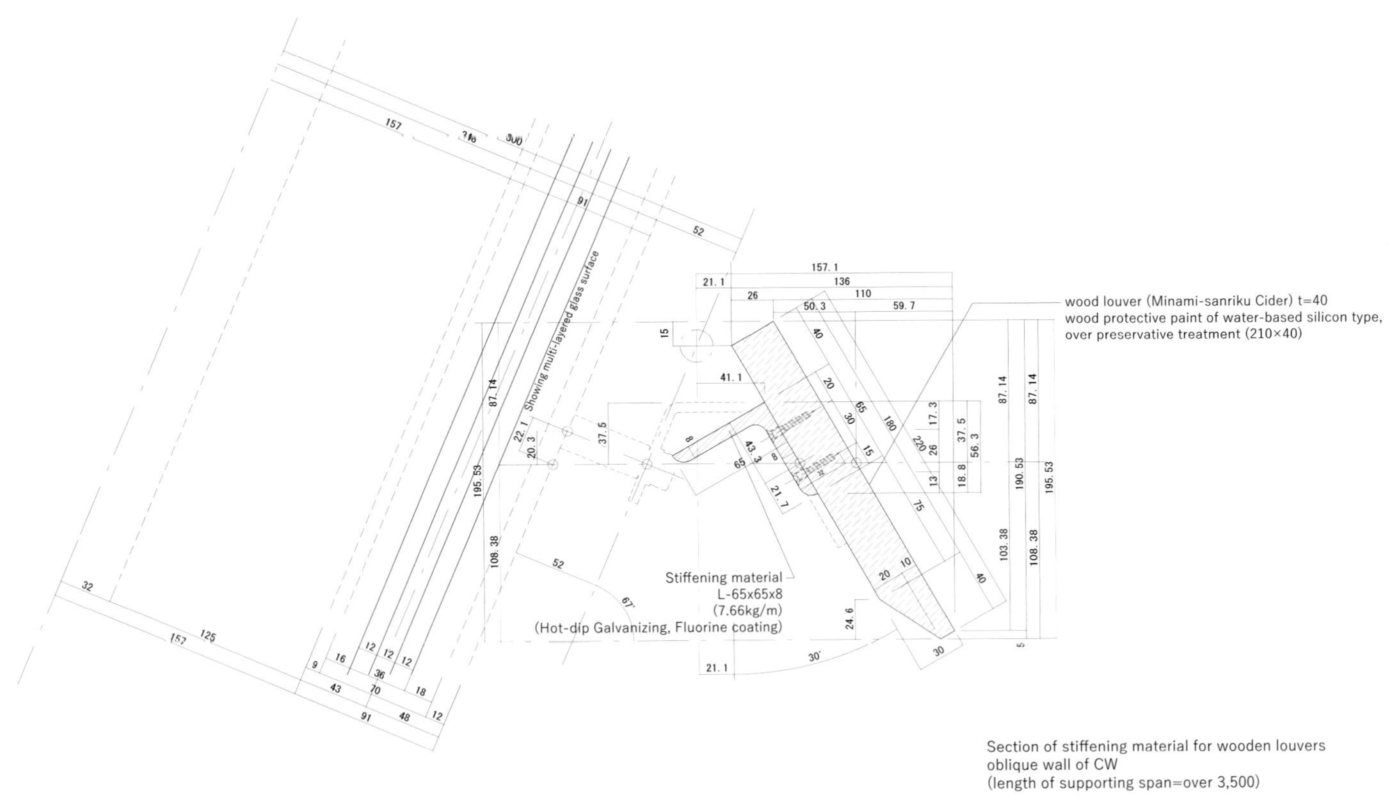

Section of stiffening material for wooden louvers
oblique wall of CW
(length of supporting span=over 3,500)

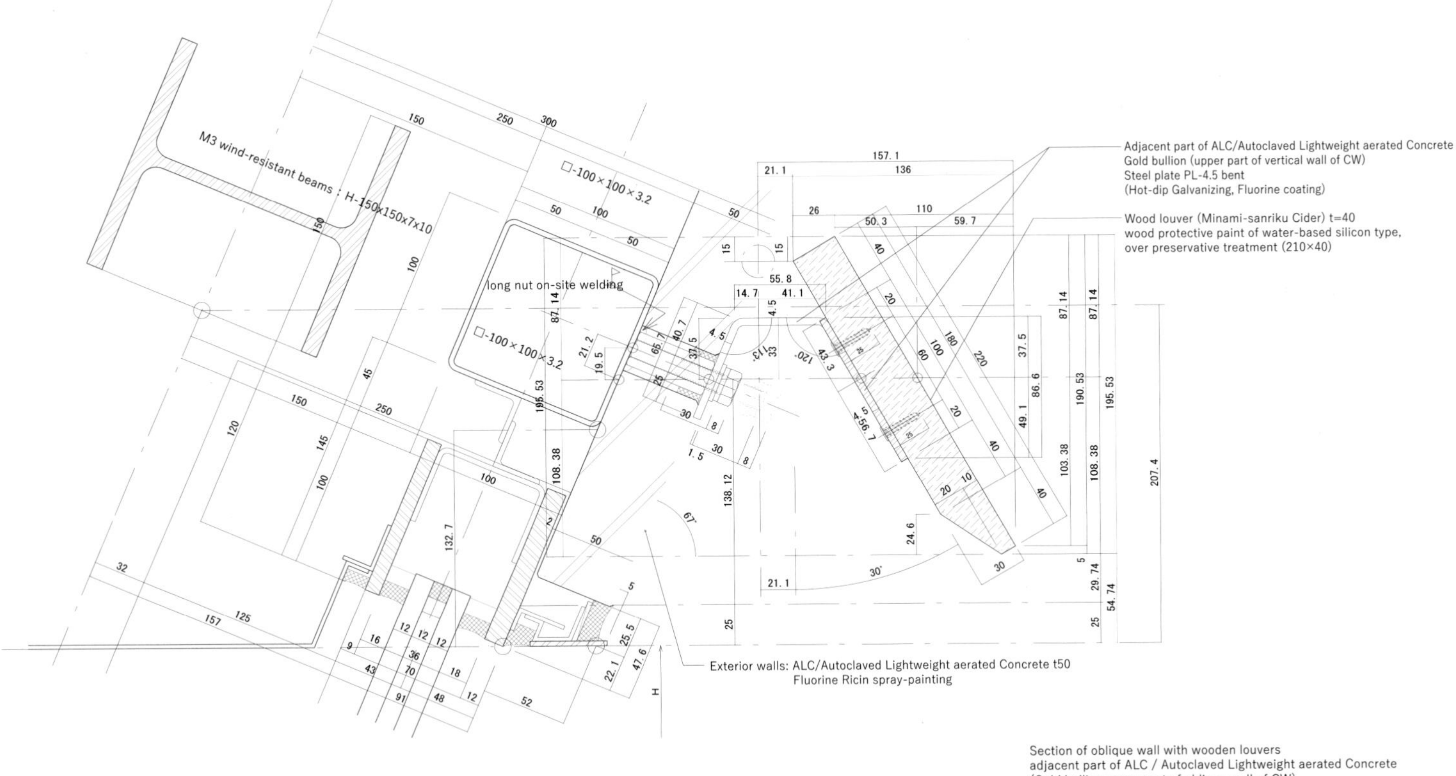

M3 wind-resistant beams : H-150x150x7x10
□-100×100×3.2
long nut on-site welding
□-100×100×3.2
Adjacent part of ALC/Autoclaved Lightweight aerated Concrete
Gold bullion (upper part of vertical wall of CW)
Steel plate PL-4.5 bent
(Hot-dip Galvanizing, Fluorine coating)
Wood louver (Minami-sanriku Cider) t=40
wood protective paint of water-based silicon type,
over preservative treatment (210×40)
Exterior walls: ALC/Autoclaved Lightweight aerated Concrete t50
Fluorine Ricin spray-painting

Section of oblique wall with wooden louvers
adjacent part of ALC / Autoclaved Lightweight aerated Concrete
(Gold bullion upper part of oblique wall of CW)

WOOD 18: MURASAKI PENGUIN PROJECT TOTSUKA

Completion year: 2022
Location: Kanagawa, Japan
Structure: wood
Building type: educational

In the varied landscape of Totsuka-ku, Yokohama City, nestled between a mountain and a residential area, we constructed a facility that houses both a daycare center and a performing-arts and multimedia-arts space for the community.

To integrate seamlessly into the irregularly shaped site, surrounded by retaining walls, we drew inspiration from Froebel blocks—Frank Lloyd Wright's favored childhood toy. The building mimics these blocks tossed onto the slope, resulting in sharp geometries and fragmented volumes. The roof, featuring exposed carbon fibers, serves not only as a structural element but also as a visual connector between the ground and the sky.

Inside, the first-floor studio is architecturally linked to the basement studio through a diagonal atrium. This design choice fosters a sense of unity across different programs and enhances the connection to the ground, facilitating a cohesive and interactive environment for users of the facility.

We envisioned a design that scattered objects resembling small gems, each dominated by triangular geometry, across a space that felt like a hollow carved out of the middle of the city.

Each gemlike element is fundamentally triangular, but we intentionally avoided the typical horizontal or vertical alignments with respect to the ground. This approach was chosen to explore the full potential of triangular shapes, allowing each facet to be perceived distinctly. To accentuate the non-Cartesian characteristics of these triangular facets, lines were strategically inserted. In the wooden sections, we used a method called "yamato-bari," where planks are alternately attached to create lines, while for the metal roof, a straightforward line-insertion technique was employed.

Additionally, carbon fiber was utilized to connect the apexes of the separate triangular forms, providing structural reinforcement. The fine lines created by the carbon fiber not only add to the structural integrity but also introduce a rhythmic element reminiscent of jazz into the city's gaps and spaces. This rhythmic interplay sometimes presents as dynamic and vigorous, weaving together with the lines drawn from the facets to create a harmonious yet visually striking urban tapestry.

Saclass

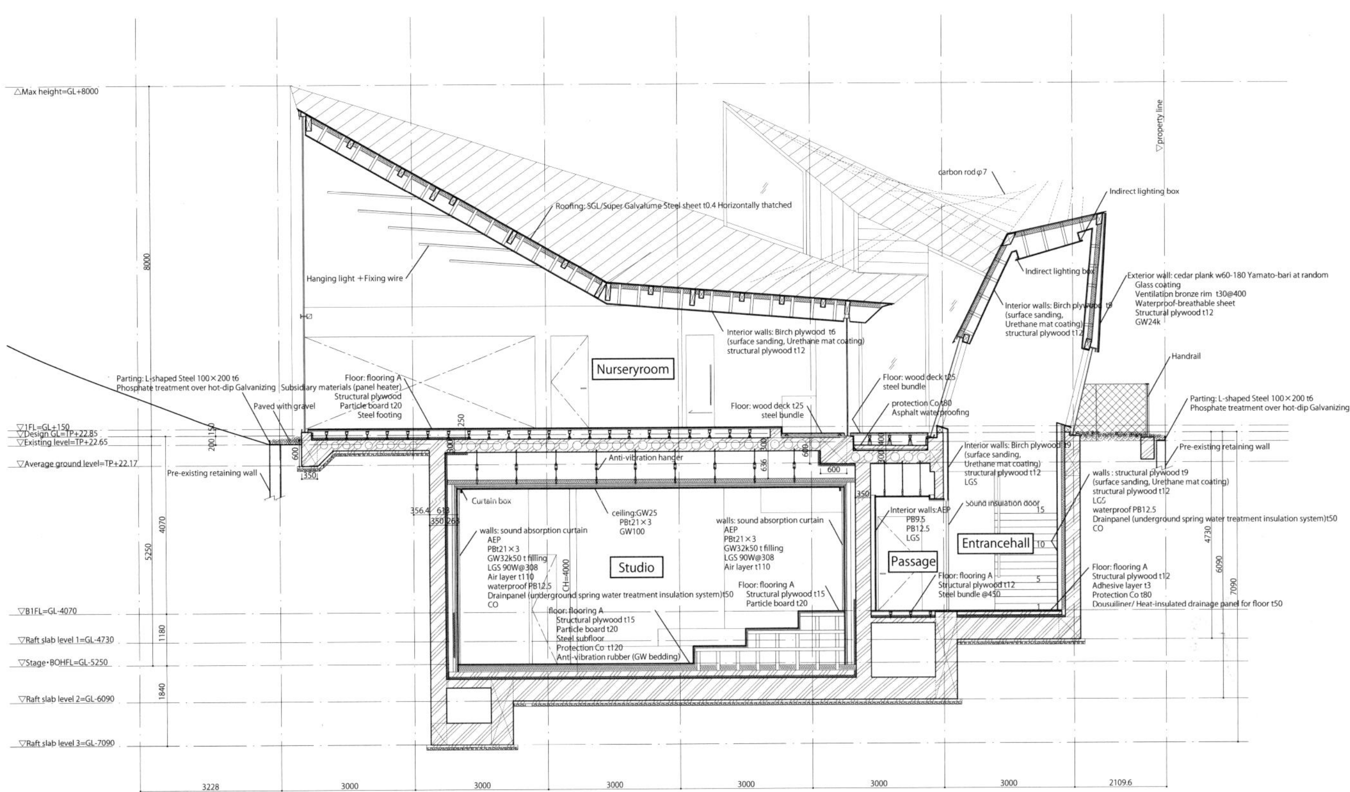

Section Detail

ABOUT THE AUTHOR

Kengo Kuma was born in 1954. He established Kengo Kuma & Associates in 1990. He is currently a University Professor and Professor Emeritus at the University of Tokyo and a member of the Japan Art Academy after teaching at Keio University and the University of Tokyo. KKAA projects are currently underway in more than 50 countries. Kengo Kuma proposes architecture that opens up new relationships between nature, technology, and human beings.

PHOTO CREDITS

Alessio Guarino: pp. 190–192, p. 193 (*above*);
Daici Ano: p. 55, pp. 62–65, p. 161, pp. 174–176, p. 193 (*below left* and *below right*);
East Japan Railway Company: pp. 42–44
Edward Caruso: p. 184 (*left*);
Eiichi Kano: pp. 84–87;
Erieta Attali: p. 77 (*right*), pp. 78–79, p. 171;
Forward Stroke, Inc.: p. 100, pp. 102–103;
Hufton+Crow: pp. 92–95;
Jeremy Bittermann: pp. 116–119;
Katsumasa Tanaka: pp. 248–250;
Kawasumi–Kobayashi Kenji Photograph Office: p. 9, pp. 48–51, pp. 106–108, p. 115, pp. 122–125, pp. 138–140, pp. 150–156, pp. 204–205, pp. 226–229, pp. 252–253
Kenshu Shintsubo: p. 101;
Kengo Kuma & Associates: p. 17 (*above*), pp. 22–25, p. 133 (*below left*);
Magnum: p. 68
Marco Introini: pp. 69–70
Martin Mischkulnig: pp. 214–217;
Masao Nishikawa: pp. 180–182;
Michel Denance: pp. 238–239;
Mitsumasa Fujitsuka: pp. 56–59, p. 162, p. 163 (*above*), p. 164;
Nicolas Waltefaugle: p. 13 (*right*), pp. 74–76, p. 77 (*left*)
Olivier Ravoire: p. 236;
Satoshi Asakawa: pp. 145–147;
SHINKENCHIKU: p. 163 (*below*);
SS Tokyo: pp. 196–199; **Keishin Horikosh /SS Tokyo**: p. 13 (*left*), pp. 256–259, pp. 268–270; **Keishin Horikoshi–Kosuke Nakao /SS Tokyo**: pp. 220–224, pp. 262–264;
Taisei Corporation, Azusa Sekkei Co., Ltd., Kengo Kuma and Associates Joint Venture: pp. 208–211;
Takeshi Yamagishi: p. 184 (*right*), pp. 185–186;
Takumi Ota: p. 15, pp. 34–37, pp. 131–132, p. 133 (*above, below right*), p. 134, pp. 168–170;
Think Utopia: p. 237;
Yoshie Nishikawa: p. 16, 17 (*below left* and *below right*), pp. 18–19

DRAWINGS

East Japan Railway Company: pp. 45–47